History of Multicultural Education, Volume III

Instruction and Assessment

History of Multicultural Education

Edited by Carl A. Grant and Thandeka K. Chapman

Volume I: Conceptual Frameworks and Curricular Issues

Volume II: Foundations and Stratifications

Volume III: Instruction and Assessment

Volume IV: Policy and Policy Initiatives

Volume V: Students and Student Learning

Volume VI: Teachers and Teacher Education

History of Multicultural Education, Volume III

Instruction and Assessment

Edited by

Carl A. Grant
University of Wisconsin, Madison

Thandeka K. Chapman
University of Wisconsin, Milwaukee

NEW YORK AND LONDON

First published 2008
by Routledge
270 Madison Ave, New York, NY 10016

Simultaneously published in the UK
by Routledge
2 Park Square, Milton Park, Abingdon, Oxon OX14 4RN

Routledge is an imprint of the Taylor & Francis Group, an informa business

Typeset in Sabon by
RefineCatch Limited, Bungay, Suffolk

Library of Congress Cataloging in Publication Data
History of multicultural education / edited by Carl A. Grant and Thandeka K. Chapman.
p.cm.
Includes bibliographical references and index.

ISBN 978-0-8058-5439-8 (hardback, volume i : alk. paper) – ISBN 978-0-8058-5441-1 (hardback, volume ii : alk. paper) – ISBN 978-0-8058-5443-5 (hardback, volume iii : alk. paper) – ISBN 978-0-8058-5445-9 (hardback, volume iv : alk. paper) – ISBN 978-0-8058-5447-3 (hardback, volume v : alk. paper) – ISBN 978-0-8058-5449-7 (hardback, volume vi : alk. paper)

1. Multicultural education–United States. I. Grant, Carl A. II. Chapman, Thandeka K.
LC1099.3.H57 2008
370.1170973–dc22 2008016735

ISBN 10: 0–8058–5443–6 (hbk)
ISBN 10: 0–415–98889–6 (set)

ISBN 13: 978–0–8058–5443–5 (hbk)
ISBN 13: 978–0–415–98889–6 (set)

CONTENTS

PREFACE TO THE SIX-VOLUME SET

How we came to this work

We were invited by a large publishing house to create a multi-volume set on what we are calling the history of multicultural education. A change within the organizational structure of the publishing house resulted in the discontinuation of the initial project. However, over the course of the last seven years, the project was embraced by a second publishing house that later merged with our first publishing home. Our 360 degree turn has been both a professional challenge and an amazing opportunity. The project has grown and expanded with these changes, and given us the opportunity to work with many different people in the publishing industry.

We relate this series of events for multiple reasons. First we want to encourage new scholars to maintain their course of publication, even when manuscripts are not accepted on the first or second attempt to publish. Second, we would like to publicly thank Naomi Silverman and Lawrence Erlbaum Associates for throwing us a necessary lifeline for the project and for their vision concerning this project. Lastly, we would also like to thank Routledge Press for warmly welcoming us back to their publishing house and providing ample resources to support the publication of the six-volume set.

What we got out of it and what we saw

Over the course of six years, we have worked to complete these volumes. These volumes, separately or as a set, were marketed for libraries and resources rooms that maintain historical collections. For Thandeka it was an opportunity to explore the field of multicultural education in deep and multifaceted ways. For Carl, it was a bittersweet exploration of things past and an opportunity to reflect on and re-conceptualize those events and movements that have shaped multicultural education. Collectively, the time we spent viewing the articles, conceptualizing the volumes, and writing the introductions was also a meaningful chance to discuss, critique, lament, and celebrate the work of past and present scholars who have devoted time to building and expanding the literature on equity and social justice in schools.

Looking across journals and articles we noticed patterns of school reform that are related to political and social ideas that constantly influence and are influenced by the public's perceptions of the state of education and by professionals working in the field of education. We would also like to recognize authors who have made consistent contributions in journals to multicultural education. These authors have cultivated lines of inquiry concerning multicultural education with regard to teachers, students, parents, and classroom events for decades. Although we would like to list these scholars, the fear of missing even one significant name keeps us from making this list.

Moreover, we recognize that a good deal of the significant work in the field was not published in journal articles or that articles were greatly altered (titles, tone, examples, word choice) to suit the editors and perceived constituents of the journal. There are many stories that are told between the lines of these articles that may go unnoticed by readers who are less familiar with the field, such as the difficulty authors had with finding publication outlets, and questions and criticism from colleagues about conducting research and scholarship in the areas of multicultural education. Although these pressures cannot be compared across groups, scholars of color, white scholars, men and women all felt marginalized because they chose to plant their careers in the rich but treacherous soil of multicultural education.

Just as we can see career patterns, we also saw patterns of journals that were willing to publish articles that focused on multicultural education. While many journals have created an *occasional* special issue around topics of equity, social justice, and students of color, there are journals that have consistently provided outlets for the work of multicultural scholars over the past three decades.

Our hopes for the use of the volumes

We began this project with the desire to preserve and recount the work conducted in multicultural education over the past three decades. As scholars rely more heavily on electronic resources, and funding for ERIC and other national databases is decreased, we are concerned that older articles (articles from the late 60s thru the early 80s) that may never be placed in this medium would eventually be lost. The volume set is one attempt to provide students, teacher educators, and researchers with a historical memory of debates, conceptualizations, and program accounts that formed and expanded the knowledge-base of multicultural education.

GENERAL INTRODUCTION TO THE VOLUMES

Multicultural education's rich and contested history is more than thirty years old; and is presently having an impact on the field of education, in particular, and society in general. It is time to provide a record of its history in order that the multiple accounts and interpretations which have contributed to the knowledge base, are maintained and documented. Whereas this account is not comprehensive, it nevertheless serves as a historically contextualized view of the development of the field and the people who have contributed to the field of multicultural education.

The paradigm of multicultural education as social reconstruction asserts the need to reform the institutional structures and schooling practices that maintain the societal status quo. These reforms are fashioned by socially reconstructing the ways that educators and politicians approach issues of equity and equality in our public schools. Multicultural education has become the umbrella under which various theoretical frameworks, pedagogical approaches, and policy applications are created, shared, critiqued, and implemented through on-going struggles for social justice in education. These campaigns for educational reform influence and benefit all citizens in the United States.

As a movement, multicultural education has brought forth an awareness of and sensitivity to cultural differences and similarities that continues to permeate the highest institutional infrastructures of our nation. Although the movement is rooted in struggles for racial equality, multicultural education readily includes physical disabilities, sexual orientation, issues of class and power, and other forms of bias affecting students' opportunities for academic and social success. The inclusion of other forms of difference beyond skin color is one way that multicultural education acknowledges diversity in a myriad of forms and dismantles the assumptions of homogeneity within racial groups.

The purpose of this set of volumes on the history of multicultural education is to locate, document, and give voice to the body of research and scholarship in the field. Through published articles spanning the past thirty years, this set of books provides readers with a means for knowing, understanding, and envisioning the ways in which multicultural education has developed; been implemented and resisted; and been interpreted in educational settings. By no means consistent in definition, purpose, or philosophy, multicultural education has influenced policy, pedagogy, and content in schools around the United States and the world. In addition, it has stimulated rigorous debates around the nature and purpose of schooling and how students and teachers should be educated to satisfy those purposes.

This set of volumes draws attention to how scholars, administrators, teachers, students, and parents have interpreted and reacted to various political and social events that have informed school policy and practices. Each volume in the set documents and tells a story of educators' attempts to explicate and advocate for the social and academic needs of heterogeneous and homogeneous communities. Through their struggles to achieve access and equity for all children, different scholars have conceptualized the goals, roles, and participants of multicultural education in numerous ways. Through the academic arena of scholarly publications, and using diverse voices from the past thirty years, the *History of Multicultural Education* acknowledges the challenges and successes distinguished through struggles for equity in education.

Methods for collecting articles and composing the volumes

It is because of the multifaceted nature of multicultural education that we have taken multiple steps in researching and collecting articles for this volume set. Keeping in mind the many ways in which this set of volumes will enrich the study and teaching of education, we have approached the task of creating the texts using various methods. These methods reflect the spirit of inclusion intrinsic to scholarship in multicultural education and respect for diversity in the academic communities that promote and critique multicultural education. This was a multiple step process that included the following stages of data collection.

In the Spring of 2000, we began collecting articles using an electronic data bank called the *Web of Science*. This program allows the Editors to discover the number of times articles have been referenced in a significant number of refereed journals. We submitted proper names, article titles, and subject headings to create lists of articles that have been cited numerous times. The number of citations gave us an initial idea of how frequently the article had been cited in refereed journals. Using the *Web of Science* we established a list of articles, which because of their extensive referencing, have become seminal and historical works in the field of multicultural education. The authors cited in these pieces generated the names of over forty scholars who are both highly recognized or not immediately recognized for their scholarship in the area of multicultural education.

To extend the breadth and depth of these volumes, we returned to the *Web of Science* and used various subject headings to uncover other articles. The articles found in our second round of searching were also highly referenced by various scholars. The two searches were then cross-referenced for articles and authors. Through this process we attempted to reveal as many significant articles that dealt with multicultural education as possible. Some articles are foundational pieces of literature that have been copiously cited since their publication, while other articles represent a specific area of scholarship that has received less attention. For example, articles specific to early childhood and middle school education were not as easily identified as conceptual pieces that articulated various aspects of multicultural education.

The *Web of Science* program has some limitations. Articles that were published in less mainstream or more radical journals may not appear. The creation of a list of articles based solely on this program begs the questions of "What knowledge is of most worth?" and "How do we validate and acknowledge those significant contributions that have been marginalized in educational discourses?"

As multicultural educators, we were cautious not to re-instantiate those very discourses and practices that marginalize academic conversations. Therefore we used other educational and social science databases and traditional library-stack searches to present a more comprehensive set of texts that represent the field of multicultural education. For example, the reference sections in the first two searches were cross-referenced for articles that may not have appeared on-line. These articles were manually located, assessed, and used for their reference pages as well.

The main program limitation that haunted us was the lack of articles from the late 1960s and early 1970s that appeared in the electronic searches. We realized that educational research is lacking a comprehensive knowledge of its history because many scholars only cite articles written in the last ten to fifteen years when reporting their findings in academic journals. The lack of citations from the early years of multicultural education scholarship forced us to take a third approach to researching articles.

Using the ERIC files from 1966–1981 and manually sifting through bounded journals from the 1960s and 1970s, we were able to uncover other significant articles to include in the volumes. The decision to include or exclude certain articles rested primarily on the editors and other scholars who reviewed earlier drafts of the introductions to each volume and the references cited for that volume. We used the feedback from these scholars to complete our search for articles.

The volumes are a reflection of the field of research in multicultural education as well as a reflection of the community of scholars who contribute to the discourse(s) concerning issues of equity and equality in public schools. Our concern with shouldering such an awesome responsibility and our desire to include the voices from the many communities of multicultural education scholarship lead us to the final approach to finding quality articles. We solicited the opinions of over twenty multiculturalists. We asked them to choose the articles they believed belong in the volumes and suggest articles or areas that were not represented. Several scholars such as Sonia Nieto, Carlos Ovando, and Christine Sleeter answered our request and provided us with valuable feedback.

Polling various academic communities made the project a more inclusive effort, but also served as a tool to communicate the work of multicultural scholars. We appreciated the opportunity to engage with other scholars during the creation of these volumes. The multi-step research methodology for this project strengthens and enhances the finished product, making the volumes a valuable contribution to the field of education. This set of volumes, because it represents the voices of many scholars, is a spirited set of articles that reflects the tenets of multicultural education, its history, its present, its ideas for the future, and the people who believe in equity and social justice for all citizenry.

Features of the volumes

Each volume in the set includes a diverse group of authors that have written in the field of multicultural education. The array of work is based on the article's contribution to educational scholarship; they represent well-known and lesser-known points of view and areas of scholarship. The volumes do not promote one scholar's vision of multicultural education, but include conflicting ideals that inform multiple interpretations of the field.

Many of the articles from the early 1970s and 1980s are difficult for students to obtain because technology limits the number of years that volumes can be accessed through web databases. Volumes in the set provide students with access to the foundational articles that remain solely in print. Students and veteran scholars doing historical research may be especially interested in the volumes because of the rich primary sources.

The volumes are delineated by six subject groupings: *Conceptual Frameworks and Curricular Content, Foundations and Stratifications, Instruction and Assessment, Policy and Governance, Students and Student Learning*, and *Teachers and Teacher Education*. These six, broadly defined areas reflect the diversity of scholarship dealing with issues of equity and social justice in schooling. The articles illustrate the progression of research and theory and provide a means for readers to reflect upon the changes in language and thought processes concerning educational scholarship. Readers also will see how language, pedagogical issues, policy reforms, and a variety of proposed solutions for equity attainment have been constructed, assimilated, and mutated over the thirty year time period.

Volume I: Conceptual Frameworks and Curricular Issues

The articles in this volume illustrate the initial and continued debates over the concepts, definitions, meanings, and practices that constitute multicultural education. The authors articulate how best to represent the history and citizens of the United States, what types of content should be covered in public schools, and the types of learning environments that best serve the needs of all students. For example, this volume shows how multicultural education challenged the representations of people of color that are presented or ignored in textbooks. Conversely, articles that challenge conceptions of multicultural education are also included. Content wars over the infusion of authors of color, the inclusion of multiple historical perspectives, and an appreciation for various scientific and social contributions from people of color that reflect challenges to Eurocentric knowledge and perspectives are presented in this volume.

Volume II: Foundations and Stratifications

This volume presents theoretical and empirical articles that discuss the institutional factors that influence schooling. Issues such as the historical configurations of schools, ideologies of reproduction and resistance, and administrative structures that often maintain imbalances of power and equity in schools are discussed. In addition, articles explicating the various ways that students and educational opportunities are racially and socio-economically stratified are present in this volume.

Volume III: Instruction and Assessment

The articles in this volume elucidate general pedagogical approaches and specific instructional approaches with consideration given to content areas and grade level. Diverse instructional practices and the relationships between students and their teachers are discussed. Although content and pedagogy are difficult to separate, the work in this volume addresses the dispositions of the teacher and his/her awareness of learning styles, and his/her ability to incorporate aspects of students' culture and community affiliations into pedagogy. Also included in this volume are theories and models of multicultural assessment tools that reflect the needs of diverse learning communities.

Volume IV: Policy and Policy Initiatives

This volume on policy and governance explores the effects of federal and state mandates on school reforms dealing with equity in education. The articles in this volume show how educational organizations and associations have attempted to influence and guide school policy, instructional practices, and teacher-education programs. In addition, the volume presents articles that discuss how interest groups (e.g., parents and concerned teachers) influence enactments of education policy in schools.

Volume V: Students and Student Learning

This volume on "Students and Student Learning" focuses on students as individuals, scholars, and members of various social and cultural groups. The articles highlight different aspects of students' lives and how they influence their academic behaviors and includes students' affective responses to their schooling and their beliefs about the value of education. The articles also address how schools socially construct student learning through the lenses of race, class, and gender. In addition, the articles show how students act as political agents to structure, direct, and often derail their academic progress. Arguing that multicultural education is necessary for everyone, the articles highlight specific racial and cultural groups as well as offer generalizations about the academic needs of all students.

Volume VI: Teachers and Teacher Education

The teacher education volume addresses issues of multicultural education for preservice and experienced teachers. The articles cover the racial and social demographics of the past and current teaching force in the United States and the impact of these demographics on the structure of multicultural teacher education programs. Several articles speak to the role(s) of the university concerning multicultural preservice and in-service education classes, field placements, and institutional support for veteran teachers. These articles explore the nature of teaching for social justice in higher education, the desire to attract teachers of color, and the juncture between theory and practice for newly licensed teachers.

ACKNOWLEDGEMENTS

There are many who deserve a public thank you for their support of and participation in this project. We would like to thank the many colleagues and graduate students who offered constructive criticism, suggested articles, read drafts of the introductions, and helped to conceptualize the placement of articles in the different volumes. These people include: Barbara Bales, Anthony Brown, Keffrelyn Brown, Nikola Hobbel, Etta Hollins, Gloria Ladson-Billings, Sonia Nieto, Carlos Ovando, Christine Sleeter, and Michael Zambon.

We would like to offer a special thank you to the journals that, because of the nature of the project, reduced or forgave their fees for re-printing.

Thanks to Director JoAnn Carr and the staff in the Center for Instructional Materials and Computing (CIMC) for putting up with our large piles of bound and unbound journals that we pulled from the shelves and made unavailable for others for days at a time. Thank you for re-shelving all the publications (sometimes over and over again) and never reprimanding us for the amount of work we created.

A super big thank you to Jennifer Austin for compiling, organizing, and maintaining our files of publishers' permission requests. Jennifer also contacted and reasonably harassed folks for us until they gave her the answers we needed. Brava!

Thank you to our families for their support and only occasionally asking "Aren't you finished yet?"

STATEMENT CONCERNING ARTICLE AVAILABILITY AND THE CONFLICT WITH REPRINT COST

During this insightful, extensive process, the goal was to share re-printings of all the articles with our readers. However, as we moved to the end of our journey, we discovered that it was financially unfeasible to secure permissions from the publishers of all the articles. We found most publishers more than willing to either donate articles or grant us significant breaks on their re-printing prices. Other publishers were more intractable with their fees. Even if the budget allowed for the purchasing of the 200-plus articles, the price of the books would have become prohibitive for most readers. Therefore, the printed articles found in the volumes do not represent all the articles that met the criteria outlined in the Preface and are discussed in each of the volumes' introductions.

At first we decided not to summarize these articles and use them solely as support for the rest of the volume(s). As we refined our introductions and re-read (and read again) the articles, we could not discount how these pieces continued to provide significant knowledge and historical reflections of the field that are unique and timely. Therefore, if the volumes are to represent the most often referenced examples and keenly situated representations of multicultural education and paint a historically conceptualized picture of the field, we had no choice but to include the works of these scholars in our introductions. Unfortunately, for the reasons explained here, some of these articles are not included in these volumes. In Appendix 2, we have provided a list of all the publishers and publishing houses so that individuals and organizations may access these articles from their local or university libraries or web services free of charge.

LIST OF JOURNALS REPRESENTED IN THE SIX-VOLUME SET

Action in Teacher Education
American Association of Colleges for Teacher Education
American Educational Research Association
American Journal of Education
American Sociological Association
Anthropology and Education
Association for Supervision and Curriculum Development
Comparative Education Review
Curriculum and Teaching
Education
Education and Urban Society
Educational Horizons
Educational Leadership
Educational Research Quarterly
Educators for Urban Minorities
English Journal
Exceptional Children
FOCUS
Harvard Educational Review
Interchange
Journal of Curriculum Studies
Journal of Curriculum and Supervision
Journal of Teacher Education
Journal of Research and Development in Education
Journal of Negro Education
Journal of Literacy Research (formerly *Journal of Reading Behavior*)
Journal of Educational Thought
Journal of Teacher Education
Language Arts
Momentum
Multicultural Education
National Catholic Educational Association
National Council for the Social Studies
National Educational Service
Negro Educational Review
Peabody Journal of Education

Phi Delta Kappan
Race, Class, and Gender in Education
Radical Teacher
Researching Today's Youth: The Community Circle of Caring Journal
Review of Educational Research
Southeastern Association of Educational Opportunity Program Personnel (SAEOPP)
Teacher Education and Special Education
Teachers College Record
The American Scholar
The Educational Forum
The High School Journal
The Journal of Educational Research
The New Advocate
The Social Studies
The Teacher Educator
The Urban Review
Theory into Practice
Viewpoints in Teaching and Learning
Young Children

INTRODUCTION TO VOLUME III

In the multicultural education (MCE) scholarship, the focus was bifurcated between the infusion of diverse content and relationships between teachers and their students. Scholars generally dealt with teaching teachers to relate to students of color and create an atmosphere of acceptance, as opposed to how to use content to discuss difficult issues of race, class, and culture that affect students' lives. The early battles for multicultural education fought to change the content of the curriculum, the nature of culturally appropriate assessments, and the perceptions white teachers held about their students. Not until the mid-1980s are discussions of instructional practices and critical pedagogies incorporated into multiculturalism. During this time people became increasingly concerned with norm-referenced standardized tests that were used to guide public education policy and further center white middle-class students as the model students of American schools. The move towards learning styles, multiple intelligences, non-traditional assessments and discussions over teaching racially diverse students became partnered with diverse instructional techniques, such as academically stratified groups or project-based learning, that served the needs of all children. The shift from lecture and IRE (information, response, evaluation) practices to varied instructional techniques were less readily adopted by subject areas such as math and science which claimed that the scientific research process and conceptualizations of mathematics were culturally neutral.

Multicultural scholars critiqued supposedly culturally neutral models and techniques of instruction for their limited understanding of the impact teachers' backgrounds and experiences have on their ability to reach all children. They argued that if students do not share the teacher's frames of reference, the culture of the teacher, as performed through language, becomes another hurdle students must traverse to learn the materials. In contrast, those students who are akin to the teacher's background are able to make the connections between examples and content and have their cultural understandings reinforced by the adult figure in the classroom. Multicultural scholars asserted that the illustrations and analogies teachers used to facilitate discussions, teach skills, model concepts, and pose assessment questions mainly came from their own experiences and unexamined cultural lenses.

Additionally, multicultural scholars criticized new instructional techniques for the lack of critical pedagogy. In this volume, the reader will better understand how MCE has addressed battles over provisions for rigorous instruction, the creation of critical informed citizens, and the caring ethic of the teacher. Thus, teaching and relationship building are the primary mechanisms to be examined in the body of literature on instruction and assessment in multicultural education.

Some scholars may take issue with the separation of content and pedagogy because the two are inextricably intertwined. Yet, the articles show that teachers' content, pedagogy, and assessment choices are culturally constructed and groomed from their own experiences as students, their personal predilections, and their levels of knowledge and comfort with the content. Thus it is not always the content that must be changed, but rather what the teacher chooses to explore within the content that is a vital issue. For example, in *Playing in the Dark*, Toni Morrison demonstrates how issues of race are imbedded in the most canonized of Early American literature, but rarely taught in ways that would lead students to think about constructions of "othering." In the 1980s multicultural education turned to using critical approaches with all texts, textbooks, and canonical literature. This approach differed from previous uses of content that explored issues of society exclusively among authors of color or female authors (eg. *Native Son* or *A Room with a View*), specific historical events (e.g., The Civil Rights Movement or The Civil War), or people of color who are historical figures (George Washington Carver or Crispus Attucks).

To articulate the multiple examples of instruction and assessment in multicultural education, the volume is divided into four main categories: state, local, and classroom assessment; instruction; examples of practice; and grade specific/subject specific applications of multicultural education. These four sections were created to provide both breadth and depth for the readers of the volume. The breadth spans the various conversations that have continued to occur over the past thirty years. The depth of each section highlights how the field has grown and refined its articulations of classroom and school practices.

State, Local, and Classroom Assessment

Multicultural educators have struggled to create large-scale assessments that measure students' skill ability and conceptual understanding and not their ability to identify with specific racial, class, and cultural cues that obstruct the test validity. In the United States, test and measurements of intellectual ability have been used to solidify stereotypes of racial inferiority and cultural dissonance. Norm referenced testing, with its premise that only a certain percentage of the population can be allowed to score in the normal range of the test, means others must be outside of the norm, and therefore not normal at all. Scholars assert that because of the challenges of creating linguistically and culturally appropriate tests, students of color and students living in poverty most often fall outside these norms and fill the deviant space.

Issues of testing occur at all levels: federal, state, local (e.g., city, town), school, and classroom. The articles in this volume show the range of issues (e.g., test mis-match due to language and cultural issues and the need for diverse content in test examples) that multicultural scholars discussed. Bigelow (1999) stated that tests do not take into account diverse content and critical thinking. He argued that standardized tests run counter to the work of multiculturalism because they do not leave room for alternative content nor do they reward critical thinking about the individual or the world. His article is a cautionary tale that interrogates the goals of testing versus the goals of multicultural education and democratic citizenry.

Figueroa and Garcia (1994) tackled the center piece issues in assessment. They contested the white middle-class reference point used to assess all students and the various embedded assumptions about commonalities in student knowledge and experiences. They also believed that such assessments serve to disadvantage students whose backgrounds do not match the norm of white middle-class students and assert that testing has yet to "cope with culture" (1994, p. 16).

The growing body of literature addressing the cultural context of testing was enhance by the contribution from Smith-Maddox (1998). The author used National Education

Longitudinal Study [NELS:88] data to construct a vision of how cultural contexts affect students' lives and influence their ability to perform on tests. She used her analysis to demonstrate the strong connections that exist between students' communities and their learning experiences. Smith-Maddox's article is one in a special issue of the *Journal of Negro Education* devoted to multicultural education and assessment. We encourage readers to explore other articles in this issue that explicate the complex nature of testing and culturally relevant practices.

Because of the problems associated with norm reference testing, several scholars have proposed alternatives. The study by Garcia, Casimir, Irminger, Wiese, and Garcia (1999), of authentic literacy assessment (ALA) poses new questions for assessment. They studied how two schools designed and dispensed ALA to students with various levels of English proficiency and from different racial groups. The experience of designing, administering, and grading the ALA led them to outline a set of principles for further guidance and future work. Garcia *et al.* call for more research to focus on culturally relevant assessments. While the MCE scholars are quite clear about what does not provide meaningful indicators of student success, i.e., culturally hegemonic representations of white middle-class America, test-makers are far from producing alternatives that meet the needs of all children.

For example, Darling-Hammond (1994) made the case for performance assessments as opposed to standardized tests for public schools. She asserted that a greater range of assessments would allow decision-makers to have a clearer picture of student achievement and academic growth. In response to policy-makers who want to increase standardized testing, Darling-Hammond shared examples of states where large testing initiatives failed to give stake-holders what they hoped to gain. Although she recognized the problems inherent in authentic assessments, she suggested that more formative and alternative summative assessments be created for all children to learn and teachers to teach, rather than settle for the limited assessments available to schools and districts. Moreover, she proposed that testing reforms must be accompanied by other policies that evaluated the uses of testing in schools and taught teachers to properly read, critique, and create assessments.

Instruction

Using assessment as one component of teacher pedagogy, this next section presents scholars who have theorized the challenges of creating multicultural spaces through teachers' instructional choices and dispositions towards their students. Scholars contend that academic instruction in school is not only about teaching the 3Rs, but also teaching students to assimilate into the mainstream of the United States and other countries. The understanding that teachers serve as agents of culture transmission and assimilation is grounded in the history of public education and comprehensive schooling. Historically, the education of European immigrants stood as the crux of concerns over the necessary transmission of values and ideal behaviors. More recently, as the global world shrinks and the populations of other racial groups continue to grow, African American, Latino, and Asian American students have become the focus of educational debates of assimilation.

In the early days of MCE, multicultural scholars fought for the representation of diverse groups in the curriculum and quality instruction that would allow all children to become educated citizens. Before integration, the struggle to connect teachers with their students in positive and culturally affirming ways was fought by German, Swedish, Italian, and Slavic immigrants that flooded inner-city schools. After desegregation, the challenge became to help white teachers, who were prioritized over African American teachers for limited teaching positions, to understand how to value the cultures of African American and Latino students in newly integrated schools. Moreover, teachers had to unlearn stereotypes and deficit paradigms of students of color in order to become effective teachers in racially diverse settings. Thus, debates over instruction shifted from deficit notions of students' intellectual abilities to questioning who could teach and reach all children.

Interestingly, the articles in this volume illustrate how the "inferiority thesis" about people of color has been nuanced and manipulated over the past thirty years. When the articles are read as one text, the debate over the intellectual capacity of students of color shifts from arguments about biological and cultural inferiority to discussions of the teacher's pedagogical ability. While ideologies of racial and cultural inferiority seemly will never be extinguished, multicultural scholars have pushed for teachers to stop pointing the finger of failure at students, and to use their talents and training to teach all students. In MCE, good teaching means that teachers must be cognizant of their personal and professional beliefs about children and the cultural markers and associations they employ when teaching. Thus, the white teacher, who has never reflected on her culture and how it impacts her practice, becomes the focus of multicultural education and the primary audience for much of the literature.

Pre-dating multicultural education, Johnson (1964) advocates for diversity of instruction to match the diversity among poor students and students of color. Given President Lyndon Johnson's "War on Poverty" and the creation of Title I monies to decrease the educational gap between students living in poverty and middle class students, G. Orville Johnson's negative descriptions of various groups of people were not uncommon for scholars in the sixties who, ironically, were advocating for curricular changes to meet the needs of diverse student populations. As the movement gained momentum in the 1970s, the language of multiculturalism changed to reflect a more positive understanding of students of color and students in poverty. For example Chinn (1979) makes the paradigmatic shift from Johnson by using the language of cultural difference to replace cultural deficit. Chinn and Johnson both maintain that fair education does not mean giving students the same education; it means meeting the needs of children in an equitable manner. The scholars' differentiations between issues of equal education and equitable education are a main tenet of multicultural education and a theme that continues through the volume.

Chinn also expanded early deliberations over content and pedagogy by integrating special education into discussions of multicultural education. He argued that students of color who also have special needs face multiple challenges that are integrated with issues of race, class, and culture. He proposed that students need an education that is relevant to their lives and communities with scaffolded learning experiences that incorporate their ways of understanding and functioning in the world.

Payne's (1983) article demonstrates how educators incorporated a human relations (Grant & Sleeter, 1997) approach to multicultural education into the curricula. Payne asks teachers to view all subjects as dependent upon four areas: skills, knowledge, values, and thinking. Using these four areas, Payne argues teachers can incorporate discussions on the differences and similarities between groups in ways that expand student knowledge about groups beyond their own affiliation.

Delpit's (1988) article is in response to strong debates over skills versus critical thinking in curricula for poor and African American students. Her article received immediate attention from multicultural advocates and other educators because she not only contended that students of color needed to learn their history; but argued that teachers needed to teach the "Codes of power" to children who are unfamiliar with how white supremacy is an institutionalized element in the lives of U.S. citizens.

Giroux (1991) argued that instruction should include a critique of systems of oppression. He criticized educators for promoting an ahistorical cultural pluralism that depicts schools as static, intellectually harmonious spaces devoid of the constant battles of curriculum and pedagogy that are endemic to the politically charged arena of public education. He also suggested that students be encouraged to critique all institutions that affect their lives and argued that white teachers must be ready to discuss and critique systems of oppression from those standpoints in which they feel comfortable, using their abilities to sympathize if they cannot empathize with their students. His article represents a turning point in conversations around instruction in which he advocated for teachers to teach all content with a critical lens and understand large issues of oppression and equity that influence student outcomes.

Several articles highlight the role of the students' backgrounds when shaping instruction. Au (1998) recognizes the need to understand the backgrounds and cultural contexts of students in order to teach in socio-cultural ways. She advocates for teachers to design and implement student-centered lessons that build upon the strengths of the students' backgrounds as well as their current interests. Huber (1996) explores how the content can marginalize students. She promotes the desire for teachers to have an in-depth understanding of their students cultural backgrounds and how content is interpreted through their socio-cultural lenses. She demonstrates how point of view and the position of the story-teller affect the story and what students are implicitly and explicitly instructed to learn and value. Banks and Banks (1995) contend that the debates around MCE, which have focused on practice, have largely ignored some important dimensions of multicultural education such as classroom contexts, the curriculum and assessments, and teachers' beliefs about children. Their argument parallels the composites of successful teachers created by Luis Moll and Gloria Ladson-Billings in the next section on examples of practice.

Examples of Practice

Most of the work done in multicultural education has revolved around theory and conceptualizations of practice. Although there is a substantial number of studies that report how systems of inequality manifest themselves in classrooms (Fine, 1987; Oakes, 1986; Rist, 1970), there are few models of how teachers and schools successfully build multicultural classrooms. Arguably, this is because multicultural education is constantly evolving and teachers are reluctant to highlight their attempts—successful and unsuccessful—as models of practice. However, what the articles in this volume do tell us is that elements of the paradigm exist in most teachers' pedagogy, but few teachers have fully embraced the higher levels of multicultural typologies as they have been espoused by Nieto (2000), Banks and Banks (1995), and Grant and Sleeter (1997).

In this section the studies highlight how teachers design and/or alter their classrooms to support and compliment students' home backgrounds, languages, community ties, and racial identities. In addition, this section includes studies that counter earlier research which suggested that students of color were less capable learners.

Moll shared data from two teachers' practices that demonstrate how they "arranged, improved, or modified social situations to teach at the highest level possible" (1988, p. 465). As part of a larger study and on-going line of action research, Moll's work with teachers illustrates that professional development and advanced education in research on students' cultural backgrounds can translate to greater student achievement.

Bigelow (1990) uses his own classroom to experiment with new pedagogical strategies that facilitate critical literacy. His objective is "to find social meaning in individual experience—push students to use their own stories as windows not only on their lives, but on society" (1990, p. 439). Biglow used literature, writing, and simulated activities to explore historical events and concepts of power and empowerment. He discussed the successful moments of this project as well as the unforeseen unsuccessful outcomes and the difficulties of doing critical, multicultural work in public school classrooms.

Ladson-Billings (1995) documented the advanced skills necessary for creating what she calls culturally relevant pedagogy (CRP). She campaigned for students to have culturally relevant instruction which takes into account their community ties and multiple identities. She also stated that difference is not a form of intellectual or behavioral deficiency and that students of color should be given the opportunity to demonstrate that they are capable of learning in numerous ways. Birthed out of critical theory and multicultural education, CRP focuses on how teachers extend their pedagogy to include the backgrounds and lives of their students in ways that transfer to an expanded vision of learning about themselves and the world in which they live. Community members, colleagues, and former students identified her participants as exemplary teachers. To help scholars recognize these practices, Ladson-Billings created a three-pronged theory that blends together elements of these teachers' practices and ideologies towards teaching.

Fine, Weis, and Powell (1997) contrast different situations where diverse groups of students occupy the same educational spaces. They provide three textually rich examples of how teachers and students function in highly racially and socio-economically stratified school contexts. This example by Fine *et al.* provides a vivid account of how teachers and students struggled to change their relationships and attack social issues in an untracked ninth-grade classroom. These authors provide a contribution to the field as they show the difficult, but rewarding task, of creating multicultural spaces for learning.

Grade Specific/Subject Specific Applications of MCE

The race and ethnic studies movements brought about an intense focus on what students learned in the classrooms about their histories in the United States. This question of curriculum content eventually led to questions of pedagogy with regard to teachers' abilities to relate to diverse populations of students at every level of schooling.

The belief that teachers should become sensitive to various types of classroom diversity regardless of grade level and subject discipline has been formally stated by many professional teaching organizations such as: National Council for Teachers of English (NCTE), National Council for Teachers of Mathematics (NCTM), National Council for Social Studies (NCSS), National Science Teachers Association (NSTA), National Council for Accreditation of Teacher Education (NCATE), and American Association of Colleges for Teacher Education (AACTE).

These organizations stipulate recommendations that push for teachers and teacher education programs to tailor their goals and outcomes to reflect multicultural education curricula and pedagogy. A few of these organizations wrote position statements for respecting and accommodating diversity almost thirty years ago, thus revealing how MCE has remained an elusive but desired goal for educators of all grade levels and subject areas. The following articles are not chronological but are presented in ascending grade level.

A major question that teachers have contemplated is: "At which grade level can I begin introducing multicultural education? How can I introduce grade/age appropriate multicultural education?" Ramsey (1982) theorized about the inclusion of multicultural education at the early childhood level. She presented teachers with concrete strategies and pedagogical areas of teaching that coincide with multicultural education. She built a compelling argument for ways to scaffold MCE in keeping with the age, maturity, and stages of development for early childhood students.

Gay (1979) used students' maturity and development as a strategic element of her elementary school plan. She explained how teachers can create multicultural classrooms for lower and upper elementary students that maintain a rigorous focus on academic learning, but also build character and self-confidence among children from diverse racial and socio-economic backgrounds. Gay and later Ramsey assert that the early formative years are a primary time for students to learn about culture, difference and similarities, and social responsibility.

Pang and Park (1992) believe that middle school students can analyze discussions and debates with contrasting views, design and carry out activities that serve their school or community, and still maintain an open-mind that absorbs new opinions and information. Using an issues-centered approach, these authors designed a curriculum that interrogates prejudice and facilitates social justice.

At the high school level, the process of incorporating multicultural education becomes splintered by the disciplinary ideologies embedded with the independent subjects. In English, Lee (1991) takes up the notion of the teacher's responsibilities towards the students. She describes strategies that incorporate multiple texts and media presentations to teach literary analysis of canonical texts. She models scaffolded instruction that allows students to build their confidence in textual analysis techniques through lessons that rely on familiar elements of media and their communities.

Sheets (1995) also used the canonical curriculum of the Spanish AP test to develop culturally relevant instruction. Similar to Lee, she changed various aspects of the class culture, the instruction styles, the relationship to the community, and the relationships between students and the teacher in order to demonstrate that all students, regardless of race or social-economic standing were capable of high achievement. She created beneficial learning activities and a classroom ethos that posed cultural differences and home language skills as strengths rather than as deficits to the curriculum.

In the physical sciences, Atwater and Riley (1993) used examples from two different contexts to describe the mismatch between teachers and their students in an urban setting. These authors recognized the challenges of integrating multicultural education into the sciences. Atwater and Riley argued that multicultural education is an imperative part of the curriculum in order to encourage more students of color and women into science related careers.

Dodds (1983) pushed for music to become more inclusive and accepting of students' interests and cultures. He proposed that when students are allowed to share their music with the class, the teacher should be able to connect new music to existing works and structures. Dodds believed in music's capacity for exploring issues, gaining an appreciation of diversity, understanding the influences of indigenous music on 20th century music, gaining a tolerance and respect for others and their music, and connecting society and history with music. He broaches social justice because he posed music as a means for challenging social barriers and advocating for multicultural education to impact the lives of white students who need exposure to people and cultures beyond themselves.

Conclusion

Throughout the four themes of the volume and the selected articles there remains a bifurcation between the teaching of content and the relationships between the teacher and student. However, just as content and instruction are seemingly inseparable, so too are trust and knowledge dissemination. Thus what remains lacking in the field is the articulation of how both the relationships and the teaching come together in a way that students and teachers work together in classrooms. The articles highlight the possibilities of instruction and assessment or veteran teachers being multicultural; but they do not show successful pathways for getting to a point of multicultural proficiency. As the field continues to grow, researchers must become more diligent in finding and documenting the process and the cultivation of multicultural expertise for teachers. These illuminations of practice must explore how teachers are able to relate to students and critically approach texts in the same moment. Only through ample examples will other teachers replicate these practices and continue to expand the vision of multicultural education.

References

Atwater, M., & Riley, J. P. (1993). Multicultural science education: perspectives, definitions, and research agenda. *Science Education, 77*(6), 661–668.

Au, K. H. (1998). Social constructivism and the school literacy learning of students of diverse backgrounds. *Journal of Literacy Research, 30*(2), 297–319.

Banks, C. A. M., & Banks, J. A. (1995). Equity pedagogy: An essential component of multicultural education. *Theory into Practice, 34*(3), 152–158.

Bigelow, B. (1999). Why standardize test threaten multiculturalism. *Education Leadership*, 37–39.

Bigelow, W. (1990). Inside the classroom: Social vision and critical pedagogy. *Teachers College Record, 91*(3), 437–448.

Chinn, P. (1979). Curriculum development for culturally different exceptional children. *Teacher Education and Special Education, 2*(4), 49–58.

Darling-Hammond, L. (1994). Performance-based assessment and educational equity. *Harvard Educational Review, 64*(1), 5–30.

Delpit, L. D. (1988). The silenced dialogue: Power and pedagogy in educating other people's children. *Harvard Educational Review, 58*(3), 280–297.

Dodds, J. P. B. (1983). Music as a multicultural education. *Music Education Journal, 69*, 33–34.

Figueroa, R. A., & Garcia, E. (1994). Issues in testing students from culturally and linguistically diverse backgrounds. *Multicultural Education, 2*(1).

Fine, M. (1987). Silencing in public schools. *Language Arts, 64*(2), 157–174.

Fine, M., Weis, L., & Powell, L. C. (1997). Communities of difference: A critical look at desegregated spaces for and by youth. *Harvard Educational Review, 67*(2).

Garcia, E. E., Casimir, M., Irminger, X. S., Wiese, A. M., & Garcia, E. H. (1999). Authentic literacy assessment (ALA) development: An instruction based assessment that is responsive to linguistic and cultural diversity. *Educators for Urban Minorities, 1*(1) 48–57.

Gay, G. (1979). On behalf of children: A curriculum design for multicultural education in the elementary school. *Journal of Negro Education, XLVII*(3), 324–340.

Giroux, H. (1991). Democracy and the discourse of cultural difference—Towards a politics of border pedagogy. *British Journal of Sociology of Education, 12*(4), 501–519.

Grant, C. A., & Sleeter, C. (1997). *Turning on Learning* (2 ed.). New Jersey: Merill/Prentice Hall.

Huber, T. (1996). Of pigs & wolves at the OK Coral. *Multicultural Education, 3*(4), 4–7.

Johnson, G. O. (1964). Organizing instruction and curriculum planning for the socially disadvantaged. *Journal of Negro Education, 33*(3), 254–263.

Ladson-Billings, G. (1995). Toward a theory of culturally relevant pedagogy. *American Educational Research Journal, 32*(3), 465–492.

Lee, C. D. (1991). Big picture talkers/words walking without masters: The instructional implications of ethnic voices for an expanded literacy. *Journal of Negro Education, 60*(3), 291–304.

Moll, L. (1988). Some key issues in teaching Latino students. *Language Arts, 65*(5), 465–471.

Nieto, S. (2000). *Affirming Diversity* (3 ed.). New York: Addison Wesley Longman.

Oakes, J. (1986). Keeping track: part 1: The policy and practice of curriculum inequality. *Phi Delta Kappan, 68*(1), 12–17.

Pang, V. O., & Park, C. (1992). Issues-centered approaches to multicultural education in the middle grades. *The Social Studies*, 108–119.

Payne, C. R. (1983). Multicultural education: A natural way to teach. *Contemporary Education, 54*(2), 98–104.

Ramsey, P. G. (1982). Multicultural education in early childhood. *Young Children, 37*(2), 13–24.

Rist, R. (1970). Student social class and teacher expectations: The self-fulfilling prophecy in ghetto education. *Harvard Educational Review, 40*(3), 411–451.

Sheets, R. H. (1995). From remedial to gifted: Effects of culturally centered pedagogy. *Theory into Practice, 34*(3), 186–193.

Smith-Maddox, R. (1998). Defining culture as a dimension of academic achievement: Implications for culturally responsive curriculum, instruction, and assessment. *Journal of Negro Education, 67*(3), 302–317.

PART 1

STATE, LOCAL, AND CLASSROOM ASSESSMENT

CHAPTER 1

WHY STANDARDIZED TESTS THREATEN MULTICULTURALISM (1999)

Bill Bigelow

Under the banner of "higher standards for all," Oregon has joined the national testing craze. In fall 1998, the Oregon Department of Education field-tested its first-ever statewide social studies assessments. Many teachers were dismayed to discover that the tests were a multiple-choice maze that lurched about helter-skelter, seeking answers on World War I. Constitutional amendments, global climate, rivers in India, hypothetical population projections, Supreme Court decisions, and economic terminology.

Given the broad scope of the standards and the resulting randomness of the test questions they generated, an infinite number of facts could appear on future social studies tests. Teachers worry that to prepare our students for the tests, which students must pass to earn Oregon's 10th grade Certificate of Initial Mastery, we will have to turn our classrooms into vast wading pools of information for students to memorize.

The tests in Oregon are part of a national standards movement that has a democratic veneer. Proponents insist that all students will benefit from "higher expectations" and greater teacher, principal, and school "accountability." But as the Oregon example shows, standardization of social studies curriculums and assessments is hostile to good teaching. Social studies standardization threatens a multicultural curriculum—one that attempts to explain the world as it really exists; speaks to the diversity of our society; and aims not only to teach important facts, but also to develop citizens who can make the world safer and more just.

Multiculturalism is a search to discover perspectives that have been silenced in traditional scholastic narratives. Multiculturalism attempts to uncover "the histories and experiences of people who have been left out of the curriculum," as educator Enid Lee emphasizes (1995, p. 9). Because multiculturalism is an undertaking that requires new scholarship and constant discussion, it is necessarily ongoing. Yet as researcher Harold Berlak points out, "Standardization and centralization of curriculum testing is an effort to put an end to a cacophony of voices on what constitutes truth, knowledge and learning and what the young should be taught. It insists upon one set of answers" (Berlak, in press).

A lack of critical sensibility

Creating an official, government-approved social studies curriculum is bound to be controversial. Thus, state education officials "tried to stake a neutral ground" to win approval for the state's version of social reality (Learn, 1998).

Not surprisingly, this attempt to be neutral and inoffensive means that the standards the state produced lack a critical sensibility and tend toward a conservative *Father Knows Best* portrait of society. For example, one typical 10th grade benchmark calls for students to "understand how the Constitution can be a vehicle for change and for resolving issues as well as a device for preserving values and principles of society." Only? Is this how, say. Frederick Douglass or the Seminole leader Osceola would have seen the Constitution? Shouldn't students also understand how the Constitution can be (and has been) a vehicle for preserving class and race stratification—for example, Dred Scott and *Plessy v. Ferguson*—and for maintaining the privileges of dominant social groups? Abolitionist William Lloyd Garrison called the Constitution an "agreement with Hell" for its support of slavery.

The school curriculum will inevitably reflect the contradictions between a society's myths and realities. But a critical multicultural approach examines these contradictions, whereas standardization tends to paper over them. For example, another benchmark, "Explain how laws are developed and applied to provide order, set limits, protect basic rights, and promote the common good," similarly fails the multicultural test. Whose order, whose basic rights, are protected by laws? Are all social groups included equally in the term *common good*? Between 1862 and 1890, laws in the United States gave an area the size of Texas and Oklahoma to privately owned railroad companies, but gave virtually no land to African Americans freed from slavery. Viewing the Constitution and other U.S. laws through a multicultural lens would add depth to the facile one-sidedness of Oregon's "neutral" standards.

Standards miss the multicultural mark

Indeed the "R" word, *racism*, is not mentioned in the 1998 11th grade field tests or in the social studies standards adopted in March 1998 by the Oregon board of education. Even if the only yardstick were strict historical accuracy, this would be a bizarre omission: The state was launched as a whites-only territory by the Oregon Donation Act and in racist wars of dispossession waged against indigenous peoples; the first constitution outlawed slavery but also forbade blacks from living in the state, a prohibition that remained law until 1927.

Perhaps state education officials are concerned that introducing the concept of racism to students could call into question the essentially harmonious world of "change and continuity over time" that underpins the standards project. Whatever the reason, students cannot make sense of the world today without carrying the idea of racism in their conceptual knapsack. If a key goal of multiculturalism is to account for how the past helped shape the present, and an important part of the present is social inequality, then Oregon's standards and tests earn a failing grade.

Despite the publication of state social studies standards and benchmarks, teachers or parents don't really know what students are expected to learn until they see the tests, which were developed by an out-of-state assessment corporation, MetriTech. As Wade W. Nelson points out in a frank article, "The Naked Truth About School Reform in Minnesota" (that might as well have been written about Oregon) (1998).

> The content of the standards is found only in the tests used to assess them. Access to the tests themselves is carefully controlled, making it difficult to get a handle on what these standards are. It seems ironic to me that basic

> standards—that which every student is expected to know or be able to do—are revealed only in tests accessible only to test-makers and administrators. This design avoids much of the debate about what these standards ought to be.

When we look directly at the tests, their limitations and negative implications for multiculturalism become most clear. Test questions inevitably focus on discrete facts, but cannot address the deeper, multifaceted meaning of facts. For example, in the field tests that Oregon piloted in fall 1998, one question asked which Constitutional amendment gave women the right to vote. Students could know virtually nothing about the long struggle for women's rights and get this question right. In contrast, they could know lots about the feminist movement and not recall that it was the 19th and not the 16th, 17th, or 18th Amendment (the other test choices) that gave women the vote.

Because there is no way to predict precisely which facts will be sought on the state tests, teachers feel pressured to turn courses into a "memory Olympics"; we simply cannot afford to spend the time probing beneath the headlines of history.

Last year, my students at Franklin High School in Portland performed a role-play on the 1848 Seneca Falls, New York, women's rights conference, the first formal U.S. gathering to demand greater equality for women. The original assembly was composed largely of middle- to upper-class white women. I wanted my students not only to appreciate the issues that these women addressed and their courage, but also to consider the limitations imposed by their race, class, and ethnicity. Thus in our simulated 1848 gathering, my students portrayed women who were not at the original conference—enslaved African Americans. Cherokee women who had been forcibly moved to Oklahoma on the Trail of Tears, Mexican women in the recently conquered territory of New Mexico, poor white New England mill workers—as well as the white middle- and upper-class reformers like Elizabeth Cady Stanton and Lucretia Mott who were in attendance.

In this more socially representative fictional assembly, students learned about the resolutions adopted at the original gathering and the conditions that prompted them, and they also saw firsthand how more privileged white women ignored other important issues, such as treaty rights of Mexican women, sexual abuse of enslaved African Americans, and workplace exploitation of poor white women, that a more diverse convention might have addressed.

The knowledge that my students acquired from this role-play consisted not only of "facts," although they learned plenty of these. They also exercised their multicultural social imaginations, listening for the voices that are often silenced in the traditional U.S. history narrative and becoming more alert to issues of race and class. However, this kind of teaching and learning takes time—time that could be ill-afforded in the fact-packing pedagogy required by multiple-choice tests. And after all their study, would my students have recalled which amendment gave women the right to vote? If not, they would have appeared ignorant about the struggle for women's rights.

Likewise, my Global Studies students spend the better part of a quarter reading, discussing, role-playing, and writing about the consequences of European colonialism. They read excerpts from Okot p'Bitek's poignant book-length poem, *Song of Lawino*, about the lingering psychological effects of colonialism in Uganda: role-play a trial on the colonial roots of the Irish potato famine; and examine how Asian economies were distorted to serve the needs of European ruling classes. But when confronted with multiple-choice questions that demand that they recall isolated facts about colonialism in 1914, would my students answer correctly?

As these examples illustrate, a multicultural curriculum is not so much about teaching facts as it is about nurturing a fuller understanding of society.

Misrepresenting social realities

Not surprisingly, Oregon's "one best answer" approach vastly oversimplifies complex social processes—and entirely erases ethnicity and race as categories of analysis. One question on a recent test reads: "In 1919, over 4.1 million Americans belonged to labor unions. By 1928, that number had dropped to 3.4 million. Which of the following best accounts for that drop?" It seems that the correct answer must be A: "Wages increased dramatically, so workers didn't need unions." All the other answers are clearly wrong, but is this answer "correct"? Do workers automatically leave unions when they win higher wages? Weren't mechanization and scientific management factors in undermining traditional craft unions? Did the post-World War I Red Scare, with systematic attacks on radical unions like the Industrial Workers of the World and deportations of foreign-born labor organizers, affect union membership?

And how about the Oregon test's reductive category of "worker"? Shouldn't students be alert to how race, ethnicity, and gender were and are important factors in determining one's workplace experience, including union membership? For example, in 1919, professional strikebreakers, hired by steel corporations, were told to "stir up as much bad feeling as you possibly can between the Serbians and the Italians." And more than 30,000 black workers, excluded from AFL unions, were brought in as strikebreakers (Zinn, 1980, p. 372). A multicultural awareness is vital to arriving at a full answer to this Oregon field-test question. But the state would reward students for choosing a historical sound bite that is as shallow as it is wrong.

What tests communicate

Another aspect of these tests is especially offensive to teachers: They don't merely assess, they also instruct. The tests represent the authority of the state, implicitly telling students, "Just memorize the facts, kids. That's what social studies is all about—and if teachers do any more than that, they're wasting your time." Multiple-choice tests undermine teachers' efforts to construct a rigorous multicultural curriculum because they delegitimate that curriculum in students' eyes: If it were important, it would be on the test.

At its core, multicultural teaching is an ethical, even a political, enterprise. Its aim is not just to impart lots of interesting facts—to equip students to be proficient Trivial Pursuit players—but to help make the world a better place. It highlights injustice of all kinds—racial, gender, class, linguistic, ethnic, national, environmental—to make explanations and propose solutions. It recognizes our responsibility to fellow human beings and to the earth. It has heart and soul.

Compare that with the sterile fact-collecting orientation of Oregon's standards and assessments. For example, a typical 49-question high school field test piloted in 1998 included seven questions on global climate, two on the location of rivers, and one on hypothetical world population projections. But not a single question in the test concerned the lives of people around the world or environmental conditions—nothing about increasing poverty, the global AIDS epidemic, rainforest destruction, unemployment rates, global warming, or efforts to address these crises. The test bounded aimlessly from one disjointed fact to another.

Indeed, the test's randomness may reveal another of its cultural biases. Oregon's standards and assessments make no distinction between knowledge and information. The state's version of social education would appear to have no purpose beyond the acquisition of large quantities of data. But for many cultures, the aim of knowledge is not bulk, but wisdom—insight into meaningful aspects about the nature of life. Writing in *Rethinking Schools*, Peter Kiang makes a similar point about the Massachusetts Teacher Test that calls into question the validity of enterprises such as these. He writes that

> by constructing a test based on a sequence of isolated, decontextualized questions that have no relationship to each other, the underlying epistemology embedded in the test design has a Western-cultural bias, even if individual questions include or represent "multicultural" content. Articulating and assessing a knowledge base requires examining not only what one knows, but also how one knows. (Kiang, 1998/99, p. 23)

Students "know" in different ways, and these differences are often cultural. Oregon nonetheless subjects all students to an abstract, data-heavy assessment device that does not gauge what or how they have learned. As Kiang points out, test makers address multicultural criticism by including individual questions about multicultural content—for example, by highlighting snippets of information about famous people of color like Martin Luther King Jr., Cesar Chavez, and Harriet Tubman. But these "heroes and holidays" additions cannot mask the fundamental hostility to multicultural education shown by standards and assessments like those initiated by Oregon.

The alternative? I want the state to abandon its effort to turn me into a delivery system of approved social information. I want it to support me and other teachers as we collaborate to create a curriculum that deals forthrightly with social problems, that fights racism and social injustice. I want it to acknowledge the legitimacy of a multicultural curriculum of critical questions, complexity, multiple perspectives, and social imagination. I want it to admit that wisdom is more than information—that the world can't be chopped up into multiple-choice questions and that you can't bubble-in the truth with a number-two pencil.

References

Berlak, H. (in press). Cultural politics, the science of assessment and democratic renewal of public education. In A. Filer (Ed.), *Assessment: Social practice and social product.* London: Falmer Press.

Kiang, P. (1998/99). Trivial pursuit testing. *Rethinking Schools, 12*(2), 23.

Learn, S. (1998, December 22). Oregon looks for middle ground with its draft history standards. *The Oregonian*, p. B2.

Lee, E. (1995). Taking multicultural, anti-racist education seriously. In D. Levine et al. (Eds.), *Rethinking schools: An agenda for change* (p. 9). New York: The New Press.

Nelson, W. W. (1998). The naked truth about school reform in Minnesota. *Phi Delta Kappan 79*(9), 681.

Zinn, H. (1980). *A people's history of the United States.* New York: HarperCollins.

CHAPTER 2

ISSUES IN TESTING STUDENTS FROM CULTURALLY AND LINGUISTICALLY DIVERSE BACKGROUNDS (1994)

Richard A. Figueroa and Eugene Garcia

The learning contexts of diversity

Demographic analyses sketch macro portraits of life parameters confronting ethnic families in our country. At the micro level, however, such parameters translate to living conditions that present children with cognitive and linguistic "curricula" often unimagined and incomprehensible to the larger society in general and to test protocols in particular.

Our society has children from nurturing, intact ethnic homes. The language of the home, the media that informs and entertains, and the communication patterns in many neighborhoods involve more than English and another language. They also include code-switching, varying levels of bilingualism and genres unique to such contexts. Biculturalism is a constant, evolving experience for many families as they negotiate competing practices in socialization, child-rearing and relationships. Large communities where English is seldom spoken are commonplace and provide social and linguistic contexts that are unique in what they teach and in how they socialize. Moving between countries on an annual basis creates unique conditions for shifts in language proficiencies and cultural adaptations. Families often live in housing projects where danger preoccupies the family's waking hours. Anomie permeates the condition of many homes, exacerbated by periodic deportations and exploitation in the work place. Some parents are broken by marginalization and isolation. In communities where ethnic groups are in the majority, powerlessness breeds loss of faith in authority and in the political process.

All of these conditions and life situations are not new in the history of the country (Figueroa, 1990). Every new group of immigrants has walked these same paths. What is unique at present is the demography of these conditions. In many areas of the country, a new majority is emerging.

Immigration trends: roots of diversity

From 1981 through 1990 some 7,388,062 people immigrated to the United States, marking a 63 per cent increase in the immigrant population over the previous decade (see Table 2.1). Apart from the sheer magnitude in the numbers of immigrants to the U.S., what are the characteristics of this population? That is, in relative terms, from which countries does this population originate? And perhaps more importantly, what are the greatest changes and emerging immigration trends?

Table 2.1 Immigration to the United States by region 1820–1990 with special emphasis on 1971–1980 and 1981–1990

Region and country of origin	*1820–1990*	*1971–1980*	*1981–1990*
All Countries	**56,994,014**	**4,493,314**	**7,338,062**
Europe	**37,101,060**	**800,368**	**761,550**
Austria-Hungary	4,342,782	16,028	24,885
Austria	1,828,946	9,478	18,340
Hungary	1,667,760	6,550	6,545
Belgium	210,556	5,329	7,066
Czechoslovakia	145,801	6,023	7,227
Denmark	370,412	4,439	5,370
France	787,587	25,069	32,353
Germany	7,083,465	74,414	91,961
Greece	703,904	92,369	38,377
Ireland	4,725,133	11,490	31,969
Italy	5,373,108	129,368	67,254
Netherlands	374,232	10,492	12,238
Norway-Sweden	2,145,954	10,472	15,182
Norway	801,224	3,941	4,164
Sweden	1,284,475	6,531	11,018
Poland	606,336	37,234	83,252
Portugal	501,261	101,710	40,431
Romania	204,841	12,393	30,857
Soviet Union	3,443,706	38,961	57,677
Spain	285,148	39,141	20,433
Switzerland	359,439	8,235	8,849
United Kingdom	5,119,150	137,374	159,173
Yugoslavia	136,271	30,540	18,762
Other Europe	181,974	9,287	8,234
Asia	**5,019,180**	**1,588,178**	**2,738,157**
China	914,376	124,326	346,747
Hong Kong	302,230	113,467	98,215
India	455,716	164,134	250,786
Iran	176,851	45,136	116,172
Israel	137,540	37,713	44,273
Japan	462,244	49,775	47,085
Korea	642,248	267,638	333,746
Philippines	1,026,653	354,987	584,764
Turkey	412,327	13,399	23,233
Vietnam	458,277	172,820	280,782
Other Asia	1,030,718	244,783	648,354
America	**13,067,548**	**1,982,735**	**3,615,255**
Canada	4,295,585	169,939	156,938
Mexico	3,888,729	640,294	1,655,843
Carribean	2,703,177	741,126	872,051
Cuba	748,710	264,863	144,578
Dominican Republic	510,136	148,135	252,035

(*Continued overleaf*)

Table 2.1 continued

Region and country of origin	*1820–1990*	*1971–1980*	*1981–1990*
America (continued)			
Haiti	234,757	56,335	138,379
Jamaica	429,500	137,577	208,148
Other Caribbean	780,074	134,216	128,911
Central America	**819,628**	**134,640**	**648,088**
El Salvador	274,667	34,436	213,539
Other Central America	544,961	100,204	254,549
South America	**1,250,303**	**295,741**	**461,847**
Argentina	131,118	29,897	27,327
Columbia	295,353	77,347	122,849
Ecuador	155,767	50,077	56,315
Other South America	668,065	138,420	255,356
Other America	110,126	995	458
Africa	**334,145**	**80,779**	**176,893**
Oceania	204,622	41,242	45,205
Not Specified	**267,459**	**12**	**1,032**

Over the past two decades, Mexico has remained the country of origin for the majority of immigrants to the U.S. An estimated 1,655,843 Mexican citizens have emigrated here since 1981. This figure outnumbers any other single nation of origin by over a million for the same time period. The Philippines have ranked second in number of U.S.-bound emigrants for some 20 years now (1971–1980: 354,987; and 1981–1990: 548,764). China (346,747), Korea (333,747), and Vietnam (280,782) followed. In terms of the greatest numbers, this ranking of countries of origin has remained relatively stable (since 1971), with the exception of Cuba. The U.S. has seen a decline of Cuban emigrants from 264,863 in the 1970s to 144,578 in the 1980s.

Comparing the past two decades, what countries of origin exhibit the greatest **growth** rates in migrations to the U.S.? In the last ten years more then six times as many Salvadorans have fled to the U.S. from war-torn El Salvador than in the previous decade (1980's: 213,539; 1970's: 34,346). Irish immigration has increased 178 per cent to 31,969. The numbers of Iranian and Haitian immigrants have more than doubled in this same time frame. Eastern European countries, such as Hungary, Poland, and Romania averaged approximately a 100 per cent increase (18,348; 83,252; 30,857 respectively, as of 1990). The Vietnamese community continues to grow at a rate 62 per cent greater than previously.

These statistics describe a U.S. immigrant population which is comprised of vastly different peoples. It is not only rapidly growing but rapidly intensifying in diversity as well. These immigrants come with families and often live in their own, large ethnic communities. More than ever before, we are a nation of immigrants/refugees. This reality has never existed in our country quite as it does now, and as it will increasingly do so in the future.

Future projections of student populations

At the student level, the most comprehensive report with regard to trend towards diversity was published in 1991 by The College Board and the Western Interstate Commission for Higher Education, *The Road to College: Educational Progress by Race and Ethnicity*. This report indicates that the U.S. non-White and Hispanic student population will increase from 10.4 million in 1985–86 to 13.7 million in 1994–95. These pupils will constitute 34 per cent of public elementary and secondary school enrollment in 1994–95, up from 29 per cent in 1985–86. White enrollment, meanwhile, will rise by just five per cent, from 25.8 million to 27 million, and their share of the student population will drop from 71 per cent to 66 per cent in 1994–95. Non-White and Hispanic student enrollment will grow from 10 million in 1976 to nearly 45 million in 2026. These students will grow from 23 per cent to 70 per cent of our nation's school enrollment during this relatively short period of time. **In 2026, we will have the exact inverse of student representation as we knew it in 1990 when White students made up 70 per cent of our enrolled K-12 student body.**

Of distinctive educational significance is the reality that in 1986, 30 to 35 per cent (3 million) of non-White and Hispanic students were identified as residing in homes in which English was not the primary language (August & Garcia, 1988). Using these figures and extrapolating from the projections displayed in Tables 2.1 and 2.2, by the year 2000, our schools will be the home for six million limited English proficient students. By the year 2026, that number will conservatively approximate 15 million students, or somewhere in the vicinity of 25 per cent of total elementary and secondary school enrollments.

The language minority student and testing

Within this discussion of student diversity, one distinctive subpopulation should be highlighted due to its growing size, both relatively and absolutely, and its precarious situation within our educational institutions. These students come to the schooling process without the language in which that process is imbedded. Demographic data has indicated that in the next two decades some 15 per cent of U.S., K-12 student population, will be comprised of these students. Moreover, they present a special challenge to our social and educational institutions and practices (such as testing) due to their linguistic diversity. Much of the formal, pre-K-12, teaching/learning/testing enterprise requires effective communication of specific facts, concepts, ideas, and problem solving strategies. Most of these students are able to do that, but, they do so in another language and through different communication skills (August & Garcia, 1988). These often do not match those of the service provider, teacher, school, or test.

As one searches for a comprehensive definition of the "language minority" student, a continuum of possibilities unfolds. At one end of the continuum are general definitions such as "students who come from homes in which a language other than English is spoken." At the other end of that continuum are highly operationalized definitions, "students scored in the first quartile on a standardized test of English language proficiency." Regardless of the definition adopted, these students come in a variety of linguistic shapes and forms.

The language minority population in the U.S. continues to be linguistically very heterogeneous. There are over 100 distinct language groups identified. Even in the largest language group, some are monolingual Spanish speakers while others are to some degree bilingual. Other non-English speaking minority groups in the U.S. are similarly heterogeneous. Describing the "typical" language minority student is highly problematic. However, one might agree that this student is one: (a) who is characterized by substantive participation in a non-English speaking social environment; (b) who has acquired the normal communicative abilities of that social environment; (c) who is exposed to a substantive English-speaking environment, more than likely for the first time, during the schooling process; and (d) who tests poorly on verbal, English-language tests.

Estimates of the number of language minority students have been compiled by the federal government on several occasions (O'Malley, 1981; Development Associates, 1984; Waggoner, 1991). These estimates differ because of the definition adopted for identifying these students, the particular measure utilized to obtained the estimate, and the statistical treatment utilized to generalize beyond the sample obtained. For example, O'Malley (1981) defined the language minority student population by utilizing a specific cutoff score on an English language proficiency test administered to a stratified sample of students. Development Associates (1984) estimated the population by utilizing reports from a stratified sample of local school districts. Estimates of language minority students have ranged from 1,300,000 (Development Associates, 1984) to 3,600,000 (O'Malley, 1981).

The U.S. Department of Education (1993) recently sketched a demographic and educational portrait of these students. Table 2.2 summarizes this information.

Notwithstanding, the statistical portrait of LEP children and their low status in the public schools, at an ideographic level the picture is just as dramatic. Children come to school with language genres, behavior patterns, motivations, attitudes, and expectations that are either unacknowledged by the schools or seen as developmental deficits that must be "remediated" or proscribed before school learning can begin. In the standoff between what the schools require and what ethnic children bring, the children usually loose. Instead of acknowledging that these pupils are learners with unique and intact systems of knowledge (Moll, Velez-Ibanez, Greenberg, & Rivera, 1990) and processes for learning, they are tracked into programs that attempt to "cure" the deficits or to diagnose cultural and linguistic differences as mental handicaps to be dealt with in special education.

In terms of the middle class normative frameworks that undergird tests, children from diverse learning environments have traditionally been described as developmentally deficient in language, cognition, attention, memory, perception, learning ability, IQ, and just about every major benchmark of "normal" growth and development. Virtually every "objective" test used to assess individual skills or aptitudes has been instrumental in profiling these deficits.

Ironically, from their inception, "standard" assessments, and particularly tests, have operated under a key, robust assumption. They assume equal or comparable exposure to the content of the assessments prior to the assessment. They assume a high degree of homogeneity of experiences. Regretably, when such homogeneity has not actually existed, test and test users have enforced it by labeling individuals with average scores as "normal" and those with below average scores as "deviant." This, in spite of historical admonishments about the assumption buttressing normative measures:

> . . . The validity of **all** mental testing rests on the fundamental assumption that those tested have had a **common opportunity to learn** the skills, facts,

Table 2.2 "Descriptive study of services to limited English proficient students" [U.S. Department of Education, 1993]—Summary of data

1. Since 1984, there has been a 70 per cent increase in the number of LEP students (currently totalling 2.31 million);
2. Across the country, 43 per cent of all school districts serve LEP pupils;
3. 82 per cent of the LEP student population is in grades K-9, making it an exceedingly young population of school-age children;
4. Almost 75 per cent speak Spanish, 4 per cent Vietnamese, 2 per cent speak Hmong, Cantonese, Cambodian and Korean (each), and and the rest speak from 29 Native American languages;
5. 41 per cent of LEP students were born in the U.S;
6. The larger the school district, the more likely that language assessment proficiency is measured through a standardized procedure;
7. English is the predominant language assessed; only 33 per cent of the districts measure oral language proficiency in the native language; only 12 per cent measure academic achievement in the home language;
8. The larger the number of LEP pupils in a school district, the more likely that services are provided in the native language;
9. 20 per cent of the states do not require native language services for LEP pupils and almost 33 per cent of the states require some form of primary language service in academic content areas;
10. Only 22 states make special allocations for instructing LEP students;
11. ESL is the predominant instructional adaptation for LEP pupils; only 17 per cent of schools provide a significant degree of primary language instruction;
12. Instructional aides provide a large amount of the instructional and translation services;
13. Though over 363,000 teachers provide some service to LEP pupils, only 10 per cent are credentialed bilingual teachers;
14. Only 33 per cent of the teachers serving LEP pupils have ever taken a college course on culture, language acquisition or teaching English to LEP pupils; and
15. The majority of teachers serving Spanish-speaking pupils have no proficiency in Spanish

> principles and methods of procedure exemplified in the tests. [emphasis added] (Colvin, 1921, p. 137.)

> The assumption is made that if one samples the results of learning in matters where all individuals tested have had an **equal chance** at learning, he may arrive at an estimate of the capacity to learn. [emphasis added] (Dearborn, 1921, p. 211.)

> One's actual present capacity for doing any particular thing is obviously dependent upon his training and learning, or, in general, upon his past experience: whereas in the measurement of intelligence, the attempt is always to minimize the effects of past experience by utilizing performances, the acquisition of the capacity for which is presumably **favored equally** by the past environments of all individuals measured. [emphasis added] (Woodrow, 1921, p. 207.)

The fragility of tests and testing

Tests have high status in our society. At the turn of the century, they propelled the new science of psychology into the limelight by politically enhancing nativist notions about American intelligence and by providing an efficient system for tracking army recruits into various jobs in the military during the first and second World Wars (Cronbach, 1957). Tests are perceived as scientific, objective, and useful. In high stakes assessments, they tend to carry the day in decisions about jobs, educational placements, diagnosis, etc. Yet, their true source of power has always resided in their ability to predict, to predict better than human judgment.

However, tests are quite fragile. They rest on some key assumptions (above), and they are generally plagued by shortcomings in technical properties. The *Buros Mental Measurement Yearbooks*, for example, typically fault most available normative measure on the issues of reliability or validity. However, the primary source of discontent by test reviewers resides in tests' weak or modest predictive validities. It is generally rare to find a test that predicts to real-life situations (grades, job success, program completion rates, etc.) with anything above a .5 or .6 correlation. This essentially means that anywhere from 75 to 64 per cent of the variance of the criterion (what is predicted to) remains unexplained. By and large, the further a test score gets from similar test scores (for example, from a developmental test score, to another developmental test score, to an achievement test score, to grades, to graduation rates), the lower the predictive validities become.

We have attempted to examine this with tests commonly given to young children. Table 2.3 presents the predictive coefficients or evaluations of validity reported by three well known test evaluators (Sattler, 1988; Salvia & Ysseldyke, 1988; Bredekamp & Shepard, 1989). By and large, the data in Table 2.3 show that these tests are fragile.

It should be noted that almost all the predictive coefficients cited in Table 2.3 involve achievement test scores as criteria. Few studies actually ever report on grades or other more "existential" criteria. Usually when such indices are used, test scores predict in the .2 to .3 range. In other words, they account for approximately 4 to 9 per cent of grade variance. Many argue that this is due to the low reliability and subjectivity involved in such real-life "scores." Paradoxically, it is these type of "scores" that usually decide on promotions, suspensions, and other real life outcomes. For tests, however, they remain too "subjective."

Table 2.3 Predictive validity and evaluations of validity for some of the most widely used tests of school readiness

Name of test	*Predictive coefficients*	*Evaluations*
Boehm Test of Basic Concepts	.40 (Mdn. Corr; Achievement tests)*	"correlates modestly with achievement . . . has inadequate reliability and norms." *p. 442
	.54 (Spelling)**	
	.54 (Ach. Tests)**	
	.27 (Rdng. Test)**	"acceptable validity but only minimally adequate validity." **p. 344
	.27–.72 (Ach. subtests)**	
Form C	.52 (Mdn; Ach. Tests)**	
Form D	.50 (Mdn; Ach. Tests)**	
Boehm Preschool	.67 (vocabulary)**	
	.57 (vocabulary)**	

Denver Developmental Screening Test		"reliability and validity are adequate . . . although the norms are questionable." **p. 440 "has several weaknesses . . . should be used with caution" **p. 352
Metropolitan Readiness Test	.34–.65 (Ach. subtests)** .48–.83 (Ach. subtests)**	"The MRT's predictive validity particular curricula or other achievement tests is unknown and therefore . . . should not be used as a predictive devise." *p. 451 ". . . the evidence for validity is scant." *p. 453
Gessel School Readiness Test	.28–.64 (Ach. intell)***	"The psychometric properties of the Gesell test do not meet the standards of professional test development." ***p. 16
Preschool Inventory-R		". . . empirical validity is generally lacking." *p. 445
Test of Basic Experience		"Evidence for predictive validity is not reported." *p. 446
Developmental Indicators for the Assessment of Language-R		"Norms are questionnable . . . reliability is poor . . . Validity is not clearly established." *p. 449
Developmental Profile II		". . . norms are unrepresentative, the degree of reliability unknown, and evidence for validity is scant." *p. 453
Columbia Mental Maturity Scale	.31–.61 (Ach. tests)	". . . appears technically adequate." *p. 195
Detroit Test of Learning Aptitude-R	.51 (Mdn; ach. tests)	*data on validity is scarce." *p. 175
Extended Merrill Palmer		"No validity indeces are reported in the manual." **p. 307
McCarthy Scales of Children's Abilities	.66 (Mdn; ach. tests)** .58 (ach. tests)**	"Evidence about validity is still limited." *p. 139
Wechsler Preschool and Primary Scale of Intelligence	.58, .30, .37, .58, .36, .36, .60, .62, .68, .43, NS, .27, .61, .41, .73 (Ach. tests)**	"evidence on validity is . . . very limited." *p. 169 "Excellent reliability and validity . . ." **p. 214

* (Salvia & Ysseldyke, 1988)
** (Sattler, 1988)
*** (Bredekamp & Shepard, 1989)

Given the fragile nature of the technical data reviewed in Table 2.2, some of the precautions and requisites in this are worth quoting:

> There are . . . major dilemmas in assessing readiness . . . the performances of preschoolers are so variable that there is relatively little long-term prediction . . . while readiness tests are used exclusively to predict a person's success or failure in an instructional sequence or program. Therefore, certain technical characteristics, such as predictive criterion-referenced validity, are extremely important. Moreover, since readiness tests are routinely used to make individual placement decisions, these tests must conform to the highest standards of technical excellence. (Salvia & Ysseldyke, 1988, p. 454)

Recently, even the most powerful tests (IQ) have also come under criticism for not being very useful in helping to plan educational interventions (Shinn, 1989). Also, ethnographic studies of what actually happens in the most controlled testing situations also show that the much touted objectivity of the enterprise may be more illusory than real:

> Proponents of testing describe tests as objective, standardized and normreferenced. In a standardized test, procedures, apparatus, and scoring have been fixed so that precisely the same test can be given to many different students on different occasions. The emphasis here is standardization of procedure. Technically, testing kits are uniform. We found, however, that the administration of tests in practical situations is not routine. The act of testing involves a complex social relationship . . . that makes the uniform and objective measure of intelligence a social activity. (Mehan, Hertweck, & Meihls, 1986, p. 94)

Mehan also found that in testing situations inappropriate feedback was given, and incorrect cues were provided. In effect, social factors played as important a part as the test directions. The distinct impression given by Mehan's descriptions of the testing sessions he videotaped is that testing is not "reliable" in that it does not follow the script provided by the test manuals.

> We have confirmed the findings of many previous researchers . . . who have shown that treating test results as . . . facts obscures the constitutive process by which testers and students jointly produce answers in individual tests. (Mehan *et al.*, 1986, p. 100)

There is one other factor to consider. Most of the predictive correlation's cited in Table 2.3 come from studies where White, middle-class children are used as subjects. In the few studies where minority children are involved (Sattler, 1988), the outcomes are often in the direction of lowering the predictive correlations. In effect, for many minority populations, evidence is beginning to accumulate indicating that test fragility may well be test bias.

The historical context

Virtually every ethnic group in the U.S. since the early 1900s has fared badly on American tests (Brigham, 1923; Figueroa, 1990; Valdes & Figueroa, in press):

> On the other hand, with regard to more purely intellectual traits, the Japanese are judged as inferior. This is shown in the ratings of general intelligence, desire to know and originality. (Darsie, 1926, p. 76)

In a comprehensive review of intelligence and achievement testing with linguistic minorities, Figueroa (1990) outlined some of the key historical issues and findings regarding the effects of culture and bilingualism on these two categories of American tests.

With respect to culture, Figueroa (1990) found that the typical way in which test researchers dealt with this variable was to operationally define it in a group. Rather than set forth a continua of factors associated with a culture, test researchers ascribed it to a group. Hence, when American Indian culture was being studied, it resided in the test scores of the American Indian group being investigated. Accordingly, Garth (1920) talked about the "mental fatigue" trait in American-Indian and Mexican-American culture. The effects of poverty, segregation, biased teacher perceptions, and the general anti-immigrant social and political sentiment of the early part of this century played no part in explaining the large differences between the test scores of "minority" populations and the dominant cultural group. Test scores had the force of science behind them and differences in group scores were seen as real differences in mental abilities and genetic potential.

Similar to culture, bilingualism was not taken seriously. However, as Figueroa (1990) demonstrates, this variable left its imprint on every study on intelligence and achievement test conducted with populations from non-English backgrounds. First, any test that required the use of English in even the most elemental task (*e.g.*, repeating digits in English) and even with groups that already spoke English, registered the impact of the second language in a lower than expected score. Interestingly, some of the most conservative test makers and advocates came to appreciate the pervasive impact of a second language on test scores:

> For purposes of comparing individuals or groups, it is apparent that tests in the vernacular [English] must be used only with individuals having equal opportunities to acquire the vernacular of the test. This requirement precludes the use of such tests in making comparative studies of individuals brought up in homes in which the vernacular of the test is not used, or in which two vernaculars are used. The last condition is frequently violated here in studies of children born in this country whose parents speak another tongue. It is important, as the effects of bilingualism are not entirely known. (Brigham, 1930, p. 165)

Second, bilingualism never affected internal indices (reliability, concurrence) of test adequacy. But in several studies, there was evidence that bilingualism lowered predictive validity (Figueroa, 1990). Third, anomalous data showed up: for bilinguals, recalling digits backward was easier than recalling them forward; middle class bilingual test-takers often did better than middle-class English speakers; and finally, older bilinguals who had been educated in their primary language also often did better than English speakers. Fourth, though verbal tests were always hypersensitive to bilingualism, school grades were not.

The solutions that test users and test makers often tried to apply when it came to testing bilingual populations pre-1950s included the following: (a) ignore bilingualism and test in English, (b) use non-verbal tests, (c) translate the test into the native language and use the same norms, and (d) norm the test in the primary language. Some of these solutions exist to the present. However, as Figueroa (1989, 1990) has pointed out, none of them have any merit. In many ways, the caveats that were articulated in the 1920s and 1930s about the bilingual pupil and testing remain just as poignant today (Brigham, 1930, above).

It is regrettable, however, that test users and test makers have chosen to repeat the mistakes of the past when it comes to culturally and linguistically diverse students. Since the 1960s, the federal courts and Congress have had to step in and legislate testing practices. This is uniquely the case in special education.

Special education testing

The contemporary issue of testing and minorities first came to the attention of the courts in a non-special education case, *Hobsen v. Hansen*. In this case, Black children in the Washington, D.C. area, after being integrated at the high school level (as per *Brown v. Board of Education*), began failing in large numbers. The district superintendent initiated a testing system designed to tailor educational programs to individual abilities. An elaborate testing system was set in place to direct the students into their most appropriate program. Since neither the tests nor the test givers paid attention to the fact that pre-integration, Black pupils attended "disadvantaged" school and were exposed to "disadvantaged" curricula, in a few years the vocational tracks in the high schools were all Black and the academic tracks were all White. In the subsequent trial, the judge in *Hobsen v. Hansen* ruled that the tests were responsible for the new segregation and that these instruments could not measure the learning potential of Black students because they did not account for their cultural background.

Hobsen v. Hansen is a benchmark in the field of testing because all the language linked to prejudice, racism and segregation became associated with the adverse impact that tests often have on culturally diverse pupils. From this case, the stage was set for a legal challenge to the sort of testing that goes on in special education.

In the early 1960s. an old phenomenon (Reynolds, 1933) began receiving attention from researchers (Mercer, 1973). Classes for the mildly handicapped (mild mental retardation, learning handicaps) were found to be over-populated by Black and Hispanic pupils (the same could have been reported about American Indian children). In *Diana v. California Board of Education*, the Ninth Circuit oversaw an out of court settlement entitling bilingual pupils to testing in English and in their primary language. The settlement also called for yearly monitoring of the effects of testing on overrepresentation rates in classes for the mildly handicapped.

In *Larry P. v. Riles*, the same Ninth District federal judge ruled, after a lengthy trial, that IQ tests were biased against Black children because they did not take into account their cultural background. He banned the use of such tests for Black children who were being considered for placement into the Educable Mentally Retarded programs.

Since these two cases, there have been a series of similar legal challenges to testing in special education (*Lora v. Board of Education of the City of New York; Jose P. v. Ambach; PASE v. Hannon*). Most of these have been framed within the facts and issues surrounding *Diana* and *Larry P.* Most of the time the rulings have gone in the same direction as *Diana*. In the matter of *Larry P.*, some judges have ruled in a diametrically different direction and at present a legal challenge to *Larry P.* in California (*Crawford v. Honig*) is moving the state on the side of Black children and possibly towards the elimination of IQ tests, psychometric tests, the Medical Model used to "diagnose" problem learners as handicapped learners, and the very existence of separate classes for the mildly handicapped. These moves, it should be pointed out, are not without support from the research community (Skrtic, 1991).

In 1975, in P.L. 94–142, Congress included testing language that flowed directly from the court cases. In special education for young children and for the K-12 population, tests and testing have to be racially and culturally non-discriminatory and have to be provided in the primary language, if it is at all feasible to do so.

The regulatory context

Since the 1960s, the testing professions have published many editions of the testing *Standards* (American Psychological Association, 1954; American Educational Research Association & National Council on Measurement, 1955; American Psychological Association, American Educational Research Association, & National Council on Measurement, 1966, 1974; American Educational Research Association, American Psychological Association, National Council on Measurement, 1985), and periodic texts on issues confronting testing (Cleary, Humphreys, Kendrick, & Wesman, 1975; Wigdor & Garner, 1982; Heller, Holtzman, & Messick, 1982). Most have either asserted that cultural bias in testing cannot be found (Cleary, Humphreys, Kendrick, & Wesman, 1975) or they have reiterated the same historical cautions about bilingualism and testing without any real sense of sanctions or proscriptions. Among these, however, there are two key exceptions.

First, the National Academy of Sciences, in an indirect way, has framed some of the cultural concerns surrounding the testing of ethnic pupils in an interesting manner (Heller, Holtzman, & Messick, 1982). In its report on the overrepresentation of minority pupils in special education, the Academy endorsed one suggestion (pp. 68–72): before the very high-stakes testing for special education, there should be an assessment of the **instructional context** where the student is currently placed. In effect, the recommendation is for educators to take into account at least one of the key background variables that affects children's learning: the quality of their learning experience in the classroom.

Specifically, the Academy set four dimensions in order to gauge the effectiveness of the classroom: (a) there should be evidence that the curriculum offered works with the pupil's cultural group, (b) there should be documented evidence that such curriculum is effectively implemented by the teacher, (c) there should be evidence that the child in question has not really learned the material taught, (d) there should be evidence of early intervention when the problems in learning first appeared. If all these conditions are met, then and only then does the assessment move on to consider the possibility that the problem resides in the pupil. This is a major departure in the history of testing. For once, there is now a directive to examine the historical caveats and assumptions on which tests rest: the homogeneity of experience. This is to be done prior to the administration of the test and prior to the interpretation of any score.

Second, all the major national organizations involved with testing, in the *Standards for Educational and Psychological Testing*, (AERA, APA, NCM, 1985) finally come to terms with the historical, complex, intervening variable of bilingualism. In a chapter on "Testing Linguistic Minorities" the *Standards*, like the

National Academy of Sciences, break new ground. First, it is acknowledged that for bilingual learners who may not have had "substantial" exposure to English, any test given in English becomes in unknown degrees a test of English language or English literacy.

Third, a bilingual individual's linguistic background must be taken into account in any type of testing. "Bilingualism" is multifactorial and includes individuals with a broad range of speaking, reading, writing, and understanding abilities in each language. Further, some "bilinguals" not only speak two languages they also codeswitch as per the social demands of communicative events. Also, for some bilingual individuals, processing information in the weaker language is a more demanding undertaking than for a monolingual.

Fourth, translating tests does not translate psychometric properties. The same vocabulary item in two languages can have different frequency (p) values, degrees of propriety and meaningfulness.

Fifth, there is a need for multifactorial language tests ("communicative competence, literacy, grammar, pronunciation, comprehension" p. 74) in English and in primary languages in order to help make educational placement decisions.

Sixth, linguistic proficiency in English is at least a dual phenomenon: that which is manifest in informal communication and that which is required in formal and academic situations.

Seventh, language is culturally embedded, and the unique linguistic genre typically used in testing ("an adult who is probing for elaborate speech with only short phrases" p. 74) may elicit culturally appropriate ways of responding rather than test appropriate ways of answering ("short phrases or . . . shrugging their shoulders" p. 74) leading to "interpretations and prescriptions of treatment [that] may be invalid and potentially harmful to the individual being tested" (p. 74).

The issues raised in the chapter on "Testing Linguistic Minorities" in the *Standards* virtually preclude the use of psychometric and normative tests with linguistically and culturally diverse individuals in the U.S. Paradoxically, this paper and the *Standards* themselves barely scratch the surface on the biasing effects of culture and bilingualism. The *Standards* are currently being revised. It will be interesting to see whether the testing professions retreat from their 1985 directives or actually move towards correcting the testing abuses of the last 75 years.

Culture and bilingualism

Testing psychology has yet to cope with culture. In studies on test bias, "culture" continues to be defined by the group that supposedly has the "culture" (Sandoval, 1979; Sandoval, Zimmerman & Woo-Sam, 1980).

As a variable, "culture" in testing psychology is a black box. The one large attempt to operationally define it, the *System of Multicultural Pluralistic Assessment* (SOMPA) (Mercer, 1979), failed because it relied on more testing (as a way to capture its complexity) while ignoring any sources of test variance unique to African-American or Hispanic cultures. At its core, SOMPA failed because it did not know how to cope with bias in the criteria to which tests are expected to predict and because it did not dare to really measure those elements in African-American and Latino cultures which constitute the curricula, pedagogy, and contexts to which cross-cultural children in our society are exposed (Tharp, 1989; Moll *et al.*, 1990; Miller-Jones, 1989).

SOMPA did do something unique. It treated each ethnic group as a separate norming population of 700 youngsters. But it used this wonderful sampling opportunity to norm the same White, culture-bound tests on culturally different children and then expected these tests to provide something more than measures of sociological distance from the majority culture. As diagnostic tools, the SOMPA tests continued the tradition of mismeasuring children because of their differentness all the while ignoring what they had learned in their unique demographic and cultural worlds. In the end, the SOMPA tests also proved to be just as fragile and modest in helping to predict future performance (Figueroa & Sassenrarth, 1989; Figueroa, 1989).

The Courts have been just as unspecific in operationalizing "culture." But, paradoxically, they have been insistent that since neither in their development nor validation have tests taken "culture" into account, they are inappropriate and invalid for pupils from diverse cultural backgrounds.

Notwithstanding, the breakthrough re-presented by the *Standards*, bilingualism also continues to be ignored by test developers and test users. The current, favorite "solution" to the challenge of bilingualism for testing is to either have a bilingual adult translate a test extemporaneously while testing a child (a practice that is widespread and proscribed by the current *Standards*) or to produce seemingly comparable versions of the U.S. tests in another language. The Spanish versions of the *Woodcock Johnson Psychoeducational Battery* and the *Boehm Test of Basic Concepts* are primary examples of this trend.

This "solution" has a unique appeal since it appears to solve the problem. But it is naive and misguided. To begin with, a bilingual learner in the U.S. is not like a monolingual English learner nor like a monolingual Spanish speaker. As Grosjean (1989) explains, the last 20 years of educational, psychological, neurological, and information-processing research has shown that:

> A bilingual (or holistic) view of bilingualism proposes that the bilingual is an integrated whole which cannot be decomposed into two separate parts. The bilingual is NOT the sum of two complete or incomplete monolinguals, rather, he or she has a unique and specific linguistic configuration. The coexistence and constant interaction of the two languages in the bilingual has produced a different but complete linguistic entity. (Grosjean, 1989, p. 6)

Because of the *Lau v. Nichols* Supreme Court decision in 1975, bilingualism and bilingual education have received an unparalleled degree of attention and debate (Hakuta, 1986). The extant knowledge base about bilingualism in the U.S. and abroad is very large and continues to document the complexity of this human trait and the complexity of learners who operate in bilingual contexts. Because of the available knowledge and because of the demographic profile of our country as an emerging bilingual society, there is a growing understanding of the multivariate, developmental conditions that can affect a bilingual learner.

Children learn two languages either simultaneously or sequentially. The latter is the more common phenomenon and includes wide differences in linguistic varieties (*e.g.* dialect, codeswitching); in second language (L2) acquisition rates and correlates (proficiency in L1, access to L2 peers, extroversion, motivation, formal instruction); in proficiencies (in L1 and L2); and in degrees of loss (either of L1 when it is not supported in the instructional setting or L2 when there is migration between countries).

At a more psychological level, several theoretical formulations have been proposed to account for the range of linguistic differences and the reasons for bilingual underachievement. Among the most widely known is the following: The Threshold Hypothesis—"the degree to which proficiencies in L1 and L2 are developed is positively associated with academic achievement" (Office of Bilingual, Bicultural Education, 1982, p. 7). The worst case scenario for bilingual children is when neither their primary nor their secondary languages are developed to near native capacity. Bilingualism in this situation is "subtractive," leading to underachievement (Skutnabb-Kangas & Toukomaa, 1976) and limited access to language-mediated cognitive functions (metaphor, similarities, analogy). This is most often caused by an emphasis on the acquisition of English above everything else.

At an atomistic level, other features of bilingualism have been mapped out with considerable specificity by research on information processing. Studies not only suggest topographical differences in the left cerebral hemisphere of bilingual individuals (Figueroa, 1991), they also indicate that bilinguals may have memory storage systems with non-overlapping and overlapping areas. In the former, the implication is that in one language, say English, a particular piece of information, such as the meaning of a vocabulary item on a test, may not be accessible even though it is known in the other, primary language. Extensive research from both Europe and the U.S. also points to the disadvantage that bilingual learners face when asked to perform encoding tasks in the weaker language. Not only is the process potentially slower, it is also more amenable to blockage due to stress, task complexity or noise. For tasks such as reading, where naming speed is critical for comprehension, the bilingual learner can be put at a considerable disadvantage when artificially induced speed or timed tasks (such as in tests) are required.

It should be pointed out that this line of research has also mapped out the strategic advantages of bilingualism. For example, using two languages to process information (with tasks as simple as taking bilingual notes) produces greater learning. There is some indication that creativity is enhanced in bilingual processing. Children who are taught in effective bilingual classrooms show greater academic gains than those taught in English-only programs. There is even the possibility of enhanced cognitive functioning in bilingual individuals.

This knowledge base exists with virtually no influence on the field of assessment. However, the imprint of bilingualism is being discovered in the key *raison d'être* of tests: predictive validity. This is new ground in the field of psychometrics and assessment in general. From their very beginnings, formal assessments have registered large ethnic and racial differences on group averages. But the argument has always been that this is not evidence of bias. The true test of bias resides in demonstrating differential rates of predictive validities. These have seldom if ever been demonstrated. Table 2.4 presents some of the emerging findings on the impact of linguistic backgrounds on predictive validities. As the available studies now show, the greater the use of a non-English language in the home, the lower the predictive validity of some of the most well known and respected psychometric instruments of mental ability. Table 2.4 shows how this applies to children's and to **young** children's measures. Interestingly, the data also indicate that non-verbal measures may be the most hypersensitive to linguistic background and the most flawed with respect to bias in predictive validity.

What is the alternative?

The testing technology currently in existence is very fragile and has not improved its percent reduction in total error beyond 40 per cent (predictive coefficients above .6). This has been the case for over 75 years in spite of progressively more

Table 2.4 Comparison of predictive validity coefficients of several tests of ability [predicting to standardized measures of reading and math] for Hispanic children from three home-language groups [E = English, E/S = English/Spanish, S = Spanish] and for Anglo children

	Reading				*Math*			
	Hispanic			*Anglo+*	*Hispanic*			*Anglo+*
	E	*E/S*	*S*		*E*	*E/S*	*S*	
WISC-R								
VIQ								
(a)*	.60	.50	.45	.66	.55	.50	.42	.56
(b)			.37	.57			.42	.62
(c)			.33	.66			.43	.56
PIQ								
(a)	.52	.40	.39	.47	.54	.44	.23	.48
(b)			.34	.50			.41	.59
(c)			.26	.47			.20	.48
FSIQ								
(a)	.61	.53	.47	.65	.60	.55	.37	.58
(b)			.35	.62			.42	.52
(c)			.37	.65			.41	.58
Binet								
3 yrs								
(c)			.34				.33	
4 yrs								
(c)			.27				.31	
McCarthy Scales								
(c)			.37	.66			.41	.66
K-ABC Mntl Procss Compos								
(d)		.23		.56		.32		.56**
K-ABC Achieve.								
(d)		.67		.80		.49		.80**
Bohem.								
(e)	.66		NS	.67	.64		.47	.65**
Tchers. Ratings Pre K to End 1st Grade								
(f)	NS		NS	.49	NS		NS	.64
Number Profic.								
(f)	.31		NS	.57	.21		.60	.51

+ Values taken from Sattler (1988); unless otherwise indicated.

* Sources: (a) Figueroa, 1990; (b) Mishra, 1983; (c) Johnson & McGowan, 1984; (d) Valencia & Ranking; 1988; (e) Pilkington, Piercel & Pontorotto, 1981; (f) Gandara, Keogh & Yoshioka-Maxwell, 1980.

** Values taken from row sources.

and more sophisticated statistical tools for analyzing scores. When it comes to testing young children the tests are extremely tenuous in what they can do. Add to this the complex, multifactorial challenges posed by the variables of culture and bilingualism and the "objective," "scientific," "accurate," and "useful" attributions made to testing become more myth than fact. It should be recalled that the diverse contexts in which children develop in our country is growing geometrically as the diversity of our population grows arithmetically.

Taking all these considerations into account: (1) psychometric, norm-based assessments of school readiness and high-stakes testing for all diverse learners in schools and outside of schools should be abandoned, and (2) the Medical Model paradigm which undergirds testing should also be abandoned. The first recommendation is not new. It has been proposed since the 1970s when the court cases involving tests received a great deal of media and public attention. Recent versions of this recommendation (Diversity and Equity in Assessment Network, 1993; Neill, 1993), however, break new ground in not just calling for the removal of "multiple-choice, norm-referenced, standardized tests in the U.S." They also call for redefining the principles that govern school-based testing: appropriateness, instructional validity, and limited role in decision-making. The most critical dimension in the new debate on the tests and testing, however, is the call for authentic, performance-based assessments. This includes the recognition, sometimes underemphasized, that authentic assessments must hold the instructional setting accountable and must also assess its impact on the learner.

What is often missing in the new demands for a sea change in assessments is the call for a change in paradigm. The psychology of "individual differences" has been such a powerful influence that entire professions view IQs as measures of intelligence, achievement test scores as measures of what children know, personality profiles as what a person is, and vocational aptitude scores as indicators of what a person can do. Scores derived from one, two, or three hours of small responses to small stimuli (test items) do not account for much of real-life functioning, nor for the situated and unpredictable nature of human behavior. The same student with the same academic task can use many different cognitive strategies depending on the day, the teacher, or the mood. Only assessments that recognize that contexts often influence or even define outcomes actually begin to work under a different paradigm, and under a more contextualist and constructivist view of human functioning and human measurement. Such assessments are by nature longitudinal and bifocal. That is, they inherently measure the individual's work and the context in which it happened.

In education, the movement towards portfolio assessment is particularly promising. Attempts, however, at using old psychometric benchmarks in order to legitimize portfolio assessments, or at attributing portfolio work-products exclusively to individual mentation (the "individual differences" model), or at developing portfolio measurement systems that do not account or build on cultural and linguistic diversity (*e.g.*, Resnick & Resnick, 1989) are not really reform efforts. A paradigm shift begins with a refutation of the Medical Model myth that what is behaviorally measured is really what is inside the individual in actuality and inmutably (like "intelligence," or "mental retardation," or "learning disabilities"). Without such a change, dynamic assessment, criterion-referenced and "authentic" assessment models will still lead to ethnic overrepresentation in special education classes because the search will still be for the broken mental process, for the disability **inside** the individual.

Portfolio assessment is uniquely intriguing since it inherently provides a portrait of the type of educational opportunity that a pupil has been given. In classrooms that are driven by a Reductionist pedagogical model (Poplin, 1988a,b), the portfolio will include worksheets, phonics drills, and spelling lists. In classrooms that are taught without regard for the use of the primary language, the portfolios of limited English-speakers will provide a portrait of many futile struggles at making meaning. In classrooms that are optimal learning environments (where constructivism, biliteracy, literature, and authentic writing projects occur) the portfolio will track development and academic achievement in-context.

References

American Educational Research Association, American Psychological Association, The National Council on Measurement. (1985). *Standards for educational and psychological testing*. Washington, DC: American Psychological Association.

American Educational Research Association, The National Council on Measurement. (1955). *Technical recommendations for achievement tests*. Washington, DC: National Education Association.

American Psychological Association (1954). *Technical recommendations for psychological tests and diagnostic techniques*. New York: American Psychological Association.

American Psychological Association, American Educational Research Association, The National Council on Measurement. (1966). *Standards for educational and psychological tests and manuals*. Washington, DC: American Psychological Association.

American Psychological Association, American Educational Research Association, The National Council on Measurement. (1974). *Standards for educational and psychological tests*. Washington, DC: American Psychological Association.

August, D. & Garcia, E. (1988). *Language minority education in the U.S.: Research, policy and practice*. Chicago, IL: Charles C. Thomas.

Bredekamp, S. & Shepard, L. (1989). How best to protest children from inappropriate school expectations, practices and policies. *Young Children*, 44(3), 14–24.

Brigham, C. C. (1923). *A study of American intelligence*. Princeton: Princeton University Press.

Brigham, C. C. (1930). Intelligence tests of immigrant groups. *Psychological Review*, 37, 15–165.

California Department of Education. (1992). LEP growth in the last two decades. *Bulletin of the California State Department of Education*, 12, 3–4.

Cleary, T. A., Humphreys, L. G., Kendrick, S. A. & Wesman, A. (1975). Educational uses of tests with disadvantaged students. *American Psychologist*, 30, 15–40.

Colvin, S. S. (1921). Intelligence and its measurement: A symposium (IV). *Journal of Educational Psychology*, 12, 136–139.

Cronbach, L. J. (1957). The two disciplines of scientific psychology. *American Psychologist*, 12, 671–684.

Darsie, M. L. (1926). The mental capacity of American-born Japanese children. *Comparative Psychology Monographs*, 3(15), 1–89.

Dearborn, W. F. (1921). Intelligence and its measurement: A symposium (XII). *Journal of Educational Psychology*, 12, 210–212.

Development Associates (1984). *Final report descriptive study phase of the national longitudinal evaluation of the effectiveness of services for language minority limited English proficient students*. Arlington, VA: Author.

Diversity and Equity in Assessment Network (1993). Guidelines for Equitable Assessment. Cambridge, MA: Fair Test.

Figueroa, R. A. (1989). Psychological testing of linguistic minority students in special education. *Exceptional Children*, 56(2), 145–152.

Figueroa, R. A. (1990). Assessment of linguistic minority group children. In C. R. Reynolds & R. W. Kamphaus (Eds.), *Handbook of psychological and educational assessment of children: Intelligence and achievement*. New York: Guilford Press.

Figueroa, R. A. (1991). Bilingualism and psychometrics. *Diagnostique*, 17(1), 70–85.

Figueroa, R. A. & Sassenvath, J. M. (1989). A longitudinal study of the predictive validity of the system multicultural pluralistic assessment (SOMPA). *Psychology in the Schools*, 26(1), 5–19.

Gandara, P., Keogh, B. K., & Yoshioka-Maxwell, B. (1980). Predicting academic performance of Anglo and Mexican American kindergarten children. *Psychology in the Schools*, 17(2), 174–177.

Garth, T. R. (1920). Racial differences in mental fatigue. *Journal of Applied Psychology*, 4, 235–244.

Grosjean, F. (1989). Neurolinguists, beware! The bilingual is not two monolinguals in one person. *Brain and Language*, 36, 3–15.

Hakuta, K. (1986). *Mirror of language: The debate on bilingualism*. New York: Basic Books.

Heller, K. A., Holtzman, W. H., & Messick, S. (1982). *Placing children in special education: A strategy for equity*. Washington, DC: National Academy Press.

Johnson, D. L. & McGowan, R. J. (1984). Comparison of three intelligence tests as predictors of academic achievement and classroom behaviors of Mexican American children. *Journal of Psychoeducational Assessment*, 2, 345–352.

Mehan, H., Hertweck, H. & Meihls, J. L. (1986). *Handicapping the handicapped*. Palo Alto, CA: Stanford University Press.

Meisels, S. J. (1987). Uses and abuses of developmental screening and school readiness testing. *Young Children*, 42(2), 4–6.

Mercer, J. R. (1973). *Labeling the mentally retarded*. Berkeley, CA: University of California Press.

Mercer, J. R. (1979). *The System of Multicultural Pluralistic Assessment*. New York: The Psychological Corporation.

Miller-Jones, D. (1989). Culture and testing. *American Psychologist*, 44(2), 360–366.

Mishra, S. P. (1983). Validity of WISC-R IQs and factor scores in predicting achievement for Mexican-American children. *Psychology in the Schools*, 20(4), 442–444.

Moll, L. C., Velez-Ibanez, C., Greenberg, J., & Rivera, C. (1990). *Community knowledge and classroom practice: Combining resources for literacy instruction*. Tucson: The University of Arizona, College of Education.

Neill, M. (1993). Some pre-requisites for the establishment of equitable, inclusive multicultural assessment systems. Cambridge, MA: Fair Test.

Office of Bilingual Bicultural Education. (1982). *Basic principles for the education of language minority students: An overview 1982 Edition*. Sacramento, CA: California State Department of Education.

O'Malley, M. J. (1981). *Language minority children with limited English proficiency in the U.S. Children's English and services study*. Rosslyn, VA: National Clearinghouse for Bilingual Education.

Pilkington, C., Piersel, W. & Ponterotto, J. (1988). Home language as a predictor of first-grade achievement for Anglo- and Mexican-American children. *Contemporary Educational Psychology*, 13(1), 1–14.

Poplin, M. S. (1988a). The reductionist fallacy in learning disabilities: Replicating the past by reducing the present. *Journal of Learning Disabilities*, 7, 389–400.

Poplin, M. S. (1988b). Holistic/Constructivist principles of the teaching/learning process: Implications for the field of learning disabilities. *Journal of Learning Disabilities*, 21, 401–423.

Resnick, L. B. & Renick, D. P. (1989). Assessing the thinking curriculum: New tools for educational reform. In B.R. Gifford & M.C. O'Connor (Eds.), *Future assessments: Changing view of aptitude, achievement, and instruction*. Boston, MA: Kluwer.

Reynolds, A. (1933). *The education of Spanish-speaking children in five southwestern states (Bulletin No. 11)*. Washington, DC: U.S. Department of the Interior.

Salvia, J. & Ysseldyke, J. E. (1988). *Assessment in special and remedial education (Fourth Edition)*. Dallas, TX: Houghton Mifflin.

Sandoval, J. (1979). The WISC-R and internal evidence of test bias with minority groups. *Journal of Consulting and Clinical Psychology*, 47(5), 919–926.

Sandoval, J., Zimmerman, I.L. & Woo-Sam, J.M. (1980, September), *Cultural differences on WIS-R verbal items*. Paper presented at the annual convention of the American Psychological Association, Montreal, Canada.

Sattler, J. M. (1988). *Assessment of children (Third Edition)*. San Diego: Jerome M. Sattler.

Skrtic, T. M. (1991). The special education paradox. Equity as the way to excellence. *Harvard Educational Review*, 61(2), 148–206.

Skutnabb-Kangas, T. & Toukomaa, P. (1976). *Teaching migrant children's mother tongue and learning the language of the host country in the context of the sociocultural situation of the migrant family*. Helsinki, Finland: Finnish National Commission for UNESCO.

Tharp, R. G. (1989). Psychocultural variables and constants. *American Psychologist*, 44(2), 349–359.

Valdes, G. & Figueroa, R. A. (in press). *Bilingualism and psychometrics: A special case of bias*. New York: Ablex.

Valencia, R. R. & Rankin, R. J. (1988). Evidence of bias in predictive validity on the Kaufman assessment battery for children in samples of Anglo and Mexican American children. *Psychology in the Schools*, 25(3), 257–263.

Waggoner, D. (1991). *Language minority census newsletter*. Washington, DC: Waggoner Incorporated.

Wigdor, A. & Garner, W. R. (Eds.). (1982). *Ability testing: Uses, consequences and controversies*. Washington, DC: National Academy Press.

Woodrow, H. (1921). Intelligence and its measurement: A symposium (XI). *Journal of Educational Psychology*, 12, 207–210.

CHAPTER 3

DEFINING CULTURE AS A DIMENSION OF ACADEMIC ACHIEVEMENT (1998)

Implications for culturally responsive curriculum, instruction, and assessment

Renée Smith-Maddox

In approaching the next millennium, it appears that the concerns for educational equity and excellence that have characterized the rhetoric of American schooling during the current century are destined to accompany us unto the next. Many advocates of these goals argue that schools must promote academic excellence and create the conditions necessary for all students to achieve it (Darling-Hammond, 1995; Kirst, 1984; Oakes, 1985). Though educational reform efforts addressing these issues are numerous and promising, widespread discussions about achieving both excellence and equity often minimize the relationship between the home, community, and school cultures. According to Gay (1995), what is needed is the incorporation of cultural pluralism in all aspects of the educational process, and curriculum design is a key function in this process. Thus, any discussion of education within a multicultural context must consider the implications of personal and cultural knowledge, values, and language for the learning process. Significant to this standpoint is the view that culturally responsive education must acknowledge the relevance of approaches that incorporate students' cultures into the curricular and instructional strategies used in schools (Au & Kawakami, 1994; Delpit, 1995; Ladson-Billings, 1994a, 1994b; Nieto, 1997).

As Banks (1995) maintains, multicultural education is a broad concept encompassing many different dimensions. Any definition of multicultural education must wrestle not only with the question of what multicultural education is but also with the question of what it is not. This, however, is the terrain upon which social, political, and ideological struggles related to this concept are waged. These struggles have been most evident in the educational reform process. As a result, an understanding of the competing ideas about what students should know and what their intellectual capabilities might be is critical for proponents of multicultural education who are trying to mount any educational reform effort.

Efforts to impact the standards movement present a similar challenge. Current standard-setting efforts involve states and major school districts in working together to articulate both content and performance standards as well as benchmark those standards against world-class achievement in mathematics (New Standards Project, 1993; Resnick, Nolan, & Resnick, 1995). They also involve states (California, for example) in developing curriculum frameworks (Smith & O'Day, 1991). Curriculum frameworks, school curricula, professional development, in-service professional development, assessment, a restructured governance system, and the implementation of a coherent instructional guidance system are often seen as necessary components of systemic reform. However, given the political nature of most educational reforms, additional aspects must be considered, such as:

- how equity issues become central to the agenda,
- what knowledge related to ethnic and cultural diversity should be taught in schools,
- how cultural knowledge can be genuinely acknowledged, and
- how to draw on culturally specific norms that align with national standards.

Although the contemporary standards-based movement reflects a long-held belief that states need a national benchmark for comparing student achievement, that movement is complicated by the political struggle that is being waged over its content and meaning. It remains to be seen what steps must be taken to ensure that current proposals for national standards and tests reflect the complex nature of student learning and that the nation's schools move closer toward achieving the goal of equity, in both processes and outcomes of learning for all students.

Another critical concern associated with the national standards movement pertains to the call for tests to serve as indicators for determining whether the desired standards are being met and learning has occurred. Smith and O'Day (1991) have pointed out that assessment systems in the United States are plagued with myriad problems, including confusion about the purpose of testing in schools, inconsistencies related to the lack of a common curriculum, and concerns that performance on standardized tests is being used as a mechanism to sort out and limit educational access for some students, particularly students of color. As numerous multicultural educators have noted, these problems, along with conflicting reform objectives, have resulted in the tendency of new educational reform initiatives to ignore ongoing efforts aimed at improving the education of students whose cultures and backgrounds have been maligned, diminished, or omitted in school curricula (Banks, 1996; Delpit, 1988; Foster, 1993; Gordon, 1994; Grant & Sleeter, 1985; King, 1994; Irvine, 1990; Ladson-Billings, 1994a, 1994b, 1995; Lee, 1994; McLaren, 1989; Nieto, 1992). These educators, whose work has broadened our understandings of cultural issues in U.S. education and society, affirm the strong role that marginalized students' cultural experiences, identity, and knowledge play in matters related to educational outcomes. They are keenly aware of the politics of cultural difference, and make profound use of their insights to provide a vision for what might be done in the areas of pedagogy and curriculum.

The ways in which cultural differences are manifested in schools has been an issue of particular interest to educational researchers concerned with equity for students of color. For example, studies have shown that educational testing works to the disadvantage of various minority groups (Oakes, 1985, 1990; Ogbu, 1991). Erickson (1987, 1997) and Piestrup (1973) have conducted similar work showing that student failure is situated in the cultural mismatch between students and school. Conclusions such as these have led Apple (1993) and Martin (1994) to contend that it is difficult to see how calls for more stringent standards and more complex tests will do anything other than further entrench the discriminatory status quo in U.S. education.

If, as Boykin (1983) maintains, culture is an interlocking system of beliefs, values, and behavioral expressions, then the critical challenge for educators is understanding how culture is distributed within students' multiple contexts and how to define its implications for learning and school success. Given this dual focus, the present article explores the various meanings of culture and considers its implications for student learning and assessment. In doing so, it addresses a critical question: Does culture matter in a child's education?

Conceptions of culture

Let us begin by operationalizing the construct of culture, then by examining how the various dimensions of culture affect achievement. The concept of culture has been studied extensively. Spradley (1972) defines it as "the acquired knowledge people use to interpret experience and generate behavior" (p. 6). For Hall (1959), culture is a set of patterns experienced by individuals as normal ways of acting, feeling, and being. As is evident in Erickson's (1997) view, the important attributes of culture as it relates to education are both explicit (such as habits of people) and implicit (such as values, assumptions, and beliefs):

> Culture, as it is more or less visible and invisible to its users, is profoundly involved in the processes and contents of education. Culture shapes and is shaped by the learning and teaching that happen during the practical conduct of daily life within all the educational settings we encounter as learning environments throughout the human life span, in families, in school classrooms, in community setting, and in the workplace. . . . Educators address these issues every time they teach and every time they design curriculum. They may be addressed by educators explicitly and within the conscious awareness, or they may be addressed implicitly and outside conscious awareness. But, at every momentum the conduct of educational practice, cultural issues and choices are at stake. (pp. 33–34)

Culture is thus seen as involving not only everyday practices (patterns of discrete behaviors, traditions, habits, or customs) but also the way that people understand ideas and ascribe meaning to everyday life. These meanings serve as a foundation for learning, instruction, and assessment.

Fundamental insights into the nature of culture elucidate how it is represented and transmitted in various styles for learning. For example, "psychological verve" is the term that Boykin (1979, 1982, 1983) uses to characterize the variability and intensity qualities of stimulation that he maintains are factors within the domain of African American cultural motifs. Boykin argues that children, particularly African American children, may be placed at educational risk because cultural and adaptive considerations are typically not considered in instructional contexts. The framing of cultural differences can also provide evidence for changing the ways student performance and knowledge are assessed.

Research that addresses the presence of cultural differences insofar as standardized testing is concerned highlights this point. For example, standardized testing measures such as achievement and IQ tests have traditionally indicated that African Americans score lower on IQ tests, and thus have lower IQs, than do European American students (Ogbu, 1995). Moreover, trends in academic progress among American students between 1969 and 1990 on the National Assessment of Educational Progress (NAEP) show that African American and Latino students continue to score significantly below European Americans on every measure (Mullis, Dossey, Foertsch, Jones, & Gentile, 1991). Although standardized testing will probably persist, performance-based assessment is a growing alternative that addresses cultural differences (Barton & Coley, 1994; Linn, 1994).

In the theoretical frameworks of many researchers, culture plays a significant role in teaching and learning. Hargreaves (1996) distinguishes the content and form of "teacher culture" when he argues that:

> . . . the content of culture refers to the substantive attitudes, beliefs, values and ways of life that members of an organization, or a sub-group hold in common. The content of a teacher culture may be found in allegiances to subject knowledge, commitments to child-centeredness, acceptance of low standards, placing strong focus on caring and community, concentrating upon the academic elite, giving pride to sports. . . . The form of teachers cultures, by contrast describe the pattern of relationships and forms of association among members of that culture. . . . It is through the cultures of teaching, that teachers learn what it means to teach, and what kind of teacher they want to be within their school . . . (pp. 11–12)

The literature examining effective teaching strategies with African American students espouses a distinct philosophy rooted in African American cultural norms and political history (Foster, 1989, 1993; Irvine, 1990; Ladson-Billings, 1994a, 1994b, 1995). Ladson-Billings (1995), for example, draws upon the concept of culturally relevant pedagogy to describe a pedagogical practice "that not only addresses student achievement but also helps students to accept and affirm their cultural identity while developing critical perspectives that challenge inequities schools (and other institutions) perpetuate" (p. 469). She and others have shown that effective teaching strategies for African American students involve a pedagogy that "empowers students intellectually, socially, emotionally, and politically by using cultural referents to impart knowledge, skills and attitudes" (pp. 17–18). This cultural synchronization, according to Irvine, describes the necessary interpersonal context that must exist between teachers and African American students to maximize learning.

Culture and structure

Along with an increased emphasis on culture and effective educational practices, the last decade has seen deeper investigations showing that the relationship between schools and the social actors within them is very complex (Dimaggio, 1982; Lareau, 1987; Wells & Serna, 1996). Much of this research has been influenced by the French sociologist Pierre Bourdieu (1977), who contends that culture is a mediating factor linking both agency and structure. Bourdieu argues that culture is the medium through which dominant classes maintain their positions in a society. His notions of "cultural capital" and "habitus" have been used to study the complex ways in which schools perpetuate inequality and why this process of social reproduction is so readily accepted by the oppressor and the oppressed.

According to Bourdieu, culture takes on different forms and functions. As a form of capital, it consists of societally valued tastes and consumption patterns that reflect the cultural background, knowledge, disposition, and skills that are passed on from one generation to the next. Class position and family life are social and cultural resources that must be invested or activated to become a form of cultural capital. However, the social and cultural resources of all students are not valued equally. As Bourdieu maintains, schools validate the culture of the dominant class while they delegitimize the forms of knowledge brought to school by groups not in power. As a result, those who participate in elite-status cultures are particularly valued and rewarded by schools. Moreover, their social and cultural resources are invaluable assets insofar as access to educational and occupational opportunities is concerned.

Because socially valuable cultural capital is a desirable resource, systematic institutional exclusion usually results for those who do not have it (Lamont & Lareau, 1988; Lareau, 1987). Schools, in turn, reproduce social inequality by valuing one form of cultural capital over others (Lareau, 1987). Throughout the educational system, the interplay between class and culture leads parents with different cultural knowledge, strategies, routines, rituals, and practices to negotiate different pathways for their children's educational success. The schools, however, continue to inculcate a set of values and social skills that are congruent with the culture of dominant, elite-status groups. This enculturation becomes a mechanism for maintaining class and status divisions and privileging the dominant group across generations (Bourdieu, 1977; Bourdieu & Passeron, 1977; Lareau, 1987; Wells & Serna, 1996).

Bourdieu (1977) also looks specifically at how different cultural knowledge and social positions explain the structure of opportunity in Western society and the way in which individuals proceed through that structure. This perspective points to the structure of family life and the process of schooling, which are mediated by what Bourdieu calls habitus, or "a system of lasting, transposable dispositions which, integrating past experiences, functions at every moment as a matrix of perceptions, appreciation, and action" (pp. 82–83). Put simply, habitus is an internalized system of beliefs and notions about the world that an individual gains from his or her environment. This outlook shapes an individual's attitudes, such as those toward schooling.

Through the concepts of cultural capital and habitus, Bourdieu attempts to explain the relative autonomy of individuals and how social inequality is perpetuated. Within the educational system, for example, Fordham and Ogbu (1986) suggest that some African American students who strive for academic success are seen as "acting White" and therefore may, for fear of betraying their collective group identity, resist or oppose the idea of achieving academic success. Although the development of such oppositional behavior could be viewed optimistically because it proves that students do in fact actively shape their academic experience and opportunities through the choices they make, the act of resistance often reflects an understanding of the structure of schooling and its high regard for the cultural capital of the upper classes.

The interaction of culture and structure within the school plays out in a number of ways for students. Evidence of the U.S. public school system's failure to equalize the life chances for students, especially for low-income and African American students, is overwhelming (Braddock & Dawkins, 1993; Carnegie Council on Adolescent Development, 1989; Hallinan, 1987; Oakes, 1985, 1990). These and other studies have examined the discriminatory character of schools and the school processes that reproduce social inequality by looking at educational practices such as tracking. Oakes (1985) found that tracking leads to very different learning opportunities for students. This occurs as a result of schools' providing high- and low-track students with vastly different levels of access to knowledge and opportunities to learn. For example, students in high-track English classes were exposed to content (i.e., topics and skills that are required for college, classic and modern fiction, characteristics of literary genres, and elements of good narrative writing) that can be called "high-status knowledge" while those in low-track English classes rarely, if ever, encountered similar types of knowledge. Oakes and other researchers have argued that the structure of tracking is perpetuated partly because elite-status White parents continue to lobby for advanced placement courses and gifted and talented programs or their children (Oakes, 1990; Wells & Oakes, 1996, Wells & Serna, 1996). Upon examining this issue in a study of detracking in racially mixed schools, Wells and Serna found that the politics of cultural differences is sometimes powerfully attached to how the political and cultural capital of elite-status White parents enables them to influence and resist efforts to dismantle tracking.

As these studies show, the U.S. educational system structures inequality. Although individuals do have agency, they are typically constrained by a school culture that is alienating and inconsistent with their cultural experiences, hopes, dreams, and struggles. Thus, the answer to achieving equity and excellence lies in reforms that reflect a cultural paradigm that emphasizes specific ways in which personal and cultural knowledge can be drawn upon to improve education for culturally and linguistically diverse groups of students.

Home and community culture

Over the past two decades, studies on student achievement and its relationship to home–school connections have focused on parental involvement (Epstein, 1988; Lareau, 1987; Muller & Kerbow, 1993; Useem, 1991) and parental participation (Irvine, 1990; Slaughter, 1977) as key to children's academic success. Clark (1983) provides a detailed description of the parenting styles of high- and low-achieving poor African American students. He found that African American parents of high achievers talked often with their children; visited their children's schools frequently; assisted, coached, and instructed their children; established clear and consistent rules for them regarding behavior; and had high expectations for their school success and future college attainment. By contrast, the parents of low achievers had low expectations for their children; seldom went to visit their children's schools; did not expect them to attend college; did not encourage, assist, or support them academically; did not define rules of conduct or the boundaries of the parent and child roles; and failed to monitor the way their children spent their time.

Another sphere of influence on student's academic success that has been widely researched is the community, which offers varied social and cultural resources to support children's learning (Unger & Sussman, 1990) and development (Nettles, 1991). Community resources have been shown to greatly benefit children of all ages when they are organized and deployed in school, family, and community partnerships (Coleman, 1988; Epstein, 1988; Kagan, 1989; Kirst & McLaughlin, 1990). As evident throughout the literature on how culture is defined, knowledge of culture and its influence on educational outcomes for children is likely to be enhanced as teachers, researchers, and policymakers understand students' community and home lives.

Framing the analysis

How do we begin to organize the prevailing definitions of culture to present a more coherent picture of the role it plays in achievement? Given that most students arrive at their assumptions, beliefs, and values about education from their personal experiences in their home, school, and community cultures, cultural factors are essential to understanding student outcomes. Despite the complexity of capturing the cultural context, data from the base year survey of the National Longitudinal Study of 1988 (NELS:88), provides a basis for evaluating the effects of contextual influences (home, school, and community) and culturally relevant strategies on academic achievement by racial–ethnic groups. Given the limitations of the data available for analysis, however, these findings must be understood as suggestive rather than definitive. This analysis is useful in understanding the role of culture in students' schooling experiences.

Method

Data and sample

The data examined in this analysis are from the National Educational Longitudinal Survey of 1988 (NELS:88), a longitudinal study of 24,599 eighth graders from 1,052 schools in the U.S. NELS:88 was funded and designed by the National Center for Education Statistics (NCES) to collect data on students' experiences as they transition from middle or junior high school to high school. The unique feature of this data set is that NELS:88 researchers resurveyed students biannually until 1992 and collected longitudinal supporting data from parents, teachers, and school administrators.

In the present study, NELS:88 data from the base-year student, parent, and teacher questionnaires were merged. Of interest to this investigation were those items on the questionnaire pertaining to the various dimensions of culture. The sample examined was representative of eighth-grade students at both the regional and national level.

Measures

Means, standard deviations, and a brief description for all the variables used in the analysis are shown in Table 3.1. The 13 variables employed in the analyses are operationalized as follows (the variable labels and source variables from the NELS:88 are indicated in parentheses).

Dependent Variable. The dependent variable, Academic Performance, was measured by a composite standardized test score in mathematics (BYTXMSTD).

Independent Variables. Four domains were constructed to represent the contextual dimensions of culture: student, family, school, and teacher.

The first domain captures student characteristics, including demographic variables, attitude, and behaviors. Seven variables were considered for this domain. Two demographic variables were constructed as dummy variables:

(1) Race (1 = African American; 0 = European American); and
(2) Gender (SEX) (1 = Male; 0 = Female).

A measure of student attitudes consisted of the following:

(3) Attitudes (Aspirations, BYS45)—This variable was based on students' responses to the questionnaire item, "How far in school do you think you will get?" The response choices for this item were: (1) "won't finish

Table 3.1 Weighted means, standard deviations, and description of variables

Variables	*Mean*	*SD*	*Min*	*Max*	*Description*
STUDENT CHARACTERISTICS					
Test Score	50.64	10.22	26.75	71.22	Mathematics standardized test
African American	0.16	0.36	0	1	Race = 1; European American = 0
Female	0.50	0.50	0	1	Gender = 1
Educational Aspirations	4.61	1.29	1	6	How far in school student thinks he/she will go
Homework Habits	4.18	1.51	1	8	Homework composite
Activities	1.82	1.11	0	4	Outside school activity
Cultural Synchronization	0.66	0.47	0	1	Talks to teacher about studies
Culturally Relevant Content	0.13	0.34	0	2	Explicit teaching of culture
FAMILY CHARACTERISTICS					
SES	−0.07	0.80	−2.97	2.56	SES composite
Parental Involvement	4.14	1.52	0	6	Communication with parents
Parent's Educational Expectations	8.71	2.80	1	12	How far in school parents expect student to go
SCHOOL CHARACTERISTICS					
Percentage of Minority Students	3.01	2.17	0	7	Percentage of minority students
TEACHER PERCEPTIONS					
Placement in Low-Ability Group	0.40	0.66	0	2	Placement in low-ability group

high school"; (2) "will graduate from high school but won't go any further"; (3) "will go to vocational, trade, or business school after high school"; (4) "will attend college"; (5) "will graduate from college"; and (6) "will attend a higher level of school after graduating from college."

Two behavioral variables were included in the student domain:

(4) Homework Habits (Homework, BYHOMEWK)—a measure of students' response to the NELS:88 item on homework habits ("[Indicate the] number of hours spent on homework per week"); and
(5) Activities (Activities)—a dummy variable indicating parents' response to the item, "Does your eighth grader take part in any of the following activities?" The response choices were: (a) "[borrows] books from the public library" (BYP61AB); (b) "[studies] computer outside regular school class" (BYP60G); and (c) "[involved] in religious group" (BYP63E). Responses were coded 1 (yes) and 0 (otherwise).

Variables reflecting culturally relevant strategies included the following:

(6) Cultural Synchronization (BYS51EB)—a dummy variable indicating students' response to the item, "[I] talk to [my] teacher about studies in class" (responses were coded 1 = yes, 0 = no); and
(7) Culturally Relevant Content—a composite factor that includes (a) students' reports about whether their racial/ethnic group's history, government, and social studies were taught in English during the first two years of middle school (BYS28F1); and (b) students' reports of whether their racial/ethnic group's history, government, and social studies were taught in their group's language during the first two years of middle school (BYS28F2).

The second domain of variables captured family characteristics. The first variable represents a traditional measure of economic status: socioeconomic status (BYSES), a composite measure developed by NCES. The second type of family-related variable attempted to capture specific aspects of students' home cultures, namely parental involvement in and expectations for their children's education. The Parental Involvement variable was a measure of students' responses to the item regarding parents' communication with their children. Responses to three items were summed to construct this variable: (BYS36A) ("[I] discuss programs at school with parents"); (BYS36B) ("[I] discuss school activities with parents"); and (BYS36C) ("[I] discuss things studied in class with parents"). The variable of Parent's Expectation was constructed from responses to the following NELS:88 item: "How far in school [does parent] expect child to go?" (BYP76). Response choices included: (1) less than high school diploma; (2) GED; (3) high school graduation; (4) vocational, trade, or business school after high school (sub-options: less than one year, one or two years, two years or more); (5) college program (sub-options: less than two years of college, two or more years of college, finish a two-year program, finish a four- or five-year program, master's degree or equivalent, Ph.D, or other advanced degree).

The third domain represents a school characteristic. This domain was measured by the percentage of minority students enrolled in school (G8MINOR).

The last domain was constructed to measure teachers' perception of their students' achievement level. This dummy variable indicates teachers' responses to the NELS:88 item, "Which of the following best describes the achievement level of the eighth graders in this class compared with the average eighth-grade student in this school?" The question was coded to identify four levels: (a) higher achievement, (b) average achievement, (c) lower achievement, and (d) heterogeneous classes with widely differing achievement levels. Data from the responses of two of the four teachers reporting for each student in the NELS:88 sample were examined, in the following subject areas: mathematics (MBYT2_2), English (EBYT2_2), science (SBYT2_2), and history (HBYT2_2). The classes that consisted of students with lower achievement levels were summed (1 = low-ability group if two teachers reported "Student performs below ability"; 0 = otherwise).[1]

Results

How does cultural context influence academic achievement? Table 3.2 reports the results of regression analysis on the NELS:88 data selected for this study. The results reveal that the cultural factors that influence academic achievement in this aggregate model for eighth graders are many. Students' aspirations, homework habits, and participation in extracurricular activities as well as parents' socioeconomic status, parental involvement, expectations, and regular communication with teachers about classroom activities were shown to have a positive effect on students' academic achievement. Concurrently, placement in low-ability groups,

Table 3.2 Effects of cultural influences on eighth graders' academic achievement

	Total	
Independent variables	*Sig T*	*Beta*
STUDENT CHARACTERISTICS		
African American	−.155	.000
Gender	.060	.000
Aspirations	.157	.000
Homework Habits	.088	.000
Activities	.141	.000
Teacher–Student Interaction	.009	.158
Culturally Relevant Content	−.014	.026
FAMILY CHARACTERISTICS		
SES	.204	.000
Parental Involvement	.085	.000
Parents' Expectations	.157	.000
SCHOOL CHARACTERISTICS		
Percentage of Minorities Enrolled in School	−.048	.000
TEACHERS' PERCEPTIONS		
Placement in Low-Ability Group	−.169	.000

$R^2 = .379$

cultural content, and percentage of minorities in school had a negative effect. Although all these variables were significant ($p < .05$ or better), the effects were strongest for parents' socioeconomic status ($\beta = .204$), placement in low-ability groups ($\beta = .169$), and parents' expectations ($\beta = .157$). The R^2-value obtained reveals that the model accounts for 38% of the variation in students' academic performance.

The data reported in Table 3.2 suggest that gender has a significant effect on academic achievement. These effects show that the eighth-grade females in the NELS:88 sample are more likely than males to have high academic performance. Table 3.2 also provides information on the effects of race on student achievement—that is, race was significant when cultural context was taken into account. The negative effects indicate that African American eighth graders were more likely to have lower academic performance than were European American eighth graders.

Although the focus of this investigation was on the effect of cultural measures on academic performance, the findings on culturally relevant strategies influencing student outcomes are also of interest. As shown in Table 3.3, the effect of cultural content was inconsistent across racial/ethnic subgroups. The effects shown are unstandardized regression coefficients, or the net effects after controlling for gender, student aspirations, homework habits, participation in extracurricular activities, parents' socioeconomic status, parental involvement, parents' expectations, parents' regular communication with teacher about classroom activities, placement in low-ability groups, and percentage of minorities enrolled in school. Table 3.3 also reveals that the strongest effect for cultural content was for American Indians ($\beta = .115$) while the weakest effects for this variable were evidenced for African Americans ($\beta = .009$). Both of these results, however, were not significant. Interestingly, the effects for European Americans ($\beta = .019$), Asian Americans ($\beta = .079$), and Latino Americans ($\beta = .037$) were negative but significant.

To what extent can academic achievement be explained by teacher–student interaction? Table 3.4 shows that across most racial/ethnic subgroups, regular communication with teachers enhanced academic achievement. Overall, it appears that the strongest effect on academic achievement was experienced by European

Table 3.3 Effects of culturally relevant content on eighth graders' academic achievement, by ethnicity, with selected controls[a]

	Beta	*t*
African Americans (3,009)	.009	.472
American Indians (299)	.115	1.782
European Americans (16,317)	–.019	–2.647*
Asian Americans (1,527)	–.079	–3.22**
Latino Americans (3,171)	–.037	–1.94*

[a]Controls = gender, student's aspirations, homework habits, participation in extracurricular activities, parents' SES, parental involvement, parents' expectations, regular communication with teacher about classroom activities, placement in low-ability groups, and percentage of minorities enrolled in school.

* $p = .05$

** $p = .001$

Table 3.4 Effects of teacher–student interaction on eighth graders' academic achievement, by ethnicity, with selected controls[a]

	Beta	*t*
African Americans (3,009)	.013	.715*
American Indians (299)	.001	.020
European Americans (16,317)	–.007	.997*
Asian Americans (1,527)	.020	.791*
Latino Americans (3,171)	–.017	–.873*

[a] Controls = gender, student's aspirations, homework habits, participation in extracurricular activities, parents' SES, parental involvement, parents' expectations, regular communication with teacher about classroom activities, placement in low-ability groups, and percentage of minorities enrolled in school.
* $p = .05$

Americans (β = .997), Asian Americans (β = .791), and African Americans (β = .715). This effect was not significant for American Indians, but was shown to negatively affect the achievement outcomes of Latino Americans.

Discussion and conclusion

The present study yields valid reasons to conclude that cultural and structural theories are useful in explaining differences in student achievement across racial/ethnic lines. This view is consistent with Irvine's (1990) work on African American students and school failure. Irvine argues that students live in multiple contexts (interpersonal, societal, and institutional) that contribute to or inhibit school achievement. Within the school context, she states, "the lack of cultural synchronization and negative teacher expectations result in hidden, and often unintended, conflict between teachers and their students" (p. xvii). It follows, then, that analyses that consider the multiple contexts in which students live might provide a clearer, more indepth picture of these factors.

These findings reveal that parents' discussions with teachers are a strong predictor of academic achievement for African American, European American, and Asian American students. Although the data does not yield a vivid description of the quality and content of the communication, it confirms that teacher–student interaction is significant to students' achievement in school. By contrast, a negative and insignificant result for this measure of cultural synchronization may indicate that students are experiencing cultural discontinuity. When this occurs, teacher–student communication is diminished, instruction is ineffective, and positive teacher affect is minimized. In turn, the lack of communication influences both teacher–student interaction and teacher expectations. Consequently, teachers' low expectations become self-fulfilling prophecies that either contribute to or hinder student achievement.

Many formidable challenges are presented when unpacking cultural content. In the present study, the measure for this construct referenced the explicit teaching of culture in various subjects. The findings were inconsistent among racial/ethnic groups. Perhaps this is because the NELS:88 survey did not explicitly focus on the dimensions of cultural content. Thus, this result should be interpreted with caution. However, lack of cultural congruence in the classroom seems to have had a negative effect on the achievement of some students. For other students, their personal and cultural knowledge may be in opposition to the school culture or marginalized in the curriculum.

The most important family cultural predictors of academic achievement revealed in this study were parental involvement, parents' socioeconomic status, and parents' expectations for students' education. This result suggests that the academic performance of eighth graders tends to be influenced by their families' economic and cultural capital. On one hand, the effects of familial influence point to the importance of strong ties between the parent and the child in setting and achieving educational goals. On the other hand, although parents may impress upon their children the importance of education and stress that education is a key resource for opportunities, their socioeconomic status may lead them to construct different pathways for helping their children acquire the knowledge and skills necessary to negotiate the educational experience.

The findings also corroborate those of Oakes (1985) and Braddock (1990) regarding the negative effect of students' placement in low-ability groups. The similarity of the findings provides support for efforts aimed at ameliorating the entrenched patterns of ability grouping in our nation's schools that often result in differentiated classroom learning environments and opportunities for students (Darling-Hammond, 1994). Further, these findings illustrate that participation in extracurricular activities has a significant effect on student achievement. An explanation for the connection between this community factor and achievement may be attributed to the finding that these activities provide opportunities to capture students' interests and cultivate the knowledge and skills students need to learn to succeed in school. This is not surprising, given the special prominence that the literature concedes to the role of community involvement (Braddock, Royster, Winfield, & Hawkins, 1991; Nettles, 1989, 1991).

Overall, the findings from this study present a resounding argument for the importance of culture in teaching and learning, but the story is not complete. Although it is obvious that culture permeates the activities of teaching and learning, cultural influences are very difficult to capture. These influences can vary dramatically according to families' cultural capital, teacher–student interactions, and the structure of inequality in different schools. This conclusion suggests that within-group and cross-cultural research designs should be used to capture these differences.

The results also raise questions about the limitations of the study. Until more work is done in this area, caution should be attached to any conclusions drawn. More refined studies are needed to operationalize key variables such as cultural content and cultural capital in different ways. New databases should also include measures of culturally relevant teaching and family cultural capital. For example, cultural content could be measured by underlying constructs such as content relevance, teacher discourse, classroom life, racial/ethnic identity, values, beliefs, and assumptions, rather than by frequency of culturally related discussions. The reexamining and rethinking of what knowledge should be taught in the school curriculum and what teaching strategies are effective for students from diverse cultural backgrounds will also depend on a variety of innovative measurement tools (e.g., classroom participation assessments, teachers' observations, student portfolios). These new tools can help to better measure academic performance and create new construct validity arguments.

Moreover, the models for culturally responsive educational reform developed by Banks (1993), Banks and Banks (1993), Ladson-Billings (1994a, 1994b, 1995), and Lee (1994) provide a compelling case for the reassessment and reappraisal of pedagogical practices. Further examination into the multiple dimensions of culturally relevant pedagogy will not only enhance our understanding of this practice, but focus our attention on culturally relevant performance assessments and the consequences for failing to develop them. A prerequisite to this call for linking pedagogical style with assessment methods is making use of students' personal and cultural knowledge.

The use of culturally responsive instructional strategies changes the form and content of instruction. The energy and effort put forth by educators who use these strategies create the conditions for students to not only affirm their cultural identity but to express their thoughts, insights, and learning about a product or process. This new paradigm deconstructs and challenges dominant relations of power and knowledge. If one acknowledges this perspective, the distinctive features of culturally responsive pedagogy have important implications for emerging culturally relevant assessment systems and their evaluation.

Though considerable progress is being made in improving the assessment of academic performances and knowledge production, the current debate about standards and tests tends to lose sight of the primary purpose of assessment, which is to improve student learning. Current assessment reform efforts focus on rewards and sanctions rather than on the way test results are used, the influence of testing in the classroom, and changes in practice (Darling-Hammond, 1997; Hornbeck, 1992; Tucker, 1992). In schools around the nation, traditional standardized, norm-referenced tests tend to measure the amount of information remembered and the ability to take a test under a limited timespan. They are not necessarily well-suited to measure complex thinking, problem solving, language ability, or actual student work. As Wiggins (1992), an advocate of "tests worth taking" points out, these traditional tests, even the more demanding ones, tend to over-assess student "knowledge" and under-assess student "know-how with knowledge" (p. 27). Implementing standards and assessments that make a difference can support teacher learning and stimulate widespread rethinking of culturally responsive assessments.

Firmer conclusions await analysis of the impact of culturally relevant instructional strategies; however, analyzing the role of culture in teaching, learning, and assessment provides a theoretical framework for understanding how to promote academic excellence and provide the conditions for all students to achieve it. As the standards for what students should know change from the mastery of facts to the construction of knowledge and critical thinking, the conceptions of culture in educational practices also need to become more constructivistic and less essentialistic. Nonetheless, research focusing on the role of culture is helpful to standard setters and test developers who must continue to struggle to develop reliable and valid measures. Most importantly, culturally conscious practitioners, researchers, and policymakers must persist in viewing the call for "higher" standards and "better" tests as an opportunity to develop culturally relevant curriculum, pedagogy, and assessment strategies that reflect the ideological framework of diverse cultures while simultaneously placing priority on excellence and educational inequality.

Note

1 Given that grouping categories may vary from school to school, the wording of the ability grouping question can be easily misinterpreted. Therefore, some caution

should be taken in interpreting the ability-grouping variable. To directly assess or demonstrate the mediating role of ability grouping, it is essential to differentiate the types of ability-grouped assignments because it is not clear whether students are grouped by ability or achievement. Additionally, the question may encourage teachers to rectify school policy randomly, particularly when some schools have grouping but no formal grouping policy. This information was matched with each of the subject variables (mathematics, English, science, and social studies) to determine ability-group assignment.

References

Apple, M. (1993). The politics of knowledge: Does a national curriculum makes sense? *Teachers College Record, 95*(2), 222–241.

Au, K. A., & Kawakami, A. J. (1994). Cultural congruence in instruction. In E. R. Hollis, J. E. King, & W. C. Hayman (Eds.), *Teaching diverse populations: Formulating a knowledge base* (pp. 5–24). New York: State University of New York Press.

Banks, J. A. (1993). Multicultural education: Characteristics and goals. In J. A. Banks & C. A. M. Banks (Eds.), *Multicultural education: Issues and perspectives* (2nd ed., pp. 195–214). Boston: Allyn & Bacon.

Banks, J. A. (1995). Multicultural education: Historical development, dimensions, and practice. In J. A. Banks & C. A. M. Banks (Eds.), *Multicultural education: Issues and perspectives* (pp. 3–24). Needham Heights, MA: Allyn & Bacon.

Banks, J. A. (Ed.). (1996). *Multicultural education, transformative knowledge, and action: Historical and contemporary perspectives*. New York: Teachers College Press.

Banks, J. A., & Banks, C. A. M. (Eds.). (1993). *Multicultural education: Issues and perspectives* (2nd ed.). Boston: Allyn & Bacon.

Barton, P. E., & Coley, R. J. (1994). *Testing in America's schools*. Princeton, NJ: Educational Testing Service, Policy Information Center.

Bourdieu, P. (1977). Cultural reproduction and social reproduction. In J. Karabel & A. H. Halsey (Eds.), *Power and ideology in education* (pp. 487–511). New York: Oxford University Press.

Bourdieu, P., & Passeron, J. (1977). *Reproduction in education, society, and culture.* Beverly Hills, CA: Sage.

Braddock, J. H., II. (1990, February). *Tracking: Implications for student race–ethnic subgroups* (Report No. 1). Baltimore, MD: The Johns Hopkins University, Center for Research on Effective Schooling for Disadvantaged Students.

Braddock, J. H., II, & Dawkins, M. P. (1993). Ability grouping, aspirations, and attainments: Evidence from the national educational longitudinal study of 1988. *Journal of Negro Education*, 62(3), 324–336.

Braddock, J. H., II, Royster, D. A., Winfield, L. F., & Hawkins, R. (1991). Sports and academic resilience among African-American males. In L. F. Winfield (Ed.), *Resilience, schooling and development in African-American youth* (pp. 113–131). Beverly Hills, CA: Sage.

Boykin, A. W. (1979). Psychological–behavioral verve: Some theoretical explorations and empirical manifestations. In A. W. Boykin, A. J. Franklin, & J. F. Yates (Eds.), *Research directions of Black psychologists* (pp. 351–367). New York: Russell Sage.

Boykin, A. W. (1982). Task variability and the performance of Black and White school children: Vervistic explorations. *Journal of Black Studies, 12*, 469–485.

Boykin, A. W. (1983). The academic performance of Afro-American children. In J. Spence (Ed.), *Achievement and achievement motives* (pp. 321–371). San Francisco: W. Freeman.

Carnegie Council on Adolescent Development. (1989, June). *Turning points: Preparing American youth for the 21st century*. New York: Author.

Clark, R. M. (1983). *Family life and school achievement: Why poor Black children succeed or fail*. Chicago, IL: The University of Chicago Press.

Coleman, J. S. (1988). Social capital in the creation of human capital. *American Journal of Sociology, 94*, 95–120.

Darling-Hammond, L. (1994). Performance-based assessment and educational equity. *Harvard Educational Review, 64*, 5–30.

Darling-Hammond, L. (1995). Inequality and access to knowledge. In J. A. Banks & C. A. M. Banks (Eds.), *Handbook of research on multicultural education* (pp. 465–483). New York: Macmillan.

Darling-Hammond, L. (1997). *The right to learn: A blueprint for creating schools that work*. San Francisco: Jossey-Bass.

Delpit, L. (1988). The silenced dialogue: Power and pedagogy in educating other people's children. *Harvard Educational Review, 58*(3), 280–298.

Delpit, L. (1995). *Other people's children: Cultural conflict in the classroom*. New York: The New Press.

Dimaggio, P. (1982). Cultural capital and school success: The impact of status culture participation on the grades of U.S. high school students. *American Sociological Review, 47*, 189–201.

Epstein, J. L. (1988). *Schools in the center: School, family, peer, and community connections for more effective middle grades schools and students*. Baltimore, MD: The Johns Hopkins University Center for Research on Elementary and Middle Schools.

Erickson, F. (1987). Transformation and school success: The politics and culture of educational achievement. *Anthropology and Education, 18*, 335–356.

Erickson, F. (1997). Culture in society and in educational practices. In J. A. Banks & C. A. M. Banks (Eds.), *Multicultural education: Issues and perspectives* (pp. 32–60). Needham Heights, MA: Allyn & Bacon.

Fordham, S., & Ogbu, J. (1986). Black students' school success: Coping with the burden of "acting White." *Urban Review, 18*(3), 1–31.

Foster, M. (1989). It's cookin' now: An ethnographic study of a successful Black teacher in an urban community college. *Language in Society, 18*(1), 1–29.

Foster, M. (1993). Education for competence in community and culture: Exploring the views of exemplary African-American teachers. *Urban Education; 27*(4), 370–394.

Gay, G. (1995). Curriculum theory and multicultural education. In J. A. Banks & C. A. M. Banks (Eds.), *Handbook of research on multicultural education* (pp. 25–43). New York: Macmillan.

Gordon, B. (1994). African-American cultural knowledge and liberatory education: Dilemmas, problems, and potentials in a postmodern American society. In M. J. Shujaa (Ed.), *Too much schooling, too little education* (pp. 57–78). Trenton, NJ: Africa World Press.

Grant, C. A., & Sleeter, C. E. (1985). The literature on multicultural education: Review and analyses. *Educational Review, 37*, 97–118.

Hall, E. (1959). *The silent language*. New York: Anchor Books.

Hallinan, M. T. (1987). Ability grouping and student learning. In M.T. Hallinan (Ed.), *The social organization of schools: New conceptualizations of the learning process* (pp. 41–69). New York: Plenum.

Hargreaves, A. (1996, April). *Cultures of teaching and educational change*. Paper presented at the annual meeting of the American Educational Research Association, New York, NY.

Hornbeck, D. W. (1992, May 6). The true road to equity. *Education Week*, pp. 32, 25.

Irvine, J. (1990). *Black students and school failure*. Westport, CT: Greenwood Press.

Kagan, S. L. (1989). Early care and education: Beyond the schoolhouse doors. *Phi Delta Kappan, 71*, 107–112.

King, J. E. (1994). The purpose of schooling for African American children: Including cultural knowledge. In E. R. Hollins, J. E. King, & W. C. Hayman (Eds.), *Teaching diverse populations: Formulating a knowledge base* (pp. 25–56). Albany: State University of New York Press.

Kirst, M. (1984). *Who controls our schools: American values in conflict*. New York: Freeman.

Kirst, M. W., & McLaughlin, M. M. (1990). Rethinking policy for children: Implications for educational administration. In B. Mitchell & L. L. Cunningham (Eds.), *Educational leadership and changing contexts of families, communities, and schools* (pp. 69–90). Chicago: The University of Chicago Press.

Ladson-Billings, G. (1994a). *The dreamkeepers: Successful teaching for African American students*. San Francisco: Jossey–Bass.

Ladson-Billings, G. (1994b). Who will teach our children? Preparing teachers to successfully teach African American students. In E. R. Hollis, J. E. King, & W. C. Hayman (Eds.), *Teaching diverse populations: Formulating a knowledge base* (pp. 129–142). New York: State University of New York Press.

Ladson-Billings, G. (1995). Toward a theory of culturally relevant pedagogy. *American Educational Research Journal, 32*(3), 465–491.

Lamont, M., & Lareau, A. (1988). Cultural capital: Allusions, gaps and glissandos in recent theoretical developments. *Sociological Theory, 6*, 153–168.

Lareau, A. (1987). Social class differences in family–school relationships: The importance of cultural capital. *Sociology of Education, 60*, 73–85.

Lee, C. (1994). African-centered pedagogy: Complexities and possibilities. In M. J. Shujaa (Ed.), *Too much schooling, too little education* (pp. 295–318). Trenton, NJ: Africa World Press.

Linn, R. L. (1994). Performance assessment: Policy promises and technical measurement standards. *Educational Researcher, 23*(9), 4–14.

Martin, J. R. (1994). Curriculum and the mirror of knowledge. In J. Martin (Ed.), *Changing the educational landscape* (pp. 212–227). New York: Routledge.

McLaren, P. (1989). *Life in schools*. White Plains, NY: Longman.

Muller, C., & Kerbow, D. (1993). Parent involvement in the home, school, and community. In B. Schneider & J. Coleman (Eds.), *Parents, their children and schools* (pp. 13–42). Boulder, CO: Westview Press.

Mullis, I. V., Dossey, J. A., Foertsch, M. A., Jones, L. R., & Gentile, C. A. (1991). *Trends in academic progress: Achievement of U.S. students in science, 1969–70 to 1990*. Washington, DC: Office of Educational Research and Improvement, U.S. Department of Education.

Nettles, S. M. (1989). The role of community involvement in fostering investment behavior in low-income Black adolescents: A theoretical perspective. *Journal of Adolescent Research, 4*, 190–201.

Nettles, S. M. (1991). Community contributions to school outcomes of African American students. In L. F. Winfield (Ed.), *Resilience, schooling and development in African-American youth* (pp. 132–147). Beverly Hills, CA: Sage.

New Standards Project. (1993). *Effective public engagement* (Report prepared by the Public Agenda Foundation). Washington, DC: Author.

Nieto, S. (1992). *Affirming diversity*. New York: Longman.

Nieto, S. (1997). School reform and student achievement: A multicultural perspective. In J. A. Banks & C. A. M. Banks (Eds.), *Multicultural education: Issues and perspectives* (pp. 387–407). Needham Heights, MA: Allyn & Bacon.

Oakes, J. (1985). *Keeping track: How schools structure inequality*. New Haven, CT: Yale University Press.

Oakes, J. (1990). *Multiplying inequalities: The effects of race, social class, and tracking on opportunities to learn mathematics and science*. Santa Monica, CA: The RAND Corporation.

Ogbu, J. (1995). Understanding cultural diversity and learning. In J. A. Banks & C. A. M. Banks (Eds.), *Handbook of research in multicultural education* (pp. 582–593). New York: Macmillan.

Piestrup, A. (1973). *Black dialect interference and accommodation of reading instruction, first grade* (Monograph No. 4). Berkeley, CA: Language Behavior Research Laboratory.

Resnick, L. B., Nolan, K. J., & Resnick, D. (1995). Benchmarking education standards. *Educational Evaluation and Policy Analysis, 17*(4), 438–461.

Slaughter, D. (1977). Relation of early parent–teacher socialization influences to achievement orientation and self-esteem in middle childhood among low-income Black children. In J. Gidewell (Ed.), *The social context of learning and development* (pp. 101–131). New York: Gardner.

Spradley, J. (1972). Foundations of cultural knowledge. In J. Spradley (Ed.), *Culture and cognition* (pp. 3–38). San Francisco: Chandler.

Smith, M. S., & O'Day, J. (1991). Systemic school reform. In S. H. Fuhrman & B. Malen (Eds), *The politic of curriculum and testing: 1990 yearbook of the Politics of Education Association* (pp. 233–267). New York: Falmer Press.

Tucker, M. (1992, June 17). Quoted in the roundtable: A new "social compact" for mastery in education. *Education Week* [Special Report].

Unger, D. G., & Sussman, M. B. (Eds.). (1990). *Introduction to families in community settings: Interdisciplinary perspectives*. New York: Haworth.

U.S. Department of Education, National Center for Education Statistics. (1990, December). *National Education Longitudinal Study of 1988* (ICPSR 9389). Ann Arbor, MI: Inter-University Consortium for Political and Social Research.

Useem, E. L. (1991). Student selection into course sequences in mathematics: The impact of parental involvement and school policies. *Journal of Research on Adolescence, 1*(3), 231–250.

Wells, A. S., & Oakes, J. (1996). Potential pitfalls of systemic reform: Early lessons from detracking research. *Sociology of Education* [Extra Issue], 135–143.

Wells, A. S., & Serna, I. (1996). The politics of culture: Understanding local political resistance to detracking in racially mixed schools. *Harvard Educational Review, 66*(1), 93–118.

Wiggins, G. (1992, May). Creating test worth taking. *Educational Leadership, 49*(8), 23–26.

CHAPTER 4

AUTHENTIC LITERACY ASSESSMENT (ALA) DEVELOPMENT (1999)

An instruction based assessment that is responsive to linguistic and cultural diversity

Eugene E. Garcia, Myriam Casimir, Xiaoquin (Alice) Sun Irminger, Ann Marie Wiese, and Erminda H. Garcia

Introduction and background

Over the past two decades, teachers of literacy influenced by a growing body of research about language and literacy learning and by their own observations of how children develop as writers, have shifted their practice from a product to a process orientation (Calkins 1986, Graves 1994). Most educators see this as positively impacting students' literacy skills, but problems abound in how to document student progress and program effectiveness due to inadequate assessment tools and over reliance on standardized achievement tests, including English and primary language tests (Wiggins 1994). One problem is the perceived lack of validity between standardized tests and new, more process-oriented curricula. Many schools now implement authentic assessments, including portfolio assessment to supplement or replace these tests (Hewitt 1995, Porter & Cleland 1995). In the spirit of a "working paper," this description of an authentic assessment work-in-progress attempts to describe our recent efforts to co-develop and implement an assessment process and tool that is of particular significance to multicultural and multilingual instructional setting.

Holistic assessments have the potential to solve the problem of tracking individual achievement (Hewitt 1995). However, the validity and reliability of the rubrics and scoring guides intended to convert such data into quantifiable data are often unknown. Thus, standardized tests which can and do report validity and reliability are used for assessing curricula, programs, or for providing peer comparison information. Efforts to make fundamental changes in assessments are frequently undermined at the local levels by this dual system of assessment.

Given this dilemma, it is appropriate to conclude that there are many challenges in assessing writing. The complexity of the writing process itself is a primary contributor to these challenges. We know, based on the research of writing specialists including Atwell (1987), Calkins (1986), Graves (1994), Murray (1982) and others, that writing is a process involving multiple steps. These steps are not sequential in nature but rather are recursive, with the writer bouncing from one to another and back again during the course of writing. Each writer has a unique individual strategy for addressing this process. These strategies emerge following equally unique and individual developmental time lines. In writing assessment, developmental issues also pose a challenge to teachers of children in K-12 schools. At early ages (K-2) literacy skills develop rapidly. Students often undergo rapid growth followed by regression and renewed growth. Few developmentally appropriate assessment tools exist to document this early literacy development.

The qualities of an individual's writing are profoundly influenced by the context in which it develops including the intended purpose and audience. For most writers, and for all developing writers, there is a wide variability from piece to piece. In his landmark text, Graves reflected on the topic of variability, stating: "writing is a highly idiosyncratic process that varies from day to day" (p. 270). Graves went on to identify eight factors that contribute to variability in writing of both adults and children alike. The first of these eight factors is topic. Qualities of an individual's writing are influenced by topic selection, and in some cases, previous experience for young and linguistically and culturally diverse writers topic is a critical issue because of their limited and unique experiences in the world (Dyson 1995; Garcia 1994a,b). In addition, fluency in developing writers is inhibited by strict adherence to and emphasis on conventional correctness usually only in English (Calkins 1986).

Traditional writing evaluation instruments emphasize language conventions including grammar and spelling. The tasks of organization, development, establishment of voice, tone or mood, and audience awareness are overlooked and undervalued. Calkins stated that we had "elevated form over content," (Calkins 1986, p.14). Proponents of the writing process hold that breaking writing tasks into isolated drills in basic grammer fails to produce students capable of real, substantive writing (Edelsky et al. 1991).

The influence of variability, topic selection, time limitations, demands for conventionally, and isolated samples in traditional forms of direct writing assessment are profound. Most direct assessments require students to write from a predetermined prompt, for a specified amount of time, under "test" conditions (Williamson 1993). Occasionally, the best of these writing assessment will allow a follow-up session during which the writers are directed to edit, proofread, and revise the work on a subsequent day. Most large-scale assessments do not allow for these limited elements of the writing process to be included. Neither do they allow for assessments in languages other than English. In addition, in an effort to equalize the "playing field" and adhere to the expectations of a standardized testing paradigm, resource access is prohibited or extremely limited. The assessment requires a decontextualized setting in which to conduct an artificial writing task for removed from the needs, interests, or passions of the writer (Camp 1993; Garcia 1994a; Moss 1994b).

To provide educators, particularly those serving mulitilingual/multicultural students, with meaningful and consistent writing assessment tools and methods of quantifying data from their classroom observations and students' portfolios, new assessments must be developed, field-tested, and researched to determine their validity and reliability (Camp, 1993). Assessment procedures must match classroom practices and current research in order to provide valid and reliable information (Williamson, 1993). According to Wiggins (1994), "an authentic and pedagogically-supportive writing assessment would educate students and teachers alike as to the qualities sought in finished products and the processes deemed likely to yield exemplary products" (p.130). The Authentic Literacy Assessment (ALA) described here attempts to meet this goal in English, Spanish and Cantonese.

One critical concern is the relationship between, and importance of, content versus form. Socio- and psycholinguistics remind us that the purpose of language is to make meaning (Garcia, 1994b). The content of the message is the first and most important aspect of writing a teacher must address. For young writers, form takes a great deal of time and a lot of exposure to printed text in order to develop. Few adults would claim to have perfected their writing. For young writers (and perhaps for all writers) emphasis must first be placed on the content of the written message and secondarily on the form. The work of Calkins (1986), Keenan (1994), and many others supports this contention. The ALA is designed to separate the "telling of the story" from the conventions used by the young writers, thus placing emphasis on content first and form second.

Conventionality adds ease to the meaning-making task of the reader. As a result, there is a bias for highly conventional writings. The ALA is designed to allow conventions to be scored separately. In addition, the collaborative process for use of the scales allows only one rater to interact with the written text at a time. The team can then focus all their attention on the quality of the child's story or narrative development and listen for growing evidence of conscious control, indicating audience awareness on the part of the writer.

Frederiksen and Collins (1989) raised concerns over the potential negative effects of some forms of assessment on instructional practice. The purpose of the ALA is to inform instruction in a way consistent with the theoretical constructs of language acquisition theory and writing process theory. Thus, the process is designed to support and enhance teaching of the writing process. Toward this goal, writing samples to be assessed by the ALA are taken from student writing which is embedded in a writing process. The context of the writing task is authentic. The pieces to be assessed are real examples of students' work, not samples produced for a test in a 45 minute sitting on a standard topic or prompt. Samples are carefully prompted and are part of a process-to-product interaction.

Students are provided with one or more carefully developed topics which are strategically selected by the teacher. Pre-writing activities always precede the writing activity. The ALA assessment process involves eliminating time-limitations, providing access to reference materials, and opportunities for rehearsal, limited revision, editing, and proof reading. With this support, the ALA is helpful to the student writer who has no opportunity to think about what he or she wants to say (or write) in an otherwise constrained setting.

During the pilot period, when multiple samples from the same children were assessed, teacher-defined rubrics were used to score the writing product. Topic and rubric development were developed with teacher input and after reviewing examination of actual student writing.

Huot (1990) has signaled the potential lack of inter-rater reliability when writing samples are independently scored. The ALA requires a collaborative process for larger scale assessments. Thus, multiple readers evaluate the writing samples and then discuss them in relation to the rubric criteria. Multiple-takes on an individual's writing are afforded by this collaborative approach. Consensus is required at the close of the discussion. This collaborative process also constitutes a rigorous, hands-on professional development opportunity for teachers that encourages professional discourse about the qualities of student writing across broad developmental levels beginning with emergent literacy. Hewitt (1995) calls for such staff development as a critical part of any assessment program.

August and Hakuta (1997) claim that several "uses of assessment are unique to English language learners and bilingual children." These uses include: identifying children whose English proficiency is limited; determining eligibility for placement in specific language programs (e.g., bilingual education or English as a second language [ESL]); and monitoring student progress in and readiness to exit from special language service programs. In addition, tests are used to place culturally and linguistically diverse (CLD) students in categorically specific programs, such as Title I, remedial or advanced coursework, and monitor them in compliance with state and federal programs.

Gonzalez et al. (1996) argue that CLD students tend to be over-identified, under-identified, or mis-identified, and more often than not, CLD students are mis-identified as either "culturally and linguistically inferior as well as academically and socially incapable due to their disabling condition," (p. 7) or "with mental retardation" (p. 8). As a consequence of being inappropriately diagnosed by certain test batteries, CLD students are more likely to suffer either low self-esteem, or ill-fitted curriculum and programs. To "correct" this, Gonzalez et al. argue for assessment administered in the child's native language, validated for the purposes the test is used.

Cumming and Mellow (1994) propose that assessments have to have "valid assessment procedures that measure specific aspects of language" (p. 73). They further caution that ill-structured tests or test items might have the negative influence of encouraging fossilization among CLD students in their language development.

In writing assessment, standardized multiple-choice tests are especially problematic for measuring children's real ability because of the recursive nature of the writing process, involving multiple steps in a non-sequential way. "Even professional testing institutions are unable to construct indirect tests which measure writing ability accurately" (Hughes 1989, p. 75). Hughes further proposes that for a writing assessment instrument to be an accurate tool to measure writing ability, three factors should be taken into account: (1) The writing task should be "properly representative of the population" that "we should expect students to be able to perform;" (2) The assessment should directly "elicit samples of writing which truly represent the students ability", and nothing else; and (3) the samples should be scored reliably. Gonzalez et al. (1996) come to the conclusion that to best assess CLD students, alternative assessment methods should be used, such as portfolio assessment, regular observation, anecdotal records, checklists, and performance assessment as "bits of curriculum".

Stiggins (1995) proposes three basic methodological ingredients for sound performance tests: The assessment system has to have a clearly defined specification of performance to be tested; the testing task or testing exercises should be able to just elicit that performance; and, the design of administration procedures and scoring process should be sound and reliable. Stiggins further suggests that the criterion for selecting a performance to be tested should be based on judgments about whether this performance is a key to academic success and embodies standards that could be naturally applied to classroom tasks. He also emphasizes the importance of inter-rater reliability in the scoring process with well-designed scoring guides and specific holistic rating criteria.

The above brief discussion of assessment issues regarding CLD students has demonstrated a clear recognition among scholars that although standardized assessments might have validity, reliability and practicality of administration, they are problematic and unable to provide accurate and sufficient assessment of writing development. Standardized tests tend to be biased against CLD students, and may have negative effects on them. Performance assessment, on the other hand, seems to have the potential to provide avenues to make measurement more accurate and direct. But we are also cautioned about its possible lack of validity and reliability. Furthermore, there does not seem to be much research regarding writing assessments for CLD students. There are, however, discussions of how to test ESL writing development, and how to use native language to test CLD students so that they can understand the task and the test. The above two kinds of consideration do not take into consideration the following issues, which a sound bilingual writing assessment should be able to address:

(1) Since assessment can elicit behaviors that are seen as valued in the test, writing assessment should also promote bilingual abilities. In other words, the use of native language is not just seen as an aid but rather as a means and an end of the writing assessment.
(2) The parallel writing assessments in two languages, English and the children's native language, should specify a similar performance with equal standards, and design parallel testing procedures, also both in English and in the L1, so that the construct and content validity can be achieved.
(3) The scoring processes should also be in both languages and with similar scoring guides and guidance.

The ALA provides teachers and entire elementary school systems with the critical information necessary to consider assessment of literacy development and instruction in their Spanish, Cantonese and English language classrooms. The process is intended to broaden teachers' knowledge about writing across multiple grade levels and to generate discussion about instructional issues such as topic selection or technical versus creative writing. Thus, it is also a powerful tool for staff development. Determining the degree of construct validity and inter-rater reliability of this assessment tool and the collaborative process expands the potential use of the ALA and allows for comparison between the results of various schools with comparable populations. The remainder of this paper describes the co-development effort of researchers and teachers at two multilingual/multicultural schools.

The schools

Cesar Chavez elementary school

This school serves students in kindergarten through fifth grade and is located in the heart of the Mission District in San Francisco. Students come from the Western Addition, Chinatown, and the Mission District. It is a magnet school focusing on Science, Technology, and Foreign Language Development. There are Chinese/English, Spanish/English, and American Sign Language/English bilingual classes as well as African-centered and multicultural classes. Some classes are multi-age—grades one and two are combined, etc. The school also has a Pre-K and a Center for childcare. Cesar Chavez is also a school-wide Title I school.

During the fall of 1996 Cesar Chavez had a population of 546 students (according to SFUSD school profile). There were 354 limited English proficient (LEP) and non-English proficient (NEP) students (65%), 44 special education students, 185 educationally disadvantaged youth (EDY) students, and 447 students (82%) on free or reduced lunch. Latino students made up the largest ethnic student population at Cesar Chavez at 44.9% (245 students). Chinese-American students represented 27.5% of the student population (150 students). African-American students represented 9.9% of the population (54 students). White students madeup 5.7% of the population (31 students) while there were two Japanese-American students, five Native American students, and 18 Filipino students. Finally, 7.5% of the students are categorized as Other Non-White (41 students); this would include students from the Middle East.

In the Chinese Bilingual Program there are five self-contained classes of 140 K-5th grade students with six Cantonese bilingual teachers and three Cantonese bilingual instructional aides. The program has adopted a maintenance philosophy using primary language to teach certain content areas and curriculum while also enhancing English acquisition. On-going parent workshops are provided to bridge the home-school connection with teachers and the school's Chinese bilingual mental health consultant. The Spanish Bilingual Program is composed of two Spanish immersion classes K-5th and six late-exit bilingual classes also K-5th. All are multi-age classes with three age/grade groups in each classroom. A Spanish Bilingual Special Education class (grades 3rd through 5th) is also part of the program. The Deaf Education Program consists of three self-contained classrooms of pre-K through fifth grade. The staff consists of six deaf and three hearing staff, all fluent in American Sign Language (ASL). ASL is the primary language for classroom instruction and written English is used as the primary form of English expression. The program provides weekly ASL classes for parents and staff. Parents are also invited to educational workshops to learn about the academic program, deaf culture, and different class projects.

During the 1995–1996 school year, students at Cesar Chavez participated in the Comprehensive Test of Basic Skills (CTBS). The overall normal curve equipment (NCE) for the school in Reading was 31.9. For Math the overall NCE was 35.7.

Fairmount elementary school

This school serves students in kindergarten through fifth grade and is located in the Glen Park District of San Francisco. Students come from Noe Valley, Bernal Heights, Bayview/Hunter's Point, and the Mission District. Fairmount offers a developmental Spanish bilingual program (K-5) focusing on language maintenance and cultural appreciation, and offering English speakers an opportunity to learn a second language. There are three special day classes and an inclusion program for students with special needs. The school offers a school-wide Friday cross-age integration of all students and an after school mathematics tutorial program. Additional funds for educationally disadvantaged youths (EDY) have provided additional support in the form of a program resource teacher, a librarian, a Reading Recovery teacher in Spanish, a Reading Recovery teacher in English, a mathematics resource teacher, para-professionals, and two elementary advisors. There is also a coordinated-services team which includes a nurse, a psychologist, and a lead teacher one day a week. A bilingual speech therapist is available to students with special needs, as well as a play therapist.

During the fall of 1996 Fairmount had a population of 383 students (according to SFUSD school profile). There were 104 limited English proficient (LEP) and non English proficient (NEP) students (27.2%), 38 special education students, 164 educationally disadvantaged youth (EDY) students, and 311 students (81.2%) on free or reduced lunch. Latino students made up the largest ethnic student population at Fairmount at 46% (176 students). African-American students represented 33.2% of the population (127 students). White students made-up 7.3% of the population (28 students), while there were eleven Chinese-American students, five Native American students, and 18 Filipino students. Finally, 4.7% of the students are categorized as Other Non-White (18 students); this would include students from the Middle East.

During the 1995–1996 school year, students at Fairmount participated in the Comprehensive Test of Basic Skills (CTBS). In Reading, at first grade the national percentile (NP) was 22 and the normal curve equivalent (NCE) was 34.5. For Math the NP at first grade was 24 and the NCE was 35.8.

The absence of any on-going, non-standardized, non-English literacy assessment led the staff at these two schools to begin the development of a school-wide assessment in English, Spanish and Cantonese. A consensus emerged among the staffs that such an assessment and its related analysis could inform literacy instruction. As a by-product, this effort was intended to produce a school-wide, standards-based articulation within and between grade levels in the area of literacy.

Development and implementation

Designing the ALA

Along with teachers and administrators, researchers planned and implemented the ALA with the understanding that it would allow students to explore writing as a process in the context of the curriculum; and would not be constrained by traditional standardized assessment tools. It would take place in the different languages of instruction; and would occur several times during the school year, giving teachers periodic indicators of their students' strengths and needs.

Administering the ALA

The procedures for administering the ALA were established and piloted during the first year of the study. Teachers and students were to read a literature selection at grade-level together. They would then engage in approximately two pre-writing activities. For instance, the teacher might lead students in a whole-class discussion of a central theme of the reading, taking notes on chart paper. Students might then work in pairs or in cooperative groups to reflect, in writing, on how their personal experiences related to ideas in the reading. After preparing for the written assessment in this way, all students were to write a personal response to a prompt that involved themes treated in the literature selection.

An example

The following excerpt from field notes taken during an ALA event in a third to fourth grade Chinese-bilingual classroom illustrates the Assessment:

> The teacher started the English session by passing out the assessment packet, and reminded students that they had done this activity before. She then started to read the instructions, and explained them briefly.
>
> She began to read the story, "A Gift for my Mother" by Vera B. Williams, as students followed along in their packets. After reading approximately a third of the story, she stopped and asked volunteers to answer a few comprehension questions orally. She continued, stopping soon to ask a few more questions. She finished reading the story, and asked more comprehension questions again.

The teacher moved to Part A: "Prewriting Activities." Since the purpose of the pre-writing activities was to engage students in a reflection of the themes that surfaced in the readings, they were allowed to complete individual and group pre-writing activities in their first or second language. However, she spoke to the class in English throughout the administration of the ALA.

For the first pre-writing activity the teacher asked students to reflect individually on two questions:

1. What do you remember best about "A Gift for my Mother"? You can draw a picture, make a story map, or write about what the story made you think about or remember.
2. Draw or write about the young girl's thoughts as she saves money to buy her mother a gift.

There were four students with limited-English comprehension who received special attention during the individual pre-writing activities. They were pulled out by the teacher, and she checked their comprehension of the story. (. . .) After completing the individual pre-writing activities, the teacher started Part B: Partner/Small Group Work. She read the instructions and instructed each student to take turns sharing what she/he remembered about the story. All other students were asked to take notes when this student was sharing his/her ideas. The table monitor of each cooperative group guided the discussion while the teacher walked around student tables and assisted as necessary.

After the small-group discussion, the teacher asked a few more questions about the story, and had some students tell the class what and how they would get a gift for someone special. She then explained the writing prompt: Students were to write about a personal story involving an important gift. She emphasized two issues: (a) students were to "show not tell;" describing the gift in detail; and (b) specify how the gift was obtained.

She briefly reminded students that they could look at classroom posters to review the organizational structure of compositions, punctuation, and parts of speech posters. These resources remained accessible during the writing of the compositions, as they would during other writing events in the classroom. Students were then given 30 minutes to write their composition individually. Two students who had been in the country for less than two months wrote in their first language. All other students were instructed to write in English. At the end of the writing segment of the ALA, the teacher collected the writing samples, and thanked students for their diligence.

This example provides an overview of the way the assessment is administered. Still, procedures for students in primary grades and upper elementary grades differ slightly to take into account the social and academic abilities of students of different ages. For example, the second grade ALA involves more teacher-directed pre-writing, and the fourth grade ALA involves more cooperative group pre-writing. In the lower grades students have less time to write than students in the upper grades.

Standardizing the ALA across grade levels

The ALA was administered according to pre-set guidelines several times a year during the first (pilot) year of the study. The piece of literature, the pre-writing activities and the writing prompt were to be consistent across grade level groupings. At each grade level, teachers were to adhere to time limitations for the writing segments of the ALA. During the first year, standardizing the administration was difficult, so for the second year of implementation, instructions, including teacher scripts, have been developed.

Frequency of ALA administration

During the first year of implementation, the schools attempted to administer the ALA monthly in each language of instruction. In order to have time to analyze students' writings and develop instructional interventions, schools elected to administer the ALA quarterly in all languages of instruction during the second year of implementation.

Developing the assessments at grade level

Several times during the first year, teachers met to choose literature selections, pre-writing activities and writing prompts. This proved to be time-consuming for the grade-level teams of teachers, particularly for teachers instructing in two languages. In order to expedite the ALA selection process in preparation for the second year of implementation, a team of researchers and teachers reviewed District-adopted grade-level literature, and developed two choices for ALA activities for each grade level and in each language of instruction. Teachers then met in grade-level groups to select one of the two choices of ALA activities to administer.

Rubric development

In order to maximize the impact of the ALA, during the first year of implementation teachers worked with a school district coach to learn to identify students' literacy strengths and needs based on their written work. The coach exposed the teachers to different types of elementary level writing rubrics, and led them in thinking critically about the rubrics as tools for assessing students' writing. As a result of this process, teachers decided to develop their own school-wide writing rubrics. They worked with researchers and with the coach to develop writing rubrics in all languages of instruction. These rubrics underwent several revisions and are aligned with district-wide writing standards.[1]

Anchor papers

After developing the rubrics, teachers selected writing samples that were exemplars, or anchor papers, for the different scores in the rubrics. These are to be used by teachers to determine the holistic score of each paper that they score as the project enters its second year. Specific example of student writing and the narrative which places that writing at a particular score on the rubric have been developed for each language. It was, and is, important to provide examples of student work related to the rubric and a narrative explanation of that student's work in relationship to a score on the rubric.

Conclusion

In this "working paper," we have attempted to articulate the importance of developing and implementing a more authentic assessment of literacy for multilingual and multicultural student populations. From this work, we have developed a set of principles that guide this effort:

- The assessment process and instrument must be aligned with instructional activity existent in the classroom, including the language in which instruction is taking place.
- The assessment must maximize the student's experience and ability to demonstrate literacy competencies in several domains.
- The assessment must be on-going and able to demonstrate development/ learning over the entire academic year.
- The assessment must be tied to a theoretical and empirical knowledge base and coupled with teacher practice expertise.
- The results and analysis of the assessment must be usable by teachers to inform, adapt and maximize literacy instruction.
- Wherever possible, students should be able to participate in the development and utilization of the assessment process.

Next steps

The second year of implementation is currently underway. During fall 1998, teachers selected and administered ALA activities in the languages of instruction and for each grade level. They scored their student's writing, and "Study Teams," led by the school coach, are in the process of looking at the student data to identify trends and to develop instructional interventions.

Note

1 One school elected to have three six-point writing rubrics, one for each of the grade-level groups K-1, 2–3, 4–5. Score 4 for these rubrics would be considered the "benchmarks" for all students in grades 1, 3, and 5. The other school chose to connect the three-level rubrics into one continuous rubric for grades Pre-K-5. This resulted in a 14-point rubric where score 12, would be considered the benchmark for grade 5.

References

August, D., & Hakuta, K. (1997). *Improving Schooling for Language-Minority Children: A Research Agenda.* Washington, DC: National Academy Press.

Atwell, N. (1987). *In the middle.* Upper Montclair, NJ: Boyton/Cook.

Calkins, L.M. (1986). *The Art of Teaching Writing.* Portsmouth, NH: Heinemann.

Camp, R. (1993). Changing the model for direct assessment of writing. In M. Williamson & B. Hout (eds.), *Validating Holistic Scoring for Writing Assessment: Theoretical and empirical foundations.* Cresskill, NJ: Hampton Press, Inc., 109–141.

Cumming, A., & Berwick, R. (1994). *Validation in Language Testing.* Bristol, PA: Multilingual Matters Ltd.

Cumming, A., & Mellow, D. (1994). An Investigation into the Validity of Written Indicators of Second Language Proficiency. In Cumming, A., & Berwick, R. (eds). *Validation in Language Testing.* Bristol, PA: Multilingual Matters Ltd.

Dyson, A. (1995). *Writing Children: Reinventing the development of childhood literacy.*

Berkeley, CA: National Center for the Study of Writing, University of California: [Washington, DC]: U.S. Dept. of Education, Office of Educational Research and Improvement, Educational Resources Information Center.

Edelsky, C., Altwerger, B., & Flores, B. (1991). *Whole Language: What's the difference?* Portsmouth, NH: Heinemann.

Fredricksen, J. R. & Collins, A. (1989). A systems approach to educational testing. *Educational Researcher*, 18.

Garcia, E. (1994a). Addressing the challenges of diversity. In S.L. Kagan and B. Weissbourd (eds.), *Putting Families First*. San Francisco: Jossey-Bass, 243–275.

Garcia, E. (1994b). The impact of linguistic and cultural diversity in American schools: A need for new policy. In M.C. Wang and M.C. Reynolds (eds.), *Making a Difference for Students at Risk*. Thousand Oaks, CA: Corwin Press, 156–182.

Genishi, C., & Brainard, M. B. (1995). Assessment of Bilingual Children: A dilemma seeking solutions. In Garcia & McLaughlin (eds.), *Meeting the Challenge of Linguistic and Cultural Diversity in Early Childhood Education*. New York, NY: Teachers College, Columbia University, 49–63.

Gonzalez, V., Brusca-Vega, R., & Yawkey, T. (1996). *Assessment and Instruction of Culturally and Linguistically Diverse Students with or At-Risk of Learning Problems: From Research to Practice*. Needham Heights, MA: Allyn & Bacon.

Graves, D. (1994). *A Fresh Look at Writing*. Portsmouth, NH: Heinemann.

Hewitt, G. (1995). *A Portfolio Primer: Teaching, Collecting, and Assessing Student Writing*. Portsmouth, NH: Heinemann.

Hughes, A. (1989). *Testing for Language Teachers*. Cambridge, UK: Cambridge University Press.

Huot, B. (1990). The literature of directing writing assessment: Major concerns and prevailing trends. *Review of Educational Research* 60: 237–263.

Keenan, J. (1994). Assessing the written language abilities of beginning writers. In K. Holland, D. Bloome & J. Solsken (eds.) *Alternative Perspectives in Assessing Children's Language and Literacy*. Norwood, NJ: Ablex Publishing Corporation.

Milanovic, M., Saville, N., Pollitt, Al., & Cook, A. (1994). Developing rating scales for CASE: Theoretical concerns and analyses. In Cumming & Berwick (eds.), *Validation in Language Testing*. Bristol, PA: Multilingual Matters Ltd.

Moss, P. (1994b). Shifting conceptions of validity in educational measurement: Implications for performance assessment. *Review of Educational Research* 62: 229–258.

Murray, D. M. (1982). *The Listening Eye. Learning by teaching*. Upper Montclair, NJ: Boyton/Cook Publishers.

Porter, C., & Cleland, J. (1995). *The Portfolio as a Learning Strategy*. Portsmouth, NH: Heinemann.

Roeber, E. (1995). *Emerging Student Assessment for School Reform*. ERIC Digest. ED 389959.

Stiggins, R. J. (1995). *Sound Performance Assessments in the Guidance Context*. ERIC Digest. ED 388889.

Valdes, G. (1991). *Bilingual Minorities and Language Issues in Writing: Toward Profession-Wide Responses to a New Challenge*: Technical Report No. 54. Berkeley, CA: National Center for the Study of Writing.

Valencia, S.W., Hiebert, E.H., & Afflerbach, P.P. (1994). *Authentic Reading Assessment: Practices and Possibilities*. Newark, DE: International Reading Association.

Wiggins, G. (1994). The constant danger of sacrificing validity to reliability: Making writing assessment serve writers. *Assessing Writing* 1: 129–139.

Williamson, M. (1993). An introduction to holistic scoring: The social, historical and theoretical context for writing assessment. In M. Williamson & B. Hout (eds.), *Validating Holistic Scoring for Writing Assessment: Theoretical and empirical foundations*. Cresskill, NJ: Hampton Press, Inc., 1–44.

CHAPTER 5

PERFORMANCE-BASED ASSESSMENT AND EDUCATIONAL EQUITY (1993)

Linda Darling-Hammond

In recent years, the school reform movement has engendered widespread efforts to transform the ways in which students' work and learning are assessed in schools. These alternatives are frequently called performance-based or "authentic" assessments because they engage students in "real-world" tasks rather than multiple-choice tests, and evaluate them according to criteria that are important for actual performance in a field of work (Wiggins, 1989). Such assessments include oral presentations, debates, or exhibitions, along with collections of students' written products, videotapes of performances and other learning occasions, constructions and models, and their solutions to problems, experiments, or results of scientific and other inquiries (Archbald & Newman, 1988). They also include teacher observations and inventories of individual students' work and behavior, as well as of cooperative group work (National Association for the Education of Young Children [NAEYC], 1988).

Much of the rationale for these initiatives is based on growing evidence that traditional norm-referenced, multiple-choice tests fail to measure complex cognitive and performance abilities. Furthermore, when used for decisionmaking, they encourage instruction that tends to emphasize decontextualized, rote-oriented tasks imposing low cognitive demands rather than meaningful learning. Thus, efforts to raise standards of learning and performance must rest in part on strategies to transform assessment practices.

In addition, efforts to ensure that *all* students learn in meaningful ways resulting in high levels of performance require that teachers know as much about students and their learning as they do about subject matter. However, teachers' understandings of students' strengths, needs, and approaches to learning are not well supported by external testing programs that send secret, secured tests into the school and whisk them out again for machine scoring that produces numerical quotients many months later. Authentic assessment strategies can provide teachers with much more useful classroom information as they engage teachers in evaluating how and what students know and can do in real-life performance situations. These kinds of assessment strategies create the possibility that teachers will not only develop curricula aimed at challenging performance skills, but that they will also be able to use the resulting rich information about student learning and performance to shape their teaching in ways that can prove more effective for individual students.

Recently, interest in alternative forms of student assessment has expanded from the classroom-based efforts of individual teachers to district and statewide initiatives to overhaul entire testing programs so that they become more performance-based. Major national testing programs, such as the National Assessment of Educational Progress and the College Board's Scholastic Assessment Tests (formerly the Scholastic Aptitude Tests), are also undergoing important changes. These programs are being redesigned so that they will increasingly engage students in performance tasks requiring written and oral responses in lieu of multiple-choice questions focused on discrete facts or decontextualized bits of knowledge.

However, proposals for assessment reform differ in several important ways: 1) in the extent to which they aim to broaden the roles of educators, students, parents, and other community members in assessment; 2) in the extent to which they aim to make assessment part of the teaching and learning process, and use it to serve developmental and educational purposes rather than sorting and screening purposes; 3) in the extent to which they anticipate a problem-based interdisciplinary curriculum or a coverage-oriented curriculum that maintains traditional subject area compartments for learning; and 4) in the extent to which they see assessment reform as part of a broader national agenda to improve and equalize educational opportunities in schools. Some see assessment reform as part of a broader agenda to strengthen the national educational infrastructure (the availability of high-quality teachers, curriculum, and resources) and to equalize access so that all students start from an equal platform for learning. Others, however, view performance-based assessment as a single sledgehammer for change, without acknowledging other structural realities of schooling, such as vast inequalities in educational opportunities.

These differences in approaches to assessment reform predict very different consequences for the educational system, and dramatically different consequences for those who have been traditionally underserved in U.S. schools—students in poor communities, "minorities," immigrants, and students with distinctive learning needs. In this article, I argue in particular that *changes in the forms of assessment are unlikely to enhance equity unless we change the ways in which assessments are used as well:* from sorting mechanisms to diagnostic supports; from external monitors of performance to locally generated tools for inquiring deeply into teaching and learning; and from purveyors of sanctions for those already underserved to levers for equalizing resources and enhancing learning opportunities.

The extent to which educational testing serves to enhance teaching and learning and to support greater equality or to undermine educational opportunity depends on how a variety of issues are resolved. Among these are issues associated with the nature of assessment tools themselves:

- whether and how they avoid bias;
- how they resolve concerns about subjectivity versus objectivity in evaluating student work;
- how they influence curriculum and teaching.

A second set of issues has to do with whether and how assessment results are used to determine student placements and promotions, to reinforce differential curriculum tracking, or to allocate rewards and sanctions to teachers, programs, or schools.

A final set of issues concerns the policies and practices that surround the assessment system and determine the educational opportunities available to students to support their learning. A fundamental question is whether assessment systems will support better teaching and transform schooling for traditionally underserved students or whether they will merely reify existing inequities. This depends on the extent to which they promote equity in the allocation of resources for providing education, supports for effective teaching practices, and supports for more widespread school restructuring.

Motivations for assessment reform

The current movement to change U.S. traditions of student assessment in large-scale and systemic ways has several motivations. One is based on the recognition that assessment, especially when it is used for decisionmaking purposes, exerts powerful influences on curriculum and instruction. It can "drive" instruction in ways that mimic not only the content, but also the format and cognitive demands of tests (Darling-Hammond & Wise, 1985; Madaus, West, Harmon, Lomax, & Viator, 1992). If assessment exerts these influences, many argue, it should be carefully shaped to send signals that are consistent with the kinds of learning desired and the approaches to curriculum and instruction that will support such learning (Cohen & Spillane, 1992; O'Day & Smith, 1993).

A second and somewhat related motive for systemic approaches to assessment reform stems from the belief that if assessment can exert powerful influences on behavior, it can be used to change school organizational behavior as well as classroom work. The idea of using assessment as a lever for school change is not a new one: many accountability tools in the 1970s and 1980s tried to link policy decisions to test scores (Linn, 1987; Madaus, 1985; Wise, 1979). Unfortunately, these efforts frequently had unhappy results for teaching and learning generally, and for schools' treatment of low-scoring students in particular. Research on these initiatives has found that test-based decisionmaking has driven instruction toward lower order cognitive skills. This shift has created incentives for pushing low scorers into special education, consigning them to educationally unproductive remedial classes, holding them back in the grades, and encouraging them to drop out (Allington & McGill-Franzen, 1992; Darling-Hammond, 1991, 1993; Koretz, 1988; Shepard & Smith, 1988; Smith, 1986). In addition, school incentives tied to test scores have undermined efforts to create and sustain more inclusive and integrated student populations, as schools are punished for accepting and keeping students with special needs and are rewarded for keeping such students out of their programs through selective admissions and transfer policies. Those with clout and means "improve" education by manipulating the population of students they serve (Smith, 1986). Schools serving disadvantaged students find it increasingly hard to recruit and retain experienced and highly qualified staff when the threat of punishments for low scores hangs over them. Thus, such policies exacerbate rather than ameliorate the unequal distribution of educational opportunity.

Nonetheless, a variety of proposals have recently been put forth that involve the use of mandated performance-based assessments as external levers for school change (Commission on Chapter I, 1992; Hornbeck, 1992; O'Day & Smith, 1993). Even those who do not endorse such proposals share the view that assessment can promote change. Other proposals, raised from a different philosophical vantage point and envisioning different uses of assessment, suggest the use of alternative classroom-embedded assessments as internal supports for school-based inquiry (Darling-Hammond & Ascher, 1990; Wolf & Baron, in press).

A third reason for assessment reform addresses concerns about equity and access to educational opportunity. Over many decades, assessment results have frequently been used to define not only teaching, but also students' opportunities to learn. As a tool for tracking students into different courses, levels, and kinds of instructional programs, testing has been a primary means for limiting or expanding students' life choices and their avenues for demonstrating competence. Increasingly, these uses of tests are recognized as having the unintended consequence of limiting students' access to further learning opportunities (Darling-Hammond, 1991; Glaser, 1990; Oakes, 1985).

Some current proposals for performance-based assessment view these new kinds of tests as serving the same screening and tracking purposes as more traditional tests (Commission on the Skills of the American Workforce, 1990; Educate America, 1991; National Center on Education and the Economy, 1989). The presumption is that more "authentic" assessments will both motivate and sort students more effectively. Others see a primary goal of assessment reform as transforming the purposes and uses of testing as well as its form and content. They argue for shifting from the use of assessment as a sorting device to its use as a tool for identifying student strengths and needs so that teachers can adapt instruction more successfully (Darling-Hammond, Ancess, & Falk, in press; Glaser, 1981, 1990; Kornhaber & Gardner, 1993). Given the knowledge now available for addressing diverse learning needs and the needs of today's society for a broadly educated populace, the goals of education—and assessment—are being transformed from deciding who will be permitted to become well-educated to helping ensure that everyone will learn successfully.

Clearly, the current press to reform assessment entails many motivations and many possible consequences, depending on decisions that are made about 1) the nature of the "new" assessments; 2) the ways in which they are used; and 3) the companion efforts (if any) that accompany them to actually improve education in the schools.

In this article I outline the range of equity issues that arise with respect to testing generally, and with respect to proposals for the development of new "authentic" assessments specifically. I argue that the outcomes of the current wave of assessment reforms will depend in large measure on the extent to which assessment developers and users:

- focus on both the quality and fairness of assessment strategies;
- use assessments in ways that serve teaching and learning, rather than sorting and selecting;
- develop policies that are congruent with (and respectful of) these assessment goals, as well as with assessment strategies and limitations;
- embed assessment reform in broader reforms to improve and equalize access to educational resources and opportunities;
- support the professional development of teachers along with the organizational development of schools, so that assessment is embedded in teaching and learning, and is used to inform more skillful and adaptive teaching that enables more successful learning for all students.

Uses and consequences of testing

Historical perspectives

For over one hundred years, standardized testing has been a tool used to exert control over the schooling process and to make decisions about educational entitlements for students. Testing proved a convenient instrument of social control for those superintendents in the late nineteenth century who sought to use tests as a means for creating the "one best system" of education (Tyack, 1974). It also proved enormously useful as a means of determining how to slot students for more and less rigorous (and costly) curricula when public funding of education and compulsory attendance vastly increased access to schools in the early twentieth century.

Given the massive increase in students, the limits of public budgets, and the relatively meager training of teachers, strategies were sought to codify curriculum and to group students for differential instruction. IQ tests were widely used as a measure of educational input (with intelligence viewed as the "raw material" for schooling) to sort pupils so they could be efficiently educated according to their future roles in society (Cremin, 1961; Cubberly, 1919; Watson, in press). Frequently, they were used to exclude students from schooling opportunities altogether (Glaser, 1981).

Though many proponents argued that the use of these tests as a tool for tracking students would enhance social justice, the rationales for tracking—like those for using scores to set immigration quotas into the United States—were often frankly motivated by racial and ethnic politics. Just as Goddard's 1912 data—"proving" that 83 percent of Jews, 80 percent of Hungarians, 79 percent of Italians, and 87 percent of Russians were "feebleminded"—were used to justify low immigration quota for those groups (Kamin, 1974), so did Terman's test data "prove" that "[Indians, Mexicans, and Negroes] should be segregated in special classes. . . . They cannot master abstractions, but they can often be made efficient workers" (Terman, cited in Oakes, 1985, p. 36). Presumptions like these reinforced racial segregation and differential learning opportunities.

Terman found many inequalities in performance among groups on his IQ test, which was adapted from Binet's work in France. Most, but not all of them, seemed to confirm what he, and presumably every "intelligent" person, already knew: that various groups were inherently unequal in their mental capacities. However, when girls scored higher than boys on his 1916 version of the Stanford-Binet, he revised the test to correct for this apparent flaw by selecting items to create parity among genders in the scores (Mercer, 1989). Other inequalities —between urban and rural students, students, students of higher and lower socioeconomic status, native English speakers and immigrants, Whites and Blacks—did not occasion such revisions, since their validity seemed patently obvious to the test-makers.

The role of testing in reinforcing and extending social inequalities in educational opportunities has by now been extensively researched (Gould, 1981; Kamin, 1974; Mercer, 1989; Oakes, 1985; Watson, in press) and widely acknowledged. It began with the two fallacies Gould describes: the fallacy of reification, which allowed testers to develop and sell the abstract concept of intelligence as an innate, unitary, measurable commodity; and the fallacy of ranking, which supported the development of strategies for quantifying intelligence in ways that would allow people to be arrayed in a single series against each other (Gould, 1981). These two fallacies—recently debunked (though not yet dismantled) by understandings that intelligence has many dimensions (Gardner, 1983; Sternberg, 1985)—were made more dangerous by the social uses of testing as a tool for allocating educational and employment benefits rather than as a means for informing teaching and developing talents.

Negative consequences of standardized testing

Current standardized tests are widely criticized for placing test-takers in a passive, reactive role (Wigdor & Garner, 1982), rather than one that engages their capacities to structure tasks, produce ideas, and solve problems. Based on out-moded views of learning, intelligence, and performance, they fail to measure students' higher order cognitive abilities or to support their capacities to perform real-world tasks (Resnick, 1987a; Sternberg, 1985).

In a seminal paper on the past, present, and future of testing, Glaser (1990) makes an important distinction between testing and assessment. These two kinds of measurement have different purposes and different social and technical histories. Glaser describes testing as aimed at selection and placement: it attempts to predict success at learning by "measur[ing] human ability prior to a course of instruction so that individuals can be appropriately placed, diagnosed, included or excluded" (p. 2). Assessment, on the other hand, is aimed at gauging educational outcomes: it measures the results of a course of learning. What is important for testing is the instrument's predictive power rather than its content. What is important for assessment is the content validity of an approach—its ability to describe the nature of performance that results from learning.

Recently, another validity construct has emerged: *consequential validity*, which describes the extent to which an assessment tool *and the ways in which it is used* produce positive consequences both for the teaching and learning process and for students who may experience different educational opportunities as a result of test-based placements (Glaser, 1990; Shepard, 1993). This emerging validity standard places a much heavier burden on assessment developers and users to demonstrate that what they are doing works to the benefit of those who are assessed and to the society at large. The emergence of this standard has led many educators and researchers to question test-based program placements for students and to press for forms of assessment that can support more challenging and authentic forms of teaching and learning. Some test developers are just beginning to understand that the criteria against which their products are being evaluated are changing.

For most of this century, much of the energy of U.S. measurement experts has been invested in developing tests aimed at ranking students for sorting and selecting them into and out of particular placements. Standardized test developers have devoted much less energy to worrying about the properties of these instruments as reflections of—or influences on—instruction (Wigdor & Garner, 1982). As a consequence, the tests generally do not reflect the actual tasks educators and citizens expect students to be able to perform, nor do they stimulate forms of instruction that are closely connected to development of performance abilities. Similarly, to date, though awareness levels are heightened, virtually no attention has yet been paid to the consequences of test-based decisions in policy discussions about developing new assessment systems.

These shortcomings of U.S. tests were less problematic when they were used as only one source of information among many other kinds of information about student learning, and when they were not directly tied to decisions about students and programs. However, as test scores have been used to make important educational decisions, their flaws have become more damaging. As schools have begun to "teach to the tests," the scores have become ever poorer assessments of students' overall abilities, because class work oriented toward recognizing the answers to multiple-choice questions does not heighten students' proficiency in aspects of the subjects that are not tested, such as analysis, complex problem-solving, and written and oral expression (Darling-Hammond & Wise, 1985; Haney & Madaus, 1986; Koretz, 1988).

As the National Assessment of Educational Progress (NAEP) found: "Only 5 to 10 percent of students can move beyond initial readings of a text; most seem genuinely puzzled at requests to explain or defend their points of view." The NAEP assessors explained that current methods of testing reading require short responses and lower level cognitive thinking, resulting in "an emphasis on shallow and superficial opinions at the expense of reasoned and disciplined thought, . . . [thus] it is not surprising that students fail to develop more comprehensive thinking and analytic skills" (NAEP, 1981, p. 5).

During the 1970s, when test-oriented accountability measures were instituted in U.S. schools, there was a decline in public schools' use of teaching methods appropriate to the teaching of higher order skills, such as research projects and laboratory work, student-centered discussions, and the writing of essays or themes (National Center for Education Statistics [NCES], 1982, p. 83). Major studies by Boyer (1983), Goodlad (1984), and Sizer (1985) documented the negative effects of standardized testing on teaching and learning in high schools, while the disadvantage created for U.S. students by the rote learning stressed in U.S. standardized tests has been documented in international studies of achievement (McKnight et al., 1987).

The effects of basic skills test misuse have been most unfortunate for the students they were most intended to help. Many studies have found that students placed in the lowest tracks or in remedial programs—disproportionately low-income and minority students—are most apt to experience instruction geared only to multiple-choice tests, working at a low cognitive level on test-oriented tasks that are profoundly disconnected from the skills they need to learn. Rarely are they given the opportunity to talk about what they know, to read real books, to write, or to construct and solve problems in mathematics, science, or other subjects (Cooper & Sherk, 1989; Davis, 1986; Oakes, 1985; Trimble & Sinclair, 1986). In short, they have been denied the opportunity to develop the capacities they will need for the future, in large part because commonly used tests are so firmly pointed at educational goals of the past.

Thus, the quality of education made available to many students has been undermined by the nature of the testing programs used to monitor and shape their learning. If new performance-based assessments point at more challenging learning goals for all students, they may ameliorate some of this source of inequality. However, this will be true only to the extent that teachers who serve these students are able to teach in the ways demanded by the assessments—that is, in ways that support the development of higher order thinking and performance skills and in ways that diagnose and build upon individual learners' strengths and needs.

The uses of assessment tools in decisionmaking

As noted earlier, testing policies affect students' opportunities to learn in other important ways. In addition to determining whether students graduate, tests are increasingly used to track students and to determine whether they can be promoted from one grade to the next. Research suggests that both practices have had harmful consequences for individual students and for U.S. achievement generally. If performance-based assessments are used for the same purposes as traditional tests have been, the outcomes for underserved students are likely to be unchanged.

Tracking

In the United States, the process of tracking begins in elementary schools with the designation of instructional groups and programs based on test scores, and becomes highly formalized by junior high school. The result of this practice is that challenging curricula are rationed to a very small proportion of students. Consequently, few U.S. students ever encounter the kinds of curricula that most students in other countries typically experience (McKnight et al., 1987). As Oakes (1986) notes, these assignments are predictable:

> One finding about placements is undisputed. . . . Disproportionate percentages of poor and minority youngsters (principally black and Hispanic) are placed in tracks for low-ability or non-college-bound students (NCES, 1985; Rosenbaum, 1980); further, minority students are consistently underrepresented in programs for the gifted and talented. (College Board, 1985, p. 129)

Students placed in lower tracks are exposed to a limited, rote-oriented curriculum and ultimately achieve less than students of similar aptitude who are placed in academic programs or untracked classes. Furthermore, these curricular differences explain much of the disparity between the achievement of White and minority students and between those of higher and lower income levels (Lee & Bryk, 1988; Oakes, 1985). In this way, the uses of tests have impeded rather than supported the pursuit of high and rigorous educational goals for all students.

Grade retention

In addition, some U.S. states and local districts have enacted policies requiring that test scores be used as the sole criterion for decisions about student promotion from one grade to the next. Since the student promotion policies were enacted, a substantial body of research has demonstrated that the effects of this kind of test-based decisionmaking are much more negative than positive. When students who were retained in grade are compared to students of equal achievement levels who were promoted, the retained students are consistently behind on both achievement and social-emotional measures (Holmes & Matthews, 1984; Shepard & Smith, 1986). As Shepard and Smith put it, "Contrary to popular beliefs, repeating a grade does *not* help students gain ground academically and has a negative impact on social adjustment and self-esteem" (1986, p. 86).

Furthermore, the practice of retaining students is a major contributor to increased dropout rates. Research suggests that being retained increases the odds of dropping out by 40 to 50 percent. A second retention nearly doubles the risk (Mann, 1987; see also Carnegie Council on Adolescent Development, 1989; Massachusetts Advocacy Center, 1988; Wehlage, Rutter, Smith, Lesko, & Fernández, 1990). Thus, the policy of automatically retaining students based on their test-score performance has actually produced lower achievement for these students, lower self-esteem, and higher dropout rates for them and for the nation.

Graduation

Perhaps the ultimate test-related sanction for students is denying a diploma based on a test score. The rationale for this practice is that students should show they have mastered the "minimum skills" needed for employment or future education in order to graduate. The assumption is that tests can adequately capture whatever those skills are. While this appears plausible in theory, it is unlikely in reality, given the disjunction between multiple-choice tests of decontextualized bits of information and the demands of real jobs and adult tasks (Bailey, 1989; Carnevale, Gainer, & Meltzer, 1989; Resnick, 1987b). In fact, research indicates that neither employability nor earnings are significantly affected by students' scores on basic skills tests, while chances of employment and welfare dependency are tightly linked to graduation from high school (Eckland, 1980; Gordon & Sum, 1988; Jaeger, 1991). Thus, the use of tests as a sole determinant of graduation imposes heavy personal and societal costs, without obvious social benefits.

Rewards and sanctions

Finally, a few states and districts have also tried to use student test scores to allocate rewards or sanctions to schools or teachers. President Bush's proposal for a National Test included a suggestion to allocate some federal funds based on schools' scores on the "American Achievement Tests" (U.S. Department of Education, 1991). An independent commission on Chapter I has recently proposed, over the formal dissent of a number of its members, a rewards and sanctions system for Chapter I programs based on aggregate "performance-based" test scores (Commission on Chapter I, 1992). An analogous policy proposal has been enacted, though not yet implemented, for use with performance-based tests in the state of Kentucky. There, all schools that do not show specified percentage increases in student achievement scores each year will automatically suffer sanctions, which may include actions against staff. Those that meet the standards will be financially rewarded (Legislative Research Commission, 1990, p. 21).

Oblivious to the fact that schools' scores on any measure are sensitive to changes in the population of students taking the test, and that such changes can be induced by manipulating admission, dropouts, and pupil classifications, the policy will create and sustain a wide variety of perverse incentives, regardless of whether the tests are multiple-choice or performance-oriented. Because schools' aggregate scores on any measure are sensitive to the population of students taking the test, the policy creates incentives for schools to keep out students whom they fear may lower their scores—children who are handicapped, limited English speaking, or from educationally disadvantaged environments. Schools where average test scores are used for making decisions about rewards and sanctions have found a number of ways to manipulate their test-taking population in order to inflate artifically the school's average test scores. These strategies include labelling large numbers of low-scoring students for special education placements so that their scores won't "count" in school reports, retaining students in grade so that their relative standing will look better on "grade-equivalent" scores, excluding low-scoring students from admission to "open enrollment" schools, and encouraging such students to leave schools or drop out (Allington & McGill-Franzen, 1992; Darling-Hammond, 1991, 1993; Koretz, 1988; Shepard & Smith, 1988; Smith, 1986).

Smith explains the widespread engineering of student populations that he found in his study of a large urban school district that used performance standards as a basis for school level sanctions:

> Student selection provides the greatest leverage in the short-term accountability game. . . . The easiest way to improve one's chances of winning is (1) to add some highly likely students and (2) to drop some unlikely students, while simply hanging on to those in the middle. School admissions is a central thread in the accountability fabric. (1986, pp. 30–31)

Needless to say, this kind of policy that rewards or punishes schools for aggregate test scores creates a distorted view of accountability, in which beating the numbers by playing shell games with student placements overwhelms efforts to serve students' educational needs well. Equally important, these policies further exacerbate existing incentives for talented staff to opt for school placements where students are easy to teach, and school stability is high. Capable staff are less likely to risk losing rewards or incurring sanctions by volunteering to teach where many students have special needs and performance standards will be more difficult to attain. This compromises even further the educational chances of disadvantaged students, who are already served by a disproportionate share of those teachers who are inexperienced, unprepared, and under qualified.

Applying sanctions to schools with lower test score performance penalizes already disadvantaged students twice over: having given them inadequate schools to begin with, society will now punish them again for failing to perform as well as other students attending schools with greater resources and more capable teachers. This kind of reward system confuses the quality of education offered by schools with the needs of the students they enroll; it works against equity and integration, and against any possibilities for fair and open school choice, by discouraging good schools from opening their doors to educationally needy students. Such a reward structure places more emphasis on score manipulations and student assignments or exclusions than on school improvement and the development of more effective teaching practices.

Policies for building an equitable system

Improving teacher capacity

Because this nation has not invested heavily in teacher education and professional development, the capacity for a more complex, student-centered approach to teaching is not prevalent throughout the current teaching force. Furthermore, because teacher salaries and working conditions are inadequate to ensure a steady supply of qualified teachers in poor districts, low-income and minority students are routinely taught by the least experienced and least prepared teachers (Darling-Hammond, 1991; Oakes, 1990). Differences in achievement between White and minority students can be substantially explained by unequal access to high-quality curriculum and instruction (Barr & Dreeben, 1983; College Board, 1985; Darling-Hammond & Snyder, 1992a; Dreeben, 1987; Dreeben & Barr, 1987; Dreeben & Gamoran, 1986; Oakes, 1990).

From a policy perspective, perhaps the single greatest source of educational inequity is this disparity in the availability and distribution of highly qualified teachers (Darling-Hammond, 1990). Providing equity in the distribution of teacher quality will be required before changes in assessment strategies result in more challenging and effective instruction for currently underserved students. This, in turn, requires changing policies and long-standing incentive structures in education so that shortages of well-prepared teachers are overcome, and schools serving poor and minority students are not disadvantaged by lower salaries and poorer working conditions in the bidding war for good teachers. Fundamental changes in school funding are essential to this task. Since revenues in poor districts are often half as great as those in wealthy districts, state aid changes that equalize district resources are the first step toward ensuring access to qualified teachers (Darling-Hammond, in press).

This crucial equity concern is finally gaining some attention in the rush to improve schools by testing. The recent report of the National Council on Education Standards and Testing (NCEST), while arguing for national performance standards for students, acknowledged the importance of "school delivery standards" for educational improvements to occur. The Council's Standards Task Force noted:

> If not accompanied by measures to ensure equal opportunity to learn, national content and performance standards could help widen the achievement gap between the advantaged and the disadvantaged in our society. If national content and performance standards and assessment are not accompanied by clear school delivery standards and policy measures designed to afford all students an equal opportunity to learn, the concerns about diminished equity could easily be realized. Standards and assessments must be accompanied by policies that provide access for all students to high quality resources, including appropriate instructional materials and well-prepared teachers. High content and performance standards can be used to challenge all students with the same expectations, but high expectations will only result in common high performance if all schools provide high quality instruction designed to meet the expectations. (NCEST, 1992, pp. E12–E13)

Delivery standards make clear that the governmental agencies that are imposing standards upon students are simultaneously accepting responsibility for ensuring that students will encounter the opportunities necessary for their success (Darling-Hammond, 1993). Though this may seem a straightforward prerequisite for making judgments about students or schools, it marks an entirely different approach to accountability in U.S. education than the one that has predominated for most of the last two decades and is widespread today. Earlier approaches to outcomes-based accountability legislated minimum competency tests and sometimes punished schools or students with low scores without attempting to correct the resource disparities that contributed to poor performance in the first place.

Ensuring that all students have adequate opportunities to learn requires enhancing the capacity of all teachers—their knowledge of students and subjects, and their ability to use that knowledge—by professionalizing teaching. This means that teacher education policies must ensure that *all* teachers have a stronger understanding of how children learn and develop, how assessment can be used to evaluate what they know and how they learn, how a variety of curricular and instructional strategies can address their needs, and how changes in school and classroom organization can support their growth and achievement.

Such teacher capacities are also important for supporting the promise of authentic assessment to enable richer, more instructionally useful forms of evaluation that are also fair and informative. A major reason for the advent of externally controlled highly standardized testing systems has been the belief that teachers could not be trusted to make sound decisions about what students know and are able to do. The presumed "objectivity" of current tests derives both from the lack of reliance upon individual teacher judgment in scoring and from the fact that test-takers are anonymous to test-scorers (hence, extraneous views about the student do not bias scoring).

Of course, many forms of bias remain, as the choice of items, responses deemed appropriate, and content deemed important are the product of culturally and contextually determined judgments, as well as the privileging of certain ways of knowing and modes of performance over others (García & Pearson, in press; Gardner, 1983; Sternberg, 1985; Wigdor & Garner, 1982). And these forms of bias are equally likely to plague performance-based assessments, as the selection of tasks will rest on cultural and other referents, such as experiences, terms, and exposures to types of music, art, literature, and social experiences that are differentially accessible to test-takers of different backgrounds.

If assessment is to be used to open up as many opportunities as possible to as many students as possible, it must address a wide range of talents, a variety of life experiences, and multiple ways of knowing. Diverse and wide-ranging tasks that use many different performance modes and that involve students in choosing ways to demonstrate their competence become important for this goal (Gordon, no date; Kornhaber & Gardner, 1993). Substantial teacher and student involvement in and control over assessment strategies and uses are critical if assessment is to support the most challenging education possible for every student, taking full account of his or her special talents and ways of knowing. As Gordon puts it:

> The task is to find assessment probes which measure the same criterion from contexts and perspectives which reflect the life space and values of the learner. . . . Thus options and choices become a critical feature in any assessment system created to be responsive to equity, just as processual description and diagnosis become central purposes. (no date, pp. 8–9)

The objective of maintaining high standards with less standardization will demand teachers who are able to evaluate and eliminate sources of unfair bias in their development and scoring of instructionally embedded assessments, and who can balance subjectivity and objectivity, using their subjective knowledge of students appropriately in selecting tasks and assessment options while adhering to common, collective standards of evaluation. These same abilities will be crucial for other assessment developers. In many respects, even greater sensitivity to the sources of bias that can pervade assessment will be needed with forms that frequently eliminate the anonymity of test-takers, drawing more heavily on interpersonal interaction in tasks and on observations on the part of teachers.

"Top-down support for bottom-up reform"

The need for greater teacher knowledge and sensitivity in developing and using authentic assessments in schools will cause some to argue that they should not be attempted; that externally developed and scored "objective" tests are safer for making decisions because local judgement is avoided. However, the argument for authentic assessments rests as much on a changed conception of the *uses* of assessment as on the *form* in which assessment occurs. Rather than being used largely to determine how students rank against one another on a single, limited dimension of performance so as to determine curriculum or school placements of various kinds, many reformers hope that assessment can be used to *inform and improve* teaching and learning.

In this view, assessment should be integrally connected to the teaching and learning process so that students' strengths and needs are identified, built upon, and addressed. School-wide assessments should continually inform teachers' collective review of their practice so that improvements in curriculum, instruction, and school organization are ongoing. Thus, students should actually *learn* more as a result of assessment, rather than being more precisely classified, and schools should be able to inquire into and improve their practices more intelligently, rather than being more rigidly ranked. Assessment should increase the overall amount of learning and good practice across all schools, rather than merely measuring how much of a nonexpanding pool of knowledge is claimed by different students and schools.

If authentic assessment is to realize its potential as a tool for school change, however, policies must enable assessments to be used as a vehicle for student, teacher, and school development. Like students, teachers also learn by constructing knowledge based on their experiences, conceptions, and opportunities for first-hand inquiry. They must be deeply engaged in hands-on developmental work if they are to construct new understandings of the teaching-learning process and new possibilities for their own practices in the classroom and in the school. They must come to understand the kinds of higher order learning and integrated performance goals of current school reforms from the inside out if they are to successfully develop practices that will support these goals. They must create partnerships with parents and students toward the achievement of jointly held goals if the will to change is to overcome the inertia of familiar patterns.

This suggests a policy paradigm that provides "top-down support for bottom-up reform," rather than top-down directives for school-level implementation. Different policy proposals envision different uses for performance-based assessments. State and local district initiatives vary in their views of the uses of assessment results, and of the role of school and teacher participation in assessment development and use. At one end of the continuum is a state like Kentucky, where performance-based assessments are to be developed externally and used at every grade level above grade three, not only to rate children but also to allocate rewards and sanctions to schools. Because the planned system intends to continue the tradition of development and management of most testing by agencies external to the school—and the uses of such tests for individual and organizational decisionmaking—the costs of developing Kentucky's state assessment system are now estimated at over $100 million, excluding implementation costs (Wheelock, 1992).

Some state programs plan to change the nature of existing standardized tests, but not the locus of control of test items, scoring, and uses of results. Tests will still be used primarily for ranking students and schools and controlling instruction from outside the school. Similarly, some proposals for national testing envision NAEP-like instruments used to rank schools, districts, and states on measures that use more performance-oriented tasks, but these would enter and leave schools on "testing days" just as current assessments do.

Due to their intended uses, such tests will need to be carefully controlled and managed to ensure scoring reliability and security. This means local teachers, parents, and students can have little voice in choices of tasks and assessment opportunities or the means of configuring them; that those assessments that count will still be occasional and threatening rather than continuous and developmental; that the strategies for assessment will be limited to what can be managed with external development and reliable scoring at "reasonable" costs; and that the learning available to school people will be limited to that which can occur at several removes from hands-on participation.

If performance-based assessments are used in the same fashion as current externally developed and mandated tests are used, they are likely to highlight differences in students' learning even more keenly, but they will be unlikely to help teachers revamp their teaching or schools rethink their ways of operating. If they arrive in secured packets and leave in parcels for external scoring, teachers will have only a superficial understanding of what the assessments are trying to measure or achieve. If assessments are occasional externally controlled events used primarily for aggregated measures of student achievement levels, they are unlikely to be constructed in ways that provide rich information about the processes of student learning and their individual, idiosyncratic approaches to different kinds of tasks and opportunities. Consequently, teachers will have little opportunity to use the results to understand the complex nuances of student learning in ways that support more successful instruction, and little information on which to act in trying to rethink their daily practices. They will have no new grist for ongoing conversations with parents and with their peers about the insights and dilemmas raised through an ongoing, integrated, collaborative process of teaching, learning, and assessment.

Furthermore, if the results are used to allocate rewards and sanctions for students, teachers, and/or schools, the assessments will inspire fear and continual game playing to manipulate student populations, but they will be unlikely to open up the kinds of honest inquiry and serious innovation needed to stimulate new learning and transform practices in fundamental ways.

Another approach is exemplified in states such as New York, Vermont, Connecticut, and California. These states envision carefully targeted state assessments at a few key developmental points that will provide data for informing policymakers about program successes and needs, areas where assistance and investment are needed, and assessment models for local schools. Meanwhile, locally implemented assessment systems—including portfolios, projects, performance tasks, and structured teacher observations of learning—will provide the multiple forms of evidence about student learning needed to make sound judgments about instruction. In these models, assessment is used as a learning tool for schools and teachers rather than as a sledgehammer for sorting and sanctioning.

In the New York Plan, state assessments will provide comparable data on student performances on a periodic sampling basis, including data from longer term projects and portfolios as well as controlled performance tasks. In addition, investments in the development of local assessment systems will support schools in developing continuous, multifaceted records of achievement and information about students in authentic performance situations. Supports for school learning and equalization of resources are also included through a newly proposed equalizing formula for school funding (including an add-on factor for rates of poverty) and a school quality review process to support teacher and school learning (New York Council, 1992). Both California and New York are currently piloting such practitioner-led school review processes modeled, in part, after long-standing practices of Her Majesty's Inspectorate in Great Britain.

Reformers hope that these initiatives will use assessment as a vehicle for student development and adaptive teaching, rather than as a tool for sorting, screening, and selecting students out of educational opportunities. They also intend for assessment to inform teacher and school learning so that the possibilities of multiple pathways to student success are enhanced. These kinds of initiatives acknowledge the need to experiment with diverse methods for assessment that can support Gardner's (1991) conception of "individually configured excellence"—efforts that will tap the multiple intelligences and potentials of students obscured by traditional testing practices.

Many schools, reform networks, and professional organizations have already made inroads in the development of such assessments and their use for supporting teaching and learning. Strategies for assessing learning through exhibitions, portfolios, projects, and careful observations of children have been invented and shared among grassroots school reform initiatives stimulated by such organizations as the Coalition of Essential Schools, Project Zero, the Foxfire Teacher Outreach Network, the North Dakota Study Group, the Prospect Center, and other networks of progressive schools, along with organizations such as the National Association for Education of Young Children, the National Council of Teachers of Mathematics, and other professional associations.

These approaches to assessment development aim at strengthening teaching and learning at the school level by engaging students in more meaningful, integrative, and challenging work, and by helping teachers to look carefully at performance, to understand how students are learning and thinking, to reflect upon student strengths and needs, and to support them with adaptive teaching strategies.

Where these efforts are underway, changes in teaching and schooling practices occur—especially for students who are not as often successful at school-work. Kornhaber and Gardner (1993) illustrate how students whose strengths, interests, and talents are not visible on standardized tests can be understood and better taught. They describe how varied classroom opportunities for performance and assessments can illuminate productive "entry points" that build on children's developed intelligences and extend them into new areas of learning. Case studies of the use of such instruments as the Primary Language Record (Barrs, Ellis, Hester, & Thomas, 1988; Centre for Language in Primary Education [CLPE], 1990), an observational tool for teachers to document student language and literacy development in diverse performance contexts, also demonstrate how developing teachers' capacities to look closely at students' work and learning strategies helps them to provide more supportive experiences, especially for students who have previously had difficulties in learning or whose first language is not English (Falk & Darling-Hammond, 1993).

Teacher learning about how to support student learning has also occurred as teams of teachers have developed authentic assessment strategies at New York's International High School, whose population is 100 percent limited English proficient immigrants. Portfolios, projects, and oral debriefings on the work of cooperative learning groups have become the primary instruments for judging the effectiveness of both students' progress and teachers' own instruction. Students' portfolios and products are evaluated by the students themselves, their peers, and their teachers. These multiple perspectives on student work along with student evaluations of courses provide teachers with a steady stream of feedback about their curriculum and insights about individual students. This system of assessment makes the act of teaching itself an act of professional development, because teachers analyze student responses and use them in the development of their pedagogy. The press to cover content has been supplanted by the press to support students in successful learning, with extraordinary results for student success (Ancess & Darling-Hammond, in press).

At International, Central Park East Secondary School, the Urban Academy, and other urban high schools engaged in portfolio assessment for graduation, students who would normally fail in central city schools succeed—graduating and going on to college at rates comparable to affluent suburban schools (Darling-Hammond, Ancess, & Falk, in press; Darling-Hammond et al., 1993). As teachers learn about how students approach tasks, what helps them learn most effectively, and what assessment tasks challenge and support the kinds of learning desired, they find themselves transforming both their teaching and their assessment strategies. The more information teachers obtain about what students know and think as well as how they learn, the more capacity they have to reform their pedagogy, and the more opportunities they create for student success.

These and other assessment initiatives that embed authentic assessment in the ongoing processes of teaching and curriculum development share Glaser's (1990) view that schools must move from a selective mode "characterized by minimal variation in the conditions for learning" in which "a narrow range of instructional options and a limited number of paths to success are available" (p. 16), to an adaptive mode in which "conceptions of learning and modes of teaching are adjusted to individuals—their backgrounds, talents, interests, and the nature of their past performances and experiences" (p. 17). Fundamental agreement with this view leads to a rejection of the traditional uses of testing, even performance-based testing, as an externally controlled tool for the allocation of educational opportunities, rewards, or sanctions. As students are offered wider opportunities for learning and the assessment of their achievement becomes an integral part of learning and teaching, tests are required that provide multi-dimensional views of performance.

As an alternative to past uses of standardized testing, Glaser (1990) proposes the following criteria for evaluating how new assessments should be designed and used:

1. *Access to Educational Opportunity*: Assessments should be designed to survey possibilities for student growth, rather than to designate students as ready or not ready to profit from standard instruction.
2. *Consequential Validity*: Assessments should be interpreted and evaluated on the basis of their instructional effects; that is, their effectiveness in leading teachers to spend time on classroom activities conducive to valuable learning goals and responsive to individual student learning styles and needs.
3. *Transparency and Openness*: Knowledge and skills should be measured so that the processes and products of learning are openly displayed. The criteria of performance must be transparent rather than secret so that they can motivate and direct learning.
4. *Self-Assessment*: Because assessment and instruction will be integrally related, instructional situations should provide coaching and practice in ways that help students to set incremental standards by which they can judge their own achievement, and develop self-direction for attaining higher performance levels.
5. *Socially Situated Assessment*: Assessment situations in which the student participates in group activity should increase. In this context, not only performance, but also the facility with which a student adapts to help and guidance can be assessed.
6. *Extended Tasks and Contextualized Skills*: Assessment should be more representative of meaningful tasks and subject matter goals. Assessment opportunities will themselves provide worthwhile learning experiences that illustrate the relevance and utility of the knowledge and skills that are being acquired.
7. *Scope and Comprehensiveness*: Assessment will attend to a greater range of learning and performance processes, stimulating analysis of what students can do in terms of the cognitive demands and performance skills tasks entail, as well as their content.

These guidelines suggest strategies for creating assessment systems that serve the daily, intimate processes of teaching and learning. Though a continuing role for external assessments that provide information for policymakers and guide-posts for district and school analysis is legitimate, the broader vision of school restructuring demands a much more prominent and highly developed role for school-based assessment initiatives as well.

The relationship of assessment reform to school restructuring

At the policy level, the different approaches to developing and using performance-based assessments reflect different theories of organizational change and different views of educational purposes. One view seeks to induce change through extrinsic rewards and sanctions for both schools and students, on the assumption that the fundamental problem is a lack of will to change on the part of educators. The other view seeks to induce change by building knowledge among school practitioners and parents about alternative methods and by stimulating organizational rethinking through opportunities to work together on the design of teaching and schooling and to experiment with new approaches. This view assumes that the fundamental problem is a lack of knowledge about the possibilities for teaching and learning, combined with lack of organizational capacity for change.

The developmental view of assessment seeks to create the conditions that enable responsible and responsive practice, including teacher knowledge, school capacity for improvement and problem-solving, flexibility in meeting the actual needs of real people, shared ethical commitments among staff, and appropriate policy structures that encourage rather than punish inclusive education (Darling-Hammond & Snyder, 1992b). An emphasis on controlling school and classroom work through externally applied assessment schemes makes it difficult to produce this kind of practice.

Peter Senge (1992) explains why organizational controls operating through extrinsic rewards and sanctions undermine the development of learning organizations:

> Making continual learning a way of organizational life ... can only be achieved by breaking with the traditional authoritarian, command and control hierarchy where the top thinks and the local acts, to merge thinking and acting at all levels. This represents a profound re-orientation in the concerns of management—a shift from a predominant concern with controlling to a predominant concern with learning. (p. 2)

His assertion is borne out by research on necessary factors for restructuring schools. David (1990) describes the restructuring districts she studied:

> Teachers and principals are asked to experiment and to continuously assess the effects of their experiments. . . . District leaders encourage school staff to learn from their successes and their mistakes. School staffs are urged to experiment without fear of punishment for failures. These districts are moving from the known to the unknown, so risks are an essential part of progress. All the districts face the challenge of getting teachers and principals to imagine new ways of organizing their roles and their work. They recognize that risk taking requires knowledge of what to do and how to judge it as well as support and flexibility. (pp. 226–227)

Thus, support for learning and risk-taking are strengthened by opportunities for evaluating the results of that learning, when a safe environment for innovation has been created. Engaging teachers in assessment is a critical aspect of that process. That engagement becomes a powerful vehicle for professional development, supporting teachers in looking at and understanding student learning, in investigating the effects of teaching on learning, and in transforming their practices so that they become more effective. It is this insight into what students are really doing, thinking, and learning that is one of the greatest contributions of authentic assessment to teacher development.

This insight is greatly encouraged by opportunities for teachers to evaluate and document students' work in ways that help the teachers attend to what students can do, how they approach their work, and what types of teaching approaches seem to support what kinds of learning. In the parlance of many currently proposed performance assessment schemes, this kind of insight might be supported by participation in "scoring" activities; however, the kind of teacher participation needed for full attention to student learning must extend beyond evaluations of discrete pieces of work against a common grid or rubric. A focus on distinct tasks scored against necessarily narrowed and standardized criteria can be periodically helpful, but a more comprehensive view of teaching, learning, and the diverse capacities of students is needed to ensure that teachers have the understandings they need to help students learn. This learner-centered information can only be derived from extensive involvement in looking at children and their work from many different vantage points.

Kanevsky (1992), a teacher, explains the Descriptive Review process, a collaborative means for evaluating student learning and growth:

> The assessment we use determines the way we see children and make educational decisions. . . . Because the Descriptive Review is a collaborative process, it can contribute to the current efforts to restructure schools. The Descriptive Review process allows teachers to hear individual voices and to pursue collaborative inquiry. As teachers draw upon their experiences and knowledge, they begin to envision new roles for themselves and new structures for schools. They are also creating a body of knowledge about teaching and learning that starts with looking at a particular child in depth and ends with new insights and understandings about children and classrooms in general.
>
> Teachers must have opportunities to participate in an educational community; to examine what they care about and what is important for children; to have ongoing, thoughtful conversations about teaching and learning in order to plan meaningful restructuring. (p. 57)

Conclusion

I have argued here that, for all the promise of more authentic and performance-based forms of assessment, their value depends as much on how they are used and what supports for learning accompany them as on the new technologies they employ. Changing assessment forms and formats without changing the ways in which assessments are used will not change the outcomes of education. In order for assessment to support student learning, it must include teachers in all stages of the process and be embedded in curriculum and teaching activities. It must be aimed primarily at supporting more informed and student-centered teaching rather than at sorting students and sanctioning schools. It must be intimately understood by teachers, students, and parents, so that it can help them strive for and achieve the learning goals it embodies. It must allow for different starting points for learning and diverse ways of demonstrating competence. In order for schooling to improve, assessment must also be an integral part of ongoing teacher dialogue and school development.

In short, we must rethink the uses of assessment, since we have entered an era where the goal of schooling is to educate all children well, rather than selecting a "talented tenth" to be prepared for knowledge work. In addition, we must publicly acknowledge that inequalities in access to education must be tackled directly if all students are to be well-educated. Testing students will not provide accountability in education while some students receive only a fraction of the school resources that support the education of their more privileged counterparts. For all students to receive high-quality instruction from highly qualified teachers, financial investments in schooling must be equalized across rich and poor communities.

With these supports, authentic assessment strategies can help schools become educational communities committed to self-determined common values. When this happens, all members of the community become learners struggling to construct knowledge that they can individually and collectively use to achieve their goals. The development and practice of authentic assessment casts teachers in the role of problem-framers and problem-solvers who use their classroom and school experiences to build an empirical knowledge base to inform their practice and strengthen their effectiveness. When supported by adequate resources and learning opportunities for teachers, authentic assessment increases the capacity of schools to engage in a recursive process of self-reflection, self-critique, self-correction, and self-renewal. As schools thus become learning organizations, they can increase their capacity to ensure that all of their students learn. Under these conditions, assessment may work on behalf of equity in education, rather than perpetuating the "savage inequalities" (Kozol, 1991) that now exist.

References

Allington, R.L., & McGill-Franzen, A. (1992). Unintended effects of educational reform in New York. *Educational Policy,* 6, 397–414.

Ancess, J., & Darling-Hammond, L. (in press). *Authentic assessment as an instrument of learning and evaluation at International High School.* New York: Columbia University, Teachers College, National Center for Restructuring Education, Schools, and Teaching.

Archbald, D.A., & Newman, F.M. (1988). *Beyond standardized testing: Assessing authentic academic achievement in the secondary school.* Reston, VA: National Association of Secondary School Principals.

Bailey, T. (1989). *Changes in the nature and structure of work: Implications for skill requirements and skill formation* (Technical Paper No. 9). New York: Columbia University, Teachers College, National Center on Education and Employment.

Barr, R., & Dreeben, R. (1983). *How schools work.* Chicago: University of Chicago Press.

Barrs, M., Ellis, S., Hester, H., & Thomas, A. (1988). *The primary language record.* London: Inner London Education Authority Centre for Language in Primary Education.

Boyer, E.L. (1983). *High school.* New York: Harper & Row.

Carnegie Council on Adolescent Development. (1989). *Turning points: Preparing youth for the 21st century.* New York: Carnegie Corporation of New York.

Carnevale, A.P., Gainer, L.J., & Meltzer, A.S. (1989). *Workplace basics: The skills employers want.* Alexandria, VA: American Society for Training and Development.

Centre for Language in Primary Education. (1990). *The reading book.* London: Inner London Education Authority.

Cohen, D.K., & Spillane, J.P. (1992). Policy and practice: The relations between governance and instruction. In G. Grant (Ed.), *Review of research in education, Vol. 18* (pp. 3–50). Washington, DC: American Educational Research Association.
College Entrance Examination Board. (1985). *Equality and excellence: The educational status of black Americans*. New York: Author.
Commission on Chapter I. (1992). *High performance schools: No exceptions, no excuses*. Washington, DC: Author.
Commission on the Skills of the American Workforce. (1990). *America's choice: High skills or low wages*. Rochester, NY: National Center on Education and the Economy.
Cooper, E., & Sherk, J. (1989). Addressing urban school reform: Issues and alliances. *Journal of Negro Education, 58*, 315–331.
Cremin, L. (1961). *The transformation of the school: Progressivism in American education, 1876–1957*. New York: Vintage Books.
Cubberly, E.P. (1919). *Public education in the United States: A study and interpretation of American educational history*. Boston: Houghton Mifflin.
Darling-Hammond, L. (1990). Teacher quality and equality. In J. Goodlad & P. Keating (Eds.), *Access to knowledge: An agenda for our nation's schools* (pp. 237–258). New York: College Entrance Examination Board.
Darling-Hammond, L. (1991). The implications of testing policy for quality and equality. *Phi Delta Kappan, 73*, 220–225.
Darling-Hammond, L. (1993). Creating standards of practice and delivery for learner-centered schools. *Stanford Law and Policy Review, 4*, 37–52.
Darling-Hammond, L. (in press). Inequality and access to knowledge. In J. Banks (Ed.), *Handbook of multicultural education*. New York: Macmillan.
Darling-Hammond, L., Ancess, J., & Falk, B. (in press). *Authentic assessment in action: Case studies of students and schools at work*. New York: Teachers College Press.
Darling-Hammond, L., & Ascher, C. (1990). *Accountability in big city schools*. New York: Columbia University, Teachers College, National Center for Restructuring Education, Schools, and Teaching, and Institute for Urban and Minority Education.
Darling-Hammond, L., & Snyder, J. (1992a). Traditions of curriculum inquiry: The scientific tradition. In P. Jackson (Ed.), *Handbook of research on curriculum* (pp. 41–78). New York: Macmillan.
Darling-Hammond, L., & Snyder, J. (1992b). Reframing accountability for learner-centered practice. In A. Lieberman (Ed.), *The changing contexts of teaching: 91st Yearbook of the National Society for the Study of Education* (pp. 11–36). Chicago: University of Chicago Press.
Darling-Hammond, L., Snyder, J., Ancess, J., Einbender, L., Goodwin, A.L., & Macdonald, M. (1993). *Creating learner-centered accountability*. New York: Columbia University, Teachers College, National Center for Restructuring Education, Schools, and Teaching.
Darling-Hammond, L., & Wise, A. (1985). Beyond standardization: State standards and school improvement. *Elementary School Journal, 85*, 315–336.
David, J. (1990). Restructuring in progress: Lessons from pioneering districts. In R. Elmore (Ed.), *Restructuring schools: The next generation of educational reform* (pp. 209–250). San Francisco: Jossey-Bass.
Davis, D.G. (1986, April). *A pilot study to assess equity in selected curricular offerings across three diverse schools in a large urban school district: A search for methodology*. Paper presented at the annual meeting of the American Educational Research Association, San Francisco.
Dreeben, R. (1987). Closing the divide: What teachers and administrators can do to help black students reach their reading potential. *American Educator, 11*(4), 28–35.
Dreeben, R., & Barr, R. (1987, April). *Class composition and the design of instruction*. Paper presented at the annual meeting of the American Education Research Association, Washington, DC.
Dreeben, R., & Gamoran, A. (1986). Race, instruction, and learning. *American Sociological Review, 51*, 660–669.
Eckland, B.K. (1980). Sociodemographic implications of minimum competency testing. In R.M. Jaeger & C.K. Tittle (Eds.), *Minimum competency achievement testing: Motives, models, measures, and consequences* (pp. 124–135). Berkeley, CA: McCutchan.

Educate America. (1991). *An idea whose time has come: A national achievement test for high school seniors*. Morristown, NJ: Author.

Falk, B., & Darling-Hammond, L. (1993). *The primary language record at P.S. 261*. New York: Columbia University, Teachers College, National Center for Restructuring Education, Schools, and Teaching.

García, G., & Pearson, D. (in press). Assessment and diversity. In L. Darling-Hammond (Ed.), *Review of research in education, 20*. Washington, DC: American Educational Research Association.

Gardner, H. (1983). *Frames of mind*. New York: Basic Books.

Gardner, H. (1991). *The unschooled mind*. New York: Basic Books.

Glaser, R. (1981). The future of testing: A research agenda for cognitive psychology and psychometrics. *American Psychologist, 36*, 923–936.

Glaser, R. (1990). *Testing and assessment: O tempora! O mores!* Pittsburgh, PA: University of Pittsburgh, Learning Research and Development Center.

Goodlad, J.I. (1984). *A place called school: Prospects for the future*. New York: McGraw-Hill.

Gordon, E. (no date). *Implications of diversity in human characteristics for authentic assessment*. Unpublished manuscript, Yale University.

Gordon, B., & Sum, A. (1988). *Toward a more perfect union: Basic skills, poor families, and our economic future*. New York: Ford Foundation.

Gould, S.J. (1981). *The mismeasure of man*. New York: W.W. Norton.

Haney, W., & Madaus, G. (1986). *Effects of standardized testing and the future of the national assessment of educational progress*. Chestnut Hill, MA: Center for the Study of Testing, Evaluation, and Educational Policy.

Holmes, C.T., & Matthews, K.M. (1984). The effects of nonpromotion on elementary and junior high school pupils: A meta-analysis. *Review of Educational Research, 54*, 225–236.

Hornbeck, D. (1992, May 6). The true road to equity. *Education Week*, pp. 33, 25.

Jaeger, R.M. (1991, June 5). *Legislative perspectives on statewide testing: Goals, hopes, and desires*. Paper presented at the American Educational Research Association Forum, Washington, DC.

Kamin, L. (1974). *The science and politics of IQ*. New York: John Wiley.

Kanevsky, R.D. (1992). The descriptive review of a child: Teachers learn about values. In *Exploring values and standards: Implications for assessment* (pp. 41–58). New York: Columbia University, Teachers College, National Center for Restructuring Education, Schools, and Teaching.

Koretz, D. (1988). Arriving in Lake Wobegon: Are standardized tests exaggerating achievement and distorting instruction? *American Educator, 12*(2), 8–15, 46–52.

Kornhaber, M., & Gardner, H. (1993). *Varieties of excellence: Identifying and assessing children's talents*. New York: Columbia University, Teachers College, National Center for Restructuring Education, Schools, and Teaching.

Kozol, J. (1991). *Savage inequalities: Children in America's schools*. New York: Crown.

Lee, V., & Bryk, A. (1988). Curriculum tracking as mediating the social distribution of high school achievement. *Sociology of Education, 61*, 78–94.

Legislative Research Commission. (1990). *A guide to the Kentucky Education Reform Act of 1990*. Frankfurt, KY: Author.

Linn, R.L. (1987). Accountability: The comparison of educational systems and the quality of test results. *Educational Policy, 1*(2), 181–198.

Madaus, G., West, M.M., Harmon, M.C., Lomax, R.G., & Viator, K.A. (1992). *The influence of testing on teaching math and science in grades 4–12*. Chestnut Hill, MA: Boston College Center for the Study of Testing, Evaluation, and Educational Policy.

Madaus, G.F. (1985). Public policy and the testing profession—You've never had it so good? *Educational Measurement: Issues and Practice, 4*, 5–11.

Mann, D. (1987). Can we help dropouts? Thinking about the undoable. In G. Natriello (Ed.), *School dropouts: Patterns and policies* (pp. 3–19). New York: Teachers College Press.

Massachusetts Advocacy Center and the Center for Early Adolescence. (1988). *Before it's too late: Dropout prevention in the middle grades*. Boston: Author.

McKnight, C.C., Crosswhite, F.J., Dossey, J.A., Kifer, E., Swafford, S.O., Travers, K.J.,

& Cooney, T.J. (1987). *The underachieving curriculum: Assessing U.S. school mathematics from an international perspective*. Champaign, IL: Stipes.

Mercer, J.R. (1989). Alternative paradigms for assessment in a pluralistic society. In J.A. Banks & C.M. Banks (Eds.), *Multicultural education* (pp. 289–303). Boston: Allyn & Bacon.

National Assessment of Educational Progress. (1981). *Reading, thinking, and writing: Results from the 1979–80 National Assessment of Reading and Literature*. Denver: Education Commission of the States.

National Association for the Education of Young Children. (January, 1988). NAEYC position statement on developmentally appropriate practice in the primary grades, serving 5 through 8 year-olds. *Young Children, 47*(1), 64–84.

National Center for Education Statistics. (1982). *The condition of education, 1982*. Washington, DC: U.S. Department of Education.

National Center for Education Statistics. (1985). *High school and beyond: An analysis of course-taking patterns in secondary schools as related to student characteristics*. Washington, DC: U.S. Government Printing Office.

National Center on Education and the Economy. (1989). *To secure our future: The federal role in education*. Rochester, NY: Author.

National Council on Educational Standards and Testing. (1992). *Raising standards for American education*. Washington, DC: Author.

New York Council on Curriculum and Assessment. (1992). *Building a learning-centered curriculum for learner-centered schools: Report of the Council on Curriculum and Assessment*. Albany: New York State Education Department.

Oakes, J. (1985). *Keeping track: How schools structure inequality*. New Haven: Yale University Press.

Oakes, J. (1986). Tracking in secondary schools: A contextual perspective. *Educational Psychologist, 22*, 129–154.

Oakes, J. (1990). *Multiplying inequalities: The effects of race, social class, and tracking on opportunities to learn mathematics and science*. Santa Monica, CA: RAND.

O'Day, J.A., & Smith, M.S. (1993). Systemic school reform and educational opportunity. In S. Fuhrman (Ed.), *Designing coherent education policy: Improving the system* (pp. 250–311). San Francisco: Jossey-Bass.

Resnick, L.B. (1987a). *Education and learning to think*. Washington, DC: National Academy Press.

Resnick, L. (1987b). Learning in school and out. *Educational Researcher, 16*, 13–20.

Rosenbaum, J.E. (1980). Social implications of educational grouping. In D.C. Berliner (Ed.), *Review of Research in Education, 8* (pp. 361–401). Washington, DC: American Educational Research Association.

Senge, P.M. (1992). *Building learning organizations*. Framingham, MA: Innovation Associates.

Shepard, L. (1993). Evaluating test validity. In L. Darling-Hammond (Ed.), *Review of Research in Education, Vol. 19* (pp. 405–450). Washington, DC: American Educational Research Association.

Shepard, L., & Smith, M.L. (1986). Synthesis of research on school readiness and kindergarten retention. *Educational Leadership, 44*(3), 78–86.

Shepard, L.A., & Smith, M.L. (1988). Escalating academic demand in kindergarten: Counterproductive policies. *Elementary School Journal, 89*, 135–145.

Sizer, T. (1985). *Horace's compromise*. Boston: Houghton Mifflin.

Smith, F. (1986). *High school admission and the improvement of schooling*. New York: New York City Board of Education.

Sternberg, R.J. (1985). *Beyond IQ*. New York: Cambridge University Press.

Trimble, K., & Sinclair, R.L. (1986, April). *Ability grouping and differing conditions for learning: An analysis of content and instruction in ability-grouped classes*. Paper presented at the annual meeting of the American Educational Research Association, San Francisco.

Tyack, D. (1974). *The one best system*. Cambridge, MA: Harvard University Press.

U.S. Department of Education. (1991). *America 2000: An education strategy*. Washington, DC: Author.

Watson, B. (in press). *Essay from the underside*. Philadelphia: Temple University Press.

Wehlage, G.G., Rutter, R.A., Smith, G.A., Lesko, N., & Fernández, R.R. (1990). *Reducing the risk: Schools as communities of support*. New York: Falmer Press.
Wheelock, A. (1992). *School accountability policies: Implications for policy making in Massachusetts*. Paper prepared for the Massachusetts Department of Education.
Wigdor, A.K., & Garner, W.R. (Eds.). (1982). *Ability testing: Uses, consequences, and controversies*. Washington, DC: National Academy Press.
Wiggins, G. (1989). Teaching to the (authentic) test. *Educational Leadership*, 46(7), 41–47.
Wise, A.E. (1979). *Legislated learning*. Berkeley, CA: University of California Press.
Wolf, D.P., & Baron, J.B. (in press). A realization of a national performance-based assessment system. In D. Stevenson (Ed.), *Promises and perils of new assessments*. Englewood Cliffs, NJ: Lawrence Erlbaum.

PART 2

INSTRUCTION

CHAPTER 6

ORGANIZING INSTRUCTION AND CURRICULUM PLANNING FOR THE SOCIALLY DISADVANTAGED (1964)

G. Orville Johnson

Compulsory education laws have been on the statute books of the various states of our nation since approximately the turn of the twentieth century. Theoretically, each and every child has been required, since their passage, to attend school and thus receive a minimum number of years of education. That this general education did not meet the needs of many children has been apparent almost from the beginning. Children who prior to the passage of these laws had been encouraged not to attend school were now encouraged to "drop-out" as soon as the law would allow. Now, approximately six decades later, parents, educators, and society is still faced with the fact that one-third of the nation's children are leaving the schools before satisfactorily completing a program. It is obvious that the schools are not providing appropriate kinds of educational experiences for a substantial proportion of the children and youth. While all these "drop-outs" do not reflect a meager economic background or a socially disadvantaged position, a disproportionately large number of the children who come from low socioeconomic homes are among their number. This can only mean that education in general has provided less well for this group than for those who come from more socially advantaged homes.

There has sprung up in recent years a number of movements instrumental in stimulating educational activity ostensibly for the purpose of improving the instructional lot of the socially disadvantaged children. Like so many other efforts of "modern educators," a simple, mechanistic panacea for the reduction and alleviation of all social ills has been sought. This solution has, too often, involved a social rather than an educational approach. "Extra" school programs introducing recreation, cultural stimulation, social welfare, and so forth, have been devised. Standard curriculums and methods of instruction have attempted to be adapted to meet these children's needs. On only an occasional, rare instance (and usually on a strictly experimental basis) has there been a conscientious attempt to provide an appropriate, meaningful educational program. Of equal rarity has instructional method and technique been developed based upon fundamental learning theory and the dynamics of human adjustive behavior.

It could have been predicted that a substantial proportion of these programs were and are doomed to failure and that relatively little movement in a positive direction would or will develop. Where meaningful *educational* programs have not been provided, the drop-out rate has continued to be high. The quality of a school program can almost be measured by the holding power that the school has at the post-compulsory school age. Unfortunately, it has almost become axiomatic in the thinking of many educators that the culturally and socially disadvantaged children (and their parents) place a very low value upon the acquisition of an education. This negative value system is then, in their opinion, the primary cause for their leaving public school prior to the accomplishment of any educational objective. *Because a high drop-out rate and social and cultural deprivation are fairly highly correlated does not necessarily mean that there is a cause and effect relationship existing.*

A more accurate description of the situation would be the following. Socially disadvantaged children enter school with educational desires and objectives like (but not identical to) any other child. The school does not provide them with useful and meaningful experiences, they do not have success with the non-meaningful requirements, they become disillusioned and discouraged, and, consequently, they quit. Yet, where special programs have been developed (for the mentally handicapped particularly) based upon the children's characteristics, background of experiences, and in harmony with their cultural, social, and environmental needs, these children have demonstrated an eagerness to learn. They have shown that they can and do achieve. They, in general, do not leave school until they have completed the preparation school can provide them to become more effective individuals and better citizens capable of taking care of their own physical, social, and psychological needs.

Educational programs are, in general, based upon one of two theories: the theory of *equality* of education for all children, or the theory that all children should be provided with an *identical* education. The latter, or the identical education theory is often, unfortunately, wrongly interpreted as equality of education both by the professional educator as well as by the lay public. A basic lack of understanding of these fundamental concepts has led to innumerable malpractices and has acted to the detriment of the socially disadvantaged children.

Identical education for all children

Providing each and every child with an identical education requires that certain common experiences are equally good for all children, are equally required by all children in order that they may become the most effective persons possible, and that the sum total of these experiences then comprises the curriculum provided all children. All children should receive the same instruction at the same time and taught in the same way. Since most teachers, administrators, and school boards reflect a middle-class orientation, it is the experiences that are of particular value to the children coming from middle-class homes that are selected. Indirectly, a value of "goodness" is placed upon these educational programs and any programs that may deviate from them have a value of "less goodness" or "badness" placed upon them. Once again the programs for the mentally handicapped can be drawn upon for example. Many, many teachers hesitate to have a child who is performing inadequately in the classroom evaluated by the school psychologist because he is such a "nice boy" and he might be put in a special class. In some communities and states a mentally handicapped child must be "given a chance" in the regular class for at least one year before he can be recommended for placement in this "inferior program." The child must fail before he can be given a chance to succeed.

After innumerable failures, particularly with the socially disadvantaged children, using the common or identical educational approach it has been generally decided that something must be done. Of course, it was inconceivable that the basic hypothesis that every child needed the identical education could be wrong so the resulting action has taken one of two directions. The first attempt and also the simplest to implement was to adapt in one way or another the instruction and/or the curriculum. In order to accomplish this teachers (particularly at the elementary level) were urged to individualize their instruction and meet the needs of each child rather than teaching to the class. Some braver schools turned to tracks and homogeneous grouping. The net result has been a watering down of traditional programs for those children who were having difficulty but no positive, lasting results have been achieved.

More recently a new concept has entered the educator's thinking in seeking an approach to the solution of the dilemma in which the socially disadvantaged have placed him. The socially disadvantaged children reflect a different culture and a different set of values, insofar as education is concerned, from the middle class. But, it is still inconceivable that the "good" educational programs and instruction are not equally as good for them. Therefore, since these children are not ready to benefit from the instruction provided at the present time, the solution is to first provide them with an intensive as well as extensive background of middle-class experiences, at the same time indoctrinate them to understand and accept middle-class values, and then when they are ready, teach them the same material in the same way it is taught to the socially more advantaged children. How are these experiences provided? Simple. Merely place the children on buses and drive around to other parts of the city; visit stores, playgrounds, parks, farms, libraries, and museums; attend selected movies, lectures, and concerts; and in class look at pictures, have stories read, and carry on discussions. These experiences are "good" because the middle-class children all have them. Or do they? These experiences will enable them to learn the middle-class oriented materials. Or will they? These experiences will make them like the middle-class child and this is "good". Or is it for them?

Equal education for all children

There is probably nothing less equal than requiring each child to be provided with the identical educational experiences as every other child. Nothing is less democratic. We as a nation are committed to *equal educational opportunity for all.* This principle of equality has been recognized and implemented by the special educator. Deaf children require special programs providing them with oral communication skills that they cannot learn in the regular classroom. Blind children are provided tactual stimuli and taught to read using Braille because of their lack of vision. Similar kinds of special programs are provided the mentally handicapped, orthopedically handicapped, emotionally disturbed, and children with communication difficulties. These are not "adaptations" of the regular programs, but rather they are programs carefully designed and planned for children having specific characteristics and consequently unique educational needs. The same principle of program and instructional planning must be applied to those children whose educational needs are not as physically obvious but whose needs for unique and differentiated educational programs are fully as great.

Curriculum planning

The initial step the educator must take in planning a curriculum for socially disadvantaged children is the most difficult. He must attempt to forget all the school experiences he has had both as a student and as a teacher. He must be willing to start anew and carefully define the experiences that can and should be provided socially disadvantaged children in order that they may become the most effective children possible for them and then grow up into effective adults. Because of years of traditional school orientation the tendency is to examine science curriculums, social studies curriculums, and so forth and say, "How can I adapt them?" This tendency must be resisted if positive results are to be obtained.

Three fundamental considerations must be taken into account in the development of a realistic, meaningful curriculum. They are: one, the characteristics of the individuals for whom the program is being planned must be determined; two, a guess or prognosis concerning the future of these individuals must be made; and three, the program must reflect and be in harmony with the environmental background they bring with them to school.

To provide somewhat diverse educational programs (college preparation, industrial, commercial, and so forth) for various groups of children, categories have usually been established. Categories are convenient for programming but too often may act to the disadvantage of the individual child. Characteristics are all too often ascribed to a group or category and each child within that group is treated as if he possessed all those characteristics whether he does or not. Too often one hears the negative personality characteristics of the epileptic described although in reality only a relatively small number of them, and then usually only of a certain type, in actuality possess them.

Similarly, there is equal danger in attempting to describe the characteristics of the socially disadvantaged children. To many they may be considered to be uncouth, dirty, irresponsible, lacking in social awareness, delinquent, and so forth. Where these characteristics are true of an individual, it is too often forgotten that they may have been learned and are this individual's way of adjusting to situations. No more satisfactory modes of adjustment have been provided him. However, each one of these children will possess his own characteristics and will only possess those defined for the group as he has need for them—and then they will exist in varying degrees and intensity.

Probably the truest statement that can be made concerning the characteristics of the socially disadvantaged children is that there is a no more diverse group in the nation. Their racial, ethnic, and religious backgrounds reflect all races, creeds, and colors. These children may be descendants of pre-Revolutionary War English stock or slaves; they may be the children of recent immigrants from Puerto Rico or Europe. As a result of numerous limitations imposed upon them for one reason or another the incidence of poor health and disease tends to be relatively high. Usually one also finds a somewhat higher incidence of physical and sensory handicaps among them than among the more socially advantaged. In addition, the effects of protracted periods of inadequate diet and nutrition upon general physical development are not rare.

Intellectually and in school achievement the socially disadvantaged children do not compare favorably with the general school population. Present day intelligence tests are actually measures of intellectual performance on selected activities under prescribed conditions. Where the individual has not had the opportunity to have certain experiences, he will be penalized when his performance is compared to that of others. Nevertheless, standard intelligence tests do indicate with more than a fair degree of reliability how well an individual will perform in school programs as the majority of these programs are presently constituted. Under these conditions the socially disadvantaged provide the majority of the mentally handicapped and slow learning children attending school. In addition, a disproportionately large number are also low educational achievers even when compared to their measured mental ability. Numerous explanations have been given by sociologists and psychologists in regard to this phenomenon but space does not permit detailed evaluation and discussion of them. Suffice it to say that thinking educators who have made a study of the problem are convinced (with some supportive evidence) that at the very least the academic achievement and general behavioral levels of the socially disadvantaged children can be significantly improved through the use of appropriate instruction and curriculums.

The environmental backgrounds of the socially disadvantaged children are fully as diverse as their characteristics. They may reside in the slums of a large urban center, but, on the other hand, they may be the children of a poor tenant farmer or share-cropper. They may live in the North, South, East, West, or central portion of the country. They may be able to call no section of the country home being the children of an itinerant farm worker. Their common characteristics are that the family income is low. Their parents, relatives, and older siblings have usually had a minimum of education. There are few, if any, books, magazines, and newspapers in the home. They often reside under crowded conditions and/or in houses barely suited for human habitation when federal or municipal housing is not available. The level of unemployment in their families is significantly greater than is found in the nation or community as a whole. All too often the home is no longer intact, the father having left for one reason or another.

With home conditions reflecting relatively low academic achievement, with few high school graduates or students remaining in school until the completion of a defined program, and with an environment that, at least on the surface, appears to foster discouragement, despair, and hopelessness, what is the prognosis for these children? If instruction and program continue along the present lines of practice, the future will continue to look bleak and uninviting. But the present situation need not continue. With curriculums changed so that the instruction is in harmony with the abilities and experiences that the children bring with them to school so that the school experiences will now have value, the achievement will improve, general behavior will become more acceptable, and a prognosis of effective community participation, lower rate of unemployment, higher level of position, and more substantial income can be confidently made. These things in themselves will help the present socially disadvantaged children become less disadvantaged adults providing for themselves the many experiences that literally help one to become a more intelligent participant in the community.

Based upon the criteria established for the development of curriculum, some broad areas of experience can be defined. The curriculum, in total, can be divided into two areas—skills and content. As the modern world is examined carefully, it becomes apparent that certain basic skills are essential unless one wishes to join one of the few tribes of aborigines still in existence. These skills are communications (oral, listening, reading, and writing) and the ability to handle quantities effectively and efficiently. Thus, speaking, reading, writing, spelling, and arithmetic must have a primary place in the curriculum throughout the developmental years. The initial instruction for the purpose of preparing the child for the more formal aspects of his education should start in the kindergarten. It can only cease when he has achieved a proficiency beyond which he probably can never go to any great degree—eighth or ninth grade level.

The sciences and social sciences have been steadily introduced in regular education at earlier and lower grade levels. Insofar as the socially disadvantaged children are concerned, these are of far less value at the primary and elementary grade levels than the skills. Their introduction should never be to the detriment of the skill instruction. When they are introduced, the science experiences should be for the purpose of helping these children to better understand the physical environment in which they live and consequently be able to deal with it more effectively. The same principle of selection holds true for the choice of activities and study in the social sciences. It is of little value to a child to know the names of the continents, oceans, and important rivers when he knows nothing about the social environment of the community in which he resides. Instead of providing content instruction at a specified grade level as is now the general situation, provide it at the time of need and interest and as it is related to experiences and events.

The junior high school years are a period of transition. Final developmental skill instruction must be provided to insure utmost competency in their use. Survey or exploratory opportunities should also be provided in the special subject areas—homemaking, art, music, industrial arts, and so forth. The children are also becoming much more aware of the larger world about them and should be helped to begin to understand it better and also to understand their relationship to it. While society in general has certain responsibilities to them, they must also understand that they have certain responsibilities for themselves and to the society. This is merely an extension of earlier concepts that should have been developed relating to the homes' and parents' responsibilities to them but also their responsibilities to the home.

The senior high school provides the greatest challenge to educators as well as the greatest opportunities for the socially disadvantaged youth. With good evaluation programs, good counselling, and careful selection of courses of study (with necessary additions to the traditional offerings as the need is indicated) individual programs can be planned to meet each one's educational needs. Those who have the abilities and drives necessary for college and technical school training can be encouraged along these lines. They must also be provided with the appropriate preparatory programs. The group for whom high school will provide their terminal educational experiences can also be provided with realistic content (social studies, science, and so forth), and special subjects (commercial education, driver education, industrial arts, homemaking, and so forth), and school-work programs that will enable each one to quickly take his appropriate place in the society. If the programs are of real value, are realistic, and have meaning, the holding power of the school will materially increase with the youth remaining until they have achieved a stage of satisfactory completion. This will also reduce the trauma so often present during the period between school and productive work as well as materially reducing the period of waiting. Nothing is more debilitating and causes greater erosion of the attitudes and personality of the socially disadvantaged than the hopeless waiting and non-production that occurs following premature school drop-out.

It has been pointed out earlier that the socially disadvantaged are an extremely diverse and heterogeneous group. No one program (with the exception of the skill area instruction) meets their needs. As a result, the flexibility possible in complete individualization of programs, particularly at the senior high school level, is essential. It also needs to be re-emphasized that the very term *socially disadvantaged* carries a connotation of "lack in" or "less good." This is true only if the value of "good" is placed upon the kinds of experiences the more numerous middle-class children are provided—a concept that is not necessarily true for the socially disadvantaged.

The primary thesis that has been attempted to be developed here in relation to curriculum planning is that *it is poor practice to merely attempt to "fill in" middle-class experiences in order that the socially disadvantaged can then understand and benefit from middle-class oriented instruction.* Instead, carefully examine and evaluate the many positive attitudes, stimuli, and learnings these children bring with them to school and emphasize them. Give them something that is meaningful in their lives. Give them something they can be proud of. It is more than possible that they possess numerous positive factors that can and should be incorporated into the total attitudes and values of society and that will make communities better places in which to live. These could well be lost if the socially disadvantaged merely aspire to becoming like the majority group and attempts are only made to eliminate and displace all of their culture, values, and attitudes.

Organizing instruction

It is most difficult to dichotomize organizing for instruction (or teaching methodology) and curriculum because these two facets of education are so completely interdependent. One might, on paper, develop what appears to be the best curriculum possible and yet through the very methods used be unable to insure the children's learning or, in extreme situations, the instruction may actually be teaching something quite different. Thus, the acceptance of the teacher by the children, the attitudes he may have concerning the children and their problems, and the basic understanding he has of the socially disadvantaged and their problems all influence what the children are actually taught and what they learn.

Insofar as basic learning characteristics are concerned, there is no evidence or reason to believe that socially disadvantaged children learn any differently than other children. They are a part of, not apart from, the total population and as such their learning should follow the basic laws that apply to anyone else. That attitudes and values are important factors related to specific learning no one would question. That the socially disadvantaged may possess some different attitudes and values than those possessed by the majority group (middle-class) is also commonly accepted. The problem is to then understand and use their attitudes and values and change instruction and content so that they will contribute to rather than interfere with learning.

The following is a brief, selected list of factors (principles to be followed) relating to the instruction of the socially disadvantaged children that are important to their learning and healthy development. In no sense is the list meant to be either completely definitive nor exhaustive. Some of the principles are general, applying to all children, while others are specifically directed toward the socially disadvantaged.

1. Grouping should be organized around the developmental levels and educational needs of the children. The group of children brought together for instruction should be on relatively the same physical, social, emotional, intellectual, and educational developmental level. They should have need for similar kinds of experiences at this time. Since children learn and develop at different rates, grouping both within the class and among the classes should be flexible. Regrouping should occur whenever the existing groups become too heterogeneous on a number of the above factors so as to make instruction difficult and inefficient.

2. Both the program and the instruction should be developmental. Whatever is taught should be taught only when the child is ready intellectually and

experientially to benefit from the instruction. If the child is ready intellectually but not experientially, background experiences must first be provided. A truly developmental program is systematic and sequential. Programs and instruction, however, may be sequential and still not be developmental.

3. One of the most commonly violated principles of learning is that of readiness. Too often teachers assume that all children who have sat through certain designated grade levels are consequently all equally prepared to benefit from the instruction assigned to that grade level. Readiness to learn is based upon level of intellectual maturity, beckground of experiences and learnings, and the value, purpose, meaning, or desire the individual may have to learn the new material.

This is a particularly important principle for the culturally disadvantaged. They enter kindergarten or first grade at a designated age level and are offered a program of instruction based upon the home and neighborhood experiences provided middle-class children. Even if they were sufficiently intellectually mature to be able to benefit from the instruction, experientially they are not ready. Social promotion policies have tended to compound the problem. As these children progress from grade to grade (in terms of physical placement) they fall farther and farther behind. This principle further emphasizes the need for developmental instruction, meaningful rather than traditional curriculums and materials, and individualization of instruction.

4. Most middle-class children have been taught, indirectly, the value of a formal education long before entering school. Parents and older siblings spending time reading, unspoken assumptions of high school graduation and probable college education, the presence of reading materials in the home, intellectual discussions on varieties of topics, and so forth, all point to and emphasize the values and purposes of education. As a result they enter school with long term objectives. A grade or a subject does not become an end in itself but a means to an end—an education. And during the school years the long term objectives are continually reenforced by the home and the school.

Not so for most socially disadvantaged children. Little in the homes, among their parents or older siblings, or among their companions demonstrates the value of an education. While some immediate educational objectives may be held up to them, there is little or nothing in the way of encouraging the development of such a long-term, abstract objective as an "education." Furthermore, due to the poverty of their "educational" background they have little or no understanding when the school attempts to encourage such an objective. As a result, education for socially disadvantaged children must be placed upon a more immediate goal basis. What they are expected to learn must have meaning, value, and purpose in relation to living today rather than promoting "the better life" in some nebulous future. As they become older and have experienced some of the immediate values of school-learned skills and knowledge, the more abstract concept of the value of "education" can be introduced and comprehended.

5. Instruction should be planned in small, developmental steps; it should be programmed. In working with the socially disadvantaged one is essentially working with children who in the past have been educational disabilities. If any assurance is to be made that this condition is not to continue, step-by-step instruction must be instituted to insure no deficiencies or gaps in learning. The development of programmed instruction research and materials should be followed carefully and introduced at least upon an experimental or trial basis since it incorporates those characteristics considered essential for the socially disadvantaged—step-by-step instruction, immediate reenforcement, and immediate attainment of goals.

6. Instruction, at least initially, should be direct and to the point. If teaching the child a skill to improve his ability to read is the objective of a lesson, teach reading in such a way that he knows this is a reading lesson. Much of modern education has introduced "sugar coating," use of general rather than specific terms (social studies for geography, history and civics), and disguises to such a point that children are unaware of specific objectives for lessons and even entire courses of study. At the elementary level units have been used in such a way that children are attempting to learn about the "Circus" when they should be trying to learn to read. Direct instruction helps socially disadvantaged children establish educational goals that are in harmony with their cultural orientation to education and goals that are more immediately obtainable.

A brief summary statement concerning *Organizing Instruction and Curriculum Planning for the Socially Disadvantaged* would be, "Plan a program that has meaning, value, and purpose for them and use the best pedogical techniques and methods possible." Do not underrate them. Teach them where they are, not below, or not in reference to a culture foreign to theirs. The greatest amount of learning will take place when they can perform the assigned task but only with difficulty and with the expenditure of effort.

Selected supplementary readings

Featherstone, W. D., *Teaching the Slow Learner*. Bureau of Publications, Teachers College, Columbia University, 1951, 118 pp.

Johnson, G. Orville, *Education for the Slow Learners*. Englewood Cliffs, N.J.: Prentice-Hall, Inc., 1963, 330 pp.

Johnson, G. Orville, *The Slow Learner—A Second-Class Citizen?* The S. Richard Street Lecture for 1962, Syracuse University Press, 1962, 39 pp.

Riessman, Frank, *The Culturally Deprived Child*. New York: Harper and Row, Publishers, 1962, 140 pp.

CHAPTER 7

CURRICULUM DEVELOPMENT FOR CULTURALLY DIFFERENT EXCEPTIONAL CHILDREN (1964)

Phil Chinn

Culturally different exceptional children represent a special group. Clearly, we must provide unique services to meet their educational needs. These children are unique in themselves, as they can be considered a minority from two different perspectives. First, they are a minority because of their exceptional status, either handicapped or gifted. Secondly, they are a minority by virtue of their cultural diversity.

Cultural diversity itself is a complex issue, as there are a number of viewpoints regarding what constitutes a cultural group. Frequently cultural groups have been described strictly from an ethnic perspective. The ethnic groups within the United States most often identified as culturally diverse have been the Asian-American, the Blacks, Mexican-Americans (Chicanos), Native American Indians, and Puerto Ricans. There are, however, numerous other ethnic groups which could be considered diverse.

In 1977, the National Council for the Accreditation of Teacher Education (NCATE) issued revised standards for accreditation which include multicultural education. Included in Section 2.1.1 on Multicultural Education is the statement that:

> Multicultural education could include but not be limited to experiences which: (1) promote analytical and evaluative abilities to confront issues such as participatory democracy, racism and sexism, and the parity of power; (2) develop skills for values clarification, including the study of the manifest and latent transmission of values; (3) examine the dynamics of diverse cultures and the implications for developing teaching strategies; and (4) examine linguistic variations and diverse learning styles as a basis for the development of appropriate teaching strategies. (p. 4)

This statement clearly suggests that the parameters of multicultural education extend beyond ethnic studies. While ethnic studies will likely be a focal point for multicultural education, other groups may be considered cultural groups in our society. Multicultural education may very well be viewed from the standpoint of sex, religion, age, language, handicapping conditions (e.g., the deaf community as a cultural group), and socioeconomic level.

For the purposes of this article, we will view culture from the perspective of ethnic groups with the five previously mentioned groups as a primary concern. As a caution to you, however, there are other groups that do not come under this rubric who warrant special consideration if their educational needs are to be appropriately provided for. The Hasidic Jews, for example, are an ultraconservative group of Jews who are more likely to be viewed as a religious group than an ethnic group. Their unique religious practices set them apart even from other Jewish Americans. The Amish, likewise, are a unique cultural group which is generally classified as a religious group. Their avoidance of many mechanical and modern conveniences and their strict adherence to their religious principles also set this group apart from others. Both of these groups are diverse cultural groups whose beliefs, customs, and cultural values undoubtedly affect the development of any appropriate educational programming for them. As a side note, although the term *culturally diverse* carries with it a more positive connotation, it will be used interchangeably in this paper with *minority*.

Special curricula for culturally different exceptional children

A thorough search of two computer data bases, ERIC and ECER, yielded approximately 240 abstracts. Descriptors in the search included *culturally diverse, culturally different, culturally disadvantaged, minority*, each of the five previously identified ethnic groups, *exceptional children*, each area of exceptionality, *curriculum, instructional methods, instructional strategies*, etc. A second search included these two data bases and NIMIS to determine if any curricula exist related to ethnic studies or ethnic heritage for mentally retarded culturally diverse children.

The search for general curricula yielded an extremely limited number of program descriptions and suggested instructional strategies, which will be discussed. The search for ethnic studies curricula was fruitless. Essentially, the searches failed to yield curricula related specifically to culturally diverse exceptional children. A few suggestions for teaching strategies and approaches were cited and will be discussed.

The Council for Exceptional Children has a number of publications related to the education of culturally diverse exceptional children. Among these are selected papers from the 1973 CEC Institutes and Conference on Cultural Diversity and Exceptional Youth; audio tapes related to cultural diversity; a November, 1974, special issue of *Exceptional Children; Discovery and Nurturance of Giftedness in the Culturally Different*, by E. Paul Torrance; and *Mainstreaming and the Minority Child*, edited by Reginald Jones. Torrance suggests some strategies which are unique to gifted culturally diverse children. In general, however, most of the other publications address strategies and curricular adaptations which are appropriate to culturally diverse children but are not necessarily unique to the exceptional culturally diverse.

This absence of literature pertaining to specific curricula and instructional strategies for culturally diverse exceptional children suggests that either they do not exist or that the isolated curricula and strategies that do exist have not been published or disseminated. The reality is probably a little in between. There are few, if any, curricula that have been developed and are available for dissemination. There are few, if any, developed instructional strategies which have universal appeal and utilitarian value. However, there are probably a number of curricula that have been developed by individual teachers designed specifically to meet the needs of their own group of students. Likewise, many teachers have probably developed their own instructional strategies which are appropriate for specific culturally diverse exceptional children. The individual characteristics of these children all but preclude the development of effective cookbook approaches.

What should be taught

In the development of curricula or curricular approaches for culturally diverse exceptional children, there are some specific needs which should be considered. Only after these needs are identified can an effective curriculum be developed. Specific needs will vary from child to child, but there are some general needs which may be applicable to most of these children. Most basic academic as well as nonacademic skills that are programmed for nonminority group children are likely to be of equal value to minority group children. In addition, some areas of special concern may be appropriate to emphasize in developing the curriculum for these children.

We will now look at some topics which should be considered in curriculum development. In addition, as I have suggested (Chinn, 1979), there are many variables which contribute to the social and emotional adjustment of culturally diverse children. Poor adjustment inhibits effective educational programming and all but precludes successful employment adjustment in later years. Among the variables I cite are racism, poverty, health, and the built-in failure system for many culturally diverse children within the educational process.

Ethnic studies

The inclusion of ethnic studies in the curriculum for all children is a necessity. Ethnic studies for culturally diverse children is absolutely essential. The reasons are numerous and somewhat complex. Nearly all culturally diverse children will encounter some blatant racism throughout their lives. Even those few who are fortunate enough to escape overt racism will encounter the subtle results of racism and stereotyping which depreciate the self-concept of these children. This subtle racism may be difficult to detect, but it is as insidious as overt discrimination.

Labels

One form of subtle racism is the way in which culturally diverse groups are categorized or labeled. The term *minority* itself carries with it a connotation of being less than other groups with respect to power, status, and treatment. Even in situations where a minority group outnumbers other ethnic groups in population size, it may still be relegated to minority status due to the socioeconomic and power structure of the community (Chinn, 1979).

Terms such as *culturally deprived, culturally disadvantaged*, and *culturally different* are frequently used to identify culturally diverse individuals. The first two terms suggest a posture of arrogance, which implies that members of these cultures function at a level below that of the majority group culture. Further, these terms do not recognize the intrinsic value and uniqueness of these cultural groups and their contributions to our society (Chinn, 1979). Even *culturally different* suggests some degree of deviance and carries negative connotations.

Media

The mass media, including newspapers, television, motion pictures, and textbooks, have all contributed to the negative image of culturally diverse individuals either by stereotyping, omissions, or distortions. Stereotyping in movies and television has created distorted views of minority group members. In past years, minorities were almost totally excluded from roles as professionals. Instead they were portrayed in stereotyped roles. Only in recent years has there been any effort to correct these omissions and stereotypings. The news media continue to support biased reporting. Whites involved in criminal activities seldom are identified by ethnicity—only name, age, and sex—but reports such as "A Black male, age 29, is being held as a suspect . . ." are typical. This consistent biased reporting may suggest to the community that minority individuals are responsible for most criminal activity.

History books are filled with omissions, distortions, and stereotyping. One prime example is the credit given to engineer Pierre L'Enfant for his role in surveying and designing a master plan for Washington, D.C. Every student who studies the history of Washington or tours the city will be impressed with this man's contributions to American history. The magnificent plaza named in L'Enfant's honor serves as a visible reminder of this man's efforts. Few will read about or hear about the contributions of Benjamin Banneker, a Black, who perhaps played an equally prominent role in the designing of the city. When L'Enfant returned to France with the only set of blueprints, Banneker, who served on the surveying team with L'Enfant, was able to reproduce the plans accurately from memory and facilitated the building of the city. In contrast to the L'Enfant Plaza, only a rather obscure out-of-the-way circle bears Benjamin Banneker's name.

Perhaps the most damaging effect of stereotyping, omissions, and distortions is the negative self-perceptions which are held by many culturally diverse children. Often these children have few positive role models to identify with, either in the home or on the television or movie screen. Consequently, some perceive themselves and their cultural group as inferior to the dominant cultural group. Socially they may perceive themselves as a deviant group. Economically and politically they may view themselves as powerless. Vocationally they are often conditioned to view themselves only qualified as domestic workers, laundrymen, migrant farm workers, or pimps and prostitutes.

Ethnic studies have the potential to develop positive attitudes within both the culturally diverse and the dominant cultural group. Studying diverse cultural groups can help majority group children understand and appreciate differentness. Culturally diverse children can develop a sense of ethnic pride and identity. Carefully developed curricula could rectify much of the negative self-concept that has evolved after years of exposure (for the children and for their parents) to stereotyping, omissions, and distortions through the media.

As we have seen, at the present time there is a conspicuous absence of curricula developed specifically for culturally diverse exceptional children. However, there are a number of ethnic studies curricula available for different level children, covering a wide range of cultural groups. For a number of years Title IX has been funding projects related to curriculum development, training, and dissemination. Presently over 200 of these curricula are housed at the Ethnic Studies Clearinghouse in Boulder, Colorado. They are being catalogued as well as evaluated. Curricula have been developed for all five of the most frequently identified minority groups. In addition, a wide range of curricula for other cultural groups has also been developed. For example, the 56 projects funded for 1978–1979 included the development of curricula for Estonians, Haitians, Hawaiians, Cajun French, and Bulgarians.

Many of these curricula are appropriate for some exceptional children, while others will require various modifications to be useful in special education. But in most instances, the wheel does not need to be reinvented, simply modified to be appropriate to the needs of the student.

Poverty

The disproportionately high numbers of culturally diverse people who live at or below the poverty level is a long-standing phenomenon. Coleman (1976) suggests that nearly a third of the Blacks live in poverty, which is three times greater than for whites. The ratio for Mexican-Americans (Chicanos) is approximately the same. Poverty is not limited to these groups alone. Many immigrants who do not have the skills to enter into the competitive job market are exploited or receive below-minimum wages. The effects of poverty are potentially devastating.

While the pressures and problems associated with poverty are obvious to anyone who has gone through periods of financial stress, poverty in itself may not be as critical as poverty coupled with the individual's feelings of hopelessness. In times past, immigrants survived the early years of poverty with the anticipation of a better future. Many culturally diverse individuals today, however, see little hope of escape from their way of life. Some find the job market closed to them in spite of their educational achievements. The barriers are still up. While some Americans were generally encouraged with the drop in the unemployment figures released in the spring of 1979, there was little room for rejoicing in the Black community. In January, 1979, white unemployment dropped from 5.1 to 4.9%. At the same time, Black unemployment rates rose from 11.2 to 11.9%. Unemployment in Black America is now 243% times the rate for the white community; it is nothing short of a social disaster (Rowan, 1979).

The potential effect of poverty has frequently been cited as a factor in aggressive behavior and emotional disturbance. Levine and Kahn (1974) examined 1,000 downtown New York families to determine the relationship between psychological disadvantage and socioeconomic status. They found that lower socioeconomic status and minority ethnic group status were associated with high levels of psychiatric impairment. Frustration leads to despair, anger, aggression, and other deviant behavior, including suicide. Disproportionately high numbers of suicides have been observed among the Chinese in San Francisco and among Native Americans (Chinn, 1973a; Pepper, 1976).

The curriculum for culturally different exceptional children living in poverty situations should include some topics which may never totally alleviate the condition but can make their lives more tolerable. Among the areas of study should be instruction on how to live within the system. That is, how can these individuals learn to live within a system that can provide certain types of government services for those at poverty income levels. Curriculum should include, but not be limited to, instruction about the resources available for food assistance and health care. Even more critical is providing specific information on how to deal with bureaucratic red tape and the numerous obstacles which stand in the way of qualifying for services. Often there are stringent rules and regulations with little assistance or sympathy available for those who are not familiar with the system. Often, even the more capable individuals are discouraged and give up even though they are entitled to services. Culturally different exceptional individuals who have cognitive limitations may need specific help in overcoming their own deficiencies and dealing with intimidating behavior on the part of government officials.

A second area which needs to be strongly emphasized among economically limited students is the use and handling of finances. Special education teachers have long provided EMR students instruction in this area. With low income, minority students this is equally, if not more, critical. They need to learn the best use of their limited incomes. Among the many areas to be studied are how to budget and how and where to shop, how to find housing, how to borrow money, and how to make installment purchases. With limited financial resources and inflation, they must learn to efficiently use what little they do have.

With the disproportionately high numbers of culturally diverse individuals identified among the ranks of the unemployed, career education appears to be critical for the children in this group. Vocational education should be a critical area of curriculum emphasis, and the development of vocational skills must begin early in the educational process. Other aspects of career education such as leisure skills are also critical areas for curriculum development.

Health

Health problems are frequently associated with poverty; and poverty, as previously cited, is associated with minority groups. Problems center around poor nutrition, poor medical service (typically government-supported), and poor prenatal care. The high incidence of children born at risk (preterm and postterm) to parents of low socioeconomic status has been documented (Kernek, Osterud, & Anderson, 1966). Further, the incidence of brain injury, mental retardation, and learning disabilities has been related to children born at risk. These problems are directly related to the school problems so frequently identified with children from minority groups. Tarnapol (1970) found that minority group children had a significant degree of minimal brain damage related to learning disabilities. He suggests that delinquency and dropping out of school by minority group children may be partially related to brain dysfunction.

In a study comparing the physical well-being of third grade students as determined by a physical examination, Chinn (1973b) found a direct relationship between physical well-being and teacher ratings of the student's academic performance and social acceptance by peers. The poor health conditions of some culturally diverse students may affect their functional abilities in school.

Curricular adaptations for culturally diverse exceptional children may include information regarding access to government medical and dental care. Also, instruction on good health care procedures for themselves and their families should be an integral part of the curriculum.

Education

To the average middle-class child, school is a highly valued institution. The influences of parents, siblings, and other people in the child's environment lead to positive perceptions of school. Most children see it as a place where learning takes place; where learning is an enjoyable experience. School is also viewed as a positive social institution where the child is valued by his teachers and his peers (Chinn, 1979).

Disillusioned by their educational experiences, many minority group parents view school from a more negative perspective, and older children often share the same perceptions. Minority group children frequently begin school with little enthusiasm; for other people in their world, the school is an institution which represents failure, frustration, rejection, and at times discrimination. Too often their preconceived ideas are justified (Chinn, 1979).

The drop-out rate for minority students is alarming. About 800,000 students drop out of school each year. Twenty-two out of every 100 students who enter the fifth grade do not complete high school. Garcia (1976) reports that 45% of Mexican-American children drop out before completing the twelfth grade. The attrition rate for Native Americans is 55%. Of the dropouts, 85% are poor Blacks and Hispanics, along with poor whites. In larger cities, the majority of the drop-outs are Black, economically disadvantaged youth who have values and attitudes that are incongruent with those of the urban middle class. Many suffer from educational handicaps rooted in their poverty, deprivation, discrimination, and environmental conditions over which they personally have little or no control. In many instances, their home environment does not provide the self-concept, opportunity, motivation, or the capacity to cope with their problems (Jones, 1977).

Cultural pluralism

In 1908, Zangwill's play the *Melting Pot* saw all of the American people (particularly those of European descent) melting together in God's crucible and then emerging as a new race—as Americans. While the original melting pot concept applied to Europeans, this concept—assimilation—has prevailed. Many teachers are assimilationists who see immigrants and minority group members embracing and being absorbed into the culture, values, and language of the dominant society. In essence, a true assimilationist would have all individuals becoming as close as possible to being white Anglo-Saxon Protestants. They would, in particular, have all Americans use the same language—standard American English.

The 1974 Civil Rights Commission estimated that there were 5,000,000 linguistically different children in the United States. This figure does not include the millions of Black children who use Ebonics (Black English) as their primary medium of communication. The extreme assimilationist would have all these children develop standard English skills to the point of ridding themselves of any traces of non-English languages and non-standard English dialects. The assimilationist would have immigrants and minority group members rid themselves of their unique characteristics, to become as much as possible "model Americans."

The advocates of the melting pot theory have been effective, to a certain extent. Most European immigrants have been well assimilated in the cultural mainstream. Assimilated minorities have more doors opened to them in occupations, professions, and in other reward systems. The result has been that some Blacks, Asians, Hispanics, and Native Americans are as much a part of the dominant society as that society has allowed them to be. These individuals see assimilation as a vehicle to acceptance and success within the dominant society. Yet in spite of their efforts to embrace the new culture and to become educated, jobs are often still not available at higher echelons, and salaries are disproportionately lower. In spite of their education and cultural sophistication, they still experience social and vocational rejection (Chinn, 1979).

For these people, problems with self-identity often emerge. No longer are they a part of the ethnic community they have rejected, nor are they an integral part of the dominant society. Instead they exist between two worlds. Children who are in the process of breaking from their parents' culture often feel guilty because they are rejecting the family values. They may feel alienated from their family unit and ethnic community and rejected by the dominant group (Chinn, 1979).

Of course, self-imposed assimilation is a matter of choice and is not in itself wrong or particularly undesirable. However, assimilationist views imposed by others on the culturally diverse child and negating the value of the child's culture can only be seen as racist.

In the early and middle 1960s, the languages of culturally diverse children (e.g., Ebonics, pidgin English) were viewed as deficiencies. In more recent years, however, the language of these children has been recognized as being different rather than deficient. For instance, Hurley (1975), Cazden (1972), and Houston (1971) all have found that Black English possesses all the characteristics of any language system. Linguistically different children generally fall into one of two categories. There are large numbers of children who speak a nonstandard English dialect such as Hawaiian pidgin or Black English. Other linguistically different children come from homes where the native language is not English (e.g., Chinese, Spanish). From a legal and moral standpoint, this second group of children have received some attention of educators, who use the child's home language as a medium of instruction. This is part of bilingual education. Even though many issues in bilingual education are debatable, the legal rights of these linguistically different children have been provided for in the courts.

Nonstandard English dialects have not enjoyed the same level of support. They do not have legal support, nor do educators agree about whether or not to use these dialects in instruction. In some respects, some individuals from these cultural groups are "bilingual." They use standard English, or an approximation of it, within the educational system, with teachers, majority group peers, and authority figures. Within their own cultural groups, they use the nonstandard English dialect. The use of nonstandard English dialects as a medium of instruction is debatable, and there is not room to address that issue in this paper. What is critical, however, is that educators are aware of the implications of requiring culturally diverse children to use standard English in the classroom. This requirement may have considerable merit in that these children can learn to function linguistically in two worlds, the dominant cultural group and their own. The ability to assimilate linguistically may open social and vocational doors. However, educators should realize that while the children are learning to function in a different linguistic style, refraining from the use of the child's own cultural group language may keep the child from completely and freely expressing all of his thought patterns. More simply, the child's limited standard English skills may not be as developed as his cognitive skills, and his language limitations may cause the child to appear dull.

Educationally, it is critical that teachers realize that there is no one model American and that the strength of American society exists in a pluralistic culture. The Commission on Multicultural Education of the American Association of Colleges for Teacher Education developed a policy statement adopted in 1972 entitled "No One Model American." As the text states:

> To endorse cultural pluralism is to endorse the principle that there is no one model American. To endorse cultural pluralism is to understand and appreciate the differences that exist among the nation's citizens. It is to see these differences as a positive force in the continuing development of a society which professes a wholesome respect for the intrinsic worth of every individual.

> Cultural pluralism is more than a temporary accommodation to placate racial and ethnic minorities. It is a concept that aims toward a heightened sense of being and of wholeness of the entire society based on the unique strengths of each of its parts.

The teacher who accepts the basic tenants of this statement will likely be prepared to provide students with appropriate ethnic studies in their curriculum. The same teacher will likely provide or try to provide for the linguistic differences that any of the children may have. Legally, according to laws and court decisions such as the Lau vs. Nichols case (1974), Public Law 94-142, and Section 504, the linguistic needs of these children must be met. More important, however, is that the programming be motivated by feelings of propriety and rightfulness rather than legal compliance.

Exceptional children

Strategies for culturally diverse gifted and talented

In adapting the work of Greer and Rubinstein (1972), Frasier, Fisher, and Clinton (1977) suggested that in developing an appropriate curriculum for culturally diverse gifted children, four key dimensions should be considered: (1) what I want to teach, (2) what I want to learn, (3) what you want to learn, and (4) what you want to teach. Out of these four dimensions emerges a fifth, what we discover together.

In Dimension 1 what I want to teach, the teacher's decisions are based on diagnosis of the children's strengths and weaknesses based on both objective measures and subjective observations. Here are some considerations for working with culturally diverse gifted children. These children:

1. Are capable of operating at higher levels of thought (i.e., analysis, synthesis, evaluation);
2. May need some time in developing lower level thought processes (i.e., knowledge, comprehension, evaluation);
3. Exhibit some nonstandard abilities;
4. May need support in initial exploratory opportunities;
5. Need to have strengths emphasized and weaknesses developed (Baldwin, 1973; Frasier, et al., 1977).

Dimension 2 suggests that the teacher can also learn. The culturally diverse children sometimes bring information into the learning environment in nontraditional ways.

Dimension 3 considers what the learner views as important. This approach is congruent with the view that intrinsic motivation stimulates the learning process.

Dimension 4, which is related to Dimension 3, suggests that what the child wants to *teach* is also an integral part of the learning process.

Dimension 5 is a mutually benefitting experience where all in the learning environment can learn and grow together.

Baldwin (1973) suggests using simulation games, research through films, interviews, and computer-assisted instruction. Baldwin further emphasizes the importance of creative thinking (e.g., elaborative thinking, fluent thinking, and flexible thinking).

Torrance (1977) developed a list of 18 "creative positives" (e.g., fluency and flexibility in figural media), which are sets of characteristics he believes can assist in identifying strengths and giftedness among culturally different students. He contends that these creative positives exist to a higher degree among culturally different groups. The creative positives may be detected by tests, observation of behavior, performance, constructions, or any other means whatsoever. These abilities, Torrance states, "for the most part . . . can be observed with a high degree of frequency among culturally different students by anyone who is willing to become a sensitive, open-minded human being in situations where trust and freedom are established." Torrance further contends that the creative positives can be used to motivate learning, select learning experiences, and develop career plans. In his monograph he provides suggestions and examples on how they might be utilized in the classroom.

Culturally diverse retarded children

Hurley (1975) suggests that, while there is increasing concern about the misplacement of children in special education classes, the fact remains that a sizeable percentage of the special education population is culturally different. To better meet the needs of the culturally different in classes for the retarded, Hurley suggests that certain approaches may be used. One approach suggested is the inductive approach. In the learning processes, the child should not only learn facts, skills, and concepts, but also learn how to learn. The student must learn how to process information which he collects. To do so requires practice, an essential element in the inductive process.

Hurley (1975) cautions that some children may have linguistic limitations even in their nonstandard dialects. Thus the teacher must accommodate and meet the needs of both groups—those limited in standard English as well as those limited in both standard as well as nonstandard dialects. This accommodation may involve reading material. Hurley suggests using the experience story. Here the child dictates from his own perceptions and experiences. This may in some instances be a viable approach to reading for those for whom the regular readers hold minimal interest value.

Learning characteristics of culturally diverse children

A number of characteristics of culturally diverse children have been identified. These traits in some instances set them apart from the middle-class white child. Some of these characteristics are applicable to a particular group, while others cut across a greater number of groups. Differences in cultures are apt to be more striking among lower-class members of an ethnic group, because they tend to be less assimilated than those who are middle class.

Many educators make the erroneous assumption that culturally diverse children lived in a cultural vacuum before they entered school. In truth, often it is the school which fails to match its methods and curriculum to the child's language, cultural background, and learning style. But when the school fails, the child is regarded as deficient. Black mothers, for example, tend to be more firm and physical in discipline than white mothers. When Black children have white teachers who practice what they have learned in college, the children become uncontrollable and are labeled *discipline problems.*

The differences in white and minority group values can make the educational experience one of cognitive dissonance. For instance, Black, Mexican American, and Native-American children are often more expressive in the affective domain than white students. Their white peers, however, value the cognitive functioning which the schools value and stress (Burgress, 1978).

Open education settings, designed for the white, middle-class child, are another factor in cultural dissonance. Many Black children perform poorly using educational hardware. The technology and automation which replaces certain interactions between teachers and students creates problems for Black and Mexican-American children who are accustomed to associating learning with the interpersonal interaction found in their family settings.

With regard to cognitive style, Ramirez, Casteneda, and Herold (1974) suggest that Mexican-American children are more field dependent in their perceptions than their Anglo peers. Field dependence related to cognitive style may be a function of how traditional a group is. Traditional groups may be more field dependent, while acculturated groups are more field independent (Hsi & Lim, 1977). Ramirez and his associates (1974) found a greater degree of field dependence among children in communities where social conformity is stressed.

Anderson (1977) states that there are two types of cognitive styles, analytic or abstract and nonanalytic or concrete. School related activities and IQ tests rely heavily on analytic cognitive abilities. Minority group children, particularly Black, Mexican-American and Puerto Rican, tend to manifest the nonanalytic style of cognitive functioning. While developmental psychologists usually consider analytic style as superior to the nonanalytic, and see the latter as indicative of cognitive deficit, others (e.g., Bernstein, 1971) do not view nonanalytic thinking as a *lack* of analytic thinking. Rather, they view it as a positively different form of cognitive functioning. Cognitive style may be a function of socialization typical of an ethnic group.

Anderson (1977) suggests that no group of children can be said to have cognitive deficit in an absolute sense. The ability to perform cognitively may be more a function of experience and the context of the situation in which a culturally diverse child is expected to perform. In testing situations, these children are placed in what Labov (1972) refers to as "an asymmetrical situation where anything he says can be held against him." Anderson (1977) further suggests that teachers erroneously interpret brief communication breakdowns as evidence of cognitive deficits.

Conclusion

I have included here only a brief description of some of the learning styles and characteristics of culturally diverse children. This last section is not related specifically to exceptional children, but to culturally diverse children in general. The special educator concerned with providing for the needs of culturally diverse children will find an abundance of literature on this subject.

Special educators have developed, through necessity, the ability to adapt and extract from existing materials. For the culturally diverse, the principles remain the same. Identify the needs of your children, and adapt or modify existing materials with a special education emphasis, to meet the needs of the children.

The challenge is there for all educators. If school achievement of culturally diverse exceptional children is to improve, traditional approaches designed for Anglo students must be replaced by alternative approaches tailored to the individual learning styles of each child.

References

Anderson, K. M. *Cognitive style and school failure.* Paper presented at the symposium "Anthropology in Institutional Settings," Society for Applied Anthropology and Southwestern Anthropological Association, San Diego, April 6, 1977. (ERIC Document #ED 1514253)

Baldwin, A. Instructional planning for gifted disadavantaged children. *National Leadership Institute, Teacher Education/Early Childhood.* Stoors: University of Connecticut, 1973.

Bernstein, B. *Class, codes and control.* London: Routledge and Kegan Paul, 1971.

Burgess, B. J. Native American learning styles. In L. Morris, G. Sather, & P. Scull (Eds.), *Extracting learning styles from social/cultural diversity.* Washington, D.C.: Southwest Teacher Corps Network, 1978.

Cazden, C. B. *Child language and education.* New York: Holt, Rinehart and Winston, 1972.

Chinn, P. C. The Asian American: A search for identity. In L. Bransford, L. Baca, & K. Lane (Eds.), *Cultural diversity and the exceptional child.* Reston, Va.: The Council for Exceptional Children, 1973.(a)

Chinn, P. C. A relationship between health and school problems: A nursing assessment. *Journal of School Health*, 1973 *43*, 85–89.(b)

Chinn, P. C. *Variables affecting deviant behavior in culturally diverse adolescents.* Paper presented at the First Annual Nebraska Symposium on Current Issues in Educating the Early Adolescent with Severe Behavior Disorders. Omaha, May 10, 1979.

Coleman, J. C. *Abnormal psychology and modern life*, 5th ed. Glenview, Ill.: Scott, Foresman, 1976.

Commission on Multicultural Education. *No one model American.* Washington, D.C.: American Association for Colleges of Teacher Education, 1972.

Frasier, M., Fisher, A., & Clinton, O. R. *Help for organizing productive experiences for culturally diverse gifted and talented.* Paper presented at the Annual International Convention, The Council for Exceptional Children, Atlanta, April 15, 1977 (ERIC Document #ED141981)

Garcia, R. L. *Learning in two languages.* Bloomington, Ind.: Phi Delta Kappa Educational Foundation, 1976.

Greer, M., & Rubenstein, B. *Will the real teacher please stand up? A primer in humanistic education.* Pacific Palisades, Calif.: Goodyear, 1972.

Houston, S. H. A reexamination of some assumptions about the language of the disadvantaged child. In S. Chess & A. Thomas (Eds.), *Annual progress in child psychiatry and child development.* New York: Brunner/Mazel, 1971.

Hsi, V., & Lim, V. *A summary of selected research on cognitive and perceptual variables.* Berkeley, Calif.: Asian-American Bilingual Center, 1977. (ERIC Document #ED145003)

Hurley, O. L. Strategies for culturally different children in classes for the retarded. In E. L. Meyen, G. A. Vergason, & R. J. Whelan (Eds.), *Alternatives for teaching exceptional children.* Denver: Love Publishing, 1975.

Jones, W. M. Impact on society of youth who drop out or are undereducated. *Educational Leadership*, 1977, *34*, 411–416.

Kernek, C., Osterud, H., & Anderson, B. Patterns of prematurity in Oregon. *Northwest Medicine*, 1966, *65*, 639.

Labov, W. The logic of non-standard English. In P.P.G. Giglioli (Ed.), *Language and social concept.* London: Penguin Press, 1972.

Lau vs. Nichols, 414 U.S. 563–572 (January 21, 1974).

Levine, A. S., & Kahn, M. B. Does city living damage kids' minds? *Social and Rehabilitation Record*, 1974, *1*, 25–27.

Pepper, F. C. Teaching the American Indian in mainstream settings. In R. L. Jones (Eds.), *Mainstreaming and the minority child.* Reston, Va.: The Council for Exceptional Children, 1976.

Ramirez, M., Casteneda, A., & Herold, P. The relationship of acculturation to cognitive style among Mexican-Americans. *Journal of Cross-Cultural Psychology*, 1974, *5*, 212–220.

Rowan, C. T. Black unemployment is society's shame. *The Washington Star*, March 16, 1979, P. A-11.

Tarnopol, L. Delinquency and minimal brain dysfunction. *Journal of Learning Disabilities*, 1970, *3*, 200–207.

Torrance, E. P. *Discovery and nurturance of giftedness in the culturally different*. Reston, Va.: The Council for Exceptional Children, 1977.

CHAPTER 8

MULTICULTURAL EDUCATION (1983)

A natural way to teach

Charles R. Payne

Usually when one hears the term multicultural education, one of the following three perceptions comes to mind. The first of these views is multicultural education as product with the emphasis on ethnicity, contributions and usualness or surface aspects (pow wow, rain dances, dozens, pinatas, etc.) of ethnic groups. This aspect also emphasizes teaching about different ethnic and cultural groups.

The second focal point of multicultural education emphasizes civil rights and atonement for past injustices. This could be labeled entitlement. While this perception would still involve a study of historical data and an analysis of sociological relationships, its emphasis is primarily on certain targeted oppressed groups and an amelioration of their conditions. This aspect of multicultural education has caused the practice of implementation of cultural activities to be limited to these targeted groups and, thus, multicultural education becomes viewed as only a minority concern.

The third aspect, and the least utilized, views multicultural education as a process. This process approach includes the first two perceptions, but it goes beyond the product stage in that the primary focus is on the concept of culture, as opposed to ethnicity, on the intrinsic aspects of culture in the everyday classroom instructional process. The process approach recognizes the entitlement aspect through the fact that to obtain what one is entitled to, one must begin, first, with a fair system and, second, with an equal distribution and acquisition of social and academic skills. This view of multicultural education as process involves an essential understanding on the part of educators for such educational variables as methodology, curriculum, subject examples, and instructional techniques—in other words, the total process of teaching. Another way of stating this view is that multicultural education is simply "good teaching and good education." This approach to multicultural education also emphasizes the process of teaching all disciplines to members of various ethnic and cultural groups as opposed to teaching about diverse ethnic and cultural groups. To implement this perception of multicultural education, the implementor must define *culture* as "all of the acquired or learned behaviors" and ethnicity as "hereditary traits." There is no inherent, one-to-one correspondence between culture and ethnicity.

Minorities and low-income students are commonly perceived as not being able to achieve as well academically as white and/or middle-class students. It is the purpose of this paper to offer hypotheses and to expand the explanation of the process approach. This natural teaching technique should increase the academic achievement of all students.

Common aspects of teaching

It appears that one of the most fundamental approaches to studying different aspects of cultures is to start with the commonalities. So, in teaching students in multicultural classrooms it is imperative that the commonalities of the teaching and learning process, with respect to different cultures, be identified before cultural differences can be adequately handled in an instructional manner. Thus, Hypothesis I states:

> All teachers, regardless of subject area, teach within only four very broad categories. The difference in teaching one subject area from another is in the concepts and content of the particular discipline.

These four categories are as follows:

1. Skills—how to do something, e.g., writing, reading, typing, making music from various instruments, cooking, sewing, dancing, drawing.
2. Knowledge—that something is the case (facts), e.g., George Washington was the first President of the United States; 2 + 2 = 4; there are four basic food types; a noun is the name of a person, place or thing.
3. Values—beliefs and performances, e.g., setting goals, value clarification, attitudes toward various groups of people and diverse aspects of life, acceptance of differences either in people or opinions, acting on and defending one's beliefs.
4. Thinking—intellectual acts of reasoning, e.g., deducing, concluding, explaining, comparing, defining, justifying, sequencing of events, classifying.

The first benefit of being aware of the above categories is that the act of teaching begins to become somewhat more focused. It also begins to answer the question: What should people of other cultures be taught? Each of the above four elements is present in every subject area and, therefore, must be managed in some manner by all teachers.

The second value of such knowledge is that members of all ethnic and/or cultural groups must possess these phenomena in varying degrees, if they are to function in any society. At first this statement might sound questionable. An examination of people in the least complex cultures will reveal these aspects to be in use when solving common, everyday problems. The real trick for successful teaching appears to be in the meshing of student experiences with the subject area and the particular idea being taught at a given time. This process will be discussed in more detail later in the paper.

When reviewing the major disciplines taught in schools (i.e., mathematics, science, language, physical education, home economics, social studies, art, industrial art, music, and special education), there is not a single subject mentioned that does not have some skills to be learned, facts that must be memorized, content that can be used in the formation and clarification of values, and some use of the intellectual acts of reasoning. Therefore, the fundamental difference between subjects is the content; the academic skills to be taught are the same. Subject areas are taught separately for the purposes of organization and for expedience when studying the discipline, not because subject areas are that vastly different and unrelated in nature. The major premise in this idea of the likenesses of disciplines is that the skills of mathematics, science, language, social studies, home economics, and music are worldwide; all cultures use the intellectual acts of reasoning which involve the processes of deducing, concluding, explaining, comparing, defining, justifying, sequencing of events, and classifying. The experiences and processes through which people learn these skills are determined by culture. Because of the differences between cultures, some skills would be used more in one culture than another, thereby creating cultural strengths.

Kleinfeld (1973) has provided ample evidence of cultural strengths when she describes the figural and spatial abilities of the Eskimos:

> Anecdotal reports also contain numerous descriptions of Eskimos' exceptional performance in tasks requiring memory of visual information. Many Caucasians have asked Eskimos to draw maps of the terrain and later found them to be extraordinarily accurate both in significant detail and in spatial arrangements (Briggs, 1970; King, 1848). Indeed, Marshall (1933) reports that an Eskimo woman "once sketched for me the first fifteen miles of the Alatna River, a stream which is nothing but bends in this lower portion, and she had them all plotted from memory almost as accurately as the instrumentally constructed Geological Survey Map [p. 81]." Similarly, Carpenter (1955), found maps of Southampton Island made by Eskimos in 1929 were almost identical to maps made years later by aerial photography. (p. 347)

It would appear that natural skills and abilities which have been acquired because of a certain life style or culture would be more useful in teaching when viewed as cultural strengths and not weaknesses. The practice of labeling people from other cultures which have not provided them with the same skills or the same degree of development as our own as "culturally and academically deficient" has caused many human tragedies in the classroom.

Once the commonality of teaching, irrespective of subject area, has been established, it provides a partial explanation as to why there is a similar need for people of all cultures to master the same general activities.

Common aspects of academic concepts among and between all human groups

Hypothesis II states:

> The basic concepts of any subject area will be the same for members of all ethnic/cultural groups. Therefore, differences within concepts as they exist between cultures, are in experiences with the concept.

The formulation of this hypothesis assumes that the basic concepts of any subject will be fundamentally the same for all people. It is also assumed that differences may arise through the manifestation of the concepts within a given culture. Again, it is the experience with a given concept that is determined by culture. This does not imply that people of a different culture must necessarily have a different experience with a given concept or that every concept which exists in the culture is in the immediate awareness of all people of the culture. As an example of the relationship of the concepts of science to culture Dart and Pradhan (1976) made the following observation of Nepal's culture:

> Western technology developed out of the Western scientific revolution, which, over the last three centuries, has profoundly altered Western man's understanding of, and relation to, nature. The resulting "scientific viewpoint" has become our way of considering reality, and it is so much a part of us that it is taken for granted. The traditional cultures of Asia or Africa, however, are frequently nonscientific—nonrational in their approach to nature—and they do not always provide a ready foundation upon which to build a more scientific view. Of course people of all cultures experience many of the same familiar phenomena of nature and feel that they understand what is real and how knowledge about the real world is to be organized. Interpretations of what is meant by the "real" world, however, vary widely. Major tasks, then, are to determine what constitutes reality for persons of different cultures and to learn how the most meaningful communication about nature can be established among people holding different views of reality. (p. 339)

Quite often the comment is made that it is easy to see how cultures differ when comparing cultures that are as diverse as those of the United States and Nepal. True, this example is an extreme, but it and others are presented first to make the point clear. Second, once the extreme case is internalized it will not be unthinkable to imagine that groups of people who have lived in the U.S. for generations have had very different experiences from other groups inhabiting the U.S. for the same length of time. These differences have developed in part because of the vastness of the country. Many of our ancestors brought different cultural perspectives which have been transmitted to us. Lastly, discrimination and other artificial reasons have served well to isolate groups from each other, thereby increasing the opportunity for different experiences and perceptions.

A graphic representation of the influence of culture on academic areas

Figure 8.1 is a graphic representation of the expressed idea that academic skills and subject area concepts are common to all cultures and yet are developed and perceived differently.

From this diagram Hypothesis III states:

> It is the life experiences of the individual as well as those vicarious experiences gained from other cultural members which influence one's perception of phenomena.

When reviewing the diagram in its present form, there is a valid question as to the dominating influence of the phenomena on the formation of developing cultural patterns of the new generation. The other side of the question is: Do the existing cultural patterns into which the new members enter have the dominating influence on the acquired perception of phenomena? Maybe the arrows should point inward and not outward. It is the view of this writer that it is the individuals within a culture who create, out of real experiences, the particular relationship which exists between themselves and natural phenomena. However, this assumes that the individual is in a vacuum, isolated from others such as parents, teachers, and siblings. Possibly, a more realistic view of the influences of culture on the individual and vice versa is that of parity: The individual preceives personal experiences but in conjunction with the perceptions and experiences of others.

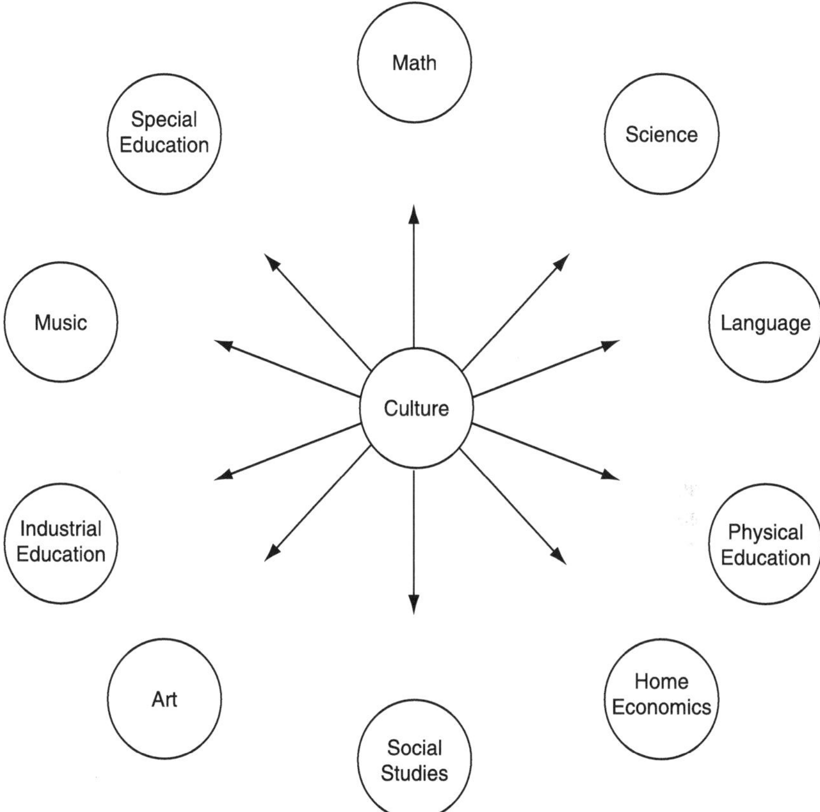

Figure 8.1

Perhaps, the diagram should reflect the experiences of older members whereby a more realistic representation would have the arrows reflect a reversible situation. This reversible situation would indicate that individuals of a culture influence their immediate culture through their own perceptions, but the individuals are also influenced by past experiences of older members of the culture. Since cultures are dynamic entities, the particular interpretation of experiences made by any given generation is going to depend heavily upon the present environment. For the purposes of this paper and for classroom planning it appears to be more practical to keep the diagram as it is.

Following are some examples of how the model can be used. First, it is essential that teachers identify the objectives that they are trying to accomplish. Many people argue that the concept of culture and its relationship to the fine arts make sense but that it has no relevance to the sciences and other related fields. The model, however, implies that the concepts of mathematics will be the same for all people, and thus its relationship to people is affected by culture. If there are cultural differences, they are found within the experiences that people of different cultures have with the particular subject area concepts.

Suppose we have an objective to teach students how to balance checkbooks. First of all, the concept that is pivotal in this objective is that of balancing, and the basic skills needed are addition and subtraction. As a teacher who is working with students unfamiliar with checkbooks and banks, the same concept of balancing and the basic skills of addition and subtraction can still be taught based on the students' encounter with the act of balancing and the process of addition and subtraction. It appears to be highly unlikely for a functioning human being anywhere on this earth not to have experienced the concept of balancing or the use of addition and subtraction. So, how many examples of different activities which represent balancing can be used in the classroom?

1. Taking inventory for a business.
2. A basketball player who scored 15 points for his/her team, but also committed five fouls that resulted in the opposing team making an additional 12 points. How many net points did this player contribute to the team?
3. An older brother is making cookies, 20 per batch, and putting them in a cookie jar but his little sister takes 3, 4, 5, 6, respectively from each batch. How many cookies are actually in the jar when he finishes?

The idea in a nutshell is that students must be able to associate concepts with their reality, and one of our real tasks as teachers is to expand their realities.

Other examples will involve the areas of art, literature, and music. These three areas are commonly viewed as means for human beings to express certain sentiments. Therefore, the concepts of love, hate, celebrations, social injustice, and happiness are used equally by people of all cultures. It is the experiences, availability of materials, and interpretations that make for differences. So the key question again is: What are the objectives to be accomplished? Once these have been established, it is a matter of selecting materials from various cultures which helps to accomplish or serve as illustration of the desired objectives. The main idea here is that the rules governing and the sentiments expressed through art, music, and literature can be found throughout most cultures.

The cognitive domain and its common use among and between human beings

Hypothesis IV states:

> The academic skills as represented by the cognitive domain, to some degree, are skills that are used by people of all ethnic/cultural groups. These same skills are also used and taught in each and every subject area.

The value of the above hypothesis for someone planning to teach is that, again, the teaching act can be focused on a given task, in this case a particular skill. It is also worthwhile to know that we teach basically the same skills, perhaps at times, emphasizing some over others, in all of our subject areas. Again the real difference in subject areas appears to be in content. So back to the question: What do you teach people of other ethnic/culture groups? Exactly the same skills.

The paramount significance of this knowledge is the fact that the cognitive domain represents the set of skills or mental tools from which people of any group must choose when attempting to solve life's problems. The task now becomes that of matching concepts, skills, and content whereby the content would actually represent the cultural aspects of the student's life. To be more specific, in many cases it would consist of the examples used to explain and illustrate ideas that would need to be associated with cultural experiences. It is being strongly suggested that content is a primary means for developing the concepts and skills of any objective. It is further being suggested that it is the successful acquisition of academic skills and concepts and the opportunity to use and apply them which serve as the equalizers among human beings. A good educational program should have among its goals the ideals that people from all groups will know how to think with respect to being able to: use the six major levels and corresponding sublevels of the cognitive domain as related to understanding specific facts and mastering a discipline; apply principles, skills, and knowledge to solving everyday life and social problems; and analyze one's own situation and be able to create an appropriate behavior. In short, the particular skills of the cognitive domain are not solely for the acquisition of academic phenomena, but the use of the skills permeates one's whole existence. This is true for all human beings. Bloom in his book, *Human Characteristics and School Learning* (1976), has stated in effect that people who do not acquire these skills cannot make good productive citizens because of the inability to make rational decisions. So these people find themselves going along with the proclaimed leader, however ordained, or they become cogs in the wheel by always resisting whatever is suggested, good or bad.

Methodology

Teaching methods have to be of the utmost concern for anyone involved in teaching for:

> No one can teach something to someone without doing it in some particular way, and that way of teaching has significant effects on the entire teaching and learning situation. . . . methods [can be] understood to mean a pattern or manner (which can be repeated) of treating people, objects, and events, that is directed—purposively and recognizably—toward the achievement of some goal. (Hyman, 1974, p. 53)

Earlier it was stated that the intended educational outcomes, as related to the development of academic skills, are very much the same for all cultural groups. Since it is the development and acquisition of academic skills and concepts along with imparting some kind of subject matter content that is of concern, can the same teaching methods be used for all cultural groups? Hypothesis V states:

> Teaching methods are culturally biased, in that they are created with the expressed intent of developing a specific behavior that is supposed to be valued by the host culture.

Since the purpose of any method is to aid the teacher in teaching something which will lead to the student's achievement of previously stated objectives, it is essential that teachers become aware of the characteristics of teaching methods. Just as methods aid in the acquisition of objectives, they also assist in developing unspoken and unwritten objectives. This does not mean that people in the culture are being devious. Because of these unconscious objectives, it is the characteristic of a given method and the behavior of the people being taught that must complement each other. For example, in working with students from cultures that stress physical ability, a teacher would do well to select or modify a method or methods to take advantage of that physical ability. This same idea is further expressed by

Miller and Swanson (Cheyney, 1967, p. 44) when they conclude from a research study that, when working with lower-class children, "If the teacher enables them to express themselves with the large muscles of the torso and limbs, her students may make surprising educational progress" (p. 44).

To further emphasize the importance of understanding culture and its influence on methodology, Eleanor Leacock (1976) writes:

> True cultural insight enables us to see behind superficial socially patterned differences to the full integrity of an individual. It prevents us from misinterpreting behavior different from that to which we are accustomed. To take an example from American Indian culture, people working with Indian children have found that they often do not respond well to teaching techniques that depend on the desire to do better than one's peers on a test, to answer a question more capably, in short, to compete successfully. Where Indian societies have retained roots with the past they are still pervaded by a cooperative spirit, and children feel uncomfortable in competitively structured situations, at least insofar as learning is concerned. This is often misinterpreted as a lack of desire to learn, but an awareness of cultural differences reveals that the motivation for learning is present, but that it is being inhibited rather than encouraged by teaching practices foreign to Indian culture.
>
> The persistence of such responses was brought home sharply to me when I assigned oral reports, seminar style, to a college class of bright, argumentative students. One of the girls, who had seldom spoken up in class, asked for permission to write rather than deliver the experience of oral delivery. She later told me that the course had given her insight into her reason for declining, and to the discomfort she had always felt in school. Her father was Indian she said and though there was little of an ongoing Indian community in Connecticut where she was raised, nonetheless the style of American Indian discourse has persisted in her family. For her, discussion should not involve the rapid-fire, essentially competitive argument to which we are accustomed. Instead, it would involve measured, considered statement, and—so difficult for us—attentive listening. Each person should listen patiently to everyone else, and the attempt should be at reaching consensus rather than winning an argument. Therefore, this student had always felt uncomfortable in classrooms, with their built-in competitive atmosphere. (pp. 418–419)

A critical analysis of the above quote should provide some insight into the relationship between the culture of the students and the effectiveness of a teaching method. Teaching methods must be chosen with a particular type of learner in mind.

Summary

This paper has defined multicultural education as good teaching and good education. There were five hypotheses presented around the following concepts:

1. the broad categories around which all teachers teach
2. the commonalities of academic concepts among and between all human groups

3. the influence of culture on the perception of and experiences with the phenomena found within a given discipline
4. the relationship of the cognitive domain and its common use among and between humanity
5. the cultural bias of teaching methodology

A diagram was also presented to graphically illustrate how the perception of academic phenomena is related to cultural experiences. Lastly some examples were given to illustrate how the proposed hypotheses and model could be implemented. It is the belief of this writer that when properly applied, the five hypotheses expressed in this paper will lead to respectable achievement by all.

References

Bloom, B. S. **Human characteristics and school learning.** New York: McGraw-Hill Book Co., 1976.

Cheyney, A. B. **Teaching culturally disadvantaged in the elementary school.** Columbus, OH: Charles E. Merrill Publishing Co., 1967.

Dart, F. E., & Pradham, P. L. Cross-cultural teaching of science. In J. I. Roberts & S. K. Akinsanya (Eds.), **Educational patterns and cultural configurations.** New York: David McKay Co., 1976.

Hyman, R. T. **Ways of teaching.** Philadelphia: J. B. Lippincott Co., 1974.

Kleinfeld, J. S. Intellectual strengths in culturally different groups: An Eskimo illustration. **Review of Educational Research,** 1973, **43,** 341–359.

Leacock, E. The concept of culture and its significance for school counselors. In J. I. Roberts & S. K. Akinsanya (Eds.), **Schooling in the cultural context.** New York: David McKay Co., 1976.

CHAPTER 9

THE SILENCED DIALOGUE (1988)

Power and pedagogy in educating other people's children

Lisa D. Delpit

A Black male graduate student who is also a special education teacher in a predominantly Black community is talking about his experiences in predominantly White university classes:

> There comes a moment in every class where we have to discuss "The Black Issue" and what's appropriate education for Black children. I tell you, I'm tired of arguing with those White people, because they won't listen. Well, I don't know if they really don't listen or if they just don't believe you. It seems like if you can't quote Vygotsky or something, then you don't have any validity to speak about your *own* kids. Anyway, I'm not bothering with it anymore, now I'm just in it for a grade.

A Black woman teacher in a multicultural urban elementary school is talking about her experiences in discussions with her predominantly White fellow teachers about how they should organize reading instruction to best serve students of color:

> When you're talking to White people they still want it to be their way. You can try to talk to them and give them examples, but they're so headstrong, they think they know what's best for *everybody*, for *everybody's* children. They won't listen, White folks are going to do what they want to do *anyway*.
>
> It's really hard. They just don't listen well. No, they listen, but they don't *hear*—you know how your mama used to say you listen to the radio, but you *hear* your mother? Well they don't *hear* me.
>
> So I just try to shut them out so I can hold my temper. You can only beat your head against a brick wall for so long before you draw blood. If I try to stop arguing with them I can't help myself from getting angry. Then I end up walking around praying all day "Please Lord, remove the bile I feel for these people so I can sleep tonight." It's funny, but it can become a cancer, a sore.
>
> So, I shut them out. I go back to my own little cubby, my classroom, and I try to teach the way I know will work, no matter what those folk say. And when I get Black kids, I just try to undo the damage they did.
>
> I'm not going to let any man, woman, or child drive me crazy—White folks will try to do that to you if you let them. You just have to stop talking to them, that's what I do. I just keep smiling, but I won't talk to them.

A soft-spoken Native Alaskan woman in her forties is a student in the Education Department of the University of Alaska. One day she storms into a Black professor's office and very uncharacteristically slams the door. She plops down in a chair and, still fuming, says, "Please tell those people, just don't help us anymore! I give up. I won't talk to them again!"

And finally, a Black woman principal who is also a doctoral student at a well-known university on the West Coast is talking about her university experiences, particularly about when a professor lectures on issues concerning educating Black children:

> If you try to suggest that that's not quite the way it is, they get defensive, then you get defensive, then they'll start reciting research.
>
> I try to give them my experiences, to explain. They just look and nod. The more I try to explain, they just look and nod, just keep looking and nodding. They don't really hear me.
>
> Then, when it's time for class to be over, the professor tells me to come to his office to talk more. So I go. He asks for more examples of what I'm talking about, and he looks and nods while I give them. Then he says that that's just my experiences. It doesn't really apply to most Black people.
>
> It becomes futile because they think they know everything about everybody. What you have to say about your life, your children, doesn't mean anything. They don't really want to hear what you have to say. They wear blinders and earplugs. They only want to go on research they've read that other White people have written.
>
> It just doesn't make any sense to keep talking to them.

Thus was the first half of the title of this text born—"The Silenced Dialogue." One of the tragedies in the field of education is that scenarios such as these are enacted daily around the country. The saddest element is that the individuals that the Black and Native American educators speak of in these statements are seldom aware that the dialogue *has* been silenced. Most likely the White educators believe that their colleagues of color did, in the end, agree with their logic. After all, they stopped disagreeing, didn't they?

I have collected these statements since completing a recently published article (Delpit, 1986). In this somewhat autobiographical account, entitled "Skills and Other Dilemmas of a Progressive Black Educator," I discussed my perspective as a product of a skills-oriented approach to writing and as a teacher of process-oriented approaches. I described the estrangement that I and many teachers of color feel from the progressive movement when writing-process advocates dismiss us as too "skills oriented." I ended the article suggesting that it was incumbent upon writing-process advocates—or indeed, advocates of any progressive movement—to enter into dialogue with teachers of color, who may not share their enthusiasm about so-called new, liberal, or progressive ideas.

In response to this article, which presented no research data and did not even cite a reference, I received numerous calls and letters from teachers, professors, and even state school personnel from around the country, both Black and White. All of the White respondents, except one, have wished to talk more about the question of skills versus process approaches—to support or reject what they perceive to be my position. On the other hand, *all* of the non-White respondents have spoken passionately on being left out of the dialogue about how best to educate children of color.

How can such complete communication blocks exist when both parties truly believe they have the same aims? How can the bitterness and resentment expressed by the educators of color be drained so that the sores can heal? What can be done?

I believe the answer to these questions lies in ethnographic analysis, that is, in identifying and giving voice to alternative world views. Thus, I will attempt to address the concerns raised by White and Black respondents to my article "Skills and Other Dilemmas" (Delpit, 1986). My charge here is not to determine the best instructional methodology; I believe that the actual practice of good teachers of all colors typically incorporates a range of pedagogical orientations. Rather, I suggest that the differing perspectives on the debate over "skills" versus "process" approaches can lead to an understanding of the alienation and miscommunication, and thereby to an understanding of the "silenced dialogue."

In thinking through these issues, I have found what I believe to be a connecting and complex theme: what I have come to call "the culture of power." There are five aspects of power I would like to propose as given for this presentation:

1. Issues of power are enacted in classrooms.
2. There are codes or rules for participating in power; that is, there is a "culture of power."
3. The rules of the culture of power are a reflection of the rules of the culture of those who have power.
4. If you are not already a participant in the culture of power, being told explicitly the rules of that culture makes acquiring power easier.
5. Those with power are frequently least aware of—or least willing to acknowledge—its existence. Those with less power are often most aware of its existence.

The first three are by now basic tenets in the literature of the sociology of education, but the last two have seldom been addressed. The following discussion will explicate these aspects of power and their relevance to the schism between liberal educational movements and that of non-White, non-middle-class teachers and communities.[1]

1. *Issues of power are enacted in classrooms.*

These issues include: the power of the teacher over the students; the power of the publishers of textbooks and of the developers of the curriculum to determine the view of the world presented; the power of the state in enforcing compulsory schooling; and the power of an individual or group to determine another's intelligence or "normalcy." Finally, if schooling prepares people for jobs, and the kind of job a person has determines her or his economic status and, therefore, power, then schooling is intimately related to that power.

2. *There are codes or rules for participating in power; that is, there is a "culture of power."*

The codes or rules I'm speaking of relate to linguistic forms, communicative strategies, and presentation of self; that is, ways of talking, ways of writing, ways of dressing, and ways of interacting.

3. *The rules of the culture of power are a reflection of the rules of the culture of those who have power.*

This means that success in institutions—schools, workplaces, and so on—is predicated upon acquisition of the culture of those who are in power. Children from middle-class homes tend to do better in school than those from non-middle-class homes because the culture of the school is based on the culture of the upper and middle classes—of those in power. The upper and middle classes send their children to school with all the accoutrements of the culture of power; children from other kinds of families operate within perfectly wonderful and viable cultures but not cultures that carry the codes or rules of power.

4. *If you are not already a participant in the culture of power, being told explicitly the rules of that culture makes acquiring power easier.*

In my work within and between diverse cultures, I have come to conclude that members of any culture transmit information implicitly to co-members. However, when implicit codes are attempted across cultures, communication frequently breaks down. Each cultural group is left saying, "Why don't those people say what they mean?" as well as, "What's wrong with them, why don't they understand?"

Anyone who has had to enter new cultures, especially to accomplish a specific task, will know of what I speak. When I lived in several Papua New Guinea villages for extended periods to collect data, and when I go to Alaskan villages for work with Alaskan Native communities, I have found it unquestionably easier—psychologically and pragmatically—when some kind soul has directly informed me about such matters as appropriate dress, interactional styles, embedded meanings, and taboo words or actions. I contend that it is much the same for anyone seeking to learn the rules of the culture of power. Unless one has the leisure of a lifetime of "immersion" to learn them, explicit presentation makes learning immeasurably easier.

And now, to the fifth and last premise:

5. *Those with power are frequently least aware of—or least willing to acknowledge—its existence. Those with less power are often most aware of its existence.*

For many who consider themselves members of liberal or radical camps, acknowledging personal power and admitting participation in the culture of power is distinctly uncomfortable. On the other hand, those who are less powerful in any situation are most likely to recognize the power variable most acutely. My guess is that the White colleagues and instructors of those previously quoted did not perceive themselves to have power over the non-White speakers. However, either by virtue of their position, their numbers, or their access to that particular code of power of calling upon research to validate one's position, the White educators had the authority to establish what was to be considered "truth" regardless of the opinions of the people of color, and the latter were well aware of that fact.

A related phenomenon is that liberals (and here I am using the term "liberal" to refer to those whose beliefs include striving for a society based upon maximum individual freedom and autonomy) seem to act under the assumption that to make any rules or expectations explicit is to act against liberal principles, to limit the freedom and autonomy of those subjected to the explicitness.

I thank Fred Erickson for a comment that led me to look again at a tape by John Gumperz[2] on cultural dissonance in cross-cultural interactions. One of the episodes showed an East Indian interviewing for a job with an all-White committee.

The interview was a complete failure, even though several of the interviewers appeared to really want to help the applicant. As the interview rolled steadily downhill, these "helpers" became more and more indirect in their questioning, which exacerbated the problems the applicant had in performing appropriately. Operating from a different cultural perspective, he got fewer and fewer clear clues as to what was expected of him, which ultimately resulted in his failure to secure the position.

I contend that as the applicant showed less and less aptitude for handling the interview, the power differential became ever more evident to the interviewers. The "helpful" interviewers, unwilling to acknowledge themselves as having power over the applicant, became more and more uncomfortable. Their indirectness was an attempt to lessen the power differential and their discomfort by lessening the power-revealing explicitness of their questions and comments.

When acknowledging and expressing power, one tends towards explicitness (as in yelling to your 10-year-old, "Turn that radio down!"). When de-emphasizing power, there is a move toward indirect communication. Therefore, in the interview setting, those who sought to help, to express their egalitarianism with the East Indian applicant, became more and more indirect—and less and less helpful—in their questions and comments.

In literacy instruction, explicitness might be equated with direct instruction. Perhaps the ultimate expression of explicitness and direct instruction in the primary classroom is Distar. This reading program is based on a behaviorist model in which reading is taught through the direct instruction of phonics generalizations and blending. The teacher's role is to maintain the full attention of the group by continuous questioning, eye contact, finger snaps, hand claps, and other gestures, and by eliciting choral responses and initiating some sort of award system.

When the program was introduced, it arrived with a flurry of research data that "proved" that all children—even those who were "culturally deprived"—could learn to read using this method. Soon there was a strong response, first from academics and later from many classroom teachers, stating that the program was terrible. What I find particularly interesting, however, is that the primary issue of the conflict over Distar has not been over its instructional efficacy—usually the students did learn to read—but the expression of explicit power in the classroom. The liberal educators opposed the methods—the direct instruction, the explicit control exhibited by the teacher. As a matter of fact, it was not unusual (even now) to hear of the program spoken of as "fascist."

I am not an advocate of Distar, but I will return to some of the issues that the program—and direct instruction in general—raises in understanding the differences between progressive White educators and educators of color.

To explore those differences, I would like to present several statements typical of those made with the best of intentions by middle-class liberal educators. To the surprise of the speakers, it is not unusual for such content to be met by vocal opposition or stony silence from people of color. My attempt here is to examine the underlying assumptions of both camps.

"I want the same thing for everyone else's children as I want for mine."

To provide schooling for everyone's children that reflects liberal, middle-class values and aspirations is to ensure the maintenance of the status quo, to ensure that power, the culture of power, remains in the hands of those who already have it. Some children come to school with more accoutrements of the culture of power already in place—"cultural capital," as some critical theorists refer to it (for example, Apple, 1979)—some with less. Many liberal educators hold that the primary goal for education is for children to become autonomous, to develop fully who they are in the classroom setting without having arbitrary, outside standards forced upon them. This is a very reasonable goal for people whose children are already participants in the culture of power and who have already internalized its codes.

But parents who don't function within that culture often want something else. It's not that they disagree with the former aim, it's just that they want something more. They want to ensure that the school provides their children with discourse patterns, interactional styles, and spoken and written language codes that will allow them success in the larger society.

It was the lack of attention to this concern that created such a negative outcry in the Black community when well-intentioned White liberal educators introduced "dialect readers." These were seen as a plot to prevent the schools from teaching the linguistic aspects of the culture of power, thus dooming Black children to a permanent outsider caste. As one parent demanded, "My kids know how to be Black—you all teach them how to be successful in the White man's world."

Several Black teachers have said to me recently that as much as they'd like to believe otherwise, they cannot help but conclude that many of the "progressive" educational strategies imposed by liberals upon Black and poor children could only be based on a desire to ensure that the liberals' children get sole access to the dwindling pool of American jobs. Some have added that the liberal educators believe themselves to be operating with good intentions, but that these good intentions are only conscious delusions about their unconscious true motives. One of Black anthropologist John Gwaltney's (1980) informants reflects this perspective with her tongue-in-cheek observation that the biggest difference between Black folks and White folks is that Black folks *know* when they're lying!

Let me try to clarify how this might work in literacy instruction. A few years ago I worked on an analysis of two popular reading programs, Distar and a progressive program that focused on higher-level critical thinking skills. In one of the first lessons of the progressive program, the children are introduced to the names of the letter *m* and *e*. In the same lesson they are then taught the sound made by each of the letters, how to write each of the letters, and that when the two are blended together they produce the word *me*.

As an experienced first-grade teacher, I am convinced that a child needs to be familiar with a significant number of these concepts to be able to assimilate so much new knowledge in one sitting. By contrast, Distar presents the same information in about forty lessons.

I would not argue for the pace of the Distar lessons; such a slow pace would only bore most kids—but what happened in the other lesson is that it merely provided an opportunity for those who already knew the content to exhibit that they knew it, or at most perhaps to build one new concept onto what was already known. This meant that the child who did not come to school already primed with what was to be presented would be labeled as needing "remedial" instruction from day one; indeed, this determination would be made before he or she was ever taught. In fact, Distar was "successful" because it actually *taught* new information to children who had not already acquired it at home. Although the more progressive system was ideal for some children, for others it was a disaster.

I do not advocate a simplistic "basic skills" approach for children outside of the culture of power. It would be (and has been) tragic to operate as if these children were incapable of critical and higher-order thinking and reasoning. Rather, I suggest that schools must provide these children the content that other families from a different cultural orientation provide at home. This does not mean separating children according to family background, but instead, ensuring that each classroom incorporate strategies appropriate for all the children in its confines.

And I do not advocate that it is the school's job to attempt to change the homes of poor and non-White children to match the homes of those in the culture of power. That may indeed be a form of cultural genocide. I have frequently heard schools call poor parents "uncaring" when parents respond to the school's urging, that they change their home life in order to facilitate their children's learning, by saying, "But that's the school's job." What the school personnel fail to understand is that if the parents were members of the culture of power and lived by its rules and codes, then they would transmit those codes to their children. In fact, they transmit another culture that children must learn at home in order to survive in their communities.

"Child-centered, whole language, and process approaches are needed in order to allow a democratic state of free, autonomous, empowered adults, and because research has shown that children learn best through these methods."

People of color are, in general, skeptical of research as a determiner of our fates. Academic research has, after all, found us genetically inferior, culturally deprived, and verbally deficient. But beyond that general caveat, and despite my or others' personal preferences, there is little research data supporting the major tenets of process approaches over other forms of literacy instruction, and virtually no evidence that such approaches are more efficacious for children of color (Siddle, 1986).

Although the problem is not necessarily inherent in the method, in some instances adherents of process approaches to writing create situations in which students ultimately find themselves held accountable for knowing a set of rules about which no one has ever directly informed them. Teachers do students no service to suggest, even implicitly, that "product" is not important. In this country, students will be judged on their product regardless of the process they utilized to achieve it. And that product, based as it is on the specific codes of a particular culture, is more readily produced when the directives of how to produce it are made explicit.

If such explicitness is not provided to students, what it feels like to people who are old enough to judge is that there are secrets being kept, that time is being wasted, that the teacher is abdicating his or her duty to teach. A doctoral student in my acquaintance was assigned to a writing class to hone his writing skills. The student was placed in the section led by a White professor who utilized a process approach, consisting primarily of having the students write essays and then assemble into groups to edit each others' papers. That procedure infuriated this particular student. He had many angry encounters with the teacher about what she was doing. In his words:

> I didn't feel she was teaching us anything. She wanted us to correct each others' papers and we were there to learn from her. She didn't teach anything, absolutely nothing.
>
> Maybe they're trying to learn what Black folks knew all the time. We

> understand how to improvise, how to express ourselves creatively. When I'm in a classroom, I'm not looking for that, I'm looking for structure, the more formal language.
>
> Now my buddy was in [a] Black teacher's class. And that lady was very good. She went through and explained and defined each part of the structure. This [White] teacher didn't get along with that Black teacher. She said that she didn't agree with her methods. But *I* don't think that White teacher *had* any methods.

When I told this gentleman that what the teacher was doing was called a process method of teaching writing, his response was, "Well, at least now I know that she *thought* she was doing *something*. I thought she was just a fool who couldn't teach and didn't want to try."

This sense of being cheated can be so strong that the student may be completely turned off to the educational system. Amanda Branscombe, an accomplished White teacher, recently wrote a letter discussing her work with working-class Black and White students at a community college in Alabama. She had given these students my "Skills and Other Dilemmas" article (Delpit, 1986) to read and discuss, and wrote that her students really understood and identified with what I was saying. To quote her letter:

> One young man said that he had dropped out of high school because he failed the exit exam. He noted that he had then passed the GED without a problem after three weeks of prep. He said that his high school English teacher claimed to use a process approach, but what she really did was hide behind fancy words to give herself permission to do nothing in the classroom.

The students I have spoken of seem to be saying that the teacher has denied them access to herself as the source of knowledge necessary to learn the forms they need to succeed. Again, I tentatively attribute the problem to teachers' resistance to exhibiting power in the classroom. Somehow, to exhibit one's personal power as expert source is viewed as disempowering one's students.

Two qualifiers are necessary, however. The teacher cannot be the only expert in the classroom. To deny students their own expert knowledge *is* to disempower them. Amanda Branscombe, when she was working with Black high school students classified as "slow learners," had the students analyze RAP songs to discover their underlying patterns. The students became the experts in explaining to the teacher the rules for creating a new RAP song. The teacher then used the patterns the students identified as a base to begin an explanation of the structure of grammar, and then of Shakespeare's plays. Both student and teacher are expert at what they know best.

The second qualifier is that merely adopting direct instruction is not the answer. Actual writing for real audiences and real purposes is a vital element in helping students to understand that they have an important voice in their own learning processes. Siddle (1988) examines the results of various kinds of interventions in a primarily process-oriented writing class for Black students. Based on readers' blind assessments, she found that the intervention that produced the most positive changes in the students' writing was a "mini-lesson" consisting of direct instruction about some standard writing convention. But what produced the *second* highest number of positive changes was a subsequent student-centered conference with the teacher. (Peer conferencing in this group of Black students who were not members of the culture of power produced the least number of changes in students' writing. However, the classroom teacher maintained—and I concur—that such activities are necessary to introduce the elements of "real audience" into the task, along with more teacher-directed strategies.)

"It's really a shame but she (that Black teacher upstairs) seems to be so authoritarian, so focused on skills and so teacher directed. Those poor kids never seem to be allowed to really express their creativity. (And she even yells at them.)"

This statement directly concerns the display of power and authority in the classroom. One way to understand the difference in perspective between Black teachers and their progressive colleagues on this issue is to explore culturally influenced oral interactions.

In *Ways With Words*, Shirley Brice Heath (1983) quotes the verbal directives given by the middle-class "townspeople" teachers (p. 280):

- "Is this where the scissors belong?"
- "You want to do your best work today."

By contrast, many Black teachers are more likely to say:

- "Put those scissors on that shelf."
- "Put your name on the papers and make sure to get the right answer for each question."

Is one oral style more authoritarian than another?

Other researchers have identified differences in middle-class and working-class speech to children. Snow et al. (1976), for example, report that working-class mothers use more directives to their children than do middle- and upper-class parents. Middle-class parents are likely to give the directive to a child to take his bath as, "Isn't it time for your bath?" Even though the utterance is couched as a question, both child and adult understand it as a directive. The child may respond with "Aw Mom, can't I wait until . . .," but whether or not negotiation is attempted, both conversants understand the intent of the utterance.

By contrast, a Black mother, in whose house I was recently a guest, said to her eight-year-old son, "Boy, get your rusty behind in that bathtub." Now I happen to know that this woman loves her son as much as any mother, but she would never have posed the directive to her son to take a bath in the form of a question. Were she to ask, "Would you like to take your bath now?" she would not have been issuing a directive but offering a true alternative. Consequently, as Heath suggests, upon entering school the child from such a family may not understand the indirect statement of the teacher as a direct command. Both White and Black working-class children in the communities Heath studied "had difficulty interpreting these indirect requests for adherence to an unstated set of rules" (p. 280).

But those veiled commands are commands nonetheless, representing true power, and with true consequences for disobedience. If veiled commands are ignored, the child will be labeled a behavior problem and possibly officially classified as behavior disordered. In other words, the attempt by the teacher to reduce an exhibition of power by expressing herself in indirect terms may remove the very explicitness that the child needs to understand the rules of the new classroom culture.

A Black elementary school principal in Fairbanks, Alaska, reported to me that she has a lot of difficulty with Black children who are placed in some White teachers' classrooms. The teachers often send the children to the office for disobeying teacher directives. Their parents are frequently called in for conferences. The parents' response to the teacher is usually the same: "They do what I say; if you just *tell* them what to do, they'll do it. I tell them at home that they have to listen to what you say." And so, does not the power still exist? Its veiled nature only makes it more difficult for some children to respond appropriately, but that in no way mitigates its existence.

I don't mean to imply, however, that the only time the Black child disobeys the teacher is when he or she misunderstands the request for certain behavior. There are other factors that may produce such behavior. Black children expect an authority figure to act with authority. When the teacher instead acts as a "chum," the message sent is that this adult has no authority, and the children react accordingly. One reason this is so is that Black people often view issues of power and authority differently than people from mainstream middle-class backgrounds.[3] Many people of color expect authority to be earned by personal efforts and exhibited by personal characteristics. In other words, "the authoritative person gets to be a teacher because she is authoritative." Some members of middle-class cultures, by contrast, expect one to achieve authority by the acquisition of an authoritative role. That is, "the teacher is the authority because she is the teacher."

In the first instance, because authority is earned, the teacher must consistently prove the characteristics that give her authority. These characteristics may vary across cultures, but in the Black community they tend to cluster around several abilities. The authoritative teacher can control the class through exhibition of personal power; establishes meaningful interpersonal relationships that garner student respect; exhibits a strong belief that all students can learn; establishes a standard of achievement and "pushes" the students to achieve that standard; and holds the attention of the students by incorporating interactional features of Black communicative style in his or her teaching.

By contrast, the teacher whose authority is vested in the role has many more options of behavior at her disposal. For instance, she does not need to express any sense of personal power because her authority does not come from anything she herself does or says. Hence, the power she actually holds may be veiled in such questions/commands as "Would you like to sit down now?" If the children in her class understand authority as she does, it is mutually agreed upon that they are to obey her no matter how indirect, soft-spoken, or unassuming she may be. Her indirectness and soft-spokenness may indeed be, as I suggested earlier, an attempt to reduce the implication of overt power in order to establish a more egalitarian and non-authoritarian classroom atmosphere.

If the children operate under another notion of authority, however, then there is trouble. The Black child may perceive the middle-class teacher as weak, ineffectual, and incapable of taking on the role of being the teacher; therefore, there is no need to follow her directives. In her dissertation, Michelle Foster (1987) quotes one young Black man describing such a teacher:

> She is boring, bo::ing.[4] She could do something creative. Instead she just stands there. She can't control the class, doesn't know how to control the class. She asked me what she was doing wrong. I told her she just stands there like she's meditating. I told her she could be meditating for all I know. She says that we're supposed to know what to do. I told her I don't know nothin'

> unless she tells me. She just can't control the class. I hope we don't have her next semester. (pp. 67–68)

But of course the teacher may not view the problem as residing in herself but in the student, and the child may once again become the behavior-disordered Black boy in special education.

What characteristics do Black students attribute to the good teacher? Again, Foster's dissertation provides a quotation that supports my experience with Black students. A young Black man is discussing a former teacher with a group of friends:

> We had fu::n in her class, but she was mean. I can remember she used to say, "Tell me what's in the story, Wayne." She pushed, she used to get on me and push me to know. She made us learn. We had to get in the books. There was this tall guy and he tried to take her on, but she was in charge of that class and she didn't let anyone run her. I still have this book we used in her class. It's a bunch of stories in it. I just read one on Coca-Cola again the other day. (p. 68)

To clarify, this student was *proud* of the teacher's "meanness," an attribute he seemed to describe as the ability to run the class and pushing and expecting students to learn. Now, does the liberal perspective of the negatively authoritarian Black teacher really hold up? I suggest that although all "explicit" Black teachers are not also good teachers, there are different attitudes in different cultural groups about which characteristics make for a good teacher. Thus, it is impossible to create a model for the good teacher without taking issues of culture and community context into account.

And now to the final comment I present for examination:

"Children have the right to their own language, their own culture. We must fight cultural hegemony and fight the system by insisting that children be allowed to express themselves in their own language style. It is not they, the children, who must change, but the schools. To push children to do anything else is repressive and reactionary."

A statement such as this originally inspired me to write the "Skills and Other Dilemmas" article. It was first written as a letter to a colleague in response to a situation that had developed in our department. I was teaching a senior-level teacher education course. Students were asked to prepare a written autobiographical document for the class that would also be shared with their placement school prior to their student teaching.

One student, a talented young Native American woman, submitted a paper in which the ideas were lost because of technical problems—from spelling to sentence structure to paragraph structure. Removing her name, I duplicated the paper for a discussion with some faculty members. I had hoped to initiate a discussion about what we could do to ensure that our students did not reach the senior level without getting assistance in technical writing skills when they needed them.

I was amazed at the response. Some faculty implied that the student should never have been allowed into the teacher education program. Others, some of the more progressive minded, suggested that I was attempting to function as gatekeeper by raising the issue and had internalized repressive and disempowering forces of the power elite to suggest that something was wrong with a Native American student just because she had another style of writing. With few exceptions, I found myself alone in arguing against both camps.

No, this student should not have been denied entry to the program. To deny her entry under the notion of upholding standards is to blame the victim for the crime. We cannot justifiably enlist exclusionary standards when the reason this student lacked the skills demanded was poor teaching at best and institutionalized racism at worst.

However, to bring this student into the program and pass her through without attending to obvious deficits in the codes needed for her to function effectively as a teacher is equally criminal—for though we may assuage our own consciences for not participating in victim blaming, she will surely be accused and convicted as soon as she leaves the university. As Native Alaskans were quick to tell me, and as I understood through my own experience in the Black community, not only would she not be hired as a teacher, but those who did not hire her would make the (false) assumption that the university was putting out only incompetent Natives and that they should stop looking seriously at any Native applicants. A White applicant who exhibits problems is an individual with problems. A person of color who exhibits problems immediately becomes a representative of her cultural group.

No, either stance is criminal. The answer is to *accept* students but also to take responsibility to *teach* them. I decided to talk to the student and found out she had recognized that she needed some assistance in the technical aspects of writing soon after she entered the university as a freshman. She had gone to various members of the education faculty and received the same two kinds of responses I met with four years later: faculty members told her either that she should not even attempt to be a teacher, or that it didn't matter and that she shouldn't worry about such trivial issues. In her desperation, she had found a helpful professor in the English Department, but he left the university when she was in her sophomore year.

We sat down together, worked out a plan for attending to specific areas of writing competence, and set up regular meetings. I stressed to her the need to use her own learning process as insight into how best to teach her future students those "skills" that her own schooling had failed to teach her. I gave her some explicit rules to follow in some areas; for others, we devised various kinds of journals that, along with readings about the structure of the language, allowed her to find her own insights into how the language worked. All that happened two years ago, and the young woman is now successfully teaching. What the experience led me to understand is that pretending that gatekeeping points don't exist is to ensure that many students will not pass through them.

Now you may have inferred that I believe that because there is a culture of power, everyone should learn the codes to participate in it, and that is how the world should be. Actually, nothing could be further from the truth. I believe in a diversity of style, and I believe the world will be diminished if cultural diversity is ever obliterated. Further, I believe strongly, as do my liberal colleagues, that each cultural group should have the right to maintain its own language style. When I speak, therefore, of the culture of power, I don't speak of how I wish things to be but of how they are.

I further believe that to act as if power does not exist is to ensure that the power status quo remains the same. To imply to children or adults (but of course the adults won't believe you anyway) that it doesn't matter how you talk or how you write is to ensure their ultimate failure. I prefer to be honest with my students. Tell them that their language and cultural style is unique and wonderful but that there is a political power game that is also being played, and if they want to be in on that game there are certain games that they too must play.

But don't think that I let the onus of change rest entirely with the students. I am also involved in political work both inside and outside of the educational system, and that political work demands that I place myself to influence as many gatekeeping points as possible. And it is there that I agitate for change—pushing gatekeepers to open their doors to a variety of styles and codes. What I'm saying, however, is that I do not believe that political change toward diversity can be effected from the bottom up, as do some of my colleagues. They seem to believe that if we accept and encourage diversity within classrooms of children, then diversity will automatically be accepted at gatekeeping points.

I believe that will never happen. What will happen is that the students who reach the gatekeeping points—like Amanda Branscombe's student who dropped out of high school because he failed his exit exam—will understand that they have been lied to and will react accordingly. No, I am certain that if we are truly to effect societal change, we cannot do so from the bottom up, but we must push and agitate from the top down. And in the meantime, we must take the responsibility to *teach*, to provide for students who do not already possess them, the additional codes of power.[5]

But I also do not believe that we should teach students to passively adopt an alternate code. They must be encouraged to understand the value of the code they already possess as well as to understand the power realities in this country. Otherwise they will be unable to work to change these realities. And how does one do that?

Martha Demientieff, a masterly Native Alaskan teacher of Athabaskan Indian students, tells me that her students, who live in a small, isolated, rural village of less than two hundred people, are not aware that there are different codes of English. She takes their writing and analyzes it for features of what has been referred to by Alaskan linguists as "Village English," and then covers half a bulletin board with words or phrases from the students' writing, which she labels "Our Heritage Language." On the other half of the bulletin board she puts the equivalent statements in "standard English," which she labels "Formal English."

She and the students spend a long time on the "Heritage English" section, savoring the words, discussing the nuances. She tells the students, "That's the way we say things. Doesn't it feel good? Isn't it the absolute best way of getting that idea across?" Then she turns to the other side of the board. She tells the students that there are people, not like those in their village, who judge others by the way they talk or write.

> We listen to the way people talk, not to judge them, but to tell what part of the river they come from. These other people are not like that. They think everybody needs to talk like them. Unlike us, they have a hard time hearing what people say if they don't talk exactly like them. Their way of talking and writing is called "Formal English."
>
> We have to feel a little sorry for them because they have only one way to talk. We're going to learn two ways to say things. Isn't that better? One way will be our Heritage way. The other will be Formal English. Then, when we go to get jobs, we'll be able to talk like those people who only know and can only really listen to one way. Maybe after we get the jobs we can help them to

> learn how it feels to have another language, like ours, that feels so good. We'll talk like them when we have to, but we'll always know our way is best.

Martha then does all sorts of activities with the notions of Formal and Heritage or informal English. She tells the students,

> In the village, everyone speaks informally most of the time unless there's a potlatch or something. You don't think about it, you don't worry about following any rules—it's sort of like how you eat food at a picnic—nobody pays attention to whether you use your fingers or a fork, and it feels *so* good. Now, Formal English is more like a formal dinner. There are rules to follow about where the knife and fork belong, about where people sit, about how you eat. That can be really nice, too, because it's nice to dress up sometimes.

The students then prepare a formal dinner in the class, for which they dress up and set a big table with fancy tablecloths, china, and silverware. They speak only Formal English at this meal. Then they prepare a picnic where only informal English is allowed.

She also contrasts the "wordy" academic way of saying things with the metaphoric style of Athabaskan. The students discuss how book language always uses more words, but in Heritage language, the shorter way of saying something is always better. Students then write papers in the academic way, discussing with Martha and with each other whether they believe they've said enough to sound like a book. Next, they take those papers and try to reduce the meaning to a few sentences. Finally, students further reduce the message to a "saying" brief enough to go on the front of a T-shirt, and the sayings are put on little paper T-shirts that the students cut out and hang throughout the room. Sometimes the students reduce other authors' wordy texts to their essential meanings as well.

The following transcript provides another example. It is from a conversation between a Black teacher and a Southern Black high school student named Joey, who is a speaker of Black English. The teacher believes it very important to discuss openly and honestly the issues of language diversity and power. She has begun the discussion by giving the student a children's book written in Black English to read.

Teacher: What do you think about that book?
Joey: I think it's nice.
Teacher: Why?
Joey: I don't know. It just told about a Black family, that's all.
Teacher: Was it difficult to read?
Joey: No.
Teacher: Was the text different from what you have seen in other books?
Joey: Yeah. The writing was.
Teacher: How?
Joey: It use more of a southern-like accent in this book.
Teacher: Uhm-hmm. Do you think that's good or bad?
Joey: Well, uh, I don't think it's good for people down this a way, cause that's the way they grow up talking anyway. They ought to get the right way to talk.
Teacher: Oh. So you think it's wrong to talk like that?
Joey: Well . . . [*Laughs*]

Teacher: Hard question, huh?
Joey: Uhm-hmm, that's a hard question. But I think they shouldn't make books like that.
Teacher: Why?
Joey: Because they not using the right way to talk and in school they take off for that and li'l chirren grow up talking like that and reading like that so they might think that's right and all the time they getting bad grades in school, talking like that and writing like that.
Teacher: Do you think they should be getting bad grades for talking like that?
Joey: [*Pauses, answers very slowly*] No . . . No.
Teacher: So you don't think that it matters whether you talk one way or another?
Joey: No, not long as you understood.
Teacher: Uhm-hmm. Well, that's a hard question for me to answer, too. It's, ah, that's a question that's come up in a lot of schools now as to whether they should correct children who speak the way we speak all the time. Cause when we're talking to each other we talk like that even though we might not talk like that when we get into other situations, and who's to say whether it's—
Joey: [*Interrupting*] Right or wrong.
Teacher: Yeah.
Joey: Maybe they ought to come up with another kind of . . . maybe Black English or something. A course in Black English. Maybe Black folks would be good in that cause people talk, I mean Black people talk like that, so . . . but I guess there's a right way and wrong way to talk, you know, not regarding what race. I don't know.
Teacher: But who decided what's right or wrong?
Joey: Well that's true . . . I guess White people did.
[*Laughter. End of tape.*]

Notice how throughout the conversation Joey's consciousness has been raised by thinking about codes of language. This teacher further advocates having students interview various personnel officers in actual workplaces about their attitudes toward divergent styles in oral and written language. Students begin to understand how arbitrary language standards are, but also how politically charged they are. They compare various pieces written in different styles, discuss the impact of different styles on the message by making translations and back translations across styles, and discuss the history, apparent purpose, and contextual appropriateness of each of the technical writing rules presented by their teacher. *And* they practice writing different forms to different audiences based on rules appropriate for each audience. Such a program not only "teaches" standard linguistic forms, but also explores aspects of power as exhibited through linguistic forms.

Tony Burgess, in a study of secondary writing in England by Britton, Burgess, Martin, McLeod, and Rosen (1975/1977), suggests that we should not teach "iron conventions . . . imposed without rationale or grounding in communicative intent," . . . but "critical and ultimately cultural awarenesses" (p. 54). Courtney Cazden (1987) calls for a two-pronged approach:

1. Continuous opportunities for writers to participate in some authentic bit of the unending conversation . . . thereby becoming part of a vital community of talkers and writers in a particular domain, and
2. Periodic, temporary focus on conventions of form, taught as cultural conventions expected in a particular community. (p. 20)

Just so that there is no confusion about what Cazden means by a focus on conventions of form, or about what I mean by "skills," let me stress that neither of us is speaking of page after page of "skill sheets" creating compound words or identifying nouns and adverbs, but rather about helping students gain a useful knowledge of the conventions of print while engaging in real and useful communicative activities. Kay Rowe Grubis, a junior high school teacher in a multicultural school, makes lists of certain technical rules for her eighth graders' review and then gives them papers from a third grade to "correct." The students not only have to correct other students' work, but also tell them why they have changed or questioned aspects of the writing.

A village teacher, Howard Cloud, teaches his high school students the conventions of formal letter writing and the formulation of careful questions in the context of issues surrounding the amendment of the Alaska Land Claims Settlement Act. Native Alaskan leaders hold differing views on this issue, critical to the future of local sovereignty and land rights. The students compose letters to leaders who reside in different areas of the state seeking their perspectives, set up audioconference calls for interview/debate sessions, and, finally, develop a videotape to present the differing views.

To summarize, I suggest that students must be *taught* the codes needed to participate fully in the mainstream of American life, not by being forced to attend to hollow, inane, decontextualized subskills, but rather within the context of meaningful communicative endeavors; that they must be allowed the resource of the teacher's expert knowledge, while being helped to acknowledge their own "expertness" as well; and that even while students are assisted in learning the culture of power, they must also be helped to learn about the arbitrariness of those codes and about the power relationships they represent.

I am also suggesting that appropriate education for poor children and children of color can only be devised in consultation with adults who share their culture. Black parents, teachers of color, and members of poor communities must be allowed to participate fully in the discussion of what kind of instruction is in their children's best interest. Good liberal intentions are not enough. In an insightful study entitled "Racism without Racists: Institutional Racism in Urban Schools," Massey, Scott, and Dornbusch (1975) found that under the pressures of teaching, and with all intentions of "being nice," teachers had essentially stopped attempting to teach Black children. In their words: "We have shown that oppression can arise out of warmth, friendliness, and concern. Paternalism and a lack of challenging standards are creating a distorted system of evaluation in the schools" (p. 10). Educators must open themselves to, and allow themselves to be affected by, these alternative voices.

In conclusion, I am proposing a resolution for the skills/process debate. In short, the debate is fallacious; the dichotomy is false. The issue is really an illusion created initially not by teachers but by academics whose world view demands the creation of categorical divisions—not for the purpose of better teaching, but for the goal of easier analysis. As I have been reminded by many teachers since the publication of my article, those who are most skillful at educating Black and poor children do not allow themselves to be placed in "skills" or "process" boxes. They understand the need for both approaches, the need to help students to establish their own voices, but to coach those voices to produce notes that will be heard clearly in the larger society.

The dilemma is not really in the debate over instructional methodology, but rather in communicating across cultures and in addressing the more fundamental issue of power, of whose voice gets to be heard in determining what is best for poor children and children of color. Will Black teachers and parents continue to be silenced by the very forces that claim to "give voice" to our children? Such an outcome would be tragic, for both groups truly have something to say to one another. As a result of careful listening to alternative points of view, I have myself come to a viable synthesis of perspectives. But both sides do need to be able to listen, and I contend that it is those with the most power, those in the majority, who must take the greater responsibility for initiating the process.

To do so takes a very special kind of listening, listening that requires not only open eyes and ears, but open hearts and minds. We do not really see through our eyes or hear through our ears, but through our beliefs. To put our beliefs on hold is to cease to exist as ourselves for a moment—and that is not easy. It is painful as well, because it means turning yourself inside out, giving up your own sense of who you are, and being willing to see yourself in the unflattering light of another's angry gaze. It is not easy, but it is the only way to learn what it might feel like to be someone else and the only way to start the dialogue.

There are several guidelines. We must keep the perspective that people are experts on their own lives. There are certainly aspects of the outside world of which they may not be aware, but they can be the only authentic chroniclers of their own experience. We must not be too quick to deny their interpretations, or accuse them of "false consciousness." We must believe that people are rational beings, and therefore always act rationally. We may not understand their rationales, but that in no way militates against the existence of these rationales or reduces our responsibility to attempt to apprehend them. And finally, we must learn to be vulnerable enough to allow our world to turn upside down in order to allow the realities of others to edge themselves into our consciousness. In other words, we must become ethnographers in the true sense.

Teachers are in an ideal position to play this role, to attempt to get all of the issues on the table in order to initiate true dialogue. This can only be done, however, by seeking out those whose perspectives may differ most, by learning to give their words complete attention, by understanding one's own power, even if that power stems merely from being in the majority, by being unafraid to raise questions about discrimination and voicelessness with people of color, and to listen, no, to *hear* what they say. I suggest that the results of such interactions may be the most powerful and empowering coalescence yet seen in the educational realm—for *all* teachers and for *all* the students they teach.

Acknowledgement

I take full responsibility for all that appears herein; however, aside from those mentioned by name in this text, I would like to thank all of the educators and students around the country who have been so willing to contribute their perspectives to the formulation of these ideas, especially Susan Jones, Catherine Blunt, Dee Stickman, Sandra Gamble, Willard Taylor, Mickey Monteiro, Denise Burden, Evelyn Higbee, Joseph Delpit, Jr., Valerie Montoya, Richard Cohen, and Mary Denise Thompson.

Notes

1 Such a discussion, limited as it is by space constraints, must treat the intersection of class and race somewhat simplistically. For the sake of clarity, however, let me define a few terms: "Black" is used herein to refer to those who share some or all aspects of "core black culture" (Gwaltney, 1980, p. xxiii), that is, the mainstream of Black America—neither those who have entered the ranks of the bourgeoisie nor those who are participants in the disenfranchised underworld. "Middle-class" is used broadly to refer to the predominantly White American "mainstream." There are, of course, non-White people who also fit into this category; at issue is their cultural identification, not necessarily the color of their skin. (I must add that there are other non-White people, as well as poor White people, who have indicated to me that their perspectives are similar to those attributed herein to Black people.)

2 *Multicultural Britain: "Crosstalk,"* National Centre of Industrial Language Training, Commission for Racial Equality, London, England, John Twitchin, Producer.

3 I would like to thank Michelle Foster, who is presently planning a more in-depth treatment of the subject, for her astute clarification of the idea.

4 *Editor's note*: The colons [::] refer to elongated vowels.

5 Bernstein (1975) makes a similar point when he proposes that different educational frames cannot be successfully institutionalized in the lower levels of education until there are fundamental changes at the post-secondary levels.

References

Apple, M. W. (1979). *Ideology and curriculum*. Boston: Routledge & Kegan Paul.

Bernstein, B. (1975). Class and pedagogies: Visible and invisible. In B. Bernstein, *Class, codes, and control* (Vol. 3). Boston: Routledge & Kegan Paul.

Britton, J., Burgess, T., Martin, N., McLeod, A., & Rosen, H. (1975/1977). *The development of writing abilities*. London: Macmillan Education for the Schools Council, and Urbana, IL: National Council of Teachers of English.

Cazden, C. (1987, January). *The myth of autonomous text*. Paper presented at the Third International Conference on Thinking, Hawaii.

Delpit, L. D. (1986). Skills and other dilemmas of a progressive Black educator. *Harvard Educational Review, 56*, (4), 379–385.

Foster, M. (1987). *"It's cookin' now": An ethnographic study of the teaching style of a successful Black teacher in an urban community college*. Unpublished doctoral dissertation, Harvard University.

Gwaltney, J. (1980). *Drylongso*. New York: Vintage Books.

Heath, S. B. (1983). *Ways with words*. Cambridge: Cambridge University Press.

Massey, G. C., Scott, M. V., & Dornbusch, S. M. (1975). Racism without racists: Institutional racism in urban schools. *The Black Scholar, 7(3)*, 2–11.

Siddle, E. V. (1986). *A critical assessment of the natural process approach to teaching writing*. Unpublished qualifying paper, Harvard University.

Siddle, E. V. (1988). *The effect of intervention strategies on the revisions ninth graders make in a narrative essay*. Unpublished doctoral dissertation, Harvard University.

Snow, C. E., Arlman-Rup, A., Hassing, Y., Josbe, J., Joosten, J., & Vorster, J. (1976). Mother's speech in three social classes. *Journal of Psycholinguistic Research, 5*, 1–20.

CHAPTER 10

SOCIAL CONSTRUCTIVISM AND THE SCHOOL LITERACY LEARNING OF STUDENTS OF DIVERSE BACKGROUNDS (1998)

Kathryn H. Au

In this article, I address issues of the school literacy learning of students of diverse backgrounds. I use the phrase *students of diverse backgrounds* to refer to students in the United States who are usually from low-income families; of African American, Asian American, Latina/o, or Native American ancestry; and speakers of a home language other than standard American English. Differences between the school literacy achievement of these students and those of mainstream backgrounds have long been documented. The National Assessment of Educational Progress has compared the reading and writing achievement of students of diverse backgrounds to that of students of mainstream backgrounds for a period of over 20 years, providing what appear to be the most comprehensive results on this issue. These results indicate that, although the achievement gap appears to be narrowing, African American and Latina/o students at all three age levels tested are not learning to read and write as well as their European American peers (Mullis & Jenkins, 1990).

The gap between the school literacy achievement of students of diverse backgrounds and those of mainstream backgrounds is a cause of growing concern, especially given demographic trends. Urban school districts in particular are faced with the task of educating an increasing number of students of diverse cultural and linguistic backgrounds from families living in poverty (Pallas, Natriello, & McDill, 1989).

The main orientation to be explored here is that of social constructivism. From the perspective of social constructivism, it may be argued that both success and failure in literacy learning are the collaborative social accomplishments of school systems; communities, teachers, students, and families (e.g., McDermott & Gospodinoff, 1981). The thesis to be developed is that a social constructivist perspective on the literacy achievement of students of diverse backgrounds can be strengthened by moving from a mainstream orientation to an orientation toward diversity, giving greater consideration to issues of ethnicity, primary language, and social class (see also Reyes, 1991). Although issues of gender play an important role, a discussion of these issues and feminist perspectives is beyond the scope of this article.

To develop the argument for a diverse constructivist perspective, I discuss social constructivism and its application to research on school literacy learning. Then I outline what appear to be the major explanations, consistent with a social constructivist position, for the achievement gap between students of diverse backgrounds and those of mainstream backgrounds. Finally, I propose a conceptual framework for improving the school literacy learning of students of diverse backgrounds. In discussing this framework, I review concerns about the largely mainstream nature of the constructivist orientation as applied to issues of school literacy learning and instruction and highlight the implications of taking a diverse constructivist orientation toward these issues.

Social constructivism

At the heart of constructivism is a concern for lived experience, or the world as it is felt and understood by social actors (Schwandt, 1994). Constructivists reject the naïve realism of the positivists, the critical realism of the post-positivists, and the historical realism of the critical theorists, in favor of a relativism based on multiple mental constructions formulated by groups and individuals (Guba & Lincoln, 1994). There are many forms of constructivism, which appear to differ along several dimensions including the relative importance of human communities versus the individual learner in the construction of knowledge (Phillips, 1995).

Spivey (1997) presented the most detailed available treatment of constructivism and its influence on contemporary literacy research. She noted that, in constructivism, communication or discourse processes are compared to processes of building, and generative acts, such as those of interpreting or composing texts, tend to be emphasized. Themes in constructivist work include active engagement in processes of meaning-making, text comprehension as a window on these processes, and the varied nature of knowledge, especially knowledge developed as a consequence of membership in a given social group. In exploring different conceptions of constructivism, Spivey highlighted the issue of agency, and whether the focus is seen as the individual, small groups and dyads, or communities and societies.

Both sociology and psychology have undergone a transformation from views of constructivism centered on the personal, subjective nature of knowledge construction to views centered on its social, intersubjective nature (Mehan, 1981). These newer views are generally called *social constructivism*. The social is seen to encompass a wide range of phenomena, from historical, political, and cultural trends to face-to-face interactions, reflecting group processes both explicit and implicit with intended and unintended consequences. In the case of literacy research, the social can include historical changes in definitions of literacy, functions and uses of literacy within communities, and the social construction of success and failure in learning to read in school, to name a few.

Social constructivists argue that the very terms by which people perceive and describe the world, including language, are social artifacts (Schwandt, 1994). Because reality is seen to be created through processes of social exchange, historically situated, social constructivists are interested in the collective generation of meaning among people. Social constructivism includes the idea that there is no objective basis for knowledge claims, because knowledge is always a human construction. The emphasis is on the process of knowledge construction by the social group and the intersubjectivity established through the interactions of the group.

Vygotsky (1987) is the theorist who appears to have had the greatest influence on literacy researchers working from a social constructivist perspective. Social, cultural, and historical factors all play a part in Vygotsky's theory of cognitive development. Vygotsky saw the focus of psychology as the study of consciousness or mind, and he wanted to discover how higher or "artificial" mental functions developed from the "natural" psychological functions that emerged through maturation. A higher mental function, such as literacy, is an aspect of human behavior, present in some form from humanity's beginnings, that has changed over time as a result of cumulative historical experience (Cole & Griffin, 1983). Vygotsky's view of consciousness included two subcomponents intellect and affect, which he regarded as inseparable (Wertsch, 1985). Social constructivist research on literacy includes attention to the motivational and emotional dimensions of literacy, as well as the cognitive and strategic ones.

Vygotsky's approach to learning was holistic, and he advocated the study of higher mental functions with all their complexity (Moll, 1990). He argued for research on units with all the basic characteristics of the whole and rejected methods based on the analysis of separate elements. Similarly, research on school literacy learning conducted from a social constructivist perspective assumes that students need to engage in authentic literacy activities, not activities contrived for practice.

Vygotsky believed that the internalization of higher mental functions involved the transfer from the interpsychological to the intrapsychological, that is, from socially supported to individually controlled performance. Perhaps the best known of Vygotsky's formulations is the *zone of proximal development*, by which he sought to explain the social origin of higher mental functions. He defined the zone as the "difference between the child's actual level of development and the level of performance that he achieves in collaboration with the adult" (Vygotsky, 1987, p. 209). Social constructivist research on literacy learning focuses on the role of teachers, peers, and family members in mediating learning, on the dynamics of classroom instruction, and on the organization of systems within which children learn or fail to learn (Moll, 1990).

Everyday and *scientific concepts* are differentiated in Vygotsky's (1987) theory. The child gains everyday (or spontaneous) concepts through daily life, whereas she learns scientific concepts through formal instruction and schooling. In Vygotsky's view, the two kinds of concepts are joined in the process of development, each contributing to the growth of the other. Research conducted from a social constructivist perspective addresses the manner in which school literacy learning activities can be restructured to allow students to acquire academic knowledge (scientific concepts) by building on the foundation of personal experience (everyday concepts). Or conversely, this research looks at how students may gain insights into their own lives through the application of academic knowledge.

Vygotsky argued that higher mental processes are always mediated by signs and tools or instruments. Wertsch (1990) pointed out that signs and tools, in Vygotsky's view, do not simply facilitate activity but shape and define it in fundamental ways. Obviously, language and writing systems are foremost among the cultural tools developed by and available to people in different societies. The forms of language and literacy within each culture have developed over time to carry the concepts that reflect the experience of that cultural group. Thus, the historical condition is joined to the cultural condition, and links among historical, cultural, and individual conditions are formed when children are learning to use language and literacy. In the next section, I draw on a social constructivist perspective and the ideas of Vygotsky in providing an overview of explanations for the literacy achievement gap.

Explanations for the achievement gap

From a social constructivist perspective, research should account for the literacy achievement gap in terms of the societal conditions that led to its creation and sustain it over time through students' daily interactions and experiences in school. As shown in Figure 10.1, five major explanations appear plausible from a social constructivist perspective. I arrived at this scheme of explanatory categories through a process that involved, first, identifying what appeared to be the major lines of educational research, consistent with a social constructivist viewpoint, that attempt to account for the achievement gap. Second, I drew on the explanatory categories proposed by other researchers (e.g., Jacob & Jordan, 1993; Strickland & Ascher, 1992).

The first explanatory category is that of *linguistic differences* and stems from the fact that many students of diverse backgrounds speak a home language other than standard American English (e.g., the home language of many Latina/o students is Spanish). Current theory and research in bilingual education, consistent with a social constructivist perspective, suggests that students' poor academic achievement generally is not due to their limited English proficiency. Rather, it is due to the exclusion or limited use of instruction in the home language in many school programs (Snow, 1990) or to the low status accorded the home language. Unlike mainstream students, students of diverse backgrounds are not encouraged to use their existing language skills as the basis for developing literacy in school, because these skills often are ignored or denigrated (Moll & Diaz, 1985). For example, Spanish-speaking students may be prevented from expressing in Spanish their thoughts about a story with an English text. Thus, linguistic differences are related to decreased opportunity to use existing language skills as the foundation for learning to read and write.

A second explanatory category is that of *cultural differences*. Proponents of this position attribute the lack of school success experienced by many students of diverse backgrounds to their preference for forms of interaction, language, and thought that conflict with the mainstream behaviors generally needed for success in school (Au & Mason, 1981; Philips, 1972). These preferences are not inborn but the result of socialization practices in the home and community, which in turn reflect cultural values. Because the school is a mainstream institution, instruction is carried out in ways following mainstream standards for behavior and reflecting mainstream cultural values. Students have difficulty learning in school because instruction does not follow their community's cultural values and standards for behavior. For example, Au and Mason (1981) found that Native Hawaiian

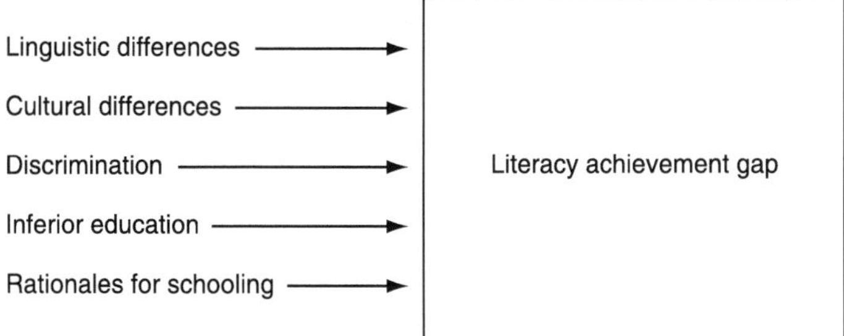

Figure 10.1 Explanations for the literacy achievement gap

students performed poorly in reading lessons, showing a considerable degree of inattentiveness, when teachers conducted these lessons following the rules for conventional classroom recitation. These students paid more attention to reading, discussed more text ideas, and made more logical inferences about the text when their reading lessons were conducted in a culturally responsive manner. In the culturally responsive lessons, the teacher allowed the students to follow rules for participation much like those in talk story, a common speech event in the Hawaiian community. In talk story-like reading lessons, unlike classroom recitation, the students could collaborate in producing responses and there was a high degree of overlapping speech.

A third explanatory category is that of *discrimination* (also called societal racism; Strickland & Ascher, 1992). From a social constructivist perspective, it can be argued that poverty and school failure are both manifestations of historical and systemic conditions rooted in discrimination. The argument is that American society and its system of schooling are structured to prevent equality of educational opportunity and outcome. For example, disproportionate numbers of students of diverse backgrounds are labeled as poor readers and placed in the lowest reading groups in the classroom, or sent from the classroom to receive remedial reading instruction. The instruction these students receive is qualitatively different from that of students placed in higher groups and tends to further hinder their learning to read. Shannon (1989) summarized research suggesting that low-group students receive the message that reading does not have to make sense, that accurate pronunciation is more important than comprehension, and that they need not be responsible for monitoring their own reading.

The fourth explanatory category suggests that differences in academic achievement are due to the *inferior education* received by students of diverse backgrounds (Strickland & Ascher, 1992). For example, urban schools with a high proportion of African American students frequently have deteriorating buildings, outdated textbooks, inexperienced teachers, and surroundings that expose students to violence. Material circumstances in these schools and in the conditions of students' lives and communities lead to savage inequalities in educational opportunity (Kozol, 1991). Schools with a high proportion of low-income students tend to devote less time to reading instruction and to rely on testing practices that limit students' opportunities to learn (Allington, 1991).

A fifth explanatory category highlights the importance of *rationales for schooling*. D'Amato (1987) noted that students who accept school and cooperate with teachers do so on the basis of rationales related to either the structural or situational implications of school. *Structural rationales* involve children's understanding of the significance of school performances to settings beyond the school, such as their relationship to employment and other life opportunities. Structural rationales allow students of mainstream backgrounds to justify their participation in school, because they usually have family histories illustrating a strong connection between schooling and life opportunities. However, structural rationales are usually not available to students of diverse backgrounds whose family histories do not show these same connections (Ogbu, 1981). *Situational rationales* are found in students' experiences with being in school, and whether or not that experience is rewarding and enjoyable. Situational rationales for accepting school are available to children when school structures and processes are compatible with the structures and processes of their peer groups (D'Amato, 1988). D'Amato argued that schools cannot rely on structural rationales but must make situational rationales available to students of diverse backgrounds as a way of motivating them to remain in school.

Considerable research supports all five of these explanations, a testimony to the complexity of the issues. Yet researchers have tended to focus on one explanatory category or another in their attempts to account for achievement differences. Few steps have been taken toward developing a comprehensive explanation of the achievement gap, by simultaneously considering the contributions of research associated with different explanatory categories.

Cummins' theoretical framework

A conceptual framework for improving the literacy achievement of students of diverse backgrounds should seek to bring together the various explanations described above and show their application to school literacy learning in particular. A starting point can be found in the work of Cummins (1986), who proposed a theoretical framework for empowering students of diverse backgrounds, as shown in Figure 10.2. His framework is consistent with a social constructivist perspective in its recognition of the links between events in the school and conditions in the larger society, the centrality of the teacher's role in mediating learning, the inseparability of affective or motivational factors and academic achievement, and the connections between schooled knowledge and personal experience. Cummins' framework has the virtue of incorporating all five explanations and, for this reason, provides an appropriate organizational structure for the diverse constructivist framework proposed here.

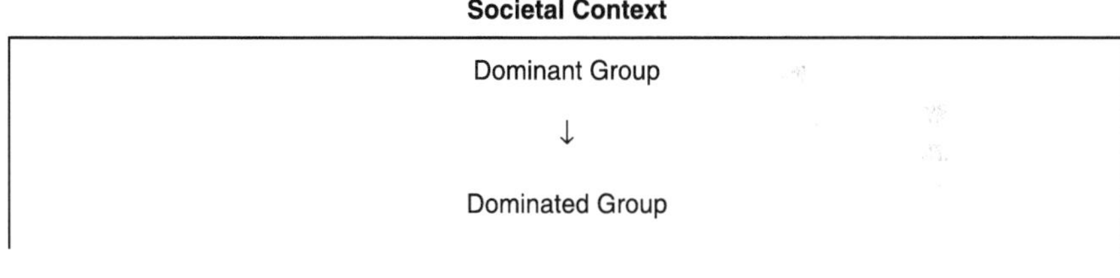

School Context

Educator Role Definitions			
Cultural/linguistic incorporation	Additive	—	Subtractive
Community participation	Collaborative	—	Exclusionary
Pedagogy	Reciprocal interaction oriented	—	Transmission oriented
Assessment	Advocacy oriented	—	Legitimization oriented
	↓		↓
	Empowered students	—	Disabled students

Figure 10.2 Cummins' Theoretical Framework for the Empowerment of Minority Students. From "Empowering Minority Students: A Framework for Intervention," by J. Cummins, 1986, Harvard Educational Review, 56, p. 24. Copyright 1986 by the President and Fellows of Harvard College. Adapted with permission.

The concept of empowerment is central to Cummins' framework. Cummins viewed empowerment as both a mediating construct and an outcome variable. Empowered students are confident in their own cultural identity, as well as knowledgeable of school structures and interactional patterns, and so can participate successfully in school learning activities. Cummins (1994) distinguished between coercive and collaborative relations of power. Coercive relations of power legitimate the subordinate status of students of diverse backgrounds on the assumption that there is a fixed amount of power, so that the sharing of power with other groups will necessarily decrease the status of the dominant group. In collaborative relations of power, no group is put above others, and power is not fixed in quantity, because it is assumed to be generated in the interactions among groups and individuals. The nature of relations of power, whether coercive or collaborative, within the larger society leads to the development of educational structures that shape the interactions among educators and students in schools. These interactions determine whether the zone of proximal development is constituted so as to help students think for themselves or accept the existing social order. Particular formulations of the zone thus contribute to students' empowerment or disempowerment.

The interactions between students and educators are mediated by the role definitions that educators assume. In Cummins' (1986) framework, these role definitions were seen to be influenced by three social contexts: (a) power relations among groups within the society as a whole, (b) relationships between schools and diverse communities, and (c) interactions between teachers and students in the classroom. Cummins urged an examination of dominant/subordinate group issues, as discussed by critical theorists, because of apparent parallels between the way students of diverse backgrounds are disabled by schools and the way their communities are disempowered by forces in the larger society. He argued that the academic success of students of diverse backgrounds depends on the extent to which patterns of interaction in the school reverse those in the larger society.

Cummins suggested that, if students of diverse backgrounds are to be empowered in school, educators must redefine their roles and assumptions in four key structural elements. For each element, the role definitions of educators are seen to lie along a continuum, with definitions at one end tending to disable students, and definitions at the other tending to empower them. The first element has to do with the incorporation of the language and culture of students of diverse backgrounds in the school program. The second element is concerned with the extent to which the involvement of community members is an integral part of the school's program. The third element refers to pedagogy that encourages students of diverse backgrounds to use language to construct their own knowledge. The fourth element, assessment, addresses the extent to which educators tend to label or disable students of diverse backgrounds, as opposed to serving as advocates for them.

Through a consideration of larger, societal influences on school, and through these four elements, Cummins provides a comprehensive framework for empowering students of diverse backgrounds through changes in the attitudes and actions of educators. Yet this framework is not without weaknesses. From the perspective of critical theory, this framework can be faulted for focusing more on the roles of educators than on issues of power in the larger society that constrain the actions of both educators and students. Another possible criticism is that Cummins' framework does not address the material circumstances with which teachers and students must contend, as illustrated in the work of Kozol (1991).

Proposed conceptual framework

The proposed framework for improving the school literacy learning of students of diverse backgrounds is shown in Figure 10.3. The seven elements in the framework reflect key areas of research on school literacy learning, especially that conducted by scholars from underrepresented groups. This research and the framework are consistent with the assumptions of social constructivism outlined in the first section. The framework attempts to capture the strengths of the five explanations for the literacy achievement gap and incorporates many of the features of Cummins' framework, although it focuses on school literacy learning in particular rather than student empowerment in general. Whereas Cummins' framework has four elements, the proposed framework requires seven in order to incorporate the major areas of literacy research I identified. The seven elements are (a) the goal of instruction, (b) the role of the home language, (c) instructional materials, (d) classroom management and interaction with students, (e) relationship to the community, (f) instructional methods, and (g) assessment.

One end of the continuum represents what I call a mainstream constructivist orientation and the other, a diverse constructivist orientation. I see differences between the mainstream and diverse constructivist orientations as a matter of emphasis and degree, rather than kind. I take the position that the social constructivist orientation can serve well to address issues of the school literacy learning of students of diverse backgrounds. However, an adequate treatment of these issues requires that discussions move beyond the boundaries usually evident in mainstream interpretations of social constructivism. In my opinion, a mainstream constructivist orientation does not take adequate account of differences in ethnicity, primary language, and social class that may affect students' school literacy learning.

A diverse constructivist orientation attempts to look at how schools devalue and could revalue the cultural capital (Bourdieu & Passeron, 1977) of students of diverse backgrounds. For this revaluing process to take place, educators can experiment with collaborative power relations that do not privilege mainstream knowledge claims over the knowledge claims of students of diverse backgrounds. A mainstream constructivist orientation recognizes that students' knowledge claims must be considered valid within students' own cultural contexts. A diverse constructivist orientation takes this line of reasoning one step further, by inquiring into the ways that knowledge claims, of educators and their students, are related to cultural identity and shaped by ethnicity, primary language, and social class. The experiences students bring to literacy events (e.g., the forms of their narratives) may depart significantly from educators' expectations. The revaluing process includes teachers' acceptance of students as cultural beings. It also encompasses the manner in which teachers receive and extend students' literacy efforts and encourage students to interact with peers and with texts.

A mainstream constructivist orientation tends to assume that similarities among students override differences related to ethnicity, primary language, and social class. In a mainstream constructivist orientation, the tendency is to propose general principles applicable to all students, although individual differences may be considered. This point of view fails to acknowledge that a given set of learning opportunities may benefit mainstream students while working to the detriment of students of diverse backgrounds within the same classroom. A diverse constructivist perspective assumes that general principles must be examined and refined so that their specific application to local contexts involving particular groups of

Societal Context

Dominant Group

↓

Subordinate Group

School Context

Educator Role Definitions

	Mainstream constructivist orientation	*Diverse constructivist orientation*
Goal of instruction	Literacy processes and attitudes	Literacy processes and attitudes, with an emphasis on ownership
Role of the home language	Additive approach; home language as vehicle for English literacy	Additive approach; biliteracy
Instructional materials	Literature plus other authentic materials	Emphasis on multicultural literature plus other authentic materials
Classroom management and interaction with students	Teacher organizes peer work groups as well as teacher-led lessons	Teacher conducts lessons and organizes peer work groups in culturally responsive manner
Relationship to the community	Classroom as a community; some parental involvement; projects such as family histories	Attention to community surrounding the school; greater parental involvement; instruction relates to community issues and funds of knowledge
Instructional methods	Authentic literacy activities; skills taught in contest; amount of explicit skill instruction may be minimal	Authentic literacy activities; skills taught in context; amount of explicit skill instruction may be considerable
Assessment	Formal and informal assessments, consistent with constructivist views of literacy	Formal and informal assessments, consistent with constructivist views of literacy, with attention to sources of bias
	↓	↓
	Students with moderate ownership and literacy achievement	Students with higher ownership and literacy achievement

Figure 10.3 Proposed conceptual framework

children can be understood. Investigations include the possible influences of ethnicity, primary language, and social class on students' responses to particular literacy learning activities and the reshaping of these activities to improve students' opportunities to learn.

Educators' recognition of the inequities possible in a given educational situation depends on an understanding of their own cultural identities as well as the cultural identities of their students. Researchers, too, should be aware of how their cultural identities shape their studies of literacy and literacy learning, in terms of research questions, methodologies, relationships with participants, and attention paid to the consequences of their work. Research conducted from a diverse constructivist orientation addresses issues of educators' and students' cultural identities and the specific ways in which ethnicity, primary language, and social class may interact in school settings effective and ineffective in bringing students of diverse backgrounds to high levels of literacy. Often, the goal of this research is not merely to describe but to improve the education of students of diverse backgrounds (Moll & Diaz, 1987).

In a mainstream constructivist orientation, it may be assumed that students primarily need to acquire the proficiency in literacy needed for self-expression and for success in the larger society. From a diverse constructivist orientation, it can be suggested that a concern for proficiency should not be allowed to override a concern for the transformative possibilities of literacy, for the individual and for the society. Garrison (1995) referred to the double bind: "the tension between the need of the students to appropriate historically entrenched tools that empower them as social actors and the simultaneous need of the culture to retool and recreate itself" (p. 729). Literacy is one such tool. With students of diverse backgrounds, conventional school literacy practices may serve as instruments of control and disempowerment, superseding and displacing the literacy practices of students' families and communities. The double bind in this instance is that current societal conditions and school practices make it difficult for students of diverse backgrounds to attain the high levels of literacy that would enable them to reflect on, critique, and address situations of inequity. Yet by virtue of their positioning with respect to ethnicity, language, and class, these students might represent the very viewpoints needed to reshape the society in significant ways.

To overcome the barriers of exclusion posed by conventional literacy instructional practices, educators must work with an expanded vision of literacy strategies and concepts in school, so that school definitions of literacy are transformed. In this way, educators create the possibility not only of helping students to become proficient in literacy but of enabling them to be empowered through literacy, to use literacy as a tool in bettering societal conditions.

The proposed framework follows that of Cummins in indicating that educator role definitions are embedded within and influenced by three social contexts: the larger society, including the power relations among groups; the school and the diverse communities it serves; and the classroom, including the interactions between teachers and students. The manner in which the framework incorporates the various explanations for the achievement gap is described below, as each of the seven elements is addressed in turn. The propositions are intended as ideas to be explored, not as final solutions. They grow not only from the research base but from my experience over a period of 25 years in classrooms with Native Hawaiian children, which includes research with teachers encompassing each of the propositions below (e.g., Au & Carroll, 1997).

Goal of instruction

Proposition. The school literacy learning of students of diverse backgrounds will be improved as educators establish students' ownership of literacy as the overarching goal of the language arts curriculum. This proposition builds on the notion of empowerment (Cummins, 1994). Ownership, in this case the notion that literacy is personally meaningful and viewed as useful for the individual's own purposes, is seen as both a mediating construct and an outcome variable, just as empowerment has both these roles in Cummins' framework.

Educators with a mainstream constructivist orientation generally define literacy in terms of students' attitudes, such as enjoyment of reading and writing, as well as in terms of cognitive processes, such as those for revising a piece of writing. However, often associated with the mainstream constructivist orientation is a reluctance to focus on particular outcomes or to give priority to any particular instructional goals. This reluctance appears to grow from the view that a focus on outcomes or goals is inconsistent with the holistic nature of literacy and literacy learning and may lead to a narrowing of instruction (e.g., Goodman, 1992).

My own view of this issue is that educators with a diverse constructivist orientation should give priority to students' ownership of literacy. Ownership is recognized in process approaches to be important for all students (Dudley-Marling & Searle, 1995). However, I have argued that it should be the major consideration or overarching goal in literacy curricula for students of diverse backgrounds (Au, 1997). This argument is grounded in D'Amato's (1987) research on the role of situational rationales discussed earlier. An explicit statement that ownership is the overaching goal has the advantage of reminding educators that literacy must be made personally meaningful to students of diverse backgrounds. Educators who wish to make literacy personally meaningful to students consistently draw on students' interests and experiences. By making literacy activities rewarding in an immediate sense, they provide students with the situational rationales for staying in school and engaging in literacy learning.

It should be noted that ownership in and of itself seems to be a necessary but not a sufficient condition for promoting the school literacy learning of students of diverse backgrounds. A study of an innovative constructivist literacy curriculum in classrooms with Hawaiian students indicated that most developed ownership of literacy, as operationally defined by the assessment measures (Au, 1994). However, high levels of ownership were not necessarily associated with high levels of reading comprehension and composition. In classrooms where teachers view ownership as the overarching goal, attention must still be paid to systematic instruction in the cognitive processes of reading and writing.

Role of the home language

Proposition. The school literacy learning of students of diverse backgrounds will improve as educators recognize the importance of students' home languages and come to see biliteracy as an attainable and desirable outcome. This proposition relates to the linguistic differences explanation and to Cummins' notion of cultural/linguistic incorporation.

Educators with a mainstream constructivist orientation usually take an additive approach. They believe that schools should add to and build on strengths in students' home languages, and they understand the value of literacy instruction in these languages. The assumption is that one only needs to learn to read and write once, and that this learning is transferable to another language (Weber, 1991).

Educators with a diverse constructivist orientation concur with these views and argue further that literacy in the home language should not be treated simply as a means for becoming literate in English. Rather, literacy in the home language should be valued in and of itself, just as literacy in a foreign language is valued at the college level. Unlike those with a mainstream orientation, educators with a diverse constructivist orientation often support biliteracy, the ability to read and write in two languages—the home language and English. Research suggests that the greater problem lies in the maintenance and development of skills in the home language rather than in students' learning of English (Pease-Alvarez & Hakuta, 1992). When biliteracy is the goal, students have the chance to use and extend literacy in the home language even after they have become literate in English.

Instructional materials

Proposition. The school literacy learning of students of diverse backgrounds will improve as educators use materials that present diverse cultures in an authentic manner, especially through the works of authors of diverse backgrounds. This element relates to the cultural differences and inferior education explanations and to the element of cultural/linguistic incorporation in Cummins' framework.

Educators with a mainstream constructivist orientation advocate the use of literature for reading instruction. They argue that the reading of literature provides students with richer, more interesting and motivating reading experiences. In a study conducted by Morrow (1992), students of diverse backgrounds who participated in a literature-based program outperformed control group students on a variety of literacy and language measures, including those for comprehension, story retelling, and story rewriting.

Educators with a diverse constructivist orientation share this view of the importance of literature, but extend it by arguing for the inclusion of multicultural literature. In particular, educators with a diverse constructivist orientation endorse the use of multicultural works, usually by authors of diverse backgrounds, that present cultures in an authentic manner (Harris, 1992). The use of literature that accurately depicts the experiences of diverse groups may improve the literacy achievement of students of diverse backgrounds by increasing their motivation to read (Spears-Bunton, 1990), their appreciation and understanding of their own language and cultural heritage (Jordan, 1988), and their valuing of their own life experience as a topic for writing. Lee (1991) found that African American students considered below-average readers could write insightful interpretations of the significance of the color purple in Alice Walker's (1982) novel.

When using multicultural literature, educators with a diverse constructivist orientation recognize that attention must be given not only to the selection of books but also to the curricular approach. Rasinski and Padak (1990) used Banks' (1989) hierarchy of approaches in multicultural educational to define different approaches for the use of multicultural literature, including the transformation and social action approaches. Teachers who follow these approaches use multicultural literature to promote critical analysis of social and historical issues and to empower students to work on the resolution of social problems.

Classroom management and interactions with students

Proposition. The school literacy learning of students of diverse backgrounds will improve as educators become culturally responsive in their management of classrooms and interactions with students. This element relates to the cultural differences explanation and the rationales for schooling explanation, as well as to the element of cultural/linguistic incorporation in Cummins' framework.

Educators with a mainstream constructivist orientation see genuine literacy activities, over which students can feel ownership, as central to classroom organization and management (Routman, 1991). These educators recognize that students may learn effectively not only in teacher-led lessons but through collaboration with peers. Discussions of literature may take the form of grand conversations (Eeds & Wells, 1989), and these conversations may have rules more like those for everyday talk than for classroom recitation.

Educators with a diverse constructivist orientation agree with the spirit of these innovations but point out that the teacher's approach to classroom management and interaction with students may need to be adjusted on the basis of differences in students' cultures. Delpit (1988) cited the expectation of African American students that the teacher act like an authority figure, displaying authority in a more direct and explicit manner than a mainstream teacher might. The authoritative teacher establishes a high standard of achievement, demands that students reach that standard, and holds students' attention by using features of Black communicative style (Foster, 1989). Considerable research has been conducted on culturally responsive instruction (for a review, see Au & Kawakami, 1994). This research suggests that students' opportunities to learn to read improve when teachers conduct lessons in a culturally responsive manner, consistent with community values and norms for interaction.

Relationship to the community

Proposition. The school literacy learning of students of diverse backgrounds will be improved as educators make stronger links to the community. This proposition builds on the idea of community participation in Cummins' framework. It relates to the discrimination explanation in pointing to the need to restructure power relations between the school and community, and to the cultural differences explanation in highlighting how the involvement of parents and other community members in the schools may increase the cultural and linguistic relevance of school situations for students of diverse backgrounds.

Educators with a mainstream constructivist orientation describe classrooms as communities of learners but do not often extend the concept of community beyond the school (Barrera, 1992). They are concerned about informing and educating parents about their children's activities in constructivist-oriented classrooms and ask parents to assist with such tasks as the publishing of the children's writing (Routman, 1991). Students write memoirs, and these projects frequently involve them in interactions with family members (Whitin, 1990).

Educators with a diverse constructivist orientation support all of these activities but go a step further. They point to the notion that literacy practices, as well as the resources available to promote literacy, differ across cultures, and that connections need to be made to the specific communities to which students belong. For example, Taylor and Dorsey-Gaines (1988) discovered a deep valuing of literacy in the homes of young African American children growing up in poverty, but the absence of a connection between the children's literacy experiences at home and at school. Students' school literacy learning would have been strengthened if connections to home literacy practices had been made. Moll (1992) described the "funds of knowledge" present among Mexican American households and how teachers motivated students to write about topics such as building and city planning, using parents and other community members as speakers.

Instructional methods

Proposition. The school literacy learning of students of diverse backgrounds will be improved as educators provide students with both authentic literacy activities and a considerable amount of instruction in the specific literacy skills needed for full participation in the culture of power. This proposition relates to the discrimination and inferior education explanations, and to the pedagogy element in Cummins' framework.

Although educators with a mainstream constructivist orientation provide students with authentic literacy activities, the amount of skill instruction in the context of these activities may vary considerably. Because the emphasis in constructivist approaches tends to be on process rather than product, educators with a mainstream constructivist orientation may see it as their role to act as facilitators of students' learning, responding to students' work but not transmitting knowledge (Reyes, 1991). Educators with this orientation may be reluctant to provide students with instruction on specific skills. However, a countervailing tendency is evident, as seen in Spiegel's (1992) work on the blending of whole language and systematic direct instruction.

Educators with a diverse constructivist perspective agree that skills should be taught within the context of authentic literacy activities. They appear to depart from the mainstream constructivist perspective in their views about the nature and degree of teacher mediation required to promote the literacy learning of students of diverse backgrounds. In a study of the literacy learning of bilingual Latina/o students, Reyes (1991) concluded that students' progress appeared to depend on a higher degree of teacher mediation and scaffolding that their process-oriented teacher felt she should provide. Delpit (1988) argued that students of diverse backgrounds are outsiders to the culture of power and deserve to gain a command of conventions and forms of discourse already known to insiders (those of mainstream backgrounds). She distinguished between what she called personal literacy and power-code literacy. Although both are important, it is the latter that is needed for success in the larger society.

Assessment

Proposition. The school literacy learning of students of diverse backgrounds will be improved when educators use forms of assessment that eliminate or reduce sources of bias (such as prior knowledge, language, and question type) and more accurately reflect students' literacy achievement. This proposition relates to the inferior education explanation and to the assessment element in Cummins' framework.

Educators with a mainstream constructivist perspective have contributed to the development of alternative forms of assessment, including portfolios and statewide tests such as those implemented in Michigan and Illinois. These new forms of assessment are consistent with current views of literacy in focusing on the process of meaning construction (Pearson & Valencia, 1987).

Educators with a diverse constructivist orientation support the development of alternatives to standardized testing. However, they recognize that innovative approaches to assessment also have the potential to work to the detriment of students of diverse backgrounds. For example, performance-based assessments tied to standards may not be sufficiently flexible to assess the literacy of Spanish-speaking children. If innovative assessments are high-stakes in nature, poor performance may carry the same negative consequences associated with standardized testing. These educators recognize that all forms of assessment, whether formal or informal, may incorporate elements of bias (García & Pearson, 1991). García (1991) compared the reading test performance of bilingual Latina/o students in the fifth and sixth grades with that of monolingual European American students in the same classrooms. She found that the tests underestimated the reading comprehension of the Latina/o students, because of their having less prior knowledge of the topics in passages and a tendency to apply strategies of literal interpretation to questions with textually implicit answers. Langer, Bartolome, Vasquez, and Lucas (1990) explored ways of tapping the text comprehension of bilingual fifth graders. One of their findings was that open-ended "envisionment" questions (e.g., What have you learned that is happening so far?) elicited more information from students than decontextualized probing questions (e.g., What order was used in the piece you just read?).

I do not propose a process-product relationship, in a positivist sense, between any particular proposition or element in the proposed framework and students' literacy achievement. All elements will operate in the context of schools and classrooms in which larger social, political, and economic forces, such as those explored by the critical theorists, play an important part. Educational change may well be prevented by material circumstances or stifled by policy decisions. Or change may take place with results that fail to be recognized, as in situations where standardized test scores are the only sanctioned outcomes. Furthermore, the complexity of school situations makes it impossible to isolate the possible effects of any single element or group of elements, and elements may interact in complex ways. Still, the overall implication is that the school literacy learning of students of diverse backgrounds will be stronger in schools and classrooms where elements of a diverse constructivist orientation are in place than in settings where they are not.

Conclusion

The thrust of this article has been to argue for the need to move from a mainstream to a diverse constructivist orientation in research on the literacy achievement gap between students of diverse backgrounds and students of mainstream backgrounds. Taking a diverse constructivist perspective, I presented a framework incorporating multiple explanations for the literacy achievement gap, while suggesting researchable actions that might be taken in schools. In concluding, I step away from the framework itself to reflect on sources of tension evident in current discussions of the literacy achievement of students of diverse backgrounds and certainly in this article as well.

A first source of tension arises from the ontological, epistemological, and methodological differences between the competing paradigms of constructivism and critical theory (Guba & Lincoln, 1994; for a discussion of epistemological issues and reading research, see Shannon, 1989). These tensions are evident in the very framing of the problem of the literacy achievement gap; what the gap signifies and what steps should be taken to address it. Without crossing from one paradigm to the other, it is difficult to link micro and macro levels of analyses, necessary to an understanding of how relations of power in the larger society play out in the way literacy instruction is organized and enacted in schools and classrooms. At the same time, attempts to incorporate critical notions into a constructivist framework, or the reverse, are likely to appear inconsistent when judged from the perspective of one paradigm or the other. I do not think these tensions can or should be resolved, but it seems desirable to have a principled importing of ideas across paradigms, as is taking place in educational anthropology.

A related source of tension arises because of differences in the political ideologies associated with liberalism and radicalism. No doubt, some will prefer a framework oriented toward more ambitious ends than those proposed here. As a researcher with liberal leanings, I am persuaded that all research is inherently political (Kincheloe & McLaren, 1994), but I do not see a research agenda and a political agenda as one and the same. As a school-oriented researcher, I have constantly been reminded of the difference between that which I see as a desired end and that increment of benefit to students and teachers which seems possible under the circumstances. Extending this view to the proposed framework, I incorporated elements that seemed researchable and achievable, at least in some school settings.

Still another source of tension resides in the differing perspectives of mainstream researchers and researchers from underrepresented groups (Willis, 1995). As I reviewed the literature, it became clear that many of the criticisms of the mainstream constructivist orientation had been formulated by researchers from underrepresented groups. This I see as no accident. These researchers may provide an insider's perspective on issues of literacy achievement with students of diverse backgrounds, through a deep understanding of issues of ethnicity, primary language, and social class, gained through personal as well as professional experience. In discussions of the literacy achievement gap, their work deserves more attention than it presently seems to receive, perhaps because of a tendency to downplay the value of studies conducted by these researchers of issues within their own communities (Frierson, 1990).

A final source of tension lies between the world of the academy and the world of the school and centers on whether researchers should keep a distance from, or be participants in, the situations being studied (Reason, 1994). Analyzing the problem is, of course, quite different from working on solutions in collaboration with educators in schools. In evaluating the contributions of critical theory to education, Giroux (1989) suggested that too much emphasis has been placed on the language of critique, too little on the language of possibility. Critical theorists, he noted, have been so concerned with the existing realities of schools that they have failed to address the question of what school should be. In a similar vein, Delpit (1991) and Ladson-Billings (1994) called for more research on situations in which students of diverse backgrounds are experiencing academic success. We are reminded, then, that the greater challenge is not in proposing frameworks but in bringing about changes in schools that will close the literacy achievement gap.

References

Allington, R. L. (1991). Children who find learning to read difficult: School responses to diversity. In E. H. Hiebert (Ed.), *Literacy for a diverse society: Perspectives, practices, and policies* (pp. 237–252). New York: Teachers College Press.

Au, K. H. (1994). Portfolio assessment: Experiences at the Kamehameha Elementary Education Program. In S. W. Valencia, E. H. Hiebert, & P. P. Afflerbach (Eds.), *Authentic reading assessment: Practices and possibilities* (pp. 103–126). Newark, DE: International Reading Association.

Au, K. H. (1997). Ownership, literacy achievement, and students of diverse cultural backgrounds. In J. T. Guthrie & A. Wigfield (Eds.), *Reading engagement: Motivating readers through integrated instruction* (pp. 168–182). Newark, DE: International Reading Association.

Au, K. H., & Carroll, J. H. (1997). Improving literacy achievement through a constructivist approach: The KEEP Demonstration Classroom Project. *Elementary School Journal, 97*, 203–221.

Au, K. H., & Kawakami, A. J. (1994). Cultural congruence in instruction. In E. R. Hollins, J. E. King, & W. Hayman (Eds.), *Teaching diverse populations: Formulating a knowledge base* (pp. 5–23). Albany, NY: State University of New York Press.

Au, K. H., & Mason, J. M. (1981). Social organizational factors in learning to read: The balance of rights hypothesis. *Reading Research Quarterly, 17*, 115–152.

Banks, J. A. (1989). Integrating the curriculum with ethnic content: Approaches and guidelines. In J. A. Banks & C. A. M. Banks (Eds.), *Multicultural education: Issues and perspectives* (pp. 189–207). Boston: Allyn & Bacon.

Barrera, R. B. (1992). The cultural gap in literature-based literacy instruction. *Education and Urban Society, 24*, 227–243.

Bourdieu, P., & Passeron, J. D. (1977). *Reproduction in education, society, and culture.* London: Sage.

Cole, M., & Griffin, P. (1983). A socio-historical approach to re-mediation. *The Quarterly Newsletter of the Laboratory of Comparative Human Cognition, 5* (4), 69–74.

Cummins, J. (1986). Empowering minority students: A framework for intervention. *Harvard Educational Review, 56*, 18–36.

Cummins, J. (1994). From coercive to collaborative relations of power in the teaching of literacy. In B. M. Ferdman, R. Weber, & A. G. Ramirez (Eds.), *Literacy across languages and cultures* (pp. 295–331). Albany, NY: State University of New York Press.

D'Amato, J. (1987). The belly of the beast: On cultural differences, castelike status, and the politics of school. *Anthropology and Education Quarterly, 18*, 357–361.

D'Amato, J. (1988). "Acting": Hawaiian children's resistance to teachers. *Elementary School Journal, 88*, 529–544.

Delpit, L. D. (1988). The silenced dialogue: Power and pedagogy in educating other people's children. *Harvard Educational Review, 58*, 280–298.

Delpit, L. D. (1991). A conversation with Lisa Delpit. *Language Arts, 68*, 541–547.

Dudley-Marling, C., & Searle, D. (Eds.), (1995). *Who owns learning: Questions of autonomy, choice, and control.* Portsmouth, NH: Heinemann.

Eeds, M., & Wells, D. (1989). Grand conversations: An exploration of meaning construction in literature study groups. *Research in the Teaching of English, 23*, 4–29.

Foster, M. (1989). "It's cookin' now": A performance analysis of the speech events of a Black teacher in an urban community college. *Language in Society, 18* (1), 1–29.

Frierson, H. T., Jr. (1990). The situation of Black educational researchers: Continuation of a crisis. *Educational Researcher, 19* (2), 12–17.

García, G. E. (1991). Factors influencing the English reading test performance of Spanish-speaking Hispanic children. *Reading Research Quarterly, 26*, 371–392.

García, G. E., & Pearson, P. D. (1991). The role of assessment in a diverse society. In E. H. Hiebert (Ed.), *Literacy for a diverse society: Perspectives, practices, and policies* (pp. 253–278). New York: Teachers College Press.

Garrison, J. (1995). Deweyan pragmatism and the epistemology of contemporary social constructivism. *American Educational Research Journal, 32*, 716–740.

Giroux, H. A. (1989). Schooling as a form of cultural politics: Toward a pedagogy of difference. In H.A. Giroux & P. McLaren (Eds.), *Critical pedagogy, the state, and cultural struggle* (pp. 125–151). Albany, NY: State University of New York Press.

Goodman, K. S. (1992). I didn't found whole language. *The Reading Teacher, 46*, 188–199.

Guba, E. G., & Lincoln, Y. S. (1994). Competing paradigms in qualitative research. In N. K. Denzin & Y. S. Lincoln (Eds.), *Handbook of qualitative research* (pp. 105–117). Thousand Oaks, CA: Sage.

Harris, V. J. (Ed.). (1992). *Teaching multicultural literature in grades K-8*. Norwood, MA: Christopher-Gordon.

Jacob, E., & Jordan, C. (1993). Understanding minority education: Framing the issues. In E. Jacob & C. Jordan (Eds.), *Minority education: Anthropological perspectives* (pp. 3–24). Norwood, NJ: Ablex.

Jordan, J. (1988). Nobody mean more to me than you and the future life of Willie Jordan. *Harvard Educational Review, 58*, 363–374.

Kincheloe, J. L., & McLaren, P. L. (1994). Rethinking critical theory and qualitative research. In N. K. Denzin & Y. S. Lincoln (Eds.), *Handbook of qualitative research* (pp. 138–157). Thousand Oaks, CA: Sage.

Kozol, J. (1991). *Savage inequalities: Children in America's schools*. New York: Crown.

Ladson-Billings, G. (1994). *The dreamkeepers: Successful teachers of African American children*. San Francisco: Jossey-Bass.

Langer, J. A., Bartolome, L., Vasquez, O., & Lucas, T. (1990). Meaning construction in school literacy tasks: A study of bilingual students. *American Educational Research Journal, 27*, 427–471.

Lee, C. D. (1991). Big picture talkers/words walking without masters: The instructional implications of ethnic voices for an expanded literacy. *Journal of Negro Education, 60*, 291–304.

McDermott, R. P., & Gospodinoff, K. (1981). Social contexts for ethnic borders and school failure. In H. T. Trueba, G. P. Guthrie, & K. H. Au (Eds.), *Culture and the bilingual classroom: Studies in classroom ethnography* (pp. 212–230). Rowley, MA: Newbury House.

Mehan, H. (1981). Social constructivism in psychology and sociology. *The Quarterly Newsletter of the Laboratory of Comparative Human Cognition, 3* (4), 71–77.

Moll, L. C. (1990). Introduction. In L. C. Moll (Ed.), *Vygotsky and education: Instructional implications and applications of sociohistorical psychology* (pp. 1–27). Cambridge, UK: Cambridge University Press.

Moll, L. C. (1992). Literacy research in community and classrooms: A sociocultural approach. In R. Beach, J. L. Green, M. L. Kamil, & T. Shanahan (Eds.), *Multidisciplinary perspectives on literacy research* (pp.211–244). Urbana, IL: National Conference on Research in English and National Council of Teachers of English.

Moll, L. C., & Diaz, S. (1985). Ethnographic pedagogy: Promoting effective bilingual instruction. In E. Garcia & R. V. Padilla (Eds.), *Advances in bilingual education research* (pp. 127–149). Tucson, AZ: University of Arizona Press.

Moll, L. C., & Diaz, S. (1987). Change as the goal of educational research. *Anthropology and Education Quarterly, 18*, 300–311.

Morrow, L. M. (1992). The impact of a literature-based program on literacy achievement, use of literature, and attitudes of children from minority backgrounds. *Reading Research Quarterly, 27*, 251–275.

Mullis, I. V. S., & Jenkins, L. B. (1990). *The reading report card, 1971–88: Trends from the nation's report card*. Princeton, NJ: National Assessment of Educational Progress, Educational Testing Service.

Ogbu, J.U. (1981). School ethnography:A multilevel approach. *Anthropology & Education Quarterly, 12*, 3–29.

Pallas, A. M., Natriello, G., & McDill, E. L. (1989). Changing nature of the disadvantaged population: Current dimensions and future trends. *Educational Researcher, 18* (5), 16–22.

Pearson, P. D., & Valencia, S. (1987). Assessment, accountability, and professional prerogative. In J.E. Readence & R.S. Baldwin (Eds.), *Research in literacy: Merging perspectives*. Thirty-sixth yearbook of the National Reading Conference (pp. 3–16). Rochester, NY: National Reading Conference.

Pease-Alvarez, L., & Hakuta, K. (1992). Enriching our views of bilingualism and bilingual education. *Educational Researcher, 21* (2), 4–6, 19.

Philips, S. (1972). Participant structures and communicative competence: Warm Springs children in community and classroom. In C. Cazden, V. John, & D. Hymes (Eds.), *Functions of language in the classroom*, New York: Teachers College Press.

Phillips, D. C. (1995). The good, the bad, and the ugly: The many faces of constructivism. *Educational Researcher, 24* (7), 5–12

Rasinski, T. V., & Padak, N. V. (1990). Multicultural learning through children's literature. *Language Arts, 67*, 576–580.

Reason, P. (1994). Three approaches to participative inquiry. In N. K. Denzin & Y. S. Lincoln (Eds.), *Handbook of qualitative research* (p. 324–339). Thousand Oaks, CA: Sage.

Reyes, M. de la Luz. (1991). A process approach to literacy instruction for Spanish-speaking students: In search of a best fit. In E. H. Hiebert (Ed.), *Literacy for a diverse society: Perspectives, practices, and policies* (pp. 157–171). New York: Teachers College Press.

Routman, R. (1991). *Invitations: Changing as teachers and learners K-12.* Portsmouth, NH: Heinemann.

Schwandt, T.A. (1994). Constructivist, interpretivist approaches to human inquiry. In N. K. Denzin & Y. S. Lincoln (Eds.), *Handbook of qualitative research* (pp. 118–137). Thousand Oaks, CA: Sage.

Shannon, P. (1989). *Broken promises: Reading instruction in twentieth-century America.* New York: Bergin & Garvey.

Snow, C. E. (1990). Rationales for native language instruction: Evidence from research. In A. M. Padilla, H. H. Fairchild, & C. M. Valadez (Eds.), *Bilingual education: Issues and strategies* (pp. 60–74). Newbury Park, CA: Sage.

Spears-Bunton, L. A. (1990). Welcome to my house: African American and European American students' responses to Virginia Hamilton's *House of Dies Drear. Journal of Negro Education, 59, 566–576.*

Spiegel, D. L. (1992). Blending whole language and systematic direct instruction. *The Reading Teacher, 46*, 38–44.

Spivey, N. N. (1997). *The constructivist metaphor: Reading, writing, and the making of meaning.* San Diego, CA: Academic Press.

Strickland, D. S., & Ascher, C. (1992). Low-income African American children and public schooling. In P. W. Jackson (Ed.), *Handbook of research on curriculum* (pp. 609–625). New York: Macmillan.

Taylor, D., & Dorsey-Gaines, C. (1988). *Growing up literate: Learning from inner-city families*. Portsmouth, NH: Heinemann.

Vygotsky, L. S. (1987). Thinking and speech. In R. W. Rieber & A. S. Carton (Eds.), *The collected works of L. S. Vygotsky: Vol. 1. Problems of general psychology* (pp. 37–285). New York: Plenum.

Walker, A. (1982). *The color purple*. New York: Harcourt Brace Jovanovich.

Weber, R. (1991). Linguistic diversity and reading in American society. In R. Barr, M. L. Kamil, P. Mosenthal, & P. D. Pearson (Eds.), *Handbook of reading research* (Vol. 2, pp. 97–119). New York: Longman.

Wertsch, J. V. (1985). *Vygotsky and the social formation of mind.* Cambridge, MA: Harvard University Press.

Wertsch, J. V. (1990). The voice of rationality in a sociocultural approach to mind. In L. C. Moll (Ed.), *Vygotsky and education: Instructional implications and applications of sociohistorical psychology* (pp. 111–126). Cambridge, UK: Cambridge University Press.

Whitin, P. E. (1990). Language learning through family history. In H. Mills & J. A. Clyde (Eds.), *Portraits of whole language classrooms: Learning for all ages* (pp. 229–241). Portsmouth, NH: Heinemann.

Willis, A. I. (1995). Reading the world of school literacy: Contextualizing the experience of a young African American male. *Harvard Educational Review, 65*, 30–49.

CHAPTER 11

OF PIGS AND WOLVES AT THE OK CORRAL (1996)

The emerging alternative paradigm and the construction of knowledge

Tonya Huber

As you begin this article, if it does not violate your spiritual beliefs, close your eyes and visualize the historical incident known as the shootout at the O.K. Corral. Imagine the physical features of the participants in the shootout and the sequence of events. Now, do the same for the chimney scene in the story of the "Three Little Pigs." Take these images with you into this reading.

In a recent box-office hit, *Tombstone* (1993), a true legend of the American West is retold in the ultimate Western showdown known most popularly as *Gunfight at the O.K. Corral*, the title of one of the earliest (1957) movie versions. On the heels of the popular Val Kilmer/Doc Holliday, Kurt Russell/Wyatt Earp dramatization followed the lengthier, reputedly more historical, version starring director Kevin Costner as Wyatt Earp, Gene Hackman as Earp's father, and an emaciated Dennis Quaid as Doc. Consideration of brief clips from these three films, along with scenes from two other early versions, John Ford's 1946 *My Darling Clementine* and the 1967 version *Hour of the Gun*, can catapult viewers into lively discussion about what **really** happened at the O.K. Corral on October 26, 1881. Did the Earp brothers take the law into their own hands or enforce it? Were the Clanton's and McLaury's a lawless gang or victims? Was Doc Holliday a dedicated, selfless friend, or a blood-thirsty, drunken killer?

That a 30-second gunfight could still create interest a century later merits discussion itself; but the topic most deserving our discussion focuses upon the difference in perspectives taken from the moment of the event through today—an issue of differing perspectives and, as such, a model for exploring the significance of multiple perspectives.

When we can clearly grasp multiple perspectives and differences in worldview, we are on our way to developing culturally responsible pedagogy. This awareness of perspectives, or paradigms, is necessary for an educator to be **responsive** to diversity and **responsible** for curriculum and instruction that reflects an understanding of diversity.

Understanding and shifting paradigms

A paradigm as defined by Maykut & Morehouse (1994) is "a set of overarching and interconnected assumptions about the nature of reality" (p. 4). To fully explore the concept of paradigms, shifting paradigms, and multiple perspectives, is a course unto itself, but at least a rudimentary understanding of the scope of the concept must be gained for those who would interact meaningfully in educational settings with others who operate from **different** paradigms.

Another way to explore paradigms that adds a deeper layer of culture to historical perspective, the aspect most clearly depicted in the O.K. Corral scenarios, is to explore a commonly accepted "reality" from other regional, lingual, cultural perspectives. I have found real enjoyment in applying this approach to the well-known story, "The Three Little Pigs." When I ask students in my teacher education courses or participants in staff development sessions to recall the story, most immediately offer that there were three pigs, they each built a different type of house, a big, bad wolf destroyed the first two houses, but the third house, built more carefully and with brick, stood the wolf's attack and saved the pigs. Participants in this experience are quick to recognize the vestiges of the Protestant work ethic at play and the moral intended for the young ears listening to the story—work hard, invest wisely, and you will be rewarded. Other perspectives on the plot suggest varied worldviews and paradigms. I like to call this exploration, with all due respect to Steinbeck,[1] "Of Pigs and Wolves."

While many of us recall a less brutal ending to the huffing and puffing, in at least one popular retelling, we read:

> Just as the wolf was coming down the chimney, the little pig took the cover off the pot, and in fell the wolf. The little pig quickly put on the cover again, boiled up the wolf, and ate him for supper. (Galdone, 1970)

The justification, implicitly, is that since the wolf has already eaten the first two little pigs, he deserves to be eaten—an application of the "eye for an eye" retribution theory.

In Milliken's *3 Piggy Opera* by Carol Kaplan and Sandi Becker (1987), the angry wolf sneaks down the chimney, burns his tail, and runs away, never to bother the pigs again—a "friendlier" plot climax, more developmentally appropriate for young children than the murder and killing involved in other versions.

Jon Scieszka turns the tale inside out with the wolf's version of the story in *The True Story of the 3 Little Pigs* (1989). The first two pigs are accidentally killed when the sick wolf sneezes and blows their houses down, and believing in "waste not, want not," eats the remains. The rude third pig, smarter than the two brothers, survives because the police arrive and take the wolf to the "pig pen." The play, with words and the "other perspective," is a delightful way to explore multiple perspectives. However, we have thus far in the comparison only reflected on difference in perspective. An awareness of cultural differences further enhances our ability to grasp the significance of paradigm and worldview.

In two of my favorite retellings of the story, the events are different. In the South-western adaptation of the story, told by Susan Lowell and illustrated by Jim Harris, the geographical setting is the Sonoran Desert, and the characters are representative of Native American and Mexican cultures: three little javelinas and a coyote who sneaks down the adobe roof stove pipe to find a lighted fire. The story concludes:

> The three little javelinas lived happily ever after in the adobe house. And if you ever hear Coyote's voice, way out in the desert at night . . . Well, you know what he's remembering! (Lowell & Harris, 1992)

Similarly, David Vozar casts the story within another cultural setting when he retells the story in Black vernacular as a nursery rap:

> Paw over paw Wolfie climbs up the shack
> To slide down the chimney in a sneak swine attack.
> Halfway down clothes are soilin', and Wolfie's recoilin'.
> In the fireplace below, the pigs' soup is boilin'.
> He pops out the chimney, hits the ground with a **boink.**
> The pigs shout, "Yahoo!" but it sounds more like **oink.**
> —Vozar & Lewin, 1993

In both of these versions, the antagonist learns his lesson when two brothers and a sister stick together and protect each other. The implication is not only a different paradigm than the more familiar retribution version, but the cultural settings imbue the retellings with contexts that enlighten as they educate about people and places, cultures and regions.

The exploration of an historical event from more than 100 years ago and a child's fairy tale provide comfortable avenues for exploring the import of recognizing and respecting difference in learners. Maxine Greene (1993) suggests that **when the learners' stories converge with other stories, they will be compelled to reach beyond themselves**—to question, to search, and ultimately to bring about change. Greene further speculates on the need for schools to provide settings that encourage such exchanges:

> It is a matter of overcoming the silences, of creating schools that are **natural habitats of learning**, schools on the way to becoming the kinds of miniature communities that embody possibility. Only under such conditions can we avoid misreading children's styles and abilities; only in this manner can we come in touch with what the young hope for themselves, how they think about what they want to be. Attending to them in their difference, we may invent ways of moving them to devise their own existential projects as they begin to articulate their stories. (p. 12)

One way of incorporating **natural habitats of learning** may involve the incorporation of multiple perspectives, multicultural worldviews, multiple intelligences, and the construction of knowledge in quality learning experiences. I propose that educators and leaders of educators must become cognizant of their own stories, overcome the silence that separates us in our different perceptions of reality, and shift our paradigms to ever more culturally responsible levels.

Research paradigms and education

Recall that **paradigm**, as defined by Maykut & Morehouse (1994), "has come to mean a set of overarching and interconnected assumptions about the nature of reality" (p. 4). First introduced into the history and sociology of science by Thomas Kuhn (1962), the concept of paradigm can, and should, be applied to the research methods of other disciplines. When applied to the research in education, review of the professional literature supports the focus given to what has been called in science the **traditional method**, or the **traditional paradigm**. As with other fields, the field of education has been dominated by the traditional paradigm—a belief in "objective observation, quantifiable data and verifiable truths"

(Maykut & Morehouse, 1994, p. 7). Because of this perceived **domination**, the concept has also been termed the **dominant paradigm**.

In *Naturalistic Inquiry*, Yvonna Lincoln and Egon Guba (1985) challenged the traditional, or dominant, paradigm as the only or most appropriate way of doing research, offering instead an **emerging paradigm** based on qualitative research. Naturalistic inquiry and the exploration of sociocultural knowledge assist the learner/educator in beginning the dialogue on questions of **why** and **how** that have for so long gone unanswered by the traditional research model that more often provides numerical or positivist answers to the questions of **which** and **what**. Expanding upon the work of Lincoln and Guba in their work *Beginning Qualitative Research*, Maykut & Morehouse (1994) have called this new set of assumptions and/or postulates the **alternate paradigm**. The differences between the two paradigms affect both the general approach to research and particular practices within each research tradition.

The **dominant paradigm**, impacted by the positivist position on research, establishes complete intellectual control over experience in terms of precise rules (Polanyi, 1958). These precise rules need only be followed to negotiate the world. The implication for education, clearly, is that a set of rules, a set of answers, a teacher's edition exists and is the ultimate authority. Research on education, from this position, posits a hypothesis and its null, then sets about to disprove one and prove the other—a simplistic, dichotomous interpretation of the world, issues, and events that.

The **emerging paradigm**, impacted by the naturalistic, qualitative approach to research, perceives knowledge as a construction of the knower. The researcher, or the knower, cannot stand independently from that which is known. The qualitative researcher seeks patterns and themes that emerge from the data, just as the learner seeks patterns and themes to construct meaning. As Maykut and Morehouse (1994) explain: "If reality is multiple and constructed, it follows that the causal links will be mutual (that is, **constructed**) and that in terms of what an event of action means, the event is not unidirectional but multidirectional" (p. 11). The implication for education, clearly, is that the teacher/educator/facilitator constructs meaning **with** the learners. Research on education, from the alternate/emerging approach, can be characterized by a close examination of people's words, actions, and documents.

The significance of the emerging paradigm to the discussion of multicultural education is at least two-fold: (a) greater importance must be assigned to qualitative, anthro-ethnographic, case study research than has heretofore been given, particularly in understanding cultural and cross-cultural concepts and ultimately in unlocking the door to sociocultural knowledge; (b) the constructionist perspective of knowledge, a corollary of the emergent paradigm, must be developed to balance the traditional positivist position on peoples, nations, and their cultures that has ignored microculture voices, experiences, and histories.

The constructionist perspective is rooted in the notion that for humans knowing is a result of continual building and rebuilding (Garcia, 1994) and that knowledge is always acquired by an individual through his or her cognitive filter. (It is not the intent of this article to review the development of new historicism, ethnohistory, or constructionist theory.) The constructionist approach to education is founded on the recognition of the learners' language and culture, in the school, the home, and the community (Spindler, 1982). This interpretation of the learning process precludes the implicit curriculum of readymade materials that all students learn the same way, at the same time, on the same day, with the same strategy, through the same modality, in the same cultural style, with the same strengths. Rather, the tenets of anthro-ethnographic and constructionist perspectives respect individual difference while promoting understanding to achieve social, political, economic, and educational equity.

The impact of paradigms on teaching multicultural education

Conceptualization of the emergent paradigm provides a key to unlocking the door to education that is culturally responsible and equitable. More traditional, linear, positivist thinking is frustrated by a perspectival response that does not provide the objective yes/no, true/false, right/wrong dichotomous answer being sought. Students enter teacher education and, in many colleges, graduate from teacher education programs, without having their traditional paradigm perspective challenged.

In multicultural education courses, the very nature of the content challenges their mechanical, linear, positivist worldview. In fact, to even begin to comprehend qualitative research and the ethnography of schooling, the history of oral tradition cultures, and the literature of people of color and women, the student of culture must leave the world of numbers, hypotheses, and proofs to journey with a multiple-perspectives worldview that hears words and discovers and builds meaning anew. This constructionist perspective of the world separates the successful student of multicultural education from the student who is expecting to prove his answer right by matching it to the teacher's edition answer key. In the emergent paradigm, no such answer key to life exists.

Because the focus of multicultural education courses is on developing the knowledge base for culturally responsible pedagogy, such courses frustrate the student who enters class believing the content will teach how to "treat" black children, the "correct" way to interact with Hispanic children, "how to," "what," "when to" *ad nauseam*—all in simple true/false and matching pairs that will insure easy test grades. Student frustration stems, in part, from lacking a conceptual foundation to approach issues of diversity. This frustration may be compounded by the admonition that major parts of the knowledge base come from data bases that a positivist worldview does not acknowledge.

Recently in a graduate-level multicultural course, a student challenged data on second language acquisition. When he queried what research supported the interpretations, several case studies were offered as supporting documentation. He retorted: "I didn't think it was real research." It seems that before we can teach multicultural education and develop empathy for others' worldviews, we must first empower ourselves to understand the alternate emerging paradigm of research and constructivist theory of knowledge. Without this open-window structure, the parameters of the knowledge base bounce off the closed doors of the positivist mind. To paraphrase Gandhi, we need to allow the winds of other lands to blow through our house, but not be knocked off of our foundation by them. Thus it must be the multiculturalist who is to construct meaning from the complexity of multiple worldviews.

While most educational reform challenges have acknowledged that the restructuring agenda for the 21st century should focus on the increasing diversity of America's students, the traditional response "has always been to accommodate student diversity within a preexisting framework designed from a mainstream perspective with little or no regard for diversity" (Brown, 1992, p. 10). This has often translated into an "Indians[2] at Thanksgiving, Black History in February" approach to diversity, also referred to as the "foods, festivals, fashions and famous people" approach to multiculturalism. As we focus on the relationship of human diversity to the knowledge base for teaching and teacher education, the restructuring must go beyond surface culture issues to explore deep structure dilemmas inherit in diversity and cross-cultural understanding. Rather than a divisive and negative process, as its adversaries have called it, truly **multicultural** efforts recognise multiple perspectives and different strengths as a growth process for a country that is beginning to ask serious questions about where it has been and where it is going.

The melting pot theory is finally being debunked as an ideology that was never operative in American society, nor in the educational system that mirrored that society. Equally, women, differently-abled peoples, lesbian and gay individuals, and the elderly have been assuming more active, creative roles in the shaping of the American mosaic. A reclaiming of history and voice by misrepresented and disenfranchised peoples continues to reshape the American identity.

The point to be made is that we face a very different set of issues than any educational paradigm has encountered heretofore. What is needed is a culturally sensitive and responsible pedagogy for **all** students in American education. The issue is not a color-bound, nor a language-specific one. Culturally responsible pedagogy subsumes **all** diversities to insure sensitivity to and responsibility for all students as learners. Rather than a goal of assimilation to the present order, the main purpose of education becomes one of maximizing learning for every student and determining how each learner can best achieve his or her potential creating anew rather than reproducing the old. Based on this inclusive orientation, G. Pritchy Smith has identified "Parameters of the Knowledge Base for Culturally Responsible and Responsive Teacher Education"[3] (in press), as the framework for structuring content in multicultural education courses. Smith posits:

> Some educators argue that there is no knowledge base for culturally responsible/responsive teacher education, that is, that there is no solid body of theory and research literature. Saying that "there is no knowledge base" is more of a statement about the limitations of the speaker's knowledge base than it is a statement about the reality of the knowledge base, and usually means that the speaker's reading has been restricted to the mainstream, generic literature that undergirds most traditional education programs. (Smith, 1992)

Notes

1 A reference to Steinbeck's classic novel, *Of Mice and Men*.

2 The term "Native American" is preferred by the author to indicate aboriginal or native claim to the country known as America. To enunciate that "American" is a label denoting citizenship rather than ethnic heritage, the author has avoided hyphenated-Americans.

American Indian, often used synonymously, reflects a misnomer—the result of Columbus' mistaken belief that he had reached the shores of India. When citing other authors, original terminology has, of course, been maintained. The terms "Native American," "American Indian," "Native," and "Indian," therefore, are used interchangeably.

3 For a more complete review of the integration of the parameters in a teacher education program see Huber, T., Kline, F. M. Bakken, L., & Clark, F. L. (in press). From Traditional teacher education to culturally responsible pedagogy: Moving a graveyard. In King, Hayman, & Hollins (Eds.) *Meeting the challenge of cultural diversity in teacher preparation.*

References

Garcia, E. (1994). *Understanding and meeting the challenge of student cultural diversity.* Boston, MA: Houghton Mifflin Company.

Greene, M. (1993). The passions of pluralism: Multiculturalism and the expanding community. *Educational Researcher*, 22(1), 13–18.

Kuhn, T. (1962). *The structure of scientific revolutions*. Chicago, IL: University of Chicago Press.

Lincoln, Y.S., & Guba, E.G. (1985). *Naturalistic inquiry*. Beverly Hills, CA: Sage.

Maykut, P., & Morehouse, R. (1994). *Beginning qualitative research: A philosophic and practical guide*. London, United Kingdom: The Falmer Press.

Polanyi, M. (1958). *Personal knowledge: Toward a post-critical philosophy*. Chicago, IL: The University of Chicago Press.

Smith, G.P. (in press). Parameters of the knowledge base for culturally responsible and responsive teacher education.

Spindler, G. (1982). *Doing the ethnography of schooling: Educational anthropology in action*. Prospect Heights, IL: Waveland Press.

CHAPTER 12

EQUITY PEDAGOGY (1995)

An essential component of multicultural education

Cherry A. McGee Banks and James A. Banks

The widespread misconceptions about multicultural education have slowed its implementation and contributed to the contentious debate about its nature and purposes (D'Souza, 1991; Schlesinger, 1991). One of the most prevalent of these misconceptions is that the integration of content about diverse cultural, ethnic, and racial groups into the mainstream curriculum is both its essence and its totality. Thus the debate about multicultural education has focused primarily on content integration (e.g., the nature of the canon) and has largely ignored other important dimensions of multicultural education (Sleeter, 1995).

To be effectively implemented in schools, colleges, and universities, multicultural education must be broadly conceptualized and its various dimensions must be more carefully delineated. In previous publications, J.A. Banks (1993b, 1993c, 1994b) has conceptualized multicultural education as consisting of five dimensions: content integration, the knowledge construction process, prejudice reduction, an equity pedagogy, and an empowering school culture and social structure.[1]

In this article, we further explicate the concept of equity pedagogy, describe how it intersects with the other four dimensions, and clarify what it means for curriculum reform and classroom teaching and learning. We also describe the characteristics that are needed by teachers to actualize this dimension of multicultural education in the classroom.

Equity pedagogy: meaning and assumptions

We define equity pedagogy as teaching strategies and classroom environments that help students from diverse racial, ethnic, and cultural groups attain the knowledge, skills, and attitudes needed to function effectively within, and help create and perpetuate, a just, humane, and democratic society. This definition suggests that it is not sufficient to help students learn to read, write, and compute within the dominant canon without learning also to question its assumptions, paradigms, and hegemonic characteristics. Helping students become reflective and active citizens of a democratic society is at the essence of our conception of equity pedagogy.

Pedagogies that merely prepare students to fit into society and to experience social class mobility within existing structures—which are characterized by pernicious class divisions and racial, ethnic, and gender stratification—are not helpful in building a democratic and just society. An education for equity enables students not only to acquire basic skills but to use those skills to become effective agents for social change. We believe education within a pluralistic democratic society should help students to gain the content, attitudes, and skills needed to know reflectively, to care deeply, and to act thoughtfully (Banks, 1994a).

The implementation of strategies such as cooperative learning and culturally relevant instruction within the context of existing assumptions and structures will not result in equity pedagogy. Instead current assumptions about teaching, students, learning, and the nature of U.S. society must be interrogated and reconstructed. Equity pedagogy also requires the dismantling of existing school structures that foster inequality. It cannot occur within a social and political context embedded with racism, sexism, and inequality.

Equity pedagogy actively involves students in a process of knowledge construction and production. It challenges the idea of instruction as transmission of facts and the image of the teacher as a citadel of knowledge and students as passive recipients of knowledge. Equity pedagogy alters the traditional power relationship between teachers and students. Most importantly, it assumes an integral relationship between knowledge and reflective action. Equity pedagogy creates an environment in which students can acquire, interrogate, and produce knowledge and envision new possibilities for the use of that knowledge for societal change (Banks, 1994b).

Our perspectives on equity pedagogy are guided by these assumptions: (a) There is an identifiable body of knowledge, skills, and attitudes that constitute critical attributes of equity pedagogy; (b) critical attributes of equity pedagogy can be identified, taught, and learned; (c) competencies in equity pedagogy can be developed through formal instruction, reflection on life experiences, and opportunities to work with students and colleagues from diverse populations; (d) all teachers need to be able to competently implement equity pedagogy and related teaching strategies because all students benefit from them; (e) in-depth knowledge of an academic discipline, pedagogy, and their students' cultures are prerequisites for teachers to successfully implement equity pedagogy; (f) competency in equity pedagogy requires a process of reflection and growth; and (g) equity pedagogy cannot be implemented in isolation from the other four dimensions of multicultural education described above. It is interrelated in a complex way with the other dimensions (Banks, 1993c).

Characteristics of equity pedagogy

Equity pedagogy is a dynamic instructional process that not only focuses on the identification and use of effective instructional techniques and methods but also on the context in which they are used. Cooperative learning, for example, can be an effective instructional technique (Cohen, 1994; Slavin, 1983). However, when it is used without an awareness of contextual issues such as status differences among students, it can reinforce stereotypes and inequality in the classroom (Cohen & Roper, 1972).

Equity pedagogy challenges teachers to use teaching strategies that facilitate the learning process. Instead of focusing on the memorization of knowledge constructed by authorities, students in classrooms where equity pedagogy is used learn to generate knowledge and create new understandings (Banks, 1993a; Brooks & Brooks, 1993). Students make connections between the autobiographical experiences of knowers and the knowledge they create. In classrooms where knowledge construction takes place, teachers enable students to identify and interrogate the positionality of knowers and to construct their own interpretations of reality (Brooks & Brooks, 1993; Code, 1991; Tetreault, 1993).

During the knowledge construction process, students relate ideas and perspectives and make judgments and evaluations. Instead of looking for *the* single answer to a problem, students are encouraged to generate multiple solutions and perspectives. They also explore how problems arise and how they are related to other problems, issues, and concepts.

Like the other dimensions of multicultural education, equity pedagogy provides a basis for addressing critical aspects of schooling and for transforming curricula and schools. The discussion that follows relates equity pedagogy to two dimensions of multicultural education: content integration and an empowering school culture and social structure.

School culture and social structure

A serious examination of the culture and social structure of the school raises significant questions about institutional characteristics such as tracking and the power relationships between students and teachers, and between teachers and administrators. The school culture and social structure are powerful determinants of how students learn to perceive themselves. These factors influence the social interactions that take place between students and teachers and among students, both inside and outside the classroom.

Tracking and power relationships within a school are important components of its deep structure (Tye, 1987). The deep structure includes the bell schedule, the physical uniformity of classrooms, test scores, and various factors that allow teachers to maintain control in the classroom (Tye, 1987). Equity pedagogy challenges the deep structure of schools because its requirements for scheduling, arrangement of physical space, and control are frequently at odds with traditional instructional methods that reinforce the structure of schools.

If students are to be involved in the production of knowledge, they need class schedules that allow time for these activities. The 50-minute time slot usually does not allow students the time they need for reflection, content integration, and synthesis. Furthermore, students who are involved in producing knowledge may need to work in places other than the classroom. Teachers may not be able to exercise as much control over students who are working in other areas of the school building, such as the library, or at sites off campus.

These elements of the deep structure of schools are important components of the hidden curriculum. When teachers use equity pedagogy that challenges the deep structure of schools, important aspects of the hidden curriculum are often revealed. Becoming aware of the relationship between the school culture, the social structure, and the deep structure of schools can heighten the teacher's awareness of the power of the hidden curriculum, or what Jackson (1992) calls the "untaught lessons."

The hidden curriculum

School teaching and learning take place primarily in groups and through social interactions. Interactions between teachers and students and among students are important parts of the relationship between equity pedagogy and the hidden curriculum. Implementing equity pedagogy requires teachers to understand how students perceive social interactions with their teachers, what they learn from them, and the extent to which students perceive their teachers as caring persons. Equity pedagogy can help reveal the nature of the hidden curriculum by encouraging teachers to raise questions such as: Is this class meaningful for my students? Would my students like a different teacher? Why or why not? What gaps exist between what I am teaching and what my students are learning? If there are gaps, why? If not, why not?

Significant adult-student interactions often occur within the context of the hidden curriculum. The number of people available to work with students in the classroom is an important part of the hidden curriculum. Some classes—often differentiated by designations such as gifted and accelerated—have many parent and community volunteers available to provide classroom help and to implement enrichment programs. The adults in these classes are able to provide students with individualized instruction. This communicates the implicit message that the students are special and important. Teachers who work in schools in which some classes have multiple adult helpers and other classes have only one adult should realize that such factors can severely limit the effectiveness of culturally sensitive pedagogy and cooperative learning.

When used in isolation, instructional strategies such as cooperative learning and constructivist techniques cannot sufficiently deal with the problems embedded in the hidden curriculum. To transform pedagogy, the adults in schools must address the social-class, racial, and ethnic inequalities embedded in the differential levels of support given to different classes and schools. The construction of equity in schools as well as the implementation of culturally-sensitive teaching methods are necessary to actualize equity pedagogy in classrooms and schools.

The physical arrangement of space in a classroom is also a cogent factor in the hidden curriculum. It communicates implicit messages to students. When chairs in a classroom are lined up in straight rows facing the teacher, the implicit message is that all students are expected to participate in the same activities simultaneously and to learn in identical ways as directed by the teacher (Tye, 1987).

Learning centers, on the other hand, suggest that students can legitimately engage in different activities, that the students are the focus in the classroom, and that learning can be interesting and rewarding. Teachers who try to implement equity pedagogy without attending to factors such as the physical arrangement of space in the classroom and the control inherent in certain types of physical conditions will rarely experience success.

Students also learn from their peers, as they are actively engaged in interactions with other students throughout the school day. Peer relationships are an important part of the social context of the classroom, and teachers need to understand these interactions. They can become potent elements in the hidden curriculum. Implementing group work without making provisions for dealing with the status differences among students based on race, gender, and social class may result in marginalizing low-status-group students rather than providing opportunities for them to learn from their peers (Cohen, 1994; Cohen & Roper, 1972).

Students learn about themselves as they acquire academic knowledge. The academic self-concept of students is highly related to their general self-concept, their ability to perform academic work, and their ability to function competently among peers (Brookover, Beady, Flood, Schweitzer, & Wisenbaker, 1979). Equity pedagogy requires teachers to deal with the dynamics of peer interactions in classroom life. Students are not one-dimensional; therefore, equity pedagogy has to reflect the complexity of student interactions and relationships.

Content integration and assessment

Equity pedagogy is tightly intertwined with content integration. How an instructor teaches is informed and shaped by what is taught. Both equity pedagogy and curriculum influence the form and function of learning (Vygotsky, 1978). Equity pedagogy is most powerful when it is integrated with transformative curricula. Most mainstream curricula do not actualize the full power of equity pedagogy. They limit equity pedagogy to incremental strategies that are characterized by ideological constraints.

Required content, however, can be taught using a transformative pedagogy, as was done by a high school physics teacher in a Seattle suburban school. He transformed a unit on torques by asking the students to identify a bridge that had collapsed, investigate why it collapsed, and determine how the collapse of the bridge affected people in the community. Working in groups, the students designed bridges that could withstand designated wind speeds and weights. This unit provided opportunities for students to connect their study of torques to a real event, draw on the strengths of their peers by working in groups, and actively engage in constructing knowledge by translating the information they collected on bridges into new designs.

Transformative curricula provide a rich context for equity pedagogy because both transformative curricula and equity pedagogy promote knowledge construction and curriculum reform. Transformative curricula and equity pedagogy also assume that the cultures of students are valid, that effective teaching must reflect the lives and interests of students (Ladson-Billings, 1990), and that students must be provided opportunities to construct meaningful knowledge. In this sense, equity pedagogy is directly related to curriculum reform.

Information is increasing at an astronomical rate. What was once packaged in a one-volume text now requires two or more. Teachers are finding it increasingly difficult to cover all the information they are expected to include in the curriculum. Equity pedagogy provides a rationale and a process that can help teachers focus on the essence of the curriculum rather than on isolated and rapidly changing facts.

Students in the 21st century, unlike those in earlier times, will have to address complex issues that cannot be answered with discrete facts. To be effective, students must know where to get the information they need, how to formulate questions that will provide access to the appropriate information, how to evaluate the information from a cognitive as well as a value perspective, how to integrate it with other information, and how to make reflective decisions based on the best information they can construct. Equity pedagogy helps students to acquire these skills.

Equity pedagogy is student focused. It incorporates issues, concepts, principles, and problems that are real and meaningful to students. Teachers who embrace equity pedagogy assume that all students can learn. They work to develop student potential and to create a classroom environment that is encouraging and filled with opportunities for success.

Equity pedagogy has important implications for assessment. Educators who embrace it must interrogate traditional tests and letter grades. Assessment strategies based on the assumption that all students can learn provide opportunities for students to improve their performances. The teacher who embraces equity pedagogy frequently gives students detailed feedback on poorly prepared assignments and asks students to "revisit" their work. Written comments instead of letter grades provide opportunities for teachers to identify areas of competence as well as to suggest strategies for improvement and remediation.

Portfolio assessment also gives students an opportunity to demonstrate their growth over time, and for teachers to give students ongoing support and encouragement (Valencia, Hiebert, & Afflerbach, 1994). Students can use portfolios to document the complexity and individuality of their work and to reflect on their progress and areas that need improvement. Portfolios contribute to sound assessment decisions and to student development. They describe and provide materials that collectively suggest the scope and quality of a student's performance. Portfolios also provide the structure needed for teachers and students to better understand and make connections between teaching and learning.

Teacher characteristics

Teachers who successfully implement equity pedagogy draw upon a sophisticated knowledge base. They can enlist a broad range of pedagogical skills and have a keen understanding of their cultural experiences, values, and attitudes toward people who are culturally, racially, and ethnically different from themselves. The skills, knowledge, and attitudes necessary to successfully implement equity pedagogy are the result of study, practical experience, and reflective self-analysis.

Reflective self-analysis requires teachers to identify, examine, and reflect on their attitudes toward different ethnic, racial, gender, and social-class groups. Many teachers are unaware of the extent to which they embrace racist and sexist attitudes and behaviors that are institutionalized within society as well as how they benefit from these societal practices (King, 1992). Reflecting on their own life journeys—by writing their life stories—can be a powerful tool for helping teachers gain a better understanding of the ways in which institutionalized conceptions of race, class, and gender have influenced their personal lives.

Autobiographical accounts and episodes provide an opportunity for teachers to reflect on times in their lives when they were the "other" who experienced discrimination or a sense of isolation because of their race, class, gender, culture, or personal characteristics. Reflective self-analysis cannot be a one-time event. Multicultural awareness can result only from in-depth work on self. It requires the unraveling of myths that perpetuate social class, gender, and racial privilege (King, 1992; McIntosh, 1990) and a commitment to maintaining multicultural awareness and action.

Equity pedagogy cannot be implemented in a vacuum. It requires more than good will and good intentions. It requires multicultural, pedagogical, and subject area knowledge (Banks, 1991, 1994a, 1994b; Banks & Banks, 1995). Our discussion focuses on multicultural knowledge. However, teachers will not be able to use it effectively without a strong background in their subject area and a sophisticated understanding of pedagogy.

Multicultural knowledge includes key concepts in multicultural education such as culture, immigration, racism, sexism, cultural assimilation, structural assimilation, ethnic groups, stereotypes, prejudice, and institutional racism (Banks, 1991, 1994a). Teachers will use their understandings of these concepts to weave them into classroom discourse, help students describe their feelings and experiences, and draw linkages among different topics.

Teachers must also be able to recognize, compare, and contrast examples of various theories related to diversity, such as cultural difference, cultural deficit, genetics, and cultural ecology (Banks, 1994b). Each of these theories has been used to explain poor academic achievement among low-income students and students of color (Baratz & Baratz, 1970). Cultural deficit theory, for example, has been used to guide the development of many early childhood intervention programs such as Head Start and Distar. An important goal of these programs is to improve the academic achievement of low-status groups.

It is not uncommon for teachers to select aspects from several theories to guide their work with students. An eclectic theoretical approach may sometimes be effective, but it can also be counterproductive. For example, after reading the book, *Making Connections*, by Gilligan, Lyons, and Hanmer (1990) a teacher may become aware that girls often equate fairness with listening. That teacher may then make a special effort to call on women and men on an equal basis. Multicultural theory, however, reveals that equity may not always mean treating different groups the same (Gay, 1993). It may sometimes be necessary to treat groups differently in order to create equal-status situations for marginalized students. Providing an equal voice for women may sometimes require an unequal focus on women's views and issues in classroom discourse. Equity pedagogy requires teachers to be able to recognize and respond to multiple student characteristics, including race, social class, and gender.

The effective implementation of equity pedagogy requires teachers to understand the histories, modal characteristics, and intragroup differences of the major racial and ethnic groups (Banks, 1991). This content and conceptual knowledge can provide a foundation to help teachers design and select appropriate instructional materials for their students (Ladson-Billings, 1990, 1994, 1995), make informed decisions about when to use culturally sensitive pedagogy, and decide when to focus on the individual characteristics of students (Nieto, 1994).

For example, research summarized by Shade (1982) indicates that Latino and African-American students often prefer a learning environment that is more personalized and contextual than that preferred by many middle-class, White students. While the learning style literature suggests that certain learning environments are more appropriate for various groups of students, it also suggests that students from all ethnic and racial groups can be found in each of the categories identified by learning style theorists (Shade & New, 1993). When reading and using learning style theories, teachers should question and analyze them carefully. The learning style paradigm is a complex one that defies simplistic classroom applications (Irvine & York, 1995). The paradigm has been criticized by researchers such as Kleinfeld and Nelson (1991), who believe it may result in the construction of new stereotypes about low-achieving students.

Teachers should look beyond the physical characteristics of students and consider the complexity of their individual and group experiences. A Latino student's biographical journey, social class, and geographical location may indicate that a teacher should not focus on modal characteristics of Latinos in determining appropriate pedagogy for the student. Instead, the teacher may need to focus on the individual characteristics of the student. Teachers must make informed decisions about when and how to use knowledge about the cultural and ethnic backgrounds of students when making pedagogical decisions.

Teaching as a multicultural encounter

Teaching is a multicultural encounter. Both teachers and students belong to diverse groups differentiated by variables such as age, social class, gender, race, and ethnicity. Teachers who are skilled in equity pedagogy are able to use diversity to enrich instruction instead of fearing or ignoring it. They are able to use diversity successfully because they understand its meaning in both their own and their students' lives. They are able to analyze, clarify, and state their personal values related to cultural diversity and to act in ways consistent with their beliefs.

Self-understanding, and knowledge of the histories, modal characteristics, and intragroup differences of ethnic groups are important competencies required for teachers to implement equity pedagogy. They provide a foundation for teachers to identify, create, and implement teaching strategies that enhance the academic achievement of students from both gender groups and from diverse racial, ethnic, and cultural groups. Equity pedagogy is not embodied in specific strategies. It is a process that locates the student at the center of schooling. When effectively implemented, equity pedagogy enriches the lives of both teachers and students and enables them to envision and to help create a more humane and caring society.

Note

1 *Content integration* consists of using examples and content from a variety of cultures and groups to teach key concepts, principles, generalizations, and theories in a subject area or discipline. In the *knowledge construction process*, students are helped to understand, investigate, and determine how implicit cultural assumptions, frames of reference, perspectives, and biases within a discipline influence the ways that knowledge is constructed within it. The *prejudice reduction* dimension focuses on helping students to develop more positive racial, gender, and ethnic attitudes (Banks, 1993c). *Equity pedagogy* consists of "techniques and methods that facilitate the academic achievement of students from diverse racial, ethnic, and social-class groups" (p. 6). An *empowering school culture and social structure* describes the process of "restructuring the culture and organization of the school so that students from diverse racial, ethnic, and social-class groups will experience equality and cultural empowerment" (p. 7). For a comprehensive discussion of the dimensions and their interrelationships, see Banks (1993c).

References

Banks, J.A. (1991). *Teaching strategies for ethnic studies* (5th ed.). Boston: Allyn & Bacon.

Banks, J.A. (1993a). The canon debate, knowledge construction, and multicultural education. *Educational Researcher, 22*(3), 4–14.

Banks, J.A. (1993b). Integrating the curriculum with ethnic content: Approaches and guidelines. In J.A. Banks & C.A.M. Banks (Eds.), *Multicultural education: Issues and perspectives* (pp. 3–28). Boston: Allyn & Bacon.

Banks, J.A. (1993c). Multicultural education: Historical development, dimensions, and practice. In L.D. Hammond (Ed.), *Review of research in education* (pp. 3–49). Washington, DC: American Educational Research Association.

Banks, J.A. (1994a). *An introduction to multicultural education*. Boston: Allyn & Bacon.

Banks, J.A. (1994b). *Multiethnic education: Theory and practice* (3rd ed.). Boston: Allyn & Bacon.

Banks, J.A., & Banks, C.A.M. (Eds.). (1995). *Handbook of research on multicultural education*. New York: Macmillan.

Baratz, S.S., & Baratz, J.C. (1970). Early childhood intervention: The social science base of institutional racism. *Harvard Educational Review, 40*, 29–50.

Brooks, J.G., & Brooks, M.G. (1993). *In search of understanding: The case for constructivist classrooms*. Arlington, VA: Association for Supervision and Curriculum Development.

Brookover, W., Beady, C., Flood, P., Schweitzer, J., & Wisenbaker, J. (1979). *School social systems and student achievement: Schools can make a difference*. New York: Praeger.

Cohen, E.G. (1994). *Designing groupwork: Strategies for the heterogeneous classrooms* (2nd ed.). New York: Teachers College Press.

Cohen, E.G., & Roper, S.S. (1972). Modification of interracial interaction disability: An application of status characteristics theory. *American Sociological Review, 37*, 643–657.

Code, L. (1991). *What can she know? Feminist theory and the construction of knowledge.* Ithaca, NY: Cornell University Press.

D'Souza, D. (1991). *Illiberal education: The politics of race and sex on campus*. New York: The Free Press.

Gay, G. (1993). Ethnic minorities and educational equality. In J.A. Banks & C.A.M. Banks (Eds.), *Multicultural education: Issues and Perspectives* (pp. 171–194). Boston: Allyn & Bacon.

Gilligan, C., Lyons, N.P., & Hanmer, T.J. (Eds.). (1990). *Making connections: The relational words of adolescent girls at Emma Willard School.* Cambridge, MA: Harvard University Press.

Irvine, J.J., & York, E.D. (1995). Learning styles and culturally diverse students: A literature review. In J.A. Banks & C.A.M. Banks (Eds.), *Handbook of research on multicultural education* (pp. 484–497). New York: Macmillan.

Jackson, P.W. (1992). *Untaught lessons*. New York: Teachers College Press.

King, J.E. (1992). Diaspora literacy and consciousness in the struggle against miseducation in the Black community. *The Journal of Negro Education, 61*(3), 317–340.

Kleinfeld, J., & Nelson, P. (1991). Adapting instruction to Native Americans' learning style: An iconoclastic view. *Journal of Cross-Cultural Psychology, 22*, 273–282.

Ladson-Billings, G. (1990). Like lightning in a bottle: Attempting to capture the pedagogical excellence of successful teachers of Black students. *Qualitative Studies in Education, 3*(4), 335–344.

Ladson-Billings, G. (1994). *The dreamkeepers: Successful teachers of African American children*. San Francisco: Jossey-Bass.

Ladson-Billings, G. (1995). Multicultural teacher education: Research, practice, and policy. In J.A. Banks & C.A.M. Banks (Eds.), *Handbook of research on multicultural education* (pp. 747–759). New York: Macmillan.

McIntosh, P. (1990). *Interactive phases of curricular and personal re-vision with regard to race*. Wellesley, MA: Wellesley College, Center for Research on Women.

Nieto, S. (1994). Lesson from students on creating a chance to dream. *Harvard Educational Review, 64*(4), 392–415.

Schlesinger, Jr., A.M. (1991). *The disuniting of America*. Knoxville, TN: Whittle Direct Books.

Shade, B.J. (1982). Afro-American cognitive style: A variable in school success? *Review of Educational Research, 52*, 219–244.

Shade, B.J., & New, C.A. (1993). Cultural influences on learning. In J.A. Banks & C.A.M. Banks (Eds.), *Multicultural education: Issues and perspectives* (2nd ed.; pp. 317–331). Boston: Allyn & Bacon.

Slavin, R.E. (1983). *Cooperative learning*. New York: Longman.

Sleeter, C.E. (1995). An analysis of the critiques of multicultural education. In J.A. Banks & C.A.M. Banks (Eds.), *Handbook of research on multicultural education* (pp. 81–94). New York: Macmillan.

Tetreault, M.K.T. (1993). Classrooms for diversity: Rethinking curriculum and pedagogy. In J.A. Banks & C.A.M. Banks (Eds.), *Multicultural education: Issues and perspectives* (2nd ed.; pp. 129–148). Boston: Allyn & Bacon.

Tye, B.B. (1987). The deep structure of schooling. *Phi Delta Kappan, 69*(4), 281–284.

Valencia, S., Hiebert, E.H., & Afflerbach, P.P. (Eds.), (1994). *Authentic reading assessment: Practices and possibilities*. Newark, DE: International Reading Association.

Vygotsky, L.S. (1978). *Mind in society: The development of higher psychological processes.* Cambridge, MA: Harvard University Press.

PART 3

EXAMPLES OF PRACTICE

CHAPTER 13

SOME KEY ISSUES IN TEACHING LATINO STUDENTS (1988)

Luis C. Moll

Latino students, as a group, have a persistent, high rate of educational failure that makes them among the most problematic groups for educators (Steinberg, Blinde, & Chan 1984). In places, however, there are positive developments. I report on a recent classroom analysis of Latino students who were doing well academically, as reflected both in teachers' assessments and in achievement tests. The study was part of a larger project on "effective" schooling conducted in three elementary schools and seven classrooms in a major metropolitan area in the southwestern United States. The teachers we selected for observation were judged by peers and administrators as outstanding or effective teachers of Latino children. Their students were achieving at or above grade level on standardized measures of academic achievement. In this paper I will report on our observations of two of the teachers: one Spanish-English bilingual and the other English monolingual, both fifth grade teachers. The findings relate to the nature of instruction in these classrooms. I will concentrate on the way teachers organized instruction for the students and why they taught the way they did. In particular, I will highlight what we have called the teachers' social mediations: the ways they arranged, changed, improved, or modified social situations to teach at the highest level possible (Moll, in press; Moll & Harper 1987).

The significance of these findings must be understood in the broader social and educational context of Latino students' education. Latino students, including the students in this study, are primarily working-class children. For years sociologists of education have reported on the social stratification of schooling and the consequences of that stratification for working-class students (see, e.g., Bowles & Gintis 1976; Giroux 1983). Classroom studies, relying primarily on participant observations, have in general provided empirical support for the thesis that the social-class standing of children influences the nature of schooling for those children (see, e.g., Anyon 1980, 1981; Wilcox 1982; Willis 1977). For example, Anyon's (1980) contrastive analysis of classrooms across social class groups discovered working-class schooling to be primarily rote work, with the students engaged in very little decision making or choice: "The teachers rarely explain why the work is being assigned, how it might connect to other assignments, or what the idea is that lies behind the procedure or gives it coherence and perhaps meaning or significance" (p. 73). More recent research (Oakes 1986), focusing on tracking and using a national data base, reached a similar conclusion about the social context of schooling: there is an unequal distribution of schooling that favors the already-privileged; white and affluent students received more of what seemed to be effective teaching than did other groups; minority and poor students received an emphasis on low-level basic literacy and computational skills. As Oakes noted, "There is no presumption that high-status knowledge is equally appropriate for all" (p. 74).

Other research has documented how these characteristics of working-class schooling are exacerbated in the schooling of Latino students. For example, there is the additional tendency to reduce even further the curriculum's level of complexity to match limited-English-speakers' level of English proficiency (Díaz, Moll, & Mehan 1986; Moll 1986). This reductionism may be manifested in several ways, most commonly by relegating the limited-English-proficient students to low-level academic work, regardless of their literate competence in Spanish, or by not allowing the students to participate in what are perceived as cognitively demanding activities, such as expository writing (Goldenberg 1984; Moll & Díaz 1986). The pervasiveness of these assumptions about working-class and minority students is revealed in recent studies of computer work in the schools: in general, affluent students do programming and problem solving; poor students do drill and practice (Center for the Social Organization of Schools 1983).

Purpose and meaning in teaching

Our findings present a striking contrast to the above profile of working-class schooling. We conducted classroom observations for six months and interviewed the teachers, formally and informally, throughout the project to get a through understanding of their teaching. In total, we collected approximately one hundred hours of observations which we supplemented with about ten hours of videotaping per classroom. In what follows we will present five findings that reveal the close relationship between the how and the why of teaching.

Central to these teachers' approaches is the belief that the essence of literacy is the understanding and communication of meaning. Both comprehension and expression are built and developed collaboratively by students and teachers through functional, relevant, and meaningful language use. Thus, a major goal of teaching is to make classrooms highly literate environments in which many language experiences can take place and different types of "literacies" can be practiced, understood, and learned. This approach explicitly and categorically rejects breaking up reading and writing into isolated skill sequences to be taught in a successive, stagelike manner. Rather, it emphasizes the creation of classroom contexts in which children learn to use, try out, and manipulate language in the service of making sense or creating meaning. The role of the teacher is to provide the necessary support and guidance so that children, through their own efforts, assume full control of the purposes and uses of oral and written language.

That the teachers held similar views about teaching does not mean they taught the same. On the contrary, how they applied their views in their specific circumstances, is at the heart of the matter. That is, each in her own way, attuned to the needs of her children and to their classroom realities, created her own instructional program. I now turn to the findings.

The intellectual level of the curriculum

In contrast to the assumption that working-class children cannot handle an academically rigorous curriculum, or in the case of limited-English-proficient students, that their lack of English fluency justifies an emphasis on low-level skills, the guiding assumption in the classrooms analyzed seemed to be the opposite: that the students were as smart as allowed by the curriculum. The teachers assumed that the children were competent and capable and that it was teaching responsibly to provide the students with a challenging, innovative, and intellectually rigorous curriculum. Rote-like learning of lower-order skills simply did not take place. Rather, the teachers emphasized the students' active use of language to obtain or express meaning and monitored closely the intellectual level of the curriculum. The idea of "watering down" the curriculum was flatly rejected as unacceptable; as one of the teacher expressed it: watering down the curriculum would be "degrading and disrespectful to the children." Students were never grouped by ability level but by student interest or as part of activities, such as reading conferences, dramatizations of readings, or science projects.

The importance of substance and content

The most prominent characteristic of these classrooms was not the teaching of specific skills or a hierarchy of subskills, but the constant emphasis on creating meaning. Every observation we collected had notations of the teachers' efforts at creating, clarifying, expanding, and monitoring the students' understanding of activities and tasks. The making of meaning permeated every instructional activity in these classrooms, regardless of topic, theme, purpose, or the children's English language competence.

Accordingly, the teachers emphasized the importance of substance and content in teaching. As one teacher viewed it: "with rich content, meaning is all around and surrounding [the students], wetting their appetites; kids love to learn." That is, the content of lessons played a leading role in organizing instruction. For example, what children read mattered. No skills-oriented basal readers were used; the teachers used trade books that contained stories that were meaningful and interesting to the students, or books related to a particular theme or topic the class was analyzing.

The principle is that when the content of reading is worthwhile, comprehension becomes the obvious goal of reading. This means not only reading comprehension but understanding how meaning is created and communicated. The teachers helped the students understand strategies authors used to convey meaning. Through their questioning, the teachers helped the students examine the writers' strategies in some depth: how writers manipulate words, phrases, descriptions, or dialogue to influence readers. The teachers also helped the students analyze the strategies they used as readers to understand text by, for example, having them make predictions and guesses about what would happen next in a story and explain why. In short, the teachers' emphasis on substance and content facilitated the frequent occurrence of what were in essence metalinguistic and metacognitive events: *the conscious examination of others' and one's own use of language and thinking*.

It also was the case that meaningful content was a key in facilitating the learning of English. In both the bilingual and monolingual classrooms, the teachers concerned themselves primarily with organizing learning activities that involved students substantively in the class. One of the teachers put it as follows: "The richer the content, the more the students had something they connected to." This idea is similar to Genesee's (1986) suggestion that second language learners will learn a second language to the extent that they are motivated by the curriculum to learn the academic material. It is the students' interest in things academic that motivates them to learn the second language or to retain and develop their first language. Thus, in both classrooms, learning English was a residual goal of academic performance.

Diversity of instruction

The teachers coordinated in various ways the students' interactions with content. This diversity of instruction was evident in the different social arrangements for learning. For example, reading and writing took place in many ways, and they were usually integrated as part of a broader activity. For example, the teachers would help their students dramatize books to analyze content and the development of characters; the students would serve as literacy tutors to younger students, which in turn gave teachers an opportunity to analyze their students' understanding of literacy; in the bilingual classroom, the students could read a book in English but write their analysis of the book in Spanish, or vice versa; and all of the students wrote regularly in journals and logs. In short, the teachers consciously tried to provide the children with practice in the greatest possible range of oral and written language uses to obtain and communicate knowledge. This is what Heath (1986) has called helping children become fully skilled in a variety of "genres of language uses." The present analysis suggests, as others have indicated, that academic success depends upon students mastering a wide range of ways of using language, especially written language (see Heath 1983, 1986; Olson 1986; Snow 1983; Wells 1986).

The teachers also used different instructional situations to assess children. As the teachers pointed out, most of their assessments were conducted by observing the students in various contexts. That is how they got to "know" the children and assess how they were doing, the type of assistance they needed, and whether the children were taking over the activity, making it their own, learning. The teachers obtained qualitatively different perspectives on students by contrasting their performance alone with their performance in collaborative situations (Minick, in press; Moll, in press).

The use of the students' experiences

The teachers set up their lessons to encourage students to use their personal experiences to make sense of the classroom content. In both classrooms the children introduced topics that came from their home or community experiences and the teacher used their comments to expand the children's understanding of the lessons (cf. Tikunoff 1985). This was most evident in reading lessons where the children often contributed personal observations and anecdotes to make a point. For example, while reading a novel about the American revolutionary war, one group was discussing how the war created strains in families' social relationships because of differences of opinion about the war. One student brought up a personal dilemma analogous to a situation one of the characters in the novel was facing and other students immediately contributed similar insights. The teacher, in turn, used the students' experiences to explain the difference between learning facts about the war, as one would in a social studies lesson, and reading a novel that possibly provided us a better understanding of how social conditions and strife affected people's lives. By eliciting social experiences the teachers facilitated the students' involvement with the content and their use of literacy as a tool for scrutiny and analysis.

Social and political support

Both teachers enjoyed considerable autonomy in their classrooms. They could set up their classrooms and teach in ways they preferred without adhering to strict curricular guidelines as determined by someone else or adhering, for example, to the limitations of certain basal readers. This autonomy was not only reflected in their teaching but in the children's learning. The students, to a great extent, had options about their own learning; they could select projects, books, tasks, and assignments and they routinely helped each other, as well as younger students, with their assignments. But it was the teachers' freedom to select or create their own curricular activities that afforded the students the opportunity to be selective and independent in their work. How did this autonomy come about?

Our analysis suggests three related factors. First is that the teachers were theoretically equipped. More than that, they were sound theorists. They could elucidate both the "hows" and "whys" of teaching. Their approach, among other things, emphasized the necessity for teachers to assume control of the curriculum to allow themselves and their children to act as thinkers in their classrooms, not as passive givers and receivers of a prepackaged curriculum. The teachers built on the idea that children learn better and more when teachers avoid reductionist approaches and instead "keep language whole and involve children in using it functionally and purposefully to meet their own needs" (Goodman 1986, p. 7). Important to this approach is the creation of social settings within which children can use language for a variety of reasons and functions, and central to the children's activities, as we have reviewed, is the communication of meaning. Thus, the teachers insisted that to implement seriously their approach they needed considerable autonomy in their classrooms.

Second, they were able to argue successfully with their principals to grant them the option of selecting texts and of implementing a curriculum that, according to their best professional judgments, would meet the children's needs. In brief, much of their autonomy was the result of difficult negotiations either with principals or the school board. Both teachers had moved to new schools and mentioned that they were willing to do it again to be with principals that allowed them the necessary instructional autonomy. One of the teachers mentioned that she interviewed several principals before deciding in which school to teach. Both teachers agreed on the difficulty of accomplishing such autonomy, especially for novice teachers. One of the teachers considered legal action in order to create the necessary conditions for her teaching. She mentioned the difficulties of "bucking the system" and how political know-how and strategies were needed by teachers; that teaching how you want is the result of a conscious political strategy (Rich 1985).

Third, the teachers also counted on the support of colleagues who shared their approach or orientation to teaching. They met regularly with teachers from other schools and with university professors who had similar views on teaching. These peers became a support and study group in providing moral encouragement and professional teaching advice. One of the teachers commented on the animosity of her peers because she taught differently and how she would receive a "silent" treatment from them. During those times she relied on her network of peers for support and encouragement.

Conclusion

I have summarized five findings from our classroom observations of outstanding teachers of Hispanic students. These teachers are important because their orientation, teaching methods, and outcomes go against the status quo. Instead of rigidity of instruction they offer flexibility; instead of basic skills they offer high-level reading and writing; instead of rote instruction they offer lessons with purpose and meaning; instead of student control they offer students options and autonomy; and instead of passivity they offer action and results.

These teachers did not accomplish their results accidentally, they have an approach that can be taught, adapted, and applied in diverse situations (see, e.g., Edelsky, Draper, & Smith 1983; Goodman 1986) and they understand the importance of political action in education. Perhaps the most encouraging aspect of our results is that teachers working in different working-class communities, and with children often considered among the most problematic, can meet their students' academic needs with a sophisticated approach that turns available resources, especially their students' considerable intellectual potential, into assets for teaching and learning.

Acknowledgements

The classroom observations reported herein formed part of the Project on Effective Schooling for Hispanics, funded by a grant to Eugene García from the Inter-University Program for Latino Research and the Social Science Research Council. Special thanks to María Harper, who collected most of the classroom observations and assisted me with the analysis reported in this paper.

References

Anyon, J. "Social Class and the Hidden Curriculum of Work." *Journal of Education*, 162(1980): 67–92.

Anyon, J. "Elementary Schooling and the Distinctions of Social Class." *Interchange*, 12(1981): 118–132.

Bowles, S., & Gintis, H. *Schooling in Capitalist America: Educational Reform and the Contradictions of Economic Life*. New York: Basic Books, 1976.

Center for the Social Organization of Schools. *Schools' Uses of Microcomputers: Reports from a National Survey*, (1,2). Baltimore: The Johns Hopkins University, 1983.

Díaz, S., Moll, L. C., & Mehan, H. "Sociocultural Resources in Instruction: A Context-Specific Approach." In *Beyond Language: Social and Cultural Factors in Schooling Language Minority Children*. Los Angeles: Evaluation, Dissemination and Assessment Center, California State University, 1986.

Edelsky, C., Draper, K., & Smith, K. "Hookin' 'Em in at the Start of School in a 'Whole Language' Classroom." *Anthropology and Education Quarterly*, 14(1983): 257–281.

Genesee, F. "The Baby and the Bathwater or, What Immersion Has to Say About Bilingual Education," *NABE Journal*, 10(1986): 227–254.

Giroux, M. *Theory and Resistance in Education: A Pedagogy for the Opposition*. South Hadley, MA: Bergin & Garvey, 1983.

Goldenberg, C. *Roads to Reading: Studies of Hispanic First Graders at Risk for Reading Failure*. Unpublished doctoral dissertation. Graduate School of Education, University of California, Los Angeles, 1984.

Goodman, K. *What's Whole in Whole Language?* Portsmouth, NH: Heinemann, 1986.

Heath, S. B. *Ways With Words: Language, Life, and Work in Communities and Classrooms*, New York: Cambridge University Press, 1983.

Heath, S. B. "Sociocultural Contexts of Language Development." In *Beyond Language:*

Social and Cultural Factors in Schooling Language Minority Children. Los Angeles: Evaluation, Dissemination and Assessment Center, California State University, 1986.
Minick, N. "The Zone of Proximal Development and Dynamic Assessment." In *Dynamic Assessment*, edited by C. Lidz. New York: Guilford Press, in press.
Moll, L. C. "Teaching Second Language Students: A Vygotskian Perspective." In *Richness in Writing: Empowering ESL Students*, edited by D. Johnson & D. Roen. New York: Longman, in press.
Moll, L. C. "Writing as Communication: Creating Strategic Learning Environments for Students." *Theory into Practice*, 25(1986): 102–108.
Moll, L. C. & Díaz, R. "Teaching Writing as Communication: The Use of Ethnographic Findings in Classroom Practice." In *Literacy and Schooling*, edited by D. Bloome. Norwood, NJ: Ablex, 1986.
Moll, L. C. & Harper, M. "*Effective Teaching of Hispanics: Preliminary Findings from Classroom Observations*." Working paper No. 6. Effective Schooling for Hispanics Project, Center for Bilingual Bicultural Education, Arizona State University, 1987.
Oakes, J. "Tracking, Inequality, and the Rhetoric of School Reform: Why Schools Don't Change." *Journal of Education*, 168(1986): 61–80.
Olson, D. "Intelligence and Literacy: The Relationship Between Intelligence and the Technologies of Representation and Communication." In *Practical Intelligence: Nature and Origins of Competence in the Everyday World*, edited by R. Stenberg & R. Wagner. New York: Cambridge University Press, 1986.
Rich, S. "Restoring Power to Teachers: The Impact of 'Whole Language.' " *Language Arts*, 62(1985): 717–724.
Snow, C. E. "Literacy and Language: Relationships During the Preschool Years." *Harvard Educational Review*, 53(1983): 165–189.
Steinberg, L., Blinde, P. L., & Chan, K. "Dropping Out Among Minority Youth." *Review of Educational Research*, 54(1982): 113–132.
Tikunoff, S. *Applying Significant Bilingual Instructional Features in the Classroom*. Rosslyn, VA: National Clearinghouse for Bilingual Education, 1985.
Wells, G. *The Meaning Makers: Children Learning Language and Using Language to Learn*. New Hampshire: Heinemann, 1986.
Wilcox, K. "Differential Socialization in the Classroom: Implications for Equal Opportunity." In *Doing the Ethnography of Schooling*, edited by G. Spindler. New York: Holt, Rinehart, & Winston, 1982.
Willis, P. *Learning to Labor*. New York: Columbia University Press, 1977.

CHAPTER 14

TOWARD A THEORY OF CULTURALLY RELEVANT PEDAGOGY (1995)

Gloria Ladson-Billings

Teacher education programs throughout the nation have coupled their efforts at reform with revised programs committed to social justice and equity. Thus, their focus has become the preparation of prospective teachers in ways that support equitable and just educational experiences for all students. Examples of such efforts include work in Alaska (Kleinfeld, 1992; Noordhoff, 1990; Noordhoff & Kleinfeld, 1991), California (King & Ladson-Billings, 1990), Illinois (Beyer, 1991), and Wisconsin (Murrell, 1990, 1991).

Currently, there are debates in the educational research literature concerning both locating efforts at social reform in schools (Popkewitz, 1991) and the possibilities of "re-educating" typical teacher candidates for the variety of student populations in U.S. public schools (Grant, 1989; Haberman, 1991a, 1991b). Rather than looking at programmatic reform, this article considers educational theorizing about teaching itself and proposes a theory of culturally focused pedagogy that might be considered in the reformation of teacher education.

Shulman's often cited article, "Knowledge and Teaching: Foundations of the New Reform" (1987), considers philosophical and psychological perspectives, underscored by case knowledge of novice and experienced practitioners. Although Shulman's work mentions the importance of both the knowledge of learners and their characteristics and knowledge of educational contexts, it generally minimizes the culturally based analyses of teaching that have preceded it. In this article, I attempt to build on the educational anthropological literature and suggest a new theoretical perspective to address the specific concerns of educating teachers for success with African-American students.

Teaching and culture

For more than a decade, anthropologists have examined ways that teaching can better match the home and community cultures of students of color who have previously not had academic success in schools. Au and Jordan (1981, p. 139) termed "culturally appropriate" the pedagogy of teachers in a Hawaiian school who incorporated aspects of students' cultural backgrounds into their reading instruction. By permitting students to use *talk-story*, a language interaction style common among Native Hawaiian children, teachers were able to help students achieve at higher than predicted levels on standardized reading tests.

Mohatt and Erickson (1981) conducted similar work with Native American students. As they observed teacher–student interactions and participation structures, they found teachers who used language interaction patterns that approximated the students' home cultural patterns were more successful in improving student academic performance. Improved student achievement also was evident among teachers who used what they termed, "mixed forms" (p. 117)—a combination of Native American and Anglo language interaction patterns. They termed this instruction, "culturally congruent" (p. 110).

Cazden and Leggett (1981) and Erickson and Mohatt (1982) used the term "culturally responsive" (p. 167) to describe similar language interactions of teachers with linguistically diverse and Native American students, respectively. Later, Jordan (1985, p. 110) and Vogt, Jordan, and Tharp (1987, p. 281) began using the term "culturally compatible" to explain the success of classroom teachers with Hawaiian children.

By observing the students in their home/community environment, teachers were able to include aspects of the students' cultural environment in the organization and instruction of the classroom. More specifically, Jordan (1985) discusses cultural compatibility in this way:

> Educational practices must match with the children's culture in ways which ensure the generation of academically important behaviors. It does not mean that all school practices need be completely congruent with natal cultural practices, in the sense of exactly or even closely matching or agreeing with them. The point of cultural compatibility is that the natal culture is used as a guide in the selection of educational program elements so that academically desired behaviors are produced and undesired behaviors are avoided. (p. 110)

These studies have several common features. Each locates the source of student failure and subsequent achievement within the nexus of speech and language interaction patterns of the teacher and the students. Each suggests that student "success" is represented in achievement within the current social structures extant in schools. Thus, the goal of education becomes how to "fit" students constructed as "other" by virtue of their race/ethnicity, language, or social class into a hierarchical structure that is defined as a *meritocracy*. However, it is unclear how these conceptions do more than reproduce the current inequities. Singer (1988) suggests that "cultural congruence in an inherently moderate pedagogical strategy that accepts that the goal of educating minority students is to train individuals in those skills needed to succeed in mainstream society" (p. 1).

Three of the terms employed by studies on cultural mismatch between school and home—culturally appropriate, culturally congruent, and culturally compatible—seem to connote accommodation of student culture to mainstream culture. Only the term *culturally responsive* appears to refer to a more dynamic or synergistic relationship between home/community culture and school culture. Erickson and Mohatt (1982) suggest their notion of culturally responsive teaching can be seen as a beginning step for bridging the gap between home and school:

> It may well be that, by discovering the small differences in social relations which make a big difference in the interactional ways children engage the content of the school curriculum, anthropologists can make practical contributions to the improvement of minority children's school achievement and to the improvement of the everyday school life for such children and their teachers. Making small changes in everyday participation structures may be

> one of the means by which more culturally responsive pedagogy can be developed. (p. 170)

For the most part, studies of cultural appropriateness, congruence, or compatibility have been conducted within small-scale communities—for example, Native Hawaiian, Native Americans. However, an earlier generation of work considered the mismatch between the language patterns of African Americans and the school in larger, urban settings (Gay & Abrahamson, 1972; Labov, 1969; Piestrup, 1973).

Villegas (1988) challenged the microsocial explanations advanced by sociolinguists by suggesting that the source of cultural mismatch is located in larger social structures and that schools as institutions serve to reproduce social inequalities. She argued that

> As long as school performs this sorting function in society, it must necessarily produce winners and losers. . . . Therefore, culturally sensitive remedies to educational problems of oppressed minority students that ignore the political aspect of schooling are doomed to failure. (pp. 262–263)

Although I would agree with Villegas's attention to the larger social structure, other scholars in the cultural ecological paradigm (Ogbu, 1981, 1983) are ahistorical and limited, particularly in their ability to explain African-American student success (Perry, 1993).[1] The long history of African-American educational struggle and achievement is well documented (Anderson, 1988; Billingsley, 1992; Bond, 1969; Bullock, 1967; Clark, 1983; Harding, 1981; Harris, 1992; Johnson, 1936; Rury, 1983; Woodson, 1919; Weinberg, 1977). This historical record contradicts the glib pronouncements that, "Black people don't value education."

Second, more recent analyses of successful schooling for African-American students (King, 1991a; Ladson-Billings, 1992a, 1994; Siddle-Walker, 1993) challenge the explanatory power of the cultural ecologists' caste-like category and raise questions about what schools can and should be doing to promote academic success for African-American students.[2]

Despite their limitations, the microanalytic work of sociolinguists and the macrostructural analysis of cultural ecologists both are important in helping scholars think about their intersections and consider possible classroom/instructional adjustments. For scholars interested in the success of students of color in complex, urban environments, this work provides some important theoretical and conceptual groundwork.

Irvine (1990) developed the concept of *cultural synchronization* to describe the necessary interpersonal context that must exist between the teacher and African-American students to maximize learning. Rather than focus solely on speech and language interactions, Irvine's work describes the acceptance of students' communication patterns, along with a constellation of African-American cultural mores such as mutuality, reciprocity, spirituality, deference, and responsibility (King & Mitchell, 1990).

Irvine's work on African-American students and school failure considers both micro- and macro-analyses, including: teacher–student interpersonal contexts, teacher and student expectations, institutional contexts, and the societal context. This work is important for its break with the cultural deficit or cultural disadvantage explanations which led to compensatory educational interventions.[3] A next step for positing effective pedagogical practice is a theoretical model that not only addresses student achievement but also helps students to accept and affirm their cultural identity while developing critical perspectives that challenge inequities that schools (and other institutions) perpetuate. I term this pedagogy, *culturally relevant pedagogy*.

Several questions, some of which are beyond the scope of this discussion, drive this attempt to formulate a theoretical model of culturally relevant pedagogy. What constitutes student success? How can academic success and cultural success complement each other in settings where student alienation and hostility characterize the school experience? How can pedagogy promote the kind of student success that engages larger social structural issues in a critical way? How do researchers recognize that pedagogy in action? And, what are the implications for teacher preparation generated by this pedagogy?

The illusion of atheoretical inquiry

Educational research is greeted with suspicion both within and outside of the academy. Among practitioners, it is regarded as *too theoretical* (Kaestle, 1993). For many academicians, it is regarded as *atheoretical* (Katzer, Cook, & Crouch, 1978). It is the latter notion that I address in this section of the article.

Clearly, much of educational research fails to make explicit its theoretical underpinnings (Argyris, 1980; Amundson, Serlin, & Lehrer, 1992). However, I want to suggest that, even without explicating a theoretical framework, researchers do have explanations for why things "work the way they do." These theories may be partial, poorly articulated, conflated, or contradictory, but they exist. What is regarded as traditional educational theory—theories of reproduction (as described by Apple & Weis, 1983; Bowles, 1977; Weiler, 1988) or neoconservative traditional theory (as described in Young, 1990)—may actually be a *default* theory that researchers feel no need to make explicit. Thus, the theory's objectivity is unquestioned, and studies undergirded by these theories are regarded as truth or objective reality.

Citing the *ranking*, or privileging, of theoretical knowledge, Code (1991) observes:

> Even when empiricist *theories* of knowledge prevail, knowledgeable *practice* constructs positions of power and privilege that are by no means as impartially ordered as strict empiricism would require. Knowledge gained from practical (untheorized) experience is commonly regarded as inferior to theoretically derived or theory-confirming knowledge, and theory is elevated above practice. (p. 243)

In education, work that recognizes the import of practical experience owes an intellectual debt to scholars such as Smith (1978), Atkin (1973), Glaser and Strauss (1967), and Lutz and Ramsey (1974) who explored notions of grounded theory as an important tool for educational research. Additionally, work by scholars in teacher education such as Stenhouse (1983), Elliott (1991), Carr and Kemmis (1986), Zeichner (1990), and Cochran-Smith and Lytle (1992) illuminates the action research tradition where teachers look reflexively at their practice to solve pedagogical problems and assist colleagues and researchers interested in teaching practice. Even some scholars in the logical positivist tradition acknowledged the value of a more experientially grounded research approach in education (Cronbach, 1975). More fundamental than arguing the merits of quantitative versus qualitative methodology (Gage, 1989) have been calls for broader understanding about the limits of any research methodology (Rist, 1990). In using selected citations from Kuhn, Patton, Becker, and Gouldner, Rist (1990) helps researchers understand the significance of research paradigms in education. For example:

> Since no paradigm ever solves all of the problems it defines and since no two paradigms leave all the same problems unsolved, paradigm debates always involve the question: Which problems is it more significant to have solved? (Kuhn, 1970, p. 46)
>
> A paradigm is a world view, a general perspective, a way of breaking down the complexity of the real world. As such, paradigms are deeply embedded in the socialization of adherents and practitioners, telling them what is important, what is reasonable. (Patton, 1975, p. 9)
>
> The issue is not research strategies, per se. Rather, the adherence to one paradigm as opposed to another predisposes one to view the world and the events within it in profoundly differing ways. (Rist, 1990, p. 83)
>
> The power and pull of a paradigm is more than simply a methodological orientation. It is a means by which to grasp reality and give it meaning and predictability. (Rist, 1990, p. 83)

It is with this orientation toward the inherent subjectivity of educational research that I have approached this work. In this next section, I discuss some of the specific perspectives that have informed my work.

The participant-observer role for researchers who are "other"

Increasingly, researchers have a story to tell about themselves as well as their work (Carter, 1993; Peterson & Neumann, in press). I, too, share a concern for situating myself as a researcher—who I am, what I believe, what experiences I have had all impact what, how, and why I research. What may make these research revelations more problematic for me is my own membership in a marginalized racial/cultural group.

One possible problem I face is the presumption of a "native" perspective (Banks, 1992; Narayan, 1993; Padilla, 1994; Rosaldo, 1989) as I study effective practice for African-American students. To this end, the questions raised by Narayan seem relevant:

> "Native" anthropologists, then, are perceived as insiders regardless of their complex backgrounds. The differences between kinds of "native" anthropologists are also obviously passed over. Can a person from an impoverished American minority background who, despite all prejudices, manages to get an education and study her own community be equated with a member of a Third World elite group who, backed by excellent schooling and parental funds, studies anthropology abroad yet returns home for fieldwork among the less privileged? Is it not insensitive to suppress the issue of location, acknowledging that a scholar who chooses an institutional base in the Third World might have a different engagement with Western-based theories, books, political stances, and technologies of written production? Is a middle-class

> white professional researching aspects of her own society also a "native" anthropologist? (p. 677)

This location of myself as native can work against me (Banks, 1992; Padilla, 1994). My work may be perceived as biased or, at the least, skewed, because of my vested interests in the African-American community. Thus, I have attempted to search for theoretical grounding that acknowledges my standpoint and simultaneously forces me to problematize it. The work of Patricia Hill Collins (1991) on Black feminist thought has been most helpful.

Briefly, Collins's work is based on four propositions: (1) concrete experiences as a criterion of meaning, (2) the use of dialogue in assessing knowledge claims, (3) the ethic of caring, and (4) the ethic of personal accountability. Below, I briefly describe the context and methodology of my study and then attempt to link each of these propositions to a 3-year study I conducted with successful teachers of African-American students.

Issues of context and methodology

While it is not possible to fully explicate the context and method of this study in this article, it is necessary to provide readers with some sense of both for better continuity. I have provided more elaborate explanations of these aspects of the work in other writings (Ladson-Billings, 1990; 1992a, 1992b, 1994). Included here is a truncated explanation of the research context and method.

In 1988, I began working as a lone investigator with a group of eight teachers in a small (less than 3,000 students) predominantly African-American, low-income elementary school district in Northern California. The teachers were identified through a process of *community nomination* (Foster, 1991), with African-American parents (in this case, all mothers) who attended local churches suggesting who they thought were outstanding teachers. The parents' criteria for teaching excellence included being accorded respect by the teacher, student enthusiasm toward school and academic tasks, and student attitudes toward themselves and others. The parents' selections were cross-checked by an independent list of excellent teachers generated by principals and some teaching colleagues. Principals' criteria for teaching excellence included excellent classroom management skills, student achievement (as measured by standardized test scores), and personal observations of teaching practice. Nine teachers' names appeared on both the parents' and principals' lists and were selected to be in the study. One teacher declined to participate because of the time commitment. The teachers were all females: five were African American and three were White.

The study was composed of four phases. During the first phase, each teacher participated in an ethnographic interview (Spradley, 1979) to discuss her background, philosophy of teaching, and ideas about curriculum, classroom management, and parent and community involvement. In the second phase of the study, teachers agreed to be observed by me. This agreement meant that the teachers gave me carte blanche to visit their classrooms. These visits were not scheduled beforehand. I visited the classrooms regularly for almost 2 years, an average of 3 days a week. During each visit, I took field notes, audiotaped the class, and talked with the teacher after the visit, either on-site or by telephone. The third phase of the study, which overlapped the second phase, involved videotaping the teachers. I made decisions about what to videotape as a result of my having become familiar with the teachers' styles and classroom routines.

The fourth and final phase of the study required that the teachers work together as a research collective or collaborative to view segments of one another's videotapes. In a series of ten 2–3-hour meetings, the teachers participated in analysis and interpretation of their own and one another's practice. It was during this phase of the study that formulations about culturally relevant pedagogy that had emerged in the initial interviews were confirmed by teaching practice.

My own interest in these issues of teaching excellence for African-American students came as a result of my desire to challenge deficit paradigms (Bloom, Davis, & Hess, 1965) that prevailed in the literature on African-American learners. Partly as a result of my own experiences as a learner, a teacher, and a parent, I was convinced that, despite the literature, there were teachers who were capable of excellent teaching for African-American students. Thus, my work required a paradigmatic shift toward looking in the classrooms of excellent teachers, *through* the reality of those teachers. In this next section, I discuss how my understanding of my own theoretical grounding connected with the study.

Concrete experiences as a criterion of meaning

According to Collins, "individuals who have lived through the experiences about which they claim to be experts are more believable and credible than those who have merely read and thought about such experience" (p. 209).

My work with successful teachers of African-American students began with a search for "expert" assessment of good teachers. The experts I chose were parents who had children attending the schools where I planned to conduct the research. The parents were willing to talk openly about who they thought were excellent teachers for their children, citing examples of teachers' respect for them as parents, their children's enthusiasm and changed attitudes toward learning, and improved academics in conjunction with support for the students' home culture. In most cases, the basis for their assessments were comparative, both from the standpoint of having had experiences with many teachers (for each individual child) and having had several school-age children. Thus, they could talk about how an individual child fared in different classrooms and how their children collectively performed at specific grade levels with specific teachers.

The second area where concrete experiences as a criterion of meaning was evident was with the teachers themselves. The eight teachers who participated in this study had from 12 to 40 years of teaching experience, most of it with African-American students. Their reflections on what was important in teaching African-American students were undergirded by their daily teaching experiences.

The use of dialogue in assessing knowledge claims

This second criterion suggests that knowledge emerges in dialectical relationships. Rather than the voice of one authority, meaning is made as a product of dialogue between and among individuals. In the case of my study, dialogue was critical in assessing knowledge claims. Early in the study, each teacher participated in an ethnographic interview (Spradley, 1979). Although I had specific areas I wanted to broach with each teacher, the teachers' own life histories and interests determined how much time was spent on the various areas. In some cases, the interviews reflect a teacher's belief in the salience of his or her family background and education. In other instances, teachers talked more about their pedagogical, philosophical, and political perspectives. Even after I began collecting data via classroom observations, it was the teachers' explanations and clarifications that helped to construct the meaning of what transpired in the classrooms.

Additionally, after I collected data from classroom observations and classroom videotaping, the teachers convened as a research collaborative to examine both their own and one another's pedagogy.[4] In these meetings, meaning was constructed through reciprocal dialogue. Instead of merely accepting Berliner's (1988) notions that "experts" operate on a level of automaticity and intuition that does not allow for accurate individual critique and interpretation—that is, they cannot explain how they do what they do—together the teachers were able to make sense of their own and their colleagues' practices. The ongoing dialogue allowed them the opportunity to re-examine and rethink their practices.

The ethic of caring

Much has been discussed in feminist literature about women and *caring* (Gilligan, 1982; Noddings, 1984, 1991). Other feminists have been critical of any essentialized notion of women (Weiler, 1988) and suggest that no empirical evidence exists to support the notion that women care in ways different from men or that any such caring informs their scholarship and work. I argue that Collins's use of caring refers not merely to affective connections between and among people but to the articulation of a greater sense of commitment to what scholarship and/or pedagogy can mean in the lives of people.

For example, in this study, the teachers were not all demonstrative and affectionate toward the students. Instead, their common thread of caring was their concern for the implications their work had on their students' lives, the welfare of the community, and unjust social arrangements. Thus, rather than the idiosyncratic caring for individual students (for whom they did seem to care), the teachers spoke of the import of their work for preparing the students for confronting inequitable and undemocratic social structures.

The ethic of personal accountability

In this final dimension, Collins addresses the notion that *who* makes knowledge claims is as important as *what* those knowledge claims are. Thus, the idea that individuals can "objectively" argue a position whether they themselves agree with the position, as in public debating, is foreign. Individuals' commitments to ideological and/or value positions are important in understanding knowledge claims.

In this study, the teachers demonstrated this ethic of personal accountability in the kind of pedagogical stands they took. Several of the teachers spoke of defying administrative mandates in order to do what they believed was right for students. Others gave examples of proactive actions they took to engage in pedagogical practices more consistent with their beliefs and values. For example, one teacher was convinced that the school district's mandated reading program was inconsistent with what she was learning about literacy teaching/learning from a critical perspective. She decided to write a proposal to the school board asking for experimental status for a literacy approach she wanted to use in her classroom. Her proposal was buttressed by current research in literacy and would not cost the district any more than the proposed program. Ultimately, she was granted permission to conduct her experiment, and its success allowed other teachers to attempt it in subsequent years.

Although Collins's work provided me with a way to think about my work as a researcher, it did not provide me with a way to theorize about the teachers' practices. Ultimately, it was my responsibility to generate theory as I practiced theory. As previously mentioned, this work builds on earlier anthropological and sociolinguistic attempts at a cultural "fit" between students' home culture and school culture. However, by situating it in a more critical paradigm, a theory of culturally relevant pedagogy would necessarily propose to do three things—produce students who can achieve academically, produce students who demonstrate cultural competence, and develop students who can both understand and critique the existing social order. The next section discusses each of these elements of culturally relevant pedagogy.

Culturally relevant pedagogy and student achievement

Much has been written about the school failure of African-American students (see, e.g., African American Male Task Force, 1990; Clark, 1983; Comer, 1984; Irvine, 1990; Ogbu, 1981; Slaughter & Kuehne, 1988). However, explanations for this failure have varied widely. One often-cited explanation situates African-American students' failure in their "caste-like minority" (p. 169) or "involuntary immigrant" status (Ogbu, 1983, p. 171). Other explanations posit *cultural difference* (Erickson, 1987, 1993; Piestrup, 1973) as the reason for this failure and, as previously mentioned, locate student failure in the cultural mismatch between students and the school.

Regardless of these failure explanations, little research has been done to examine academic success among African-American students. The *effective schools* literature (Brookover, 1985; Brookover, Beady, Flood, Schweitzer, & Wisenbaker, 1979; Edmonds, 1979) argued that a group of schoolwide correlates were a reliable predictor of student success.[5] The basis for adjudging a school "effective" in this literature was how far above predicted levels students performed on standardized achievement tests. Whether or not scholars can agree on the significance of standardized tests, their meaning in the real world serves to rank and characterize both schools and individuals. Thus, teachers in urban schools are compelled to demonstrate that their students can achieve literacy and numeracy (Delpit, 1992). No matter how good a fit develops between home and school culture, students must achieve. No theory of pedagogy can escape this reality.

Students in the eight classrooms I observed did achieve. Despite the low ranking of the school district, the teachers were able to help students perform at higher levels than their district counterparts. In general, compared to students in middle-class communities, the students still lagged behind. But, more students in these classrooms were at or above grade level on standardized achievement tests.[6] Fortunately, academic achievement in these classrooms was not limited to standardized assessments. Classroom observations revealed a variety of demonstrated student achievements too numerous to list here. Briefly, students demonstrated an ability to read, write, speak, compute, pose and solve problems at sophisticated levels—that is, pose their own questions about the nature of teacher- or text-posed problems and engage in peer review of problem solutions. Each of the teachers felt that helping the students become academically successful was one of their primary responsibilities.

Culturally relevant teaching and cultural competence

Among the scholarship that has examined academically successful African-American students, a disturbing finding has emerged—the students' academic success came at the expense of their cultural and psychosocial well-being (Fine, 1986; Fordham, 1988). Fordham and Ogbu (1986) identified a phenomenon entitled, "acting White" (p. 176) where African-American students who were academically successful were ostracized by their peers. Bacon (1981) found that, among African-American high school students identified as gifted in their elementary grades, only about half were continuing to do well at the high school level. A closer examination of the successful students' progress indicated that they were social isolates, with neither African-American nor White friends. The students believed that it was necessary for them to stand apart from other African-American students so that teachers would not attribute to them the negative characteristics they may have attributed to African-American students in general.

The dilemma for African-American students becomes one of negotiating the academic demands of school while demonstrating cultural competence.[7] Thus, culturally relevant pedagogy must provide a way for students to maintain their cultural integrity while succeeding academically. One of the teachers in the study used the lyrics of rap songs as a way to teach elements of poetry.[8] From the rap lyrics, she went on to more conventional poetry. Students who were more skilled at creating and improvising raps were encouraged and reinforced. Another teacher worked to channel the peer group leadership of her students into classroom and schoolwide leadership. One of her African-American male students who had experienced multiple suspensions and other school problems before coming to her classroom demonstrated some obvious leadership abilities. He could be described as culturally competent in his language and interaction styles and demonstrated pride in himself and his cultural heritage. Rather than attempt to minimize his influence, the teacher encouraged him to run for sixth-grade president and mobilized the entire class to organize and help run his campaign. To the young man's surprise, he was elected. His position as president provided the teacher with many opportunities to respond to potential behavior problems. This same teacher made a point of encouraging the African-American males in her classroom to assume the role of academic leaders. Their academic leadership allowed their cultural values and styles to be appreciated and affirmed. Because these African-American male students were permitted, indeed encouraged, to be themselves in dress, language style, and interaction styles while achieving in school, the other students, who regarded them highly (because of their popularity), were able to see academic engagement as "cool."

Many of the self-described African-centered public schools have focused on this notion of cultural competence.[9] To date, little data has been reported on the academic success of students in these programs. However, the work of African-American scholars such as Ratteray (1994), Lee (1994), Hilliard (1992), Murrell (1993), Asante (1991), and others indicates that African-centered education does develop students who maintain cultural competence and demonstrate academic achievement.

Culturally relevant teaching and cultural critique

Not only must teachers encourage academic success and cultural competence, they must help students to recognize, understand, and critique current social inequities. This notion presumes that teachers themselves recognize social inequities and their causes. However, teacher educators (Grant, 1989; Haberman, 1991b; King, 1991b; King & Ladson-Billings, 1990; Zeichner, 1992) have demonstrated that many prospective teachers not only lack these understandings but reject information regarding social inequity. This suggests that more work on recruiting particular kinds of students into teaching must be done. Also, we are fortunate to have models for this kind of cultural critique emanating from the work of civil rights workers here in the U. S. (Aaronsohn, 1992; Morris, 1984; Clark, 1964; Clark, with Brown, 1990) and the international work of Freire (1973, 1974) that has been incorporated into the critical and feminist work currently being done by numerous scholars (see, e.g., Ellsworth, 1989; Giroux, 1983; Hooks, 1989; Lather, 1986; McLaren, 1989). Teachers who meet the cultural critique criteria must be engaged in a critical pedagogy which is:

> a deliberate attempt to influence how and what knowledge and identities are produced within and among particular sets of social relations. It can be understood as a practice through which people are incited to acquire a particular "moral character." As both a political and practical activity, it attempts to influence the occurrence and qualities of experiences. (Giroux & Simon, 1989, p. 239)

Thus, the teachers in this study were not reluctant to identify political underpinnings of the students' community and social world. One teacher worked with her students to identify poorly utilized space in the community, examine heretofore inaccessible archival records about the early history of the community, plan alternative uses for a vacant shopping mall, and write urban plans which they presented before the city council.

In a description of similar political activity, a class of African-American, middle-school students in Dallas identified the problem of their school's being surrounded by liquor stores (Robinson, 1993). Zoning regulations in the city made some areas dry while the students' school was in a wet area. The students identified the fact that schools serving White, upper middle-class students were located in dry areas, while schools in poor communities were in wet areas. The students, assisted by their teacher, planned a strategy for exposing this inequity. By using mathematics, literacy, social, and political skills, the students were able to prove their points with reports, editorials, charts, maps, and graphs. In both of these examples, teachers allowed students to use their community circumstances as official knowledge (Apple, 1993). Their pedagogy and the students' learning became a form of cultural critique.

Theoretical underpinnings of culturally relevant pedagogy

As I looked (and listened) to exemplary teachers of African-American students, I began to develop a grounded theory of culturally relevant pedagogy. The teachers in the study met the aforementioned criteria of helping their students to be academically successful, culturally competent, and sociopolitically critical. However, the ways in which they met these criteria seemed to differ markedly on the surface. Some teachers seemed more structured or rigid in their pedagogy. Others seemed to adopt more progressive teaching strategies. What theoretical perspective(s) held them together and allowed them to meet the criteria of culturally relevant teaching?

One of the places I began to look for these commonalties was in teachers' beliefs and ideologies. Lipman (1993) has suggested that, despite massive attempts at school reform and restructuring, teacher ideologies and beliefs often remain unchanged, particularly toward African-American children and their intellectual potential. Thus, in the analysis of the teacher interviews, classroom observations, and group analysis of videotaped segments of their teaching, I was able to deduce some broad propositions (or characteristics) that serve as theoretical underpinnings of culturally relevant pedagogy.

I approach the following propositions tentatively to avoid an essentialized and/or dichotomized notion of the pedagogy of excellent teachers. What I propose represents a range or continuum of teaching behaviors, not fixed or rigid behaviors that teachers must adhere to in order to merit the designation "culturally relevant." The need for these theoretical understandings may be more academic than pragmatic. The teachers themselves feel no need to name their practice culturally relevant. However, as a researcher and teacher educator, I am compelled to try to make this practice more accessible, particularly for those prospective teachers who do not share the cultural knowledge, experiences, and understandings of their students (Haberman, 1994).

The three broad propositions that have emerged from this research center around the following:[10]

- the conceptions of self and others held by culturally relevant teachers,
- the manner in which social relations are structured by culturally relevant teachers,
- the conceptions of knowledge held by culturally relevant teachers.

Conceptions of self and others

The sociology of teaching literature suggests that, despite the increasing professionalization of teaching (Strike, 1993), the status of teaching as a profession continues to decline. The feeling of low status is exacerbated when teachers work with what they perceive to be low-status students (Foster, 1986). However, as I acted as a participant-observer in the classrooms of exemplary teachers of African-American students, both what they said and did challenged this notion. In brief, the teachers:

- believed that all the students were capable of academic success,
- saw their pedagogy as art—unpredictable, always in the process of becoming,
- saw themselves as members of the community,
- saw teaching as a way to give back to the community,
- believed in a Freirean notion of "teaching as mining" (1974, p. 76) or pulling knowledge out.

The teachers demonstrated their commitment to these conceptions of self and others in a consistent and deliberate manner. Students were not permitted to choose failure in their classrooms. They cajoled, nagged, pestered, and bribed the students to work at high intellectual levels. Absent from their discourse about students was the "language of lacking." Students were never referred to as being from a single-parent household, being on AFDC (welfare), or needing psychological evaluation. Instead, teachers talked about their own shortcomings and limitations and ways they needed to change to ensure student success.

As I observed them teach, I witnessed spontaneity and energy that came from experience and their willingness to be risk takers. In the midst of a lesson, one teacher, seemingly bewildered by her students' expressed belief that every princess had long blond hair, swiftly went to her book shelf, pulled down an African folk tale about a princess, and shared the story with the students to challenge their assertion. In our conference afterward, she commented,

> I didn't plan to insert that book, but I just couldn't let them go on thinking that only blond-haired, White women were eligible for royalty. I know where they get those ideas, but I have a responsibility to contradict some of that. The consequences of that kind of thinking are more devastating for *our* children. (sp-6, Field notes)[11]

The teachers made conscious decisions to be a part of the community from which their students come. Three of the eight teachers in this study live in the school community. The others made deliberate efforts to come to the community for goods, services, and leisure activities, demonstrating their belief in the community as an important and worthwhile place in both their lives and the lives of the students.

A final example I present here is an elaboration of a point made earlier. It reflects the teachers' attempt to support and instill community pride in the students. One teacher used the community as the basis of her curriculum. Her students searched the county historical archives, interviewed long-term residents, constructed and administered surveys and a questionnaire, and invited and listened to guest speakers to get a sense of the historical development of their community. Their ultimate goal was to develop a land use proposal for an abandoned shopping center that was a magnet for illegal drug use and other dangerous activities. The project ended with the students' making a presentation before the City Council and Urban Planning Commission. One of the students remarked to me, "This [community] is not such a bad place. There are a lot of good things that happened here, and some of that is still going on." The teacher told me that she was concerned that too many of the students believed that their only option for success involved moving out of the community, rather than participating in its reclamation.

Social relations

Much has been written about classroom social interactions (see, e.g., Brophy & Good, 1970; Rist, 1970; Wilcox, 1982). Perhaps the strength of some of the research in this area is evidenced by its impact on classroom practices. For example, teachers throughout the nation have either heard of or implemented various forms of cooperative learning (Cohen & Benton, 1988; Slavin, 1987): cross-aged, multi-aged, and heterogeneous ability groupings. While these classroom arrangements may be designed to improve student achievement, culturally relevant teachers consciously create social interactions to help them meet the three previously mentioned criteria of academic success, cultural competence, and critical consciousness. Briefly, the teachers:

- maintain fluid student-teacher relationships,

- demonstrate a connectedness with all of the students,
- develop a community of learners,
- encourage students to learn collaboratively and be responsible for another.

In these teachers' classrooms, the teacher-student relationships are equitable and reciprocal. All of the teachers gave students opportunities to act as teachers. In one class, the teacher regularly sat at a student's desk, while the student stood at the front of the room and explained a concept or some aspect of student culture. Another teacher highlighted the expertise of various students and required other students to consult those students before coming to her for help: "Did you ask Jamal how to do those math problems?" "Make sure you check with Latasha before you turn in your reading." Because she acknowledged a wide range of expertise, the individual students were not isolated from their peers as teacher's pets. Instead, all of the students were made aware that they were expected to excel at something and that the teacher would call on them to share that expertise with classmates.

The culturally relevant teachers encouraged a community of learners rather than competitive, individual achievement. By demanding a higher level of academic success for the entire class, individual success did not suffer. However, rather than lifting up individuals (and, perhaps, contributing to feelings of peer alienation), the teachers made it clear that they were working with smart classes. For many of the students, this identification with academic success was a new experience. "Calvin was a bad student last year," said one student. "And that was last year," replied the teacher, as she designated Calvin to lead a discussion group. Another example of this community of learners was exemplified by a teacher who, herself, was a graduate student. She made a conscious decision to share what she was learning with her sixth graders. Every Friday, after her Thursday evening class, the students queried her about what she had learned.

A demonstration of the students' understanding of what she was learning occurred during the principal's observation of her teaching. A few minutes into a discussion where students were required to come up with questions they wanted answered about the book they were reading, a young man seated at a table near the rear of the class remarked with seeming disgust, "We're never gonna learn anything if y'all don't stop asking all of these low level questions!" His comment was evidence of the fact that the teacher had shared Bloom's *Taxonomy of Educational Objectives* (1956) with the class. At another time, two African-American boys were arguing over a notebook. "What seems to be the problem?" asked the teacher. "He's got my metacognitive journal!" replied one of the boys. By using the language of the teacher's graduate class, the students demonstrated their ability to assimilate her language with their own experiences.

To solidify the social relationships in their classes, the teachers encouraged the students to learn collaboratively, teach each other, and be responsible for the academic success of others. These collaborative arrangements were not necessarily structured like those of cooperative learning. Instead, the teachers used a combination of formal and informal peer collaborations. One teacher used a buddy system, where each student was paired with another. The buddies checked each other's homework and class assignments. Buddies quizzed each other for tests, and, if one buddy was absent, it was the responsibility of the other to call to see why and to help with makeup work. The teachers used this ethos of reciprocity and mutuality to insist that one person's success was the success of all and one person's failure was the failure of all. These feelings were exemplified by the teacher who insisted, "We're a family. We have to care for one another as if our very survival depended on it. . . . Actually, it does!"

Conceptions of knowledge

The third proposition that emerged from this study was one that indicated how the teachers thought about knowledge—the curriculum or content they taught—and the assessment of that knowledge. Once again, I will summarize their conceptions or beliefs about knowledge:

- Knowledge is not static; it is shared, recycled, and constructed.
- Knowledge must be viewed critically.
- Teachers must be passionate about knowledge and learning.
- Teachers must *scaffold*, or build bridges, to facilitate learning.
- Assessment must be multifaceted, incorporating multiple forms of excellence.

For the teachers in this study, knowledge was about doing. The students listened and learned from one another as well as the teacher. Early in the school year, one teacher asked the students to identify one area in which they believed they had expertise. She then compiled a list of "classroom experts" for distribution to the class. Later, she developed a calendar and asked students to select a date that they would like to make a presentation in their area of expertise. When students made their presentations, their knowledge and expertise was a given. Their classmates were expected to be an attentive audience and to take seriously the knowledge that was being shared by taking notes and/or asking relevant questions. The variety of topics the students offered included rap music, basketball, gospel singing, cooking, hair braiding, and baby-sitting. Other students listed more school-like areas of expertise such as reading, writing, and mathematics. However, all students were required to share their expertise.

Another example of the teachers' conceptions of knowledge was demonstrated in the critical stance the teachers took toward the school curriculum. Although cognizant of the need to teach certain things because of a districtwide testing policy, the teachers helped their students engage in a variety of forms of critical analyses. For one teacher, this meant critique of the social studies textbooks that were under consideration by a state evaluation panel. For two of the other teachers, critique came in the form of resistance to district-approved reading materials. Both of these teachers showed the students what it was they were supposed to be using along with what they were going to use and why. They both trusted the students with this information and enlisted them as allies against the school district's policies.

A final example in this category concerns the teachers' use of complex assessment strategies. Several of the teachers actively fought the students' *right-answer* approach to school tasks without putting the students' down. They provided them with problems and situations and helped the students to say aloud the kinds of questions they had in their minds but had been taught to suppress in most other classrooms. For one teacher, it was the simple requiring of students to always be prepared to ask, "Why?" Thus, when she posed a mathematical word problem, the first question usually went something like this: "Why are we interested in knowing this?" Or, someone would simply ask, "Why are we doing this problem?" The teacher's response was sometimes another question: "Who thinks they can respond to that question?" Other times, the teacher would offer an explanation and then ask, "Are you satisfied with that answer?" If a student said "Yes," she might say, "You shouldn't be. Just because I'm the teacher doesn't mean I'm always right." The teacher was careful to help students to understand the difference between an intellectual challenge and a challenge to the authority of their parents. Thus, just as the students were affirmed in their ability to code-switch, or move with facility, in language between African-American language and a standard form of English, they were supported in the attempts at role-switching between school and home.

Another teacher helped her students to choose both the standards by which they were to be evaluated and the pieces of evidence they wanted to use as proof of their mastery of particular concepts and skills. None of the teachers or their students seemed to have test anxiety about the school district's standardized tests. Instead, they viewed the tests as necessary irritations, took them, scored better than their age-grade mates at their school, and quickly returned to the rhythm of learning in their classroom.

Conclusion

I began this article arguing for a theory of culturally relevant pedagogy. I also suggested that the tensions that surround my position as a native in the research field force me to face the theoretical and philosophical biases I bring to my work in overt and explicit ways. Thus, I situated my work in the context of Black feminist thought. I suggested that culturally relevant teaching must meet three criteria: an ability to develop students academically, a willingness to nurture and support cultural competence, and the development of a sociopolitical or critical consciousness. Next, I argued that culturally relevant teaching is distinguishable by three broad propositions or conceptions regarding self and other, social relations, and knowledge. With this theoretical perspective, I attempted to broaden notions of pedagogy beyond strictly psychological models. I also have argued that earlier sociolinguistic explanations have failed to include the larger social and cultural contexts of students and the cultural ecologists have failed to explain student success. I predicated the need for a culturally relevant theoretical perspective on the growing disparity between the racial, ethnic, and cultural characteristics of teachers and students along with the continued academic failure of African-American, Native American and Latino students.

Although I agree with Haberman's (1991b) assertion that teacher educators are unlikely to make much of a difference in the preparation of teachers to work with students in urban poverty unless they are able to recruit "better" teacher candidates, I still believe researchers are obligated to re-educate the candidates we currently attract toward a more expansive view of pedagogy (Bartolome, 1994). This can be accomplished partly by helping prospective teachers understand culture (their own and others) and the ways it functions in education. Rather than add on versions of multicultural education or human relations courses (Zeichner, 1992) that serve to exoticize diverse students as "other," a culturally relevant pedagogy is designed to problematize teaching and encourage teachers to ask about the nature of the student–teacher relationship, the curriculum, schooling, and society.

This study represents a beginning look at ways that teachers might systematically include student culture in the classroom as authorized or official knowledge.

It also is a way to encourage praxis as an important aspect of research (Lather, 1986). This kind of research needs to continue in order to support new conceptions of collaboration between teachers and researchers (practitioners and theoreticians). We need research that proposes alternate models of pedagogy, coupled with exemplars of successful pedagogues. More importantly, we need to be willing to look for exemplary practice in those classrooms and communities that too many of us are ready to dismiss as incapable of producing excellence.

The implication of continuing this kind of work means that research grounded in the practice of exemplary teachers will form a significant part of the knowledge base on which we build teacher preparation. It means that the research community will have to be willing to listen to and heed the "wisdom of practice" (Shulman, 1987, p. 12) of these excellent practitioners. Additionally, we need to consider methodologies that present more robust portraits of teaching. Meaningful combinations of quantitative and qualitative inquiries must be employed to help us understand the deeply textured, multilayered enterprise of teaching.

I presume that the work I have been doing raises more questions than it answers. A common question asked by practitioners is, "Isn't what you described just 'good teaching'?" And, while I do not deny that it is good teaching, I pose a counter question: why does so little of it seem to occur in classrooms populated by African-American students? Another question that arises is whether or not this pedagogy is so idiosyncratic that only "certain" teachers can engage in it. I would argue that the diversity of these teachers and the variety of teaching strategies they employed challenge that notion. The common feature they shared was a classroom practice grounded in what they believed about the educability of the students. Unfortunately, this raises troubling thoughts about those teachers who are not successful, but we cannot assume that they do not believe that some students are incapable (or unworthy) of being educated. The reasons for their lack of success are far too complex for this discussion.

Ultimately, my responsibility as a teacher educator who works primarily with young, middle-class, White women is to provide them with the examples of culturally relevant teaching in both theory and practice. My responsibility as a researcher is to continue to inquire in order to move toward a theory of culturally relevant pedagogy.

Notes

I am grateful to the National Academy of Education's Spencer postdoctoral fellowship program for providing me with the funding to conduct this research. However, the ideas expressed here are my own and do not necessarily reflect those of the National Academy of Education or the Spencer Foundation.

1 Although issues of culturally relevant teaching can and should be considered cross-culturally, this work looks specifically at the case of African-American students.
2 It is interesting to note that a number of trade books have emerged that detail the rage and frustration of academically successful, professional, middle-class, African-American adults, which suggests that, even with the proper educational credentials, their lives continue to be plagued by racism and a questioning of their competence. Among the more recent books are Jill Nelson's *Volunteer Slavery* (1993), Brent Staples's *Parallel Time* (1994), and Ellis Cose's *The Rage of a Privileged Class* (1993).
3 It should be noted that the "cultural deficit" notion has been reinscribed under the rubric of "at-risk" (Cuban, 1989). Initially, the U. S. Commission on Excellence in Education defined the nation as at risk. Now, almost 10 years later, it appears that only

some children are at risk. Too often, in the case of African-American students, their racial/cultural group membership defines them as at risk.

4 The research collaborative met to view portions of the classroom videotapes that I, as researcher, selected for common viewing.

5 These correlates include: a clear and focused mission, instructional leadership, a safe and orderly environment, regular monitoring of student progress, high expectations, and positive home–school relations.

6 Students in this district took the California Achievement Test (CAT) in October and May of each school year. Growth scores in the classrooms of the teachers in the study were significantly above those of others in the district.

7 This is not to suggest that cultural competence for African-American students means being a failure. The problem that African-American students face is the constant devaluation of their culture both in school and in the larger society. Thus, the styles apparent in African-American youth culture—e.g., dress, music, walk, language—are equated with poor academic performance. The student who identifies with "hip-hop" culture may be regarded as dangerous and/or a gang member for whom academic success is not expected. He (and it usually is a male) is perceived as not having the *cultural* capital (Bourdieu, 1984) necessary for academic success.

8 An examination of rap music reveals a wide variety of messages. Despite the high profile of "gansta rap," which seems to glorify violence, particularly against the police and Whites, and the misogynistic messages found in some of this music, there is a segment of rap music that serves as cultural critique and urges African Americans to educate themselves because schools fail to do so. Prominent rap artists in this tradition are Arrested Development, Diggable Planets, KRS-1, and Queen Latifah.

9 I am indebted to Mwalimu Shujaa for sharing his working paper, "Afrikan-Centered Education in Afrikan-Centered Schools: The Need for Consensus Building," which elaborates the multiplicity of thinking on this issue extant in the African-centered movement.

10 Readers should note that I have listed these as separate and distinct categories for analytical purposes. In practice, they intersect and overlap, continuously.

11 These letters and numbers represent codes I employed to distinguish among the interview data and field notes I collected during the study.

References

Aaronsohn, L. (1992). Learning to teach for empowerment. *Radical Teacher, 40*, 44–46.

African American Male Task Force. (1990). *Educating African American males: A dream deferred* (Report). Washington, DC: Author.

Amundson, R., Serlin, R. C., & Lehrer, R. (1992). On the threats that do not face educational research. *Educational Researcher, 21*(9), 19–24.

Anderson, J. (1988). *The education of Blacks in the South, 1860–1935*. Chapel Hill, NC: University of North Carolina Press.

Apple, M. (1993). *Official knowledge*. New York: Routledge.

Apple, M., & Weiss, L. (1983). *Ideology and practice in schooling*. Philadelphia: Temple University Press.

Argyris, C. (1980). *Inner contradictions of rigorous research*. New York: Academic.

Asante, M. K. (1991). The Afrocentric idea in education. *The Journal of Negro Education, 60*, 170–180.

Atkin, J. M. (1973). Practice-oriented inquiry: A third approach to research in education. *Educational Researcher, 2*(7), 3–4.

Au, K., & Jordan, C. (1981). Teaching reading to Hawaiian children: Finding a culturally appropriate solution. In H. Trueba, G. Guthrie, & K. Au (Eds.), *Culture and the bilingual classroom: Studies in classroom ethnography* (pp. 139–152). Rowley, MA: Newbury.

Bacon, M. (1981, May). *High potential children from Ravenswood Elementary School District* (Follow-up study). Redwood City, CA: Sequoia Union High School District.

Banks, J. A. (1992). African American scholarship and the evolution of multicultural education. *The Journal of Negro Education, 61*, 273–286.

Bartolome, L. (1994). Beyond the methods fetish: Toward a humanizing pedagogy. *Harvard Educational Review, 64*, 173–194.

Becker, H. S. (1967). Whose side are we on? *Social Problems, 14*, 239–247.

Berliner, D. (1988, October). *Implications of studies of expertise in pedagogy for teacher education and evaluation. New directions for teacher assessment.* Conference proceedings of the ETS Invitational Conference. Princeton, NJ: Educational Testing Service.

Beyer, L. E. (1991). Teacher education, reflective inquiry, and moral action. In B. R. Tabachnick & K. M. Zeichner (Eds.), *Inquiry-oriented practice teacher education* (pp. 112–129). London: Falmer.

Billingsley, A. (1992). *Climbing Jacob's ladder. The enduring legacy of African American families*. New York: Simon & Schuster.

Bloom, B. (1956). *Taxonomy of educational objectives* (1st ed.). New York: Longman, Green.

Bloom, B. S., Davis, A., & Hess, R. (1965). *Compensatory education for cultural deprivation.* New York: Holt.

Bond, H. M. (1969). *A Negro education: A study in cotton and steel.* NY: Octagon.

Bourdieu, P. (1984). *Distinctions: The social critique of the judgment of taste.* Cambridge, MA: Harvard University Press.

Bowles, S. (1977). Unequal education and the reproduction of the social division of labor. In J. Karabel & A. H. Halsey (Eds.), *Power and ideology in education* (pp. 137–153). New York: Oxford University Press.

Brookover, W. (1985). Can we make schools effective for minority students? *The Journal of Negro Education, 54*, 257–268.

Brookover, W., Beady, C., Flood, P., Schweitzer, J., & Wisenbaker, J. (1979). *School social systems and student achievement: Schools can make a difference.* New York: Praeger.

Brophy, J., & Good, T. (1970). Teachers' communication of differential expectations for children's classroom performance. *Journal of Educational Psychology, 61*, 365–374.

Bullock, H. A. (1967). *A history of Negro education in the South from 1614 to the present.* Cambridge, MA: Harvard University Press.

Carr, W., & Kemmis, S. (1986). *Becoming critical: Education, knowledge and action research.* (Rev. ed.). Victoria, Australia: Deakin University Press.

Carter, K. (1993). The place of story in the study of teaching and teacher education. *Educational Researcher, 22*(1), 5–12, 18.

Cazden, C., & Leggett, E. (1981). Culturally responsive education: Recommendations for achieving Lau remedies II. In H. Trueba, G. Guthrie, & K. Au (Eds.), *Culture and the bilingual classroom: Studies in classroom ethnography* (pp. 69–86). Rowley, MA: Newbury.

Clark, R. (1983). *Family life and school achievement: Why poor Black children succeed or fail.* Chicago: Chicago University Press.

Clark, S. (1964, First Quarter). Literacy and liberation. *Freedomways*, pp. 113–124.

Clark, S., with Brown, C. (1990). *Ready from within: A first person narrative.* Trenton, NJ: Africa World Press.

Cochran-Smith, M., & Lytle, S. (1992). *Inside/outside: Teachers, research, and knowledge.* NY: Teachers College Press.

Code, L. (1991). *What can she know? Feminist theory and the construction of knowledge.* Ithaca, NY: Cornell University Press.

Cohen, E., & Benton, J. (1988, Fall). Making groupwork work. *American Educator*, pp. 10–17, 45–46.

Collins, P. H. (1991). *Black feminist thought.* New York: Routledge.

Comer, J. (1984). Home school relationships as they affect the academic success of children. *Education and Urban Society, 16*, 323–337.

Cose, E. (1993). *The rage of a privileged class.* New York: HarperCollins.

Cronbach, L. J. (1975). Beyond the two disciplines of scientific psychology. *American Psychologist, 30*, 116–127.

Cuban, L. (1989). The "at-risk" label and the problem of urban school reform. *Phi Delta Kappan, 70*, 264–271.

Delpit, L. (1992). Acquisition of literate discourse: Bowing before the master? *Theory into Practice, 31*, 296–271.

Edmonds, R. (1979). Effective schools for the urban poor. *Educational Leadership, 37*, 15–24.
Elliot, J. (1991). *Action research for educational change*. Philadelphia: Open University Press.
Ellsworth, E. (1989). Why doesn't this feel empowering? Working through the repressive myths of critical pedagogy. *Harvard Educational Review, 59*, 297–324.
Erickson, F. (1987). Transformation and school success: The politics and culture of educational achievement. *Anthropology and Education, 18*, 335–356.
Erickson, F. (1993). Transformation and school success: The politics and culture of educational achievement. In E. Jacob & C. Jordan (Eds.), *Minority education: Anthropological perspectives* (pp. 27–51). Norwood, NJ: Ablex.
Erickson, F., & Mohatt, G. (1982). Cultural organization and participation structures in two classrooms of Indian students. In G. Spindler (Ed.), *Doing the ethnography of schooling* (pp. 131–174). New York: Holt, Rinehart & Winston.
Fine, M. (1986). Why urban adolescents drop into and out of high school. *Teachers College Record, 87*, 393–409.
Fordham, S. (1988). Racelessness as a factor in Black student's school success: Pragmatic strategy or pyrrhic victory? *Harvard Educational Review, 58*, 54–84.
Fordham, S., & Ogbu, J. (1986). Black students' school success: Coping with the burden of "acting white." *The Urban Review, 18*, 176–206.
Foster, H. L. (1986). *Ribbin', jivin' and playin' the dozens*. Cambridge, MA: Ballinger.
Foster, M. (1991). Constancy, connectedness, and constraints in the lives of African American teachers. *National Women's Studies Journal, 3*, 233–261.
Freire, P. (1973). *Education for critical consciousness*. New York: Seabury.
Freire, P. (1974). *Pedagogy of the oppressed*. New York: Seabury.
Gage, N. L. (1989). The paradigm wars and their aftermath. *Educational Researcher, 18* (7), 4–10.
Gay, G., & Abrahamson, R. D. (1972). Talking black in the classroom. In R. D. Abrahamson & R. Troike (Eds.), *Language and cultural diversity in education* (pp. 200–208). Englewood Cliffs, NJ: Prentice-Hall.
Gilligan, C. (1982). *In a different voice*. Cambridge, MA: Harvard University Press.
Giroux, H. (1983). *Theory and resistance: A pedagogy for the opposition*. Hadley, MA: Bergin & Garvey.
Giroux, H., & Simon, R. (1989). Popular culture and critical pedagogy: Everyday life as a basis for curriculum knowledge. In H. Giroux & P. McLaren (Eds.), *Critical pedagogy, the state, and cultural struggle* (pp. 236–252). Albany, NY: State University of New York Press.
Glaser, B. G., & Strauss, A. L. (1967). *The discovery of grounded theory: Strategies for qualitative research*. Chicago: Aldine.
Gouldner, A. (1970). *The coming crisis in western sociology*. New York: Basic.
Grant, C. A. (1989). Urban teachers: Their new colleagues and curriculum. *Phi Delta Kappan, 70*, 764–770.
Haberman, M. (1991a). The rationale for training adults as teachers. In C. E. Sleeter (Ed.), *Empowerment through multicultural education* (pp. 275–286). Albany, NY: State University of New York Press.
Haberman, M. (1991b). Can cultural awareness be taught in teacher education programs? *Teaching Education, 4*, 25–32.
Haberman, M. (1994, January 24). Redefining the "best and the brightest." *In These Times*, pp. 17–18.
Harding, V. (1981). *There is a river: The Black struggle for freedom in America*. Harcourt Brace Jovanovich.
Harris, V. (1992). African American conceptions of literacy: A historical perspective. *Theory into Practice, 31*, 276–286.
Hilliard, A. (1992). Behavioral style, culture, and teaching and learning. *The Journal of Negro Education, 61*, 370–377.
Hooks, B. (1989). *Talking back: Thinking feminist, thinking black*. Boston: South End Press.
Irvine, J. (1990). *Black students and school failure*. Westport, CT: Greenwood.
Johnson, C. (1936). The education of the Negro child. *American Sociological Review, 1*, 264–272.

Jordan, C. (1985). Translating culture: From ethnographic information to educational program. *Anthropology and Education Quarterly, 16*, 105–123.

Kaestle, C. (1993). The awful reputation of educational research. *Educational Researcher, 22* (1), 23, 26–31.

Katzer, J., Cook, K., & Crouch, W. (1978). *Evaluating information.* Menlo Park, CA: Addison-Wesley.

King, J. (1991a). Unfinished business: Black student alienation and Black teachers' emancipatory pedagogy. In M. Foster (Ed.), *Readings on equal education* (Vol. 11, pp. 245–271). New York: AMS.

King, J. (1991b). Dysconscious racism: Ideology, identity, and the miseducation of teachers. *The Journal of Negro Education, 60*, 133–146.

King, J., & Ladson-Billings, G. (1990). The teacher education challenge in elite university settings: Developing critical perspectives for teaching in a democratic and multicultural society. *European Journal of Intercultural Studies, 1*, 15–30.

King, J., & Mitchell, C. A. (1990). *Black mothers to sons: Juxtaposing African American literature with social practice.* New York: Peter Lang.

Kleinfeld, J. (1992). Learning to think like a teacher: The study of cases. In J. Shulman (Ed.), *Case methods in teacher education* (pp. 33–49). New York: Teachers College Press.

Kuhn, T. S. (1970). *The origins of scientific revolutions.* Chicago: University of Chicago Press.

Labov, W. (1969). The logic of non-standard Negro English. In J. E. Alatis (Ed.), *Linguistics and the teaching of standard English* (Monograph Series on Language and Linguistics, No. 22). Washington, DC: Georgetown University Press.

Ladson-Billings, G. (1990). Like lightning in a bottle: Attempting to capture the pedagogical excellence of successful teachers of Black students. *International Journal of Qualitative Studies in Education, 3*, 335–344.

Ladson-Billings, G. (1992a). Liberatory consequences of literacy: A case of culturally relevant instruction for African American students. *The Journal of Negro Education, 61*, 378–391.

Ladson-Billings, G. (1992b). Reading between the lines and beyond the pages: A culturally relevant approach to literacy teaching. *Theory into Practice, 31*, 312–320.

Ladson-Billings, G. (1994). *The dreamkeepers: Successful teaching for African American students.* San Francisco: Jossey-Bass.

Lather, P. (1986). Research as praxis. *Harvard Educational Review, 56*, 257–277.

Lee, C. (1994). African-centered pedagogy: Complexities and possibilities. In M. J. Shujaa (Ed.), *Too much schooling, too little education* (pp. 295–318). Trenton, NJ: Africa World Press.

Lipman, P. (1993). *The influence of restructuring on teachers' beliefs about and practices with African American students.* Unpublished doctoral dissertation, University of Wisconsin, Madison.

Lutz, F., & Ramsey, M. (1974). The use of anthropological field methods in education. *Educational Researcher, 3* (10), 5–9.

McLaren, P. (1989). *Life in schools.* White Plains, NY: Longman.

Mohatt, G., & Erickson, F. (1981). Cultural differences in teaching styles in an Odawa school: A sociolinguistic approach. In H. Trueba, G. Guthrie, & K. Au (Eds.), *Culture and the bilingual classroom: Studies in classroom ethnography* (pp. 105–119). Rowley, MA: Newbury.

Morris, A. (1984). *The origins of the civil rights movement.* New York: The Free Press.

Murrell, P. (1990, April). *Cultural politics in teacher education: What's missing in the preparation of African American teachers?* Paper presented at the Annual Meeting of the American Educational Research Association, Boston.

Murrell, P. (1991, April). *Deconstructing informal knowledge of exemplary teaching in diverse urban communities: Apprenticing preservice teachers as case study researchers in cultural sites.* Paper presented at the Annual Meeting of the American Educational Research Association, Chicago.

Murrell, P. (1993). Afrocentric immersion: Academic and personal development of African American males in public schools. In T. Perry & J. Fraser (Eds.), *Freedom's plow: Teaching in the multicultural classroom* (pp. 231–259). New York: Routledge.

Narayan, K. (1993). How native is a "native" anthropologist? *American Anthropologist, 95*, 671–686.
Nelson, J. (1993). Volunteer slavery. Chicago: Noble.
Noddings, N. (1984). *Caring*. Berkeley: University of California Press.
Noddings, N. (1991). Stories in dialogue: Caring and interpersonal reasoning. In C. Witherell & N. Noddings (Eds.), *Stories lives tell: Narrative and dialogue in education* (pp. 157–170). New York: Teachers College Press.
Noordhoff, K. (1990). Shaping the rhetoric of reflection for multicultural settings. In R. T. Cliff, W. R. Houston, & M. C. Pugach (Eds.), *Encouraging reflective practice in education* (pp. 163–185). New York: Teachers College Press.
Noordhoff, K., & Kleinfeld, J. (1991, April). *Preparing teachers for multicultural classrooms: A case study in rural Alaska*. Paper presented at the Annual Meeting of the American Educational Research Association, Chicago.
Ogbu, J. (1981). Black education: A cultural-ecological perspective. In H. P. McAdoo (Ed.), *Black families* (pp. 139–154). Beverly Hills: Sage.
Ogbu, J. (1983). Minority status and schooling in plural societies. *Comparative Education Review, 27*, 168–190.
Padilla, A. (1994). Ethnic minority scholars, research, and mentoring: Current and future issues. *Educational Researcher, 23* (4), 24–27.
Patton, M. Q. (1975). *Alternative evaluation research paradigm*. Grand Forks, ND: University of North Dakota Press.
Perry, T. (1993). *Toward a theory of African American school achievement* (Report No. 16). Wheelock College, Boston, MA: Center on Families, Communities, Schools, and Children's Learning.
Peterson, P., & Neumann, A. (Eds.), (1995). *Research and everyday life: The personal sources of educational inquiry*. New York: Teachers College Press.
Piestrup, A. (1973). *Black dialect interference and accommodation of reading instruction in first grade* (Monograph No. 4). Berkeley: Language Behavior Research Laboratory.
Popkewitz, T. S. (1991). *A political sociology of educational reform*. New York: Teachers College Press.
Ratteray, J. D. (1994). The search for access and content in the education of African Americans. In M. J. Shujaa (Ed.), *Too much schooling, too little education* (pp. 123–142). Trenton, NJ: Africa World Press.
Rist, R. (1970). Student social class and teacher expectations: The self-fulfilling prophecy in ghetto schools. *Harvard Educational Review, 40*, 411–450.
Rist, R. (1990). On the relations among educational research paradigms: From disdain to dÈtentes. In K. Dougherty & F. Hammack (Eds.), *Education and society: A reader* (pp. 81–95). New York: Harcourt Brace Javanovich.
Robinson, R. (1993, February 25). P. C. Anderson students try hand at problem-solving. *Dallas Examiner*, pp. 1, 8.
Rosaldo, R. (1989). *Culture and truth: The remaking of social analysis*. Boston: Beacon.
Rury, J. (1983). The New York African Free School, 1827–1836: Conflict over community control of Black education. *Phylon, 44*, 187, 198.
Shulman, L. (1987). Knowledge and teaching: Foundations of the new reform. *Harvard Educational Review, 63*, 161–182.
Siddle-Walker, V. (1993). Caswell County Training School, 1933–1969: Relationships between community and school. *Harvard Educational Review, 63*, 161–182.
Singer, E. (1988). *What is cultural congruence, and why are they saying such terrible things about it?* (Occasional Paper). East Lansing, MI: Institute for Research on Teaching.
Slaughter, D., & Kuehne, V. (1988). Improving Black education: Perspectives on parent involvement. *Urban League Review, 11*, 59–75.
Slavin, R. (1987). Cooperative learning and the cooperative school. *Educational Leadership, 45*, 7–13.
Smith, L. M. (1978). An evolving logic of participant observation, education ethnography, and other case studies. In L. Shulman (Ed.), *Review of research in education* (pp. 316–377). Itasca, IL: Peacock/AERA.
Spradley, J. (1979). *The ethnographic interview*. New York: Holt, Rinehart & Winston.
Staples, B. (1994). *Parallel time: Growing up in black and white*. New York: Pantheon.
Stenhouse, L. (1983). The relevance of practice to theory. *Theory into Practice, 22*, 211–215.

Strike, K. (1993). Professionalism, democracy, and discursive communities: Normative reflections on restructuring. *American Educational Research Journal, 30*, 255–275.

Villegas, A. (1988). School failure and cultural mismatch: Another view. *The Urban Review, 20*, 253–265.

Vogt, L., Jordan, C., & Tharp, R. (1987). Explaining school failure, producing school success: Two cases. *Anthropology and Education Quarterly, 18*, 276–286.

Weiler, K. (1988). *Women teaching for change*. New York: Bergin & Garvey.

Weinberg, M. (1977). *A chance to learn: A history of race and education in the United States*. Cambridge, MA: Cambridge University Press.

Wilcox, K. (1982). Differential socialization in the classroom: Implications for equal opportunity. In G. Spindler (Ed.), *Doing the ethnography of schooling* (pp. 268–309). Prospect Heights, IL: Waveland.

Woodson, C. G. (1919). *The education of the Negro prior to 1861*. Washington, DC: Associated Publishers.

Young R. (1990). *A critical theory of education*. New York: Teachers College Press.

Zeichner, K. (1990). Preparing teachers for democratic schools. *Action in Teacher Education, 11*, 5–10.

Zeichner, K. (1992). *Educating teachers for cultural diversity* (Special Report). East Lansing, MI: National Center for Research on Teacher Learning.

CHAPTER 15

COMMUNITIES OF DIFFERENCE (1995)

A critical look at desegregated spaces created for and by youth

Michelle Fine, Lois Weis, and Linda C. Powell

> The problem of the 20th century is the problem of the color line.
>
> —W. E. B. DuBois

> The problem of the 20th century is the problem of civilizing white people.
>
> —Nikki Giovanni

It appears that W. E. B. DuBois, with Giovanni's friendly amendment, might have been a two-century prophet. The color line remains, stubbornly, the defining feature of social and economic relations in twentieth-century America, confounded with class and eclipsing ethnicities. Given the persistence of racial tensions, conflicts, and, most recently, the uninhibited and vile racist rhetoric embedded in the media and national politics, it seems absurd, indeed desperate, that we as adults look to youth to accomplish what we haven't been able to accomplish—to establish rich, vibrant, and cooperative interracial relationships, contexts, communities, and projects. Yet it is with youth that our hope for the future lies.

Among us (Michelle, Lois, Linda), we have spent years consulting with teachers, studying student behavior, and even testifying for racial and gender equity within schools that have achieved what Thomas Pettigrew (1986) would call "desegregation," that is, the coexistence of students from different racial and ethnic groups within the same institution. But rarely have we had the pleasure of working with, studying, or even testifying for a truly "integrated" school (Metz, 1994), a school that self-consciously creates intellectual and social engagement across racial and ethnic groups. In this article, we distinguish between desegregated and integrated spaces, and we note that even settings of minimal desegregation are disappearing rapidly as we close the twentieth century. Today, neighborhoods are further segregating as school districts withdraw from desegregation decrees (Dreier & Moberg, 1996; Orfield & Eaton, 1996).

Our youth have had to manage the challenges of a rapidly changing racial and ethnic demography, and in some small corners of the earth they have done so, beautifully. Our objective here is to document three public school sites along a continuum from desegregated-but-racially-separate to integrated communities of differences in order to unravel systematically what it is that makes the latter work, so that these communities do not remain idiosyncratic, charisma-driven, precious, and, soon, extinct.

Having just finished editing *Off-White* (Fine, Weis, Powell, & Wong, 1997), in which we theoretically decentered Whiteness, the stance from which we launch this work takes seriously the past fifty years of extensive research on equal status and contact theory. It is our sense that the extensive, and at this moment dominant, frame on integration—equal status contact theory—must be repositioned within the broad theoretical context of community difference and democracy if we are to fully understand, document, and enable the creation and sustenance of more spaces designed for and by multiracial communities of youth.

Equal status contact theory: what we've been told

The theory of equal status contact posits four necessary conditions:

1. *Equal status*. The contact should occur in circumstances that place the two groups in an equal status.
2. *Personal interaction*. The contact should involve one-on-one interactions among individual members of the two groups.
3. *Cooperative activities*. Members of the two groups should join together in an effort to achieve superordinate goals.
4. *Social norms*. The social norms, defined in part by relevant authorities, should favor intergroup contact. (Brehm & Kassin, 1996, p. 157)

Under these conditions, children from different backgrounds—even historically unequal backgrounds—are presumed to interact in ways that produce positive task and interpersonal outcomes. As Janet Schofield (1982, 1995) reminds us, however, it is the truly exceptional school or community-based context in which we can find all of these conditions. From Gordon Allport's (1954) original work on prejudice through Muzifer and Carolyn Sherif's Robber Cave Experiments (1958), in which competitive groups of boys joined together when faced with a common enemy, to more contemporary, school-based work by David and Roger Johnson (1995), Robert Slavin (1995), and Janet Schofield (1995), we have been shown that when the conditions of equal status contact are created, interracial relations, attitudes, and networks do indeed improve. However, researchers typically find that over time these contexts develop and ultimately suffer from what Jomills Braddock, Marvin Dawkins, and George Wilson (1995) call inclusion and interaction barriers; for example, differential expectations, subtle forms of social exclusion, diminished verbal and nonverbal communication with and/or harassment of the now-included "other." All three of us have spent years in public schools and community settings as consultants, teachers, researchers, and organizers, bumping up against the stubborn persistence with which the formal structures, ideologies, informal practices of schooling, and often community life, resist inclusion. Thus we feel the need to surround equal status contact theory with a framework that draws on three traditionally independent literatures—those on community, difference, and democracy. We take as our premise that, in order for multiracial youth relations to flourish, three political and social conditions—none natural or automatic—must be intentionally set in place: a sense of community; a commitment to creative analysis of difference, power, and privilege; and an enduring investment in democratic practice with youth. In the absence of these three conditions, settings that are technically desegregated will corrode into sites of oppositional identities, racial tensions, and fractured group relations, which simply mirror the larger society. To create these conditions requires deliberate counter-hegemonic struggle by educators, activists, and youth, to invent and sustain multiracial intellectual and social sites for everyone—what integration means after all.

In our work, we are interested in understanding how to nurture these multiracial communities to be sustainable, in ways that engage groups of youth and adults who are not merely co-located but deliberately invested in a diverse group larger than self, rich in racially and ethnically diverse connections and differences. There is much evidence that designed cooperation has produced positive outcomes for such groups of youth in camps (Sherif, 1958), schools (Johnson & Johnson, 1995; Slavin, 1995), and laboratories (Gaertner, Dovidio, Anastasio, Bachman, & Rust, 1993; Gaertner et al., 1997). The beauty of these studies is that they enable us to know which micro-structures of cooperation foster positive consequences for sense of self, a more empathic view of other, and a reduction of stereotypical attitudes. But what we don't know is how a structured community of such relationships can be initiated, much less supported over time, for and by adolescents in actual communities that are porous and vulnerable to surrounding politics. Nor do we know much about how adults—enthused, hostile, ignorant, frightened, or merely unsupported—can create and sustain such communities.

Tony Bryk, Valerie Lee, and P. B. Holland (1993) have demonstrated the extent to which a communitarian ideology sits at the core of successful and diverse schools by instilling in community members a shared ideology, identity and vision. Susan Opotow (1995) has written on the interior dynamics of such moral communities (groups of individuals who share a sense of identity and extend a common set of principles of justice across the group) with an eye on what happens both within and beyond them to maintain their borders. She raises important theoretical questions about the nature of cooperative bonds, the sense of shared purpose and trust, the agreed-upon boundaries, and the demarcated out-groups inherent in community life. In studying the conditions under which separate, sometimes competing, groups of youth can be motivated to see themselves no longer as "us" and "them," but as "we," Samuel Gaertner and colleagues (1997) focused on a shared out-group, a common enemy. But we are haunted by the recurrent assumption, traced to Henri Tajfel and John Turner (1979), that in-group identities are formed inherently at the borders in opposition to out-groups. Through our research, we seek to understand the emergence of multiracial community life and to challenge Tajfel's assumption of the necessity of out-groups. That is, we hope to deepen what is known by Bryk, Opotow, Gaertner, and colleagues by discerning the conditions under which youths are willing to aspire toward an in-group identity that is sufficiently compelling, while rejecting the need to derogate out-groups (Tajfel & Turner, 1979).

Thus we complicate community with "difference." The ever-hovering questions of community—multiculturalism, inclusion, identity—of the late twentieth century inspire our second theoretical interest (see Banks, 1995; Hare-Mustin & Marecek, 1990; Minow, 1990; Rhode, 1990; Steele, 1988). Reflecting back on equal status contact theory, we worry that, by intent, the theory and its implementations have failed to analyze or deal with the rich cultural differences in biographies, passions, expectations, stereotypes, troubles, and hopes that young people bring to their cross-racial and cross-ethnic relationships (Phillips, Penn, & Gaines, 1993; Plummer, 1995; Semons, 1991; Spencer, Swanson, & Cunningham, 1991; Stevenson, 1995). Equality doubles for sameness. Differences are whited out. In theory and practice, cross-group interactions are supposed to proceed as if differences in style, history, personal and social expectations, and power could be bracketed. But like political theorist Nancy Fraser (1990), who writes on the difficulties of creating democratically accessible public spheres that bridge preexisting inequalities, we worry that the existing asymmetries in life experiences, sense of entitlement, and faculty/peer expectations can't and shouldn't simply be put aside for a moment by youth or adults. We worry that when educators ask students to bracket these differences as if we were all the same, a privileged center remains untroubled, questions of difference are suspended or suffocated, and the particular costs of bracketing differences are absorbed by students of color. Thus we seek to understand how differences disrupt or facilitate communities that are diverse in race and ethnicity. Our concern, of course, is that the bracketing assumption—leave your differences at the door—reproduces privilege, oppression, and opposition in the guise of neutrality or "color-blindness."

Following the lead of scholars such as Henry Louis Gates Jr. (1985), Stuart Hall (1991), and Martha Minow (1990), we believe that differences in race, ethnicity, class, and gender are, at this moment in history, constructed by politics, power, and biography, and are fluid and mutable. But, they are also, of course, intimately lived (Plummer, 1995; Stevenson, 1995). Differences are at once real and fictional, material and invented, enduring and mutable, rejected and embodied (Marcia, 1980; Semons, 1991). Drawing on the writings of Lani Guinier (1994), William Cross Jr. (1995), and Kimberlé Crenshaw (1992), we see race as a critical and defining feature of lived experience that young and old and people of all colors reflect upon, embody, challenge, and negotiate (see Marcia, 1980; Thorne, 1993). While race, class, ethnicity, and gender certainly influence the standpoint from which each of us views the world (Collins, 1990; Hartsock, 1984; Weis & Fine, 1993, 1996), it is as true that no one demographic box can fully contain one's point of view (Cross, 1995; Hurtado & Stewart, 1997). There is too much wonderful variety, too much moving around, and, indeed, too much playing with race for these categories to sit still. William Cross Jr. (1995), Stuart Hall (1991), and Howard Winant (1997) have taught us all that we cannot assume race to be a fixed entity. But we wonder about what conditions are in place that fix race, and what conditions must be in place in schools for such play with differences to flourish. What structures and practices, by adults and youth, enable young people to work with—not around or in spite of—race, ethnicity, and power-based differences? Within multiracial settings, when are young people invited to discuss, voice, critique, and re-view the very notions of race that feel so fixed, so hierarchical, so damaging, and so accepted in the broader culture? This invitation to re-view, we believe, marks a critical cleavage in the distinction between sites of desegregation and those of integration (Lawrence & Tatum, 1997). Merely including youth or teachers of different races and ethnicities in the same school clearly does not produce an integrated school.

The research and writings of social scientists (Clark & Saegert, in press; Putnam, 1993; Vanderslice, 1995) have convinced us that the practice of participation and democracy must be at the heart of creating, and, even more so, of sustaining multiracial communities of difference invested in and by youths and adults. Social psychologist Virginia Vanderslice (1995) writes on the power, sustainability, and vulnerabilities of worker-owned cooperatives. Without intentional structures for and (re)education in democratic practice, Vanderslice finds these cooperatives often cave in to the powerful forces of competitive capitalism in their surround. The fissures of race, class, gender, management/labor will reemerge unless deliberate democratic process is practiced. Likewise, environmental psychologists Heléne Clark and Susan Saegert (in press) have conducted participatory action research in tenant-owned versus city-managed public housing, and documented substantially better outcomes for quality of life, safety, and civic engagement in the tenant-owned housing. These researchers provide substantial evidence of the enduring positive consequence of cooperative participation and, inversely, that diverse communities are too fragile to endure if they are simply the creation of a few charismatic, visionary, or even autocratic—if well-meaning—adults.

Thus, we now seek to extend these findings to reveal how contexts of diversity and democracy in schools can generate youth leadership, voice, and participation. We are not so naive as to think that any of the positive outcomes of democratic participation would evolve spontaneously within multiracial groups of youth or without enormous coordination and collaboration by adults and youth. But we are also not sanguine that hypercontrol of the multiracial contexts by adults produces the sense of ownership or community building among youth that needs to take place to sustain long-term, profoundly integrated education.

In this country we have few models for creating, much less sustaining, communities of difference. We may have harmonious, even successful, communities of homogeneity (although their fractures, too, are growing more public). In response to this paucity of examples and exemplars, we seek to understand public spaces—indeed schools—where differences are self-consciously drawn upon to enrich and texture the community; where negotiations of difference lie at the heart of the community; and where democratic participation is a defining aspect of decision-making and daily life within the community. If schools are to produce engaged, critical citizens who are willing to imagine and build multiracial and multiethnic communities, then we presume schools must take as their task the fostering of group life that ensures equal status, but within a context that takes community-building as its task. The process of sustaining a community must include a critical interrogation of differences as the rich substance of community life and an invitation for engagement that is relentlessly democratic, diverse, participatory, and always attentive to equity and parity.

Safe spaces

> Having a sense of place and space empowers. People achieve their place through interpersonal relations, initially through family linkages and then through friendships and conjugal ties as well as work-related associations. Belonging within a space ensures safety, a zone for being and acting according to rules known and shared by others familiar with this space. Young people in inner cities, subject to the transience of frequent moves and the rapid unpredictabilities of life . . . rarely feel that they have a secure or safe place. . . .
>
> It is curious that, as the twentieth century nears its close, and economic conditions within some urban areas of the United States are such that the working together across racial and ethnic lines celebrated in theory since the 1960s is in place *in practice*. . . . Here the young as full participants have the "right to emerge from the routine of life," so as to test and challenge official and habituated hierarchical differences. (Heath, 1995, pp. 52, 65)

As Heath so eloquently articulates, there are spaces now being created by and for youth that begin to meet our criteria of community, difference, and democracy, that invite young people to work within and across traditional fault lines of identity. These may be safe spaces in which old and new identities are tried on, played with, and tossed off. We ask, can such spaces be located in schools, or is that oxymoronic?

Heath and colleagues play off of Harry Boyte and Sara Evan's (1992) notion of what they call free spaces—spaces in which people, in spite of poverty and the associated features of late-twentieth-century oppression, are able to imagine life differently, joining together to nurture hopes and dreams, often producing real changes in their individual and collective lives. Recognizing that no space is free from larger social inequities, these are sites in which young men and women have created and/or found communities in which they can challenge some of the hegemonic assumptions that surround and consume them, in which they can imagine a world that *could be* but hasn't yet been, and in which they can learn with others while teaching about policies, experiences, and lessons of young adult life. In these spaces, whispers of hope and possibility tenaciously flourish in the midst of despair located in a collapsing private economy and public sector. While there is an abundance of cool cynicism in popular youth rhetoric, there are also pockets of sweet longing—bright lights shining through cracks of demoralization.

We place the nurturing of multiracial youth communities of difference within this free space conceptualization. These spaces, in which groups of youth cross racial and ethnic boundaries, are rare and cry out for documentation. We need to understand both the interior and the borders of these spaces, find out how and why they arise, what nurtures, sustains, and threatens them, and how they can be grown in the diaspora in order to begin the slow process of transforming (de)segregated urban and suburban landscapes into integrated safe spaces.

Our research spans three schools in three different communities. Lois researched one de facto desegregated school with no sanctioned, critical, or authorized address of race or ethnicity—a site in which oppositional racism flourishes, looking quite inevitable and natural, all the while institutionally fed. Linda researched a second desegregated school while working as a professional development consultant on re-forming teacher-teacher and teacher-student relationships. Michelle researched a third, desegregated but internally tracked school in which English teachers boldly, courageously, and even under surveillance by some local politicians, chose to detrack and integrate the ninth-grade English course, and in so doing, threatened the larger, more entrenched patterns of segregation that define tracking in this school.

On this continuum of race-work in public spaces, we journey through the three sites asking what must be put in place to build a community of differences—rich in academic rigor and replete with the windows and mirrors of race, ethnicity, culture, and gender. What needs to be in place for students, faculty, staff, and administrators? How much will the State, in the body of school boards, and how much will families, especially economically elite and educationally privileged families, tolerate the decentering of their privilege to create an education for all? Is the public sphere up to the challenge? In the following sections we describe three school scenes, asking in each what sustains oppositional racism or what allows truly integrated communities of difference to emerge.

Scene one: supporting racially oppositional co-constructions (Lois Weis)

"Freeway" High School is the site of the first of these school scenes. Freeway, a small town located outside a medium-sized metropolitan area, was hit hard by the deindustrialization of the 1970s and 1980s. Freeway was particularly hurt by the downsizing and ultimate closing of Freeway Steel, a plant with a record high payroll of $168 million in 1969. In the first seven months of 1971, layoffs at the Freeway Plant numbered 4,000, and the decline continued into the 1980s. From 18,500 jobs in 1979, there were only 3,700 production and 600 supervisory workers left in 1983, and 3,600 on layoff. At the end of 1983, the plant closed, leaving in its wake unvisited "gin mills" and numerous other small businesses associated with the plant. Freeway is a true traditional working-class area, and Freeway families have been involved in the plant for generations, assuring that White male workers had jobs through which they could support their families. African Americans[1] moved up from the South after World War II to obtain jobs at Freeway Steel, and many were employed, although at far dirtier and lower-paying jobs than Whites. A small but noticeable population of Yemenites also moved to Freeway after World War II, along with an even smaller number of Puerto Ricans. Freeway remains a segregated town in terms of housing patterns, with many White former steelworkers living on one side of town, and African Americans, Puerto Ricans, and Yemenites, some of whom are also former steel workers, living on the other, although less successful White workers live among people of color. Like many U.S. cities, the side of town populated by people of color used to be inhabited by White ethnics who moved across town as they accumulated the capital necessary to buy a home. With the close of Freeway Steel and other industries located in the nearby metropolitan area, families now survive by piecing together the wages of several family members, exhibiting a sense of bitterness and loss as they try to raise the next generation. Mostly White, these workers consistently believe that affirmative action is largely responsible for their economic plight; they do not focus their criticism on the actions and policies of the elite who moved industries south of the border in search of greater profits (Weis & Fine, 1996).

The scene that follows from Freeway High describes what typically happens in a desegregated educational setting without the benefit of any meaningful interruption of racial antagonisms. This school did nothing to intervene in the production and dominance of White male culture. In fact, in many important ways it affirmed it, although not always in any conscious or intended sense (Weis, 1990). It is the institutional production and acceleration of Whiteness as center, with its associated racial tensions, that we seek to problematize. There is nothing "natural" about this story, even if it is fairly typical of American communities.

At Freeway racial tensions are high, and the school does nothing to reduce them. In fact, it does much to nourish the racially oppositional co-constructions I describe below. Data presented here were gathered as part of a large ethnographic study of Freeway High. I, Lois Weis, spent three days a week in the high school during the academic year 1986–1987 as a participant observer. I gathered data in classrooms, study halls, the cafeteria, during extracurricular activities, and conducted in-depth interviews with over sixty White juniors, and with teachers, the vice principals, social workers, guidance counselors, and others. The overall purpose of the study was to examine the identity formation processes among White working-class youth in the context of the deindustrialization of the U.S. economy. Although I certainly talked with many students of color, formal interviews were conducted only with White students, since they were the focus of this project. I was specifically concerned with the ways in which young men and women elaborated their identities and the ways in which the high school connected to these processes. Specifically, gendered identity forms were at the heart of the study. Data, therefore, were gathered from White working-class male and female students in Freeway High. Eighty individuals teach at the high school and approximately forty teach juniors; all of the teachers of juniors were interviewed. Two counselors, one social worker, two vice principals, and one principal comprise the non-teaching staff. Both counselors, the social worker, one of the vice principals, and the principal were interviewed as part of this study.

The faculty is overwhelmingly White. Three African American faculty members comprise 4 percent of the teaching population in a community that is approximately 20 percent people of color. There are no male teachers of color at Freeway High; the three African American females teach in non-academic areas. Two are in special education, where nationally a disproportionate number of African American youth is concentrated, and one is in the relatively low-paid female vocational area of secretarial studies. In terms of a broader gender breakdown, fifty-two teachers, or 65 percent, are male, with some tendency toward female ghettoization in secretarial studies, home economics, and cosmetology. All the "hard" vocational areas (which have increasingly little presence in the schools) such as automotive technology, woodworking, construction technology, machine shop, and the like, are taught by males. Females tend to spread rather evenly through the remaining subject areas, unlike the case nationally where there has been greater tendency toward academic subject matter ghettoization by gender (Kelly & Nihlen, 1982). The administrative staff is entirely White male; there is one female counselor and one male; and all the secretarial staff in the school is White female. With the exception of the three African American female teachers, then, the entire counseling, administrative, and teaching staff at Freeway High is White.

All interviews were audiotaped and transcribed with the permission of the interviewees. Data collection centered on the junior class, since this is where, in several ways, students' futures are locked in. The juniors are given a set of state-mandated tests and, during this same year, they sit for the preliminary college entrance examination, the PSAT, both of which sort students into post-secondary options.

One of the most chilling things going on at Freeway High is that the school offers a space wherein working-class White males co-construct their own identities in relation to those of African American males and females and White females. The term "co-construct" is chosen carefully here. As demonstrated below, White male students in this school construct their own identity as White at the same time they construct the identity of the other. While Whites do not author the race script in its entirety (certainly African American students have their own race script that is not examined here), they do in this context author themselves as White. This construction of self as White is, as will be shown here, absolutely dependent on the co-construction of African American students as the opposite other, and on White female students as subordinate to White male students. Although Puerto Ricans and Yemenites attend this school, White identities are not specifically elaborated in relation to these students. These students, particularly Yemenites, are largely ignored in the racial construction process outlined below, although they are seen as non-White, and, therefore, less valued. Rather, White male students, in particular, forge their raced and gendered identities in relation to what they construct as the Black other and the White female. While co-construction may suggest collaboration and shared commitment, indicating that this process is not necessarily negative, the particular content of these co-constructions, in a site perched within a racist U.S. society, is, in fact, exceptionally negative. It is a process that needs but does not receive interruption at the school level. What became clear to me over the course of the study is that the identities of young working-class White males are absolutely contingent upon the elaborated identities of the others against and with whom their own identities are woven. The discursive construction of Black males and females and White females became a means by which White males could assert themselves—a vehicle for the formation of their own positively felt identities in contrast with the constructed negative others. Heterosexuality, masculinity, and Whiteness are assertions of fierce and adversarial essentialisms sustained in the face of what these young White males construct as others—White females and African American males and females. The school provided a specific site in which these identities were encouraged to unfold. Thus Freeway High offered a space for the formation of Whiteness and enabled this Whiteness to define itself in relation to the constructed negative in the other. Curriculum could have been developed to expose and deconstruct assumptions of Whiteness. Teachers, administrations, and counselors could have intervened and attempted to derail these co-constructions. The point is that they didn't, leaving intact a set of processes that served to center White males, marginalize others, and contribute to a set of good and bad representations that undermined the building of a multiethnic and multiracial community. In this scene, "communities of difference" means the co-construction of ugly difference, difference that lays the basis for future vicious attack.

Among the White adolescent males at Freeway, Blacks are used reliably as a foil against which acceptable moral, and particularly sexual, standards are established. The goodness of White is always contrasted with the badness of Black—Blacks are involved with drugs; Blacks are unacceptable sexually; Black men attempt to invade White sexual space by talking to White women; Black women are simply filthy. This binary translated in ways that complemented White boys, as there is a virtual denial of anything at all good being associated with Blackness, and of anything bad being identified with Whiteness. Let us eavesdrop on interviews conducted at Freeway High, where much expressed racism centers on White males' perceived entitlement to White females, thus fixing Black males and females and White females as beneath them in the constructed social hierarchy. My graduate assistant, Craig Centrie, and I conducted individual interviews with White male and female students at Freeway. Held in a small nook with a closed door off the library, the interviews were private and confidential, although students understood that their interviews would be incorporated into later writing. All names used here are pseudonyms, including those of the teachers. Excerpts below illustrate points made by an overwhelming number of White males at Freeway High, whether interviewed by Craig or me.

> *Jim:* The minorities are really bad into drugs. You're talking everything. Anything you want, you get from them. A prime example, the __ ward of Freeway; about twenty years ago the ward was predominately White, my grandfather used to live there. Then Italians, Polish, the Irish people, everything was fine. The houses were maintained; there was a good standard of living. . . . The Blacks brought drugs. I'm not saying White people didn't have drugs, they had drugs, but to a certain extent. But drugs were like a social thing. But now you go down to the ward; it's amazing, it's a ghetto. Some of the houses are OK. They try to keep them up. Most of the homes are really terrible. They throw garbage on the front lawn. It's sickening. You talk to people from [surrounding suburbs]. Anywhere you talk to people, they tend to think the majority of our school is Black. They think you hang with Black people, listen to Black music. . . . A few of them [Blacks] are starting to go into the __ ward

now [the White side], so they're moving around. My parents will be around there when that happens, but I'd like to be out of there.

Lois Weis: There's no fighting and stuff here [at Freeway], is there?
Clint: Yeah, a lot between Blacks and Whites.
Lois Weis: Who starts them?
Clint: Blacks.
Lois Weis: Do Blacks and Whites hang out in the same places?
Clint: Some do. [The Blacks] live on the other side of town. . . . A lot of it [fights] starts with Blacks messing [with] White girls. That's how a lot of them start. Even if they [White guys] don't know the White girl, they don't like to see [a Black guy with a White girl].
Lois Weis: How do you feel about that yourself?
Clint: I don't like it. If I catch them [Blacks] near my sister, they'll get it. I don't like to see it like that. Most of them [his friends] see it that way [the same way he does].
Lois Weis: How about the other way around? White guys and Black girls?
Clint: There's a few that do. There's people that I know of, but no one I hang around with. I don't know many White kids that date Black girls.

Bill: Like my brother, he's in ninth grade. He's in trouble all the time. Last year he got jumped in school . . . about his girlfriend. He doesn't like Blacks. They come up to her and go, "Nice ass," and all that shit. My brother don't like that when they call her "nice ass" and stuff like that. He got suspended for saying "fucking nigger," but it's all right for a Black guy to go up to Whites and say stuff like that ["nice ass"]. . . . Sometimes the principals aren't doing their jobs. Like when my brother told [the assistant principal] that something is going to happen. Mr. __ just said, "Leave it alone, just turn your head." . . . Like they [the administrators] don't know when fights start in this school. Like there's this one guy's kid sister, a nigger—[correction]—a Black guy—grabbed her ass. He hit him a couple of times. Did the principal know about it? No!
Lois Weis: What if a White guy did that [grabbed a girl's ass]?
Bill: He'd probably have punched him. But a lot of it's 'cause they're Black.

In the above interview segments it is important to note the ways in which several discursive separations are occurring. To begin with, these White male students are constructing female students as people who need the protection of males. The young men are willing to fight for their young women, so that if anyone says, "nice ass," it is a legitimate reason to start a fight. It must be pointed out that young women did not request or require this—this protective stance is under the terrain of the males themselves, the young women never having expressed a desire for such protection during the year Lois was there, either in interviews or in any observed interactions. Black males in turn are being constructed as oversexualized: They "welcome themselves in," as Clint says more than once in the interview; they behave in ways that are inappropriate vis-à-vis White females. The complaint is communicated through the language of property rights—Black males intruding onto White property. What is at issue here is that Black males are invading White females, the property of White males, not a broader statement about the treatment of females. In addition, the discursive constructions of Black males as oversexualized enables White males to elaborate to themselves and others their own appropriate and civilized heterosexuality. At a time of heightened concern with homosexuality, by virtue of their age, the collective nature of their lives, the fear of being labeled homosexual, and the violence that often accompanies such labeling in high school, these boys are able to assert virulently their own heterosexuality and their ability to take care of their women by virtue of the co-constructions they engaged in (Messner & Sabo, 1994). This intersection of race, racism, and acting straight has not been explored, to our knowledge, but it is in serious need of analysis, as high schools such as Freeway offer a site for the simultaneous playing out of these discourses. It cannot be missed that the social construction of Black and White, good and bad, male and female, is intertwined with the construction of straight and gay (Messner & Sabo, 1994). Students elaborate identities in school, and, as we have shown, such identities are linked up with those of constructed others. We need to understand the consequences when educators choose to allow negative co-constructions to continue uninterrupted. In the worst case, educators participate in the proliferation of these co-constructions, as the following observations from my field notes illustrate:

> *March 5*
> I went to see Johnnie Aaron (the White football coach) to see if the Nautilus room could be used for my interviewing. He said, "It's always in use; there's always someone in there." William, an African American male student, was in Johnnie's room, as [was] John, a White male.
> *Johnnie:* What happened to your hair, boy?
> *William:* It fell out. I was nervous before the game. (He had shaved his head.)
> Johnnie has on other occasions referred to Black males but never White males, as "boy."
>
> *Study Hall*
> *Anthony (an African American male):* Hi girls (to two White girls).
> *Mr. Antonucci (a White teacher):* Stop talking to White girls.
> *Anthony:* Got any colored ones?
> *Mr. Antonucci:* You don't seem to understand why I moved you up here to (to the front). (He kicks Anthony out of the classroom.)

Although directly racist comments by the faculty, such as those above, were relatively infrequent, comments such as those below were not, suggesting that a deep racism lies within the teacher and school culture generally:

> *February 26, Lunchroom*
> Jean, a White business teacher, had left her lunch on top of the fridge. She threw it away, with the comment, "We all know what's in there."
> *Lois Weis:* What?
> *Susan:* Cockroaches.
> *Lois Weis:* I never saw a cockroach here.
> *Susan:* You're lucky.
> *Marsha (White teacher):* You know, I have a friend that just got a job teaching in (the nearby city), on __ and __, or something like that (right in the middle of the African American part of town). She's straight from suburbia and is teaching middle-class values. She was using a big chart, she's teaching kindergarten to teach the "M" sound. The kids were saying "M," and all of a

> sudden a cockroach walked across the paper. She stiffened; the kids did not seem to even notice; they're used to it. She just took off her shoe and killed it. Then she had the kids say, "Mommy" to practice words with a "M" sound. One little boy burst out crying and said, "Mommy got drunk and left." She said to herself, "What am I doing here?"
>
> *Barbara:* Oh yeah, and they [Black kids] love to come up and feel your hair. (She makes a face as if this is extremely distasteful to her.)
>
> *September 5, Talk with Mr. Weaver, the assistant principal*
> I ran into Mr. Weaver in the hall. He was telling me what a "good system" this is here. The kids are good. "This is a realistic situation here, about fifteen percent Black or minority." He thinks that if a school gets "too black," it is no longer "serious." "Too many of their homes are giddy places, not serious enough. If you get too many Blacks in the school, it is not serious. Fifteen percent is fine. They can't act that way [giddy] in school if they are only fifteen percent."

There is a grotesqueness about the particular set of meaning-makings in the school, meaning-makings that are not interrupted by school personnel, and at times are actively and generally encouraged by teachers; this enables White male students to write themselves as pure, straight, and superior, while authoring African American males as dirty and oversexualized. It is most interesting that not one female in this study ever discussed African American males as a "problem" in this regard. This is not to say that White females are not racist, but this particular discursive rendering of African American males is quite noticeably the terrain of White males. Not insignificantly, it is always fathers, according to young White women, who oppose interracial dating. As Suzanne, a White female student, stated, "My father would kill me if I brought home a Black guy." This is, of course, tied to the history of racism and race relations in a White working-class community, where African Americans were used to break strikes and, therefore, were pitted against White men economically. Alongside economics, however, lies the discursive realm, wherein some are authored as always being better than others. The continuation of the authoring of the [White] race script is what we see here in Freeway High.

Surely these constructions are linked dialectically to discursive and material constructions in the wider society, both historically and currently. As these young White males weave their own form of cultural superiority vis-à-vis African American males and females and White females, they are encouraged by a larger society and societal institutions. The construction of African Americans in the media, for example, as Cameron McCarthy and colleagues (1997) point out, encourages viewers to perceive this group as dangerous and drug-crazed. Historically, African Americans have been depicted less than admirably in American culture. The discursive constructions detailed here are linked to such constructions in the broader society. However, as the next scene demonstrates, we do not have to accept the Freeway set of co-constructions as an inevitable outcome in desegregated schools. The co-constructions evident at Freeway High are a specific outcome located in an institution that did nothing to undermine these constructions and even, as suggested above in the case of the teachers and staff, did some things to promote them (Weis, 1991). It is our guess that Freeway is not unique. Rather, we suspect that it exemplifies what goes on in many desegregated high schools across the nation. Freeway is a site in which bodies of historic differentiation, privilege, and oppression are huddled together with little or no adult commitment to creating common ground. The fact that the teaching, administrative, and counseling staff is almost entirely White serves to both reflect and sustain this. The battle lines are drawn. We adults either affirm them or, more typically, stand by helpless, shaking our heads in disbelief. We now turn to Scene Two, where we argue that teachers in desegregated schools can begin to challenge negative constructions of difference rather than passively accept them.

Scene two: working the authority boundary—supporting young people in a community of difference (Linda Powell)

The "Arlingdale" neighborhood, once a thriving community populated by working-class factory workers of European descent who lived and worked in the hub of the textile mill industry, has been in decline and turmoil for thirty years. Today this community is racially mixed; Whites, African Americans, and Latinos live in physical proximity, but at a psychological distance. Arlingdale High School is located in an urban area where brutal poverty is the norm, racial tensions are explosive, and crime, due principally to drug trafficking, is the worst in the city. Well over half of the complaints to the Municipal Human Rights Commissions for racially based violence and other forms of racial discrimination originate in the greater Arlingdale community. The city in which Arlingdale is located continues to be in conflict over the twenty-plus-year desegregation suit, which recently confirmed that after twenty years of effort, most of the public schools continue to be "racially isolated."

Unlike many of the 134 schools in this northeastern city, Arlingdale High School has a richly diverse student population consisting principally of Latino students (45%), White working-class students (25%), African American students (20%), and Southeast Asian students (10%). Latino students are primarily Puerto Rican, with a small number from other Caribbean countries, and from Central and South American nations. The Southeast Asian students are primarily Vietnamese, although many of their families are ethnic Chinese who resettled in Vietnam prior to coming to the United States. There are also a small number of international students who have recently immigrated from the Middle East and Eastern Europe (primarily Poland). Over half of the student body does not speak English as its first language, and approximately 15 percent of the student body is placed in support classes for limited English language proficiency.

Over time, the greatest changes have been in the Latino population, which is increasing as the African American population is decreasing. The White ethnic community had effectively boycotted Arlingdale High School for many years, sending their children to local Catholic schools. Over the past fifteen years, however, rising tuition costs and the closing of nearby Catholic schools has resulted in the reluctant return of White students.

The faculty and school staff is also multiracial—White, African American, Latino, and Asian—though not as diverse as the student body. The predominant faculty group (55%) is White, approximately 40 percent are African American, with the remaining 5 percent Latino and Asian American.

Since 1990, teachers and staff at Arlingdale have been committed to developing Family Group as a school climate intervention and a student support mechanism. Family Group creates in-school groupings of students who meet weekly with a trained facilitator. The task of the group is to talk about whatever the students need to help them be successful in school. Relationships among students are cultivated as carefully as those between the students and the facilitator. A prepared curriculum is available, based on the common topics that arise.

Joining adults from eight other public high schools, Arlingdale staff have taken the lead in attempting to implement Family Group, which requires both structural changes in the way the school day is scheduled, as well as demanding preparation and support for the adults leading the groups. Family Group has been an intergroup experience from the outset, involving groups of students with groups of adults, groups of teachers with groups of staff, and groups from various schools. The boundaries between these groupings provide opportunities for learning in a variety of ways. For example, attending to the intergroup aspect of the city-wide component has been a form of community support, giving Family Group leaders a forum to air criticism of their individual schools, gain perspective on their common and unique problems, and draw support from like-minded colleagues.

Unlike other special programs or curriculum approaches that deal with specific students, Family Group is conceived as an organizational intervention. Ideally, every student in the school has a Family Group membership. Family Group is an enhanced advisory approach that builds on the substantial dropout prevention literature, which persuasively demonstrates that a caring adult can have a profound effect on a student's achievement. Family Group is a first step toward assuring that each child has regular and continuous contact with a single adult. Elsewhere I, Linda Powell (1994), have explored the ways in which anonymity operates as a social defense (Menzies, 1960) in urban schools. This notion draws on both systems and psychoanalytic ideas about organizations, and suggests that many behaviors that appear dysfunctional may actually serve crucial organizational purposes. In urban schools, for example, "not knowing anyone well" may be an effective way of managing the anxiety associated with the immense diversity in the school, the demands of learning, the complexity of the school climate, and the many forms of violence—some interpersonal, but most often institutional. And so, any intervention that increases the opportunity for adolescents and adults to be fully present at school—whether it is Family Group, a student-centered curriculum, a peer mediation program, or a multicultural study group for teachers—is likely to meet organizational resistance as it interrupts the social defense.

Considering that it is embedded in a community immersed in racial strife, Arlingdale High School appears to be surprisingly free of racial turmoil and to be a decidedly safe environment compared to other neighborhood high schools of comparable size and location across the United States. Students and staff manage to avoid overt or violent conflict related to racial difference; few racially motivated incidents are reported, and students and adults publicly assert in Family Group, professional development sessions, and informal settings that they "love their school." Race most typically emerges as an issue in Family Group when students talk about what is important to them. In one group, a young African American man reported having a difficult experience: while he was tutoring a young White child as part of community service, the younger child called him "a nigger." As he tried to sort out his reactions, he said that he couldn't really blame the child, who was simply replaying what adults had taught him. However, the young tutor said that he "heard the teacher say nothing." He was most stung by the failure of the teacher to intervene on his behalf.

Students at Arlingdale often "hear adults say nothing." This is likely due to the fact that race is a hidden and complex issue among the staff, making it far more complicated for them to support the students. This complexity can be observed in the various adult coalitions that form in the school according to race. The most visible example is staff lunchtime seating, which is strictly by racial groups; should a new adult interrupt this pattern, they are routinely rejected and quickly reeducated about "how things are done here." This identity group strategy among teachers may be their way of managing differences and intergroup conflict. This strategy, while sufficient to keep the peace, may mask profound opportunities for learning that could be leveraged by the skilled intervention of adults. This strategy may also be teaching inadvertent lessons about power and authority that are less apparent. Adults must commit to and be trained to confront and explore rather than to shut down the clash of differences that occur when questions about race emerge through conflict.

In earlier work in this community, I report (Powell, 1994) an incident in a city-wide professional development session. A White Family Group leader was approached by a White student who reported that an African American male student had overturned her chair; the young woman described it as a racial incident, saying that he did it because she was White. The adult replied unhesitatingly, "No, it wasn't." The Family Group leader reported this incident, almost casually, as part of her description of the behavior of young men in Family Group. When the group facilitator interrupted to ask how she determined that it wasn't a racial incident, the Family Group leader was stunned by the question, as were her Family Group leader colleagues. This question drew out an extended exploration of the role of Family Group with regard to race and racial identity, which had previously been inchoate and inarticulate. The Family Group leaders' theory-in-practice had been to treat all conversations with a racial component as dangerous, and by definition to be suppressed, cut off, and treated as "not to be learned from." My belief, in contrast, is that Family Group offers a sanctioned and protected forum to treat these experiences as opportunities to build a group capacity to explore conflict and to strengthen the racial identity of every student (Carter & Helms, 1990; Helms, 1990). In the words of *How Schools Shortchange Girls* (AAUW, 1992), Family Groups and the relationships developed within them provide the environment to explore rather than avoid the "evaded curriculum" (p. 95) of power.

Another example of a missed learning opportunity occurred at Arlingdale High School following a rich and compelling multicultural assembly that celebrated the contributions of Latinos to American culture. A group of White students approached the new Puerto Rican principal and asked, "Why are Black people getting all this attention?" The principal used this as an opportunity to convince and persuade his students that not all people of color are Black, and multiculturalism was a good thing, the glue that held this school together, a democratic value they should hold. What was also there—and would have been far more incendiary—was the additional opportunity to uncover Whiteness. What different factors would have allowed the principal to gently interrogate the arrogance and entitlement the White students exhibited in raising this question?

Arlingdale students and adults have found ways to minimize and suppress conflict by avoiding negative interactions, but how could they instead learn from difference? How could their conflicts be a source of information and growth? Paraphrasing William Ayers's (1996) recent question in the *Journal of Caring and Concern*, "What is it that makes a large number of poor, immigrant children of color in this school *wonderful*?" (p. 86). One answer to that question is the profound opportunity they present to explore and transform the historic American racial categorization in a live and authentic laboratory.

This "laboratory" is shaped by internal, structural factors. In his recent course "The Health Crisis in Poor and Disenfranchised Communities," Ronald David (1996, personal communication) has reminded us that relationship is primary and everything else is derivative. This fact is well known to physicians and psychotherapists. The quality and content of information shared is a measure of the relationship existent between the participants; the greater the trust and reliability, the more authentic and risky the data shared. For example, in a recent intervention in another Family Group school, students interviewed by strangers reported that they had little or no reaction to allegations of abuse of students by a popular school administrator. Students said that they were "fine about it" and "not upset." Students interviewed by adults they knew in more intimate settings like Family Group expressed more powerful reactions to the entire situation: They were worried about what gossip this would expose them to in the neighborhood. Seniors felt that their senior year had been ruined. Several noted pointedly that violent, abusive experiences were a common part of student life in school, but "psychologists only got airlifted in" when the administrator, an adult, was at risk.

The parallel to schools seems clear; the conversation about race and ethnicity will vary greatly by time, task, and the opportunity to connect in meaningful ways. Whether young people frame their personal and group-level identities in a complex and constructive manner is related in large part to three factors: one, the values, skills, and attitudes of the adults in their environment; two, the perceived learning task at the given moment; and three, the reliability of structures in place to support them in exploring complex ideas.

For the entering ninth-grade class at Arlingdale and their advisors, those three factors are consciously manipulated by the existence of their weekly Family Group sessions. Family Group also builds on research (MEE Foundation, 1993) and commentary (Bly, 1996) that suggest that adult authority with young people is decreasing in effectiveness, and that adults are surrendering to the increasing influence of the peer culture. This powerful peer culture tends to oversimplify complex issues and demand simplistic allegiances. At its best, the very existence of and process within Family Group provides young people the opportunity to stretch and explore that culture without surrendering it. The process of discussion mitigates a certain rigidity of the peer culture, learning to express and respect differences as part of a community, not simply as a threat to cohesiveness. This succeeds in moderating "in" and "out" as givens. The impact of this intervention is to encourage positive group-based interactions among adolescents, and to build greater trust between adolescents and adults while moderating the conformist values of the peer culture.

What difference can Family Group make in the construction of the narratives about race and ethnicity? First, the task is for students to talk about whatever they need to in order to be successful in school. Encouraged and facilitated by specially trained adults, each week's topic is student directed. Often the topic is power, race, and ethnicity, although it is coded in stories about their daily interactions with their environment. In response to a direct question about race, such as, "Is race an issue here at Arlingdale?" most students of all colors will say, "It's not important. I don't see color. Not a big deal." However, students of color will spontaneously reflect on their experiences in racial terms. For example, after a sports event with a suburban school, an African American young man stated: "They wouldn't let suburban kids in a building like ours." Decoding this response yields a highly raced and classed analysis: White kids who have money would be protected from a physical plant that is cold, graffiti-covered, and asbestos-filled.

This comment is about race and power, but comes at an interesting tangent to the adult-framed question about race.

Second, preparing Family Group Leaders to facilitate rather than shut down raced conversation is absolutely crucial. In my work, I use the four-factor professional development for change model (Powell, 1997; Powell & Barry, 1995; Powell, Barry, & Davis, in press), which focuses on experiential learning, creation of safe spaces, development of complex analytic skills through the exploration of parallel processes, and the strategic use of theory. This kind of training is required to give adults access to the subtleties of their own racial identities, as well as information about group life and conflict management. For example, leaders explore their own racial and ethnic identities through activities such as constructing personal narratives of their racial identity and engaging in complex conversations about race.

The focused use of Family Group for the investigation of race in students' lives is in a new and fragile phase. Previously, Family Group was seen as a dropout prevention mechanism, and students focused on their day-to-day school life. During the next phase we pay closer attention to the impact of stability, regularity, and trained adults who facilitate the expression of narratives about race.

One of the most compelling paradoxes about Family Group is that despite an almost universal anecdotal sense that it works for students, it is almost impossible to maintain in urban schools. Schools report that Family Group improves student attendance, invigorates classroom work, and provides a structural forum to reshape school culture. It gives students a different opportunity to bring their most complex selves to schools and provides adults with sophisticated and practical professional development. This year, the commitment at Arlingdale was that every incoming ninth grader would have Family Group. Adults were trained, materials prepared, and students grouped. However, for a variety of rational and perhaps irrational reasons, sustaining the groups has been very difficult. There is often "something else" in the roster that bumps the small meetings (like a huge assembly), or there is not quite enough money for training (although other efforts with less connection to teaching/learning go forward), or there are insufficient opportunities for professional development and ongoing support (the intractability of the school day). We understand this as a form of organizational resistance and the strengthening of the social defense: Family Group does not neatly fit in an urban school because it is initially anxiety producing. If anonymity has functioned as a defense, and if we don't want to know about difference, then we certainly can't tolerate a more authentic conversation exploring race. As one reluctant Family Group Leader summed it up, "There's no doubt that it is good for the kids, but I can't stand the chaos it creates among the adults." There may be a connection between race and organizational resistance. A two-year process of investigating race relations among youth was announced at Arlingdale in the fall. Family Group leaders were invited to join a process where they, along with students, would explore multiculturalism and difference as it blossomed at Arlingdale. Since that announcement, difficulties have ensued and gotten worse. One hypothesis is that the school could not tolerate such knowledge about race, in either adult or student experience. Further, it is likely that adults are ambivalent about learning from/with young people about building community around racial difference due to the changes it might necessitate for us.

Arlingdale is at a point of cautious hope. The ingredients for a delicious experiment of knowing, being known, and making change are in place. A primary question is whether adults will use their authority to create and sustain the structures needed for students to develop and explore these questions. Will we create the relationships required for honesty and directness? Will we model approaches to difference and change that students can trust? Will we shut down conversations that make us uncomfortable with unresolved political and personal issues about race, or will we use our resources—both internal and external—to assure that these developmental conversations for adolescents will have a place? This scene is the center of a continuum—kids are struggling to create a new form of community, but adults must use their resources to support, provoke, and encourage their efforts. The kids are on track—we need to join them.

Scene three: bold pedagogies—moving toward a community of differences (Michelle Fine)

In 1991, the "Clear Mount" High School English faculty voted unanimously to detrack its ninth-grade literature course. In Clear Mount, a commuter suburb well known for ambitious racial and class integration of its pre-K through 12 system, the high school is nevertheless more tracked than many in the high school would like to admit, producing more racial segregation than most in the town would say is desirable.[2] English faculty at the high school took it upon themselves to invent an intellectually ambitious, multicultural World Literature course—heterogeneous by gender, race, ethnicity, social class, and academic history—in which all ninth graders would enroll. Committed to its public image as a progressive and intentionally integrated town in a deeply segregated state, with families ranging from quite poor to very wealthy with a substantial Black elite, Clear Mount wrestles with the lived contradictions of race, ethnicity, and class amidst dreams of integration. The World Literature course reflects and makes public those contradictions. The course, as such, is fiercely contested both within and beyond the school walls (Fields, 1996).

The course has been the site of local controversy, given the community's intense ambivalence about retaining tracking at the secondary school (see Wells & Serna, 1996, for coverage of similar dynamics nationally). This course has sustained both high academic standards and serious community scrutiny. It has been supplemented by a nationally recognized Writers Center and was recently evaluated by Dennie Palmer Wolf and Willa Spicer (1994). At a meeting of the town's board of education on the merits of the course, scores of teachers, students, and parents across racial and ethnic groups and academic histories testified to its value, with few exceptions. Quantitative and qualitative data were presented by the evaluators to demonstrate that the course represents a space in which students can critically examine literature and produce intellectual, political, and emotional work within and across groups. Students and teachers testified their support of the course:

> *A White female junior:* It is valuable to have it not tracked. First it gives all of us a common background experience. And if we all learn the same things, we become a group, a class, not just separate little groups of our own.
>
> *A White male sophomore:* I think it was actually better than if it had been ranked. It made you see how diverse the school really is. That is better than hiding out in your honors classes and always being with the same people. It is very fulfilling to see what other people are thinking. You see that there are

more cultures in the course. We have someone with Igbo ancestry, and that was very important when we were doing Africa.

A biracial female sophomore: Students, I believe as a result of heterogeneous grouping, attribute success to effort. This is critical. I also think that students realize they can contribute to the success of a class and/or small group in a variety of ways.[3]

One African American male sophomore, who had previously been tracked in low-level courses, put it boldly, "You live in the basement, you die in the basement. You know what I mean?" The combination of strong multiracial and multiethnic relationships among faculty and students, a rich multicultural curriculum, lots of support from writing coaches and the Writing Center, and high standards were presented as being sufficient factors to instill a sense of competence in substantial numbers of students, including those considered high risk.[4]

Following the external evaluation, the principal, a set of faculty, and a set of current and former students agreed to collaborate with me, Michelle Fine, on an ethnography of the course. My intent was (and is) to be a participant observer in four classes, one to two mornings a week, to meet with the faculty every other week, and to work with a group of students who will also be writing over the course of two years.[5] From this pedagogical window, I expect to learn much about the power of young adolescents' writing, the opportunities to explore their own perspectives as essential to empathic understandings of others, the consequences of differential academic histories on secondary school performance, and how to make heterogeneity real, not just in access but also in outcomes. The more time I spend with these students and teachers, the more I realize that this course is truly a window into the educational dilemmas and rich possibilities that sparkle across the school district, across public education. It is also a privileged opportunity to witness the brilliance of teaching for intellectual excellence and social justice.

As the following field notes and analyses distributed over four months suggest, we can see the critical pedagogical turns that occur as these classes shift from a discomforting desegregation to a slightly less awkward, growing, nudging integration. The critical moments include faculty trying to create community, decentering Whiteness, and youths exploring questions of "differences."

September 13: Faculty Trying to Create Community
It has only been two weeks, but I have already heard from parents and educators outside the high school that this course is "on the chopping block." The mayor "ran on a platform to get rid of it." A few vocal White parents have in the past called the superintendent, complaining, "My kid doesn't have other White students in her class," or "The class is too political, not literary enough." Many White and African American parents are stronger supporters. Rumor has it, there is a small silent but distressed group of African American middle-class parents deeply conflicted about the detracking.

In the midst, students are discussing George and Lennie's relationship at the end of *Of Mice and Men.* Carlton Jordan [one of the teachers] asks his students to form what he calls a value line: "Stand on my right if you think it was right for George to kill Lennie. Stand on my left if you don't. Stand in the middle if you are of both minds."

Much to my surprise (and dismay?), the room tips to the right. The crowd moves in those loud clumsy teenage feet over towards the "it's OK to kill" side. I look for patterns by gender, race. Nothing. To the left wander three boys, a bit surprised and embarrassed, two White and one Black, feeling like they are going to lose. "But it is never OK to kill a friend," insists Joshua.

Carlton, momentarily stunned but never stumped by his "pedagogical failure" to get equally distributed groups, undermining his "plan" to set up pairs to discuss their positions, invites them to sit in common position groups and discuss whether or not George should appeal.

The "it's OK to kill a friend" group get loud, committed, animated, vile. "Lennie stupid." "He's the biggest retard in the world. He likes to pet dead rabbits. He don't need to live," shouts Kizzy—Muslim, brassy, busty, wonderful, noisy, always the voice that provokes Darren, an African American boy, to respond with emotion. This group, however, is forming across their differences in opposition to Lennie. Here comes the Tajfel prediction about out-groups and enemies. Sofia, another young African American woman, "I study ballet 8 hours a day and they tell me I won't be able to be a famous dancer because I am Black." Kizzy puts on a "Vote for Eli Ginsburg-McCoy" sticker, with Eli, a White boy sitting next to her as Devon says, "No. Vote for Marcus Jordan." Border crossing dots the room. Kizzy declares herself a "free thinker," as she moves the sticker to her right arm where a tattoo would go, slipping it under her shirt sleeve. Sofia continues, "That Lennie could be Jeffrey Dahmer. He should have killed Lennie long ago; he's a burden." Kizzy continues: "He's stupid. He murdered cold-blooded. We got to make him bad if we're gonna get George off." Eli joins, "By killing him, it was like saving a life."

Carlton and I exchange glances. I'm thrown by the raw but vicious analyses of these young adolescents and their endless creativity. The screams of "stupid, useless, dumb" are rusting my soul.

Carlton is as visibly shaken as I am. A strong, bold African American educator, he begins to teach, to preach, to speak with his heart, his eyes, his arms, and his mouth. "Let me say something about Lennie, because as I walk around, I am disturbed. . . . What are the characteristics of Lennie?"

The class volunteers: "Stupid, slow, dumb!"

Carlton continues, "Dumb. Retarded. When you use language like that I have to speak. . . . You may say it was right for George to kill Lennie because Lennie killed someone else or Lennie would have been killed. There are many reasons. But because [he] is stupid, slow, no. Some of you have Learning Disabilities. Some of you have persons with autism or retardation in your family. And none of us know what's coming next. It is important to see Lennie as a man, as a human being, not as something that should be destroyed."

Kizzy: "But he stupid. You are coming down on our group."

My mind wanders. Remembering the calls [from some parents] to the superintendent about "Them," remembering talk at the School Board about how "those students" will hold back "the motivated ones," I am brought back to the room by Carlton's voice. "Some of you have been called stupid by others. You have to think about what it's like to be in a world where everyone seems to be getting it right, and you don't even know what you don't know. Some of you sit in lunchroom and won't eat tuna sandwiches because you are gonna save the baby whale, but you'd laugh at Lennie in our school. Some of you will send money to Rwanda and Bosnia to save children over there. But you would make fun of Lennie, throw stones or shun Lennie over here." The

> students have reproduced the discourse being narrated about them. "George should not be burdened by Lennie." That is just what some at the School Board meeting were trying to imply.
>
> Carlton: "Let me say, I take this personally. If you can't walk with Lennie, if you can't see Lennie as a human, as a brother, what future is there for our community? What possibilities are there for us as a whole?"
>
> Class is over, I'm feeling exhausted and depleted, . . . and amazed at the strength of a teacher willing to speak, interrupt, listen, and educate. After a weekend of worries and exchanged phone messages with Carlton, I returned to class on Monday to find the pedagogical genius of "community," orchestrated by Carlton, already at play.
>
> The lecture opens with a discussion of first person and third person narratives. Carlton asks students to "turn to a page of *Of Mice and Men* where George and Lennie are interacting. I want you to rewrite the passage as Lennie. In first person narrative. To see how Lennie's wheels turn."
>
> "What wheels?" snipes Paul.
>
> The students clip through the text, muttering, but writing eagerly. Carlton waits patiently for volunteers. Hands shoot up. "I am just a happy man, likin' my rabbits." "Why George callin' me a stupid so and so . . ." Hands of all hues fill the air. The room is alive with Lennies.
>
> "How do you feel?" asks Carlton. "Stupid?" The point was made. Carlton was crafting a community not yet owned by students, but the students were growing extensions with which to connect in the room and beyond.

I am profoundly moved by how much work is involved in creating community amid such an enormous range of academic biographies and social standpoints. This is a course in which students with third-grade "official reading level" sit and converse, challenge and create with students who read at far more sophisticated levels. It is a course in which questions of race and ethnicity surface and then get complicated. Students for the first eight weeks focus on "perspectives," producing "name pieces" that unravel the textured fragments of culture that braid in their genealogies. Discoveries of mixtures such as "oops, I almost forgot I'm part Native American" from one student, and "Puerto Rican Jew actually" from another student, punctuate student talk. In reading *Of Mice and Men, Twelve Angry Men, Nectar in the Sieve, The Epic of Gilgemesh, Two Old Women*, writings of Sandra Cisneros and Homer, the poetry of Walt Whitman and June Jordan, and short stories by Rudolfo Anaya, young men and women crawl back in their personal histories to discover the many selves sitting inside their skins. They practice voices sanctioned and those long smothered. And they listen to others, not always easily, not always gracefully, but always with support from faculty. While most are engaged in the talk, they are still learning to hear, to listen, and to imagine the value of another's point of view. This is the slow, not always progressive, move toward community, toward authentic education.

Dana Sherman, another World Literature teacher, is passionate about creating writers among her ninth graders. Adolescents who otherwise walk around nailed shut or performing an essentialist caricature of their demographic box come alive in her course. They stretch across borders of self and others, and in so doing, they begin to knit a community, to trust each other enough to "come out" as "Latino," "mulatto," "part Native," "not really a writer," "left back." Tanika, an African American student with a "bad"—her word—academic history, is learning to hear her own voice as she gets an audience. And Max, White Jewish, of progressive parents, who has long been reading Whitman, Morrison, and Baldwin, is learning to listen to Tanika, to shift his optics, to see through window and mirrors to re-view himself and others, to position himself and others in a community. Carlton and Dana earn their keep as they try to create a community, a world not yet.

These teachers work hard to identify both talents and needs in all, to display the treasures of each, and to remove from the closet the weaknesses in every one of us. My own elitism, racism, and anxiety surface every time one of the faculty asks students to read aloud, or poses the question, "Who has finished *Gilgemesh*? *Bhagavad-Gita*? *Nectar in the Sieve*?" And when I dare to reopen my eyes, the hands are often attached to bodies I had suspected were reading, but as often to bodies for whom I was less sure. Students read *Twelve Angry Men*. Everyone has a role to read aloud. After I exhale, I can hear clearly that, of course, everyone stumbles when reading aloud.[6]

After a few weeks of bumping through attempts to create connections and commonalities, it is clear that the unspoken center—Whiteness—needs to be complicated and shifted. At the moment it is still defended territory not yet contested. Over the course of a few weeks, questions of difference within community erupt at times in pleasure, but more often in pain.

> *September 25: Decentering Whiteness*
> Having finished *Of Mice and Men*, the class has moved on to *Two Old Women*, by Velma Wallis, a Native woman from Alaska who retells a story told by her mother. The story spins around two old women left to die, abandoned by their community.
>
> In two classes, a small set of White boys—some of the very ones who defended Lennie's right to live—are "pissed."
>
> The conversation from one class exemplifies the tensions:
>
> "She's trash," shouts Jeremy. "This woman is a terrible writer. The book has no pulse. It's not gripping."
>
> "It has the heartbeat of a dead person," adds Ethan. These young men carry on about the book. Four White boys uncharacteristically huddle together, sit and spout as critics sitting on high.
>
> "A good book," notes one of these fourteen-year-old critics, "has action, climax, movement. It's gripping."
>
> Carlton draws a phallus on the board. "Like this?"
>
> Jeremy reveals, "This book has stolen my soul."
>
> While one might have a good discussion about whether or not this is a "good" book, the energy of disgust and critique explodes. It takes me by surprise. Jeremy, we later hear, ran off to the library for some Whitman.
>
> While Carlton is trying to create a sense of entitlement, wonder, a critical voice, if you will, in Tasha, an African American girl who says little, and Pam, a White girl who says less, whose academic biographies have over-prescribed their silence, he is also trying to invite Jeremy and his friends to "get out of your box. Taste something different—even if you don't like it. Your box will be expanded."
>
> They shut down. I worry the retreat of White male energy could sabotage the class. Their silence is loud. . . . My worries are embarrassingly elitist, racist, sexist . . .
>
> With another brilliant pedagogic move, Dana (to help Carlton) searches that evening to find a Whitman poem, "On Silence." Imported to the class,

> students read it aloud. The boys are soothed. Something comforting, a blanket, has been returned to the center of the room. Velma has been exiled.
>
> But then Carlton announces the homework assignment. "Please find pages 9–11 in Wallis—where the grandson sits mute, daring not to challenge the elders as he witnesses the abandonment of his grandmother. Compare that passage to Whitman's poem 'On Silence.' Answer the question: 'Where's Whitman in Wallis? Where has she gone further?' " Jeremy reminds Carlton—with an ironic smile—"It's an insult to put Wallis and Whitman in the same sentence."

Obsessively searching for threads of connection amid difference, multiple forms of knowledge, inviting explorations and stretches, creating conversations about readers and writers who might never have known each other—Kizzy and Jeremy or Wallis and Whitman—these teachers are deliberately, carefully, and with smarts creating "safe spaces" without denying—indeed revealing and interrogating—differences.

Always working with and for talent in its many hues and registers, eager to display the cultural biographies and strengths students import, these two faculty members also demonstrate the fractures within each, the "Black boy," the "White girl," the "athlete," the "resistor," and always the "intellectual" hiding inside of us all. Questions of difference are lifted up as quickly as they are problematized and pluralized. Interested in neither diversity nor difference per se, the work these educators are performing is the work of decentering—assuring that no race, no ethnicity, no position, no gender, no stance has hegemonic authority, silencing power, or monopoly on truth. They invite writers, speakers, and readers to emerge.

So youth in these courses, over time and unevenly, recognize that they can speak and that they deserve an audience. More slowly, some learn they must listen. Those who have been sitting in advanced and gifted classes sometimes sound arrogant. Those who have been frying in special education sometimes sound jaded. By November, each knows that someone will hear, someone is waiting. So they write. Once buried, silent, pumped up with too much Ritalin, surviving under too much weight, wearing too much make-up. Student bodies swimming in pants that don't fit. Crawling out of the basement of special ed and remediation. Listening under coats and hoods. Now they are speaking and writing.

In Dana's class, a rich conversation swirls around *Two Old Women*. Dana tosses out Wallis's sentence: " 'The body needs food but the mind needs people.' What does that mean?" to which Rashin, an African American boy, offers: "Talking is another way of eating. You need it to live." Paul, an Irish American boy, joins Rashin: "If you don't have people you get lonely." April, a Jewish American girl, makes a connection to *Of Mice and Men*: "This is the perfect quote for Curly's wife." Randy, an African American girl, lays it out: "A person can go crazy if she can't let her story out. Bottled up. Doesn't matter. It gives you the challenge every day. You gonna let it out? [If not] that's how people go crazy. You need the bond."

These students couldn't have described more eloquently the community they are in the midst of creating—the one that is being created for them and with them.

As I learn in my too-hard chair on my Monday and Friday mornings, these courses have their flaws, their moments in which the magic doesn't prevail, in which the noise of the lecture drones, when looking out the window is more enticing than another round of *Nectar in the Sieve*. But these classrooms, teachers, and students are mostly magic—the magic of imagining and creating a world that does not yet exist, a world in which difference is lifted and complicated. Cultures get to speak and then fracture into beautiful, diverse, contradictory slices. Young adults narrate their still unformed selves and listen to their own brilliance and disappointments. Kizzy and Max have a conversation and learn from each other.

In the corner of this otherwise too stratified school sits this safe space for authentic integration. But even notions of integration get complicated. So, for instance, sometimes the finely balanced groups don't work academically. In some groups, African American males don't speak much. Heads fall to desks. When reading *The Odyssey* and allowed to choose "three classmates to work with," African American males in two classes chose to form their own group. They invented a (mini) historically Black school (for men), and they grew animated. This moment was a reminder to me that a flight into sameness by a marginalized group may be essential for and not a distraction from integration. This example raises questions about who benefits from presumed "balance" in integration (Cohen, 1972).

These spaces that Dana, a White woman, and Carlton, an African American man, create are sprawling, challenging, safe, and threatening; they open as a site for critical work, analysis, and sewing together fragments of self, marginalization, and questioning. Most profoundly, perhaps, this space poses a threat to the larger systems within which young people's lives sit. Tremors can be heard in the diaspora: the rest of their school, in some families, from some board members and the mayor. Safe spaces, for those of color, class, and/or of age groups that others want silenced, threaten by intent or not.

This course is chronically contested—from outside and from within. School and community members are wrestling right here, in this course, with unresolved issues of the school, the town, and the nation—issues of race, ethnicity, class, and gender. Seepage into the classroom creates an undertow. Perhaps this is too much of a burden for a small set of teachers. Or perhaps it is exactly the obligation, the responsibility, and the power of public education. How is it that a small course, one that barely creases the rigid racial and ethnic hierarchy of the school, has so traumatized a district?

We fast-forward now to November as youth in the class begin to assert the mantle of democracy themselves, redistributing power and interrogating differences within—without degenerating into difference as deficit.

> *November 22: Youths Doing "Differences"*
> Until this point, Dana and Carlton have been meticulous about creating groups of "balance," so that students who would never have spoken, do; so they hear each others' voices; so they learn to be audience for others. Usually these groups work with grace. Sometimes with incredible passion. At moments, they falter, dissembling along predictable race and class lines. On their own, among the students, there is some, and increasing, "border crossing." Often these are pairs of students who have found a common interest, in Antigone, the World Series, a poem by June Jordan. Often middle-class Black and White; some surprises too. In each class, there is consistently a group of students who coagulate like a cold, frozen white glacier, holding onto their space, their voices, their ownership of air time, defending against talk about "race all the time." As predictably, floating across these rooms, usually alone, often silent, is a very small fraction of African American boys who are not yet engaged as students in the class. Most have been doing all the reading (despite

my wrong-headed misconceptions). I know because many mumble fascinating interpretations. But only for me, or a friend, or themselves to hear. In the back. Not ready for public exposure. Meanwhile, Dana and Carlton keep dancing up front, engaging, exploring, inviting, sweating, being very smart. I now see how hard this is; how much America needs it.

We read widely, internationally, globally, critically and have now wandered into India, late 1950s, with *Nectar in the Sieve*. I haven't finished the book yet and so find myself eavesdropping on class conversations about Rukmani, the Indian mother who lives by dharma, fate, asks few questions about why or what could be and Kenny, the White, Western trained physician, who prods Rukmani about the "ignorance and patience of you people" who don't ask questions, who don't demand a better life.

Students start today's conversation in Dana's class. Rallying for Kenny as a symbol of progress, the savior, Chelsea (White) affirms, "Kenny is trying to help them see what a better life could be. You have to admit Western medicine is scientifically better." Josh, African American boy hovering in the back with me, fully clothed in jacket and hat, looking "baaad" mumbles, "I think Kenny's a racist. Rukmani ain't sad about her life." I invite him to speak up . . . his facial response suggests it may be too early in the year (or too late in his educational life).

The conversation heats up. I have been noticing, across classes, that these glaciers are now starting to melt. Some individual students have separated themselves, moving into solitary positions. Silent, but visibly withdrawn from the iceberg, moving towards some unformed "colored" polyglot. A few actively join in a inter-racial and inter-ethnic conversation, "Like she [pointing to an African American student] said . . ." There is, today, certainly more cross talk than was the case in September. Whites will now follow the comments of African American students, and will disagree with each other. Likewise, African American students will comment with and on White students' words, and even challenge what has been the heretofore unchallenged White dominance in some classes.

Amidst intense discussion about Rukmani and Kenny, Sondra—a young woman who calls herself African American but then explains, "really part Puerto Rican, Black, and part Native American"—pipes up, crawling out of her often silent mode, and says, "Sometimes I think I would like to be White. I mean to have your"—she points to Steven—"your house and cars and stuff." Steven, the implied White boy, turns and assures her, "If you try, you can have what I have." Kito, a first-generation Dominican American, emerging with barely audible insights sneaking out of a tiny mouth that has been underexercised in all his years in special education, takes the floor: "But I do try hard. I try hard all the time. And I don't have what you have." Many African Americans in the class chime in to turn on Sondra, "You should be proud of who you are." "You don't really want to be White." "That's ignorant to want to be what you ain't." Sondra tries to explain, "It ain't about bein' White. It's about having what he has. Like if I was sittin' in a soft chair and you're in a hard, uncomfortable one, you'd want to be switchin' seats. That's it." She degenerates into apology, "I'm not being clear." Dana assures her of her clarity and turns to a small square of White students—maybe four, no more, but loud—giggling in the middle of the room. She asks them for silence and respect. Tony responds to Sondra, "It's not really ignorant to want something, but it is ignorant to sit around and expect it to come. It's not

> just comin' to you, you got to get it, like Rukmani's sons." Lots of nods and "uh-huhs" around the room. Now we get a multi-voiced mini-lecture on Black empowerment, and how "we" have to do it on our own—as the world abandons them. The room, however, is now alive with commentary. Jackets start to come off. Interruptions within and across "race." The old fault lines evaporate. A community is forming.
>
> Kito is back, not letting this rest, but is cut off by Chelsea, who hitch-hikes on Tony's comment, "You think it's easy being a White girl? Getting called White bitch in the hallway?" She speaks for a long time, over seven minutes, responding in part to Sondra's muffled, "It's not easy being Black and female." Kito waits to respond, "Yeah, I know, but I just want to switch places with any one of you, for a week, live a week in my shoes and see how it feels. I just think you should be educated to all parts of the rainbow." This unexpected eloquence, vigor, and the length of his statement produces smiles and support from around the room. I note how much work some of the African American students and a few White students are exerting to create and sustain this conversation, and how hard it is for some of the White students to engage. The glacier seems to constrict, growing more defended.
>
> Then Robert speaks. Robert, like others I had coded, correctly or not, as middle class and Black, has been one of the border crossers, hanging out with White and African American students. Engaged, interesting, and interested. "This conversation is really hard for me because I am both White and Black. And I understand both sides of what you're saying. I just don't know where I belong." He's near tears and the room is fixed in silence. "I usually just talk in here, but this is really hard." He stops short. His buddy, Caleb, a serious White boy sitting next to him, moves [toward] Robert, a quiet embodiment of support visible even through peripheral, teary vision. Robert finishes. Silence. And then suddenly from across the room, Elijah applauds, thanking Robert. Then Max. Soon most of the class. Robert has both informed and muted the conversation, but created an occasion in which "difference" could be lifted, power argued, and a sense of community—possible, liberal, too soft—nevertheless, could be imagined. And it's only Thanksgiving.

For the first three months of the class, these students who import vastly different biographies carved through families, schools, passions, curiosities, racism, poverty, privilege, entitlement, and special education, wandered around but rarely into difference. Except when Dana took them there. And even then, despite invitations from faculty, students would rarely engage the unspeakable elephant sitting in the middle of the room. Until this point, when it was finally clear that "differences" in privilege are not the same as "differences" in smarts. Suddenly the responsibility for engagement swept the room. Indeed, students of color needed to talk about race in order to be intellectually "free," unburdened by structured silences. In contrast, some White students stifle in the face of such talk, claiming to be silenced.

In the beginning of the course, a shared fantasy seemed to fill the room. Differences were fixed, immutable, maybe (painfully) organized in a hierarchy of ability. But by November, students were starting to notice the many ways to be smart, engaged, critical, a writer, a social and literary analyst. Asserting their insights through writing, conversing, challenging, and building coalitions, these students —White, African American, biracial, Latino, Indian, and those whose identities are too wonderfully complicated to be captured in a simple label—are willing to play, assert, listen, and work in conversation toward community. But for most, it's tough going.

For African American students and all students read as Black, relying upon the skills of doubled consciousness that W. E. B. DuBois (1903/1990) described almost a century ago, the hard part is to voice and trust that they will be heard; to bring to bear critical analyses that probably haven't gotten warm receptions in schooling to date. But even within-group differences flourish. Some, often those most impoverished economically, need to acquire academic skills that have not yet been acquired in school. Others, often those more middle class and/or biracial, describe a sense of "loyalty tests" that litter the room like mines in an academic terrain (Fordham, 1996).

For White students, especially those reared in relative economic privilege, surrounded by educated parents, books, and an ideology of entitlement and equality that refuses to question the perverse distributions of social resources, the hard part of the task—for some, not all, maybe just a vocal few—is to listen, to enjoy others, and not to worry that their smarts (more aptly their "A"s) will disappear or be stolen if merit is multiplied. For Latinos, Asians, the one young woman who calls herself "mulatto," the virulent categorization offends. John, a Colombian-born young man, expresses outrage at this Black-White-Other categorization, explaining, "I hate this. I resent it." Over time, the categories ebb and flow, as their borders grow more and less permeable, rigid, rejecting, and, at wonderful moments, stretchy and inclusive.

This course, then, signifies possibilities for a racial democracy, social challenge, and intellectual stretch from which public education has long walked away. It may present itself as a safe place, but indeed it represents a radically transgressive site in which the work of teachers and students continually reshapes, transforms, and challenges; in which the borders on learning keep moving out. The doubled representation of this space, as a sanctuary and as a site for social change, is part of the confusion. The sweet and benign course is, actually, on the ground enormously threatening while apologies reign—"it's only ninth grade"; "it's only English"; "it's academically rigorous"—in the diaspora, in homes, at school board meetings, and in other classrooms, the power of the course bleeds, seeps, leaks, explodes, and enables. Kizzy asks, "Whose history am I learning in Social Studies class?" John, who longs to return to the name Carlos, writes poetry about his Colombian roots, closeted in other arenas. Ra, steeped in and resistant to a fixed identity as African American and female, longs to escape from the narrow boxes that have tried to contain her. Kito, whose whispers of hesitant brilliance are released from his lips, asks, "Why am I in special education?" There is a slow and quiet yearning being expressed by students to stretch, to speak, write, listen, and challenge texts and each other beyond forty minutes each day. Now it gets subversive. They are demanding education. Are we—adults—prepared to deliver our end of the bargain (see Oakes, Wells, Yonezawa, & Ray, 1997)?

Reflections on desegregation

> The act of institution is an act of social magic that can create difference *ex nihilo*, or else (as is more often the case) by exploiting as it were pre-existing differences, like the biological differences between the sexes or, as in the case of the institution of an heir on the basis of primogeniture, the difference in age. In this sense, as with religion according to Durkheim, it is a "well-founded delusion," a symbolic imposition but *cum fundamento in re*. The

> distinctions that are the most efficacious socially are those which give the appearance of being based on objective differences (I think, for example, of the notion of "natural boundary" in geography). None the less, as is clear in the case of social classes, we are always dealing with continua, with continuous distributions, due to the fact that different principles of differentiation produce different divisions that are never completely congruent. However, social magic always manages to produce discontinuity out of continuity. (Bourdieu, 1991, pp. 119–120)

We conclude by borrowing from Pierre Bourdieu, who argues that "institutions" must be rethought as "verbs," not nouns, which produce "magic." For our purposes these institutions are schools, and the magic takes the form of identities: constructed, embodied, and resisted. In desegregated schools such as Freeway, student identities are often carved through race, typically in sharp opposition to each other. On rare occasions, as at Clear Mount, identities multiply instead, within communities of fluctuating differences, where self and other are mobile and intertwined, where faculty create a context for community, for decentering, and for democracy.

Usually, increasingly, almost everywhere in the United States today, desegregation, diversity, and heterogeneity are floating signifiers: legal, political, and social strategies that sadly, if typically, manufacture relentlessness and strident differences, as Bourdieu would predict. Race, ethnicity, class, gender, sexuality, and disability, layered one upon the other, fossilize the lines of demarcation. With this analysis, we see that the Freeway White boys are all too predictable and are institutionally produced; they embody and enact oppositional identities. We see that every time we as educators refuse to interrupt such institutional productions, we help make another Freeway boy and his "colored" counterpart. They are, of course, twins.

Thus it is only through deliberate commitment, as Dana Sherman and Carlton Jordan brilliantly exercise, to decenter privilege and to refuse the fixing of differences and oppositions, that educators can sever the parasitic hierarchies of race and enable differences to be at once engaged and exploded. In such spaces multiplicities are invited; borders are crossed; retreats to home spaces are understood; voices are heard; skills are sharpened; authority is exercised. In such spaces, everyone can see why we all need to get "out of the ditch" that Fannie Lou Hammer once described:

> I'd tell the White powers that I ain't trying to take nothing from them. I'm trying to make Mississippi a better place for all of us. And I'd say "What you don't understand is that as long as you stand with your feet on my neck, you got to stand in a ditch, too. But if you move, I'm coming out. I want to get us both out of the ditch." (quoted in Beilenson & Jackson, 1992, p. 15)

Given the stakes, it seems tragically predictable that institutional leaders like those at Freeway will continue to stand in the ditch, remaining "neutral" about race and ethnicity. As we see it now, however, declarations of institutional neutrality actually produce educational hierarchy, racial and ethnic opposition, and intergroup tensions, while peer culture more than adequately patrols these racialized, classed, and gendered hierarchies (see Fine, 1991, 1997). Meanwhile, we educators can believe that we are innocent. Wringing our hands as halls fill with chants of "bitch" and "faggot," as racial slurs echo, as sexual harassment complaints go unheeded (until they hit the papers), as White boys "protect" White girls from (always colored) others, as racial tensions percolate and boil over, we lament, "What do you expect? Look at the nation." Adult responsibility flees. Institutional collusion is erased. Desegregation might seem barely worth it: "They sit separately in the cafeteria anyway."

Meanwhile, those faculty and students who dare to imbalance privilege—to incite community, to both value and pluralize difference, to make hierarchy stutter, force "smart" to listen, invite "slow" to speak, circumscribe and circumcise privilege—will likely confront backlash from the State, some families, colleagues, and students dutifully patrolling the borders. Dana and Carlton, the teachers in Arlingdale, and millions of others are throwing their bodies in front of this racialized educational avalanche. The choice to watch or interrupt is ours.

Notes

1 In this section, Lois uses the term "African American" when she writes in her voice, and "Black" when she gives what she interprets as the Freeway point of view.

2 The student body is coded as roughly 45 percent African American, 45 percent White, and the remainder coded as "Other." Most faculty are White.

3 The faculty, a team of five (two of whom were observed by Michelle) that has diverse racial and ethnic backgrounds, has been intensively involved in the study of cooperative learning, heterogenous groupings, and multicultural literature. They, too, offered their comments on the evaluation. One teacher described the aspects of heterogeneous groupings most important to her: "1) The opportunity for all their voices to be heard. 2) The opportunity for all different perspectives to be presented. 3) No prior judgements—the notions that all 'good things can happen' for all students. 4) Lively discussion and interaction because of the unique gifts each student brings. 5) Atmosphere of mutual respect!" Wolf and Spicer (1994) reported that "All the students coming from school with lower expectations for them feel the course has been a real opportunity for them. A number now see themselves as able to choose between high honors, honors, and 'regular' instead of automatically destined for the lowest track" (p. 6).

4 After their exposure to "World Lit," ninth graders return to the real world of a tracked high school, in which they have to select at what level they will study tenth-grade English. After involvement in the World Literature course, the percentage who opted for tenth-grade High Honors English swelled from 33 percent in 1992–1993 to 50 percent in 1995–1996. Indeed, even a substantial proportion of "Three Level" ability students (considered the lowest achievement group) opted for High Honors or Honors.

5 At the time of this writing, I am only into the first four months of participant observation.

6 In this class, the gap in educational opportunities, the spaces between what would typically be seen as the "top" and the "bottom," could be seen as sprawling and not easily bridged, except that these two educators, Dana and Carlton, are firmly committed to educating all and to hearing and producing the genius in all. They both, independently, recite a mantra. "I don't grade papers, that is, drafts, until I think they deserve the grade."

To redress the differences, indeed those deficits produced by very distinct academic biographies, these educators and colleagues designed a summer course for incoming freshmen who had failed English in eighth grade. In that summer experience, students were given a leg up to read and write, engage with peers and faculty about the texts they were about to encounter in the fall. The faculty, too, hang out after school. They review drafts. They narrate with exquisite explicitness what is expected, and how to get from here to there. They mine talent wherever they see it and invite students into the library club or to submit their papers for national competition. They read student papers out loud in class, making sure that students see the varied hues from which talent derives. These teachers have long abandoned pedagogical traditions designed and guaranteed to privilege only a singular best, designed to stratify, those strategies that insure fixedness, coherence, individualism, and hierarchy. Single definitions of merit have been revealed as amateur. Timed exams are distractions.

References

Allport, G. (1954). *The nature of prejudice*. Cambridge, MA: Addison-Wesley.

Ayers, W. (1996). Democracy and urban schooling for justice and care. *Journal for a Just and Caring Education, 2*(1), 85–92.

Banks, J. A. (1995). Multicultural education and the modification of students' racial attitudes. In W. D. Hawley & A. W. Jackson (Eds.), *Toward a common destiny: Improving race and ethnic relations in America* (pp. 315–339). San Francisco: Jossey-Bass.

Beilenson, J., & Jackson, H. (Eds.). (1992). *Voices of struggle, voices of pride*. White Plains, NY: Peter Pauper Press.

Bly, R. (1996). *The sibling society*. Reading, MA: Addison-Wesley.

Bourdieu, P. (1991). *Symbolic power*. Cambridge, MA: Harvard University Press.

Boyte, H. C., & Evans, S. M. (1992). *Free spaces: The sources of democratic change in America*. Chicago: University of Chicago Press.

Braddock, J. H., Dawkins, M. P., & Wilson, G. (1995). Intercultural contact and race relations among American youth. In W. D. Hawley & A. W. Jackson (Eds.), *Toward a common destiny: Improving race and ethnic relations in America* (pp. 237–256). San Francisco: Jossey-Bass.

Brehm, S. S., & Kassin, S. M. (1996). *Social psychology* (3rd ed.). Boston: Houghton Mifflin.

Bryk, A. S., Lee, V. E., & Holland, P. B. (1993). *Catholic schools and the common good*. Cambridge, MA: Harvard University Press.

Carter, R. T., & Helms, J. E. (1990). White racial identity attitudes and cultural values. In J. E. Helms (Ed.), *Black and White racial identity: Theory, research, and practice* (pp. 105–118). Westport, CT: Greenwood Press.

Clark, H., & Saegert, S. (in press). Cooperatives as places of social change. In A. Heskin & J. Leavitt (Eds.), *The hidden history of cooperatives*. Davis, CA: Center for Cooperative Change.

Cohen, E. G. (1972). Interracial interaction disability. *Human Relations, 25*(1), 9–24.

Collins, P. H. (1990). *Black feminist thought: Knowledge, consciousness, and the politics of empowerment*. Boston: Unwin Hyman.

Crenshaw, K. (1992). Whose story is it anyway? Feminist and antiracist appropriations of Anita Hill. In T. Morrison (Ed.), *Race-ing justice, en-gendering power: Essays on Anita Hall, Clarence Thomas, and the construction of social reality* (pp. 402–440). New York: Pantheon Books.

Cross, W. E., Jr. (1995). Oppositional identity and African American youth: Issues and prospects. In W. D. Hawley & A. W. Jackson (Eds.), *Toward a common destiny: Improving race and ethnic relations in America* (pp. 185–204). San Francisco: Jossey-Bass.

Dreier, P., & Moberg, D. (1996). Moving from the 'hood. The mixed success of integrating suburbia. *American Prospect, 24*, 75–79.

DuBois, W. E. B. (1990). *The souls of Black folk*. New York: Vintage Books. (Original work published 1903)

Fields, W. (1996, November/December). The myth of Montclair. *New Jersey Reporter*, pp. 17–21.

Fine, M. (1991). *Framing dropouts: Notes on the politics of an urban public high school*. Albany: State University of New York Press.

Fine, M. (1997). Witnessing whiteness. In M. Fine, L. Weis, L. Powell, & L. M. Wong (Eds.), *Off-white: Readings on race, power, and society* (pp. 57–65). New York: Routledge.

Fine, M., Weis, L., Powell, L. C., & Wong, L. M. (1997). *Off-white: Readings on race, power, and society*. New York: Routledge.

Fordham, S. (1996). *Blacked out: Dilemmas of race, identity, and success at Capital High*. Chicago: University of Chicago Press.

Fraser, N. (1990). Rethinking the public sphere: A contribution to the critique of actually existing democracy. *Social Text: Theory/Culture/Ideology, 25/26*, 56–80.

Gaertner, S., Dovidio, J., Anastasio, P., Bachman, B., & Rust, M. (1993). The common in-group identity model: Recategorization and reduction of intergroup bias. *European Review of Social Psychology, 4*, 1–26.

Gaertner, S., Dovidio, J., Banker, B., Rust, M., Nier, J., Mottola, G., & Ward, C. (1997). Does White racism necessarily mean anti-Blackness? Aversive racism and pro Whiteness. In M. Fine, L. Weis, L. Powell, & L. M. Wong (Eds.), *Off-white: Readings on race, power, and society* (pp. 167–178). New York: Routledge.

Gates, H. L., Jr. (Ed.). (1985). *"Race," writing, and difference.* Chicago: University of Chicago Press.

Giovanni, N. (1993). Black is the noun. In G. Early (Ed.), *Lure and loathing: Essays on race, identity, and the ambivalence of assimilation* (pp. 113–126). New York: Penguin.

Guinier, L. (1994). *The tyranny of the majority: Fundamental fairness and representative democracy.* New York: Free Press.

Hall, S. (1989). Identity and difference. *Radical America, 23*(4), 9–20.

Hare-Mustin, R. T., & Marecek, J. (1990). *Making a difference: Psychology and the construction of gender.* New Haven, CT: Yale University Press.

Hartsock, N. (1984). *Money, sex, and power.* Boston: Northeastern University Press.

Heath, S. B. (1995). Race, ethnicity, and the defiance of categories. In W. D. Hawley & A. W. Jackson (Eds.), *Toward a common destiny: Improving race and ethnic relations in America* (pp. 39–70). San Francisco: Jossey-Bass.

Helms, J. E. (Ed.). (1990). *Black and White racial identity: Theory, research, and practice.* Westport, CT: Greenwood Press.

Hurtado, A., & Stewart, A. (1997). Through the looking glass: Implications of studying Whiteness for feminist methods. In M. Fine, L. Powell, L. Weis, & L. M. Wong (Eds.), *Off-white: Readings on race, power, and society* (pp. 297–311). New York: Routledge.

Johnson, D. W., & Johnson, R. T. (1995). Social interdependence: Cooperative learning in education. In B. B. Bunker, J. Z. Rubin, & Associates (Eds.), *Conflict, cooperation, and justice: Essays inspired by the work of Morton Deutsch* (pp. 205–251). San Francisco: Jossey-Bass.

Kelly, G., & Nihlen, A. (1982). Schooling and the reproduction of patriarchy: Unequal workloads, unequal rewards. In M. Apple (Ed.), *Cultural and economic reproduction in education* (pp. 162–180). London: Routledge and Kegan Paul.

Lawrence, S., & Tatum, B. (1997). White educators as allies: Moving from awareness to action. In M. Fine, L. Weis, L. Powell, & L. M. Wong (Eds.), *Off-white: Readings on race, power and society* (pp. 333–342). New York: Routledge.

Marcia, J. (1980). Identity in adolescents. In J. Adelson (Ed.), *Handbook of adolescent psychology* (pp. 159–187). New York: Wiley.

McCarty, C., Rodriguez, A., Meecham, S., David, S., Wilson-Brown, C., Godina, H., Supryia, K., & Buerdia, E. (1997). Race, suburban resentment, and the representation of the inner city in contemporary film and television. In M. Fine, L. Weis, L. Powell, & L. M. Wong (Eds.), *Off-white: Readings on race, power, and society* (pp. 229–241). New York: Routledge.

MEE Foundation. (1993). Teaching the hip hop generation. In the MEE Symposium, *Final Report.* Philadelphia: MEE, Inc.

Menzies, I. E. P. (1960). A case study in the functioning of social systems as a defense against anxiety. *Human Relations, 13*, 95–121.

Messner, M., & Sabo, D. (1994). *Sex, violence, and power in sports: Rethinking masculinity.* Freedom, CA: Crossing Press.

Metz, M. H. (1994). Desegregation as necessity and challenge. *Journal of Negro Education, 63*, 64–77.

Minow, M. (1990). *Making all the difference: Inclusion, exclusion, and American law.* Ithaca, NY: Cornell University Press.

Oakes, J., Wells, A. S., Yonezawa, S., & Ray, K. (1997). Equity lessons from detracking schools. In A. Hargreaves (Ed.), *Rethinking educational change with heart and mind* (pp. 43–72). Alexandria, VA: Association for Supervision and Curriculum Development.

Opotow, S. (1995). Drawing the line: Social categorization, moral exclusion, and the scope of justice. In B. B. Bunker, J. Z. Rubin, & Associates (Eds.), *Conflict, cooperation, and justice: Essays inspired by the work of Morton Deutsch* (pp. 347–369). San Francisco: Jossey-Bass.

Orfield, G., Eaton, S. E., & the Harvard Project on School Desegregation. (1996). *Dismantling desegregation: The quiet reversal of Brown v. Board of Education.* New York: New Press.

Phillips, L., Penn, M. L., & Gaines, S. O. (1993). A hermeneutic rejoinder to ourselves and our critics. *Journal of Black Psychology, 19*, 350–357.

Plummer, D. L. (1995). Patterns of racial identity development of African American adolescent males and females. *Journal of Black Psychology, 21*, 168–180.

Powell, L. (1994). Interpreting social defenses: Family groups in an urban setting. In M. Fine (Ed.), *Chartering urban school reform: Reflections on public high schools in the midst of change* (pp. 112–121). New York: Teachers College Press.

Powell, L. (1997). The achievement (k)not: Whiteness and Black underachievement. In M. Fine, L. Weis, L. Powell, & L. M. Wong (Eds.), *Off-white: Readings on race, power, and society* (pp. 3–12). New York: Routledge.

Powell, L., & Barry, M. (1995). *Professional development for change: A working paper.* Philadelphia: Resources for Change.

Powell, L., Barry, M., & Davis, G. (in press). Facing reality in urban public schools: Using racial identity theory in family group. In L. Powell, M. Barry, & G. Davis (Eds.), *Racial identity theory: Applications for individual, group, and organizational interventions* (pp. 147–158). Mahwah. NJ: Lawrence Erlbaum.

Putnam, R. (1993). *Making democracy work: Civic traditions in modern Italy.* Princeton, NJ: Princeton University Press.

Rhode, D. L. (Ed.). (1990). *Theoretical perspectives on sexual difference.* New Haven, CT: Yale University Press.

Schofield, J. W. (1982). *Black and White in school: Trust, tension, or tolerance.* New York: Praeger.

Schofield, J. W. (1995). Promoting positive intergroup relations in school settings. In W. D. Hawley & A. W. Jackson (Eds.), *Toward a common destiny: Improving race and ethnic relations in America* (pp. 291–314). San Francisco: Jossey-Bass.

Semons, M. (1991). Ethnicity in the urban high school: A naturalistic study of student experiences. *Urban Review, 23*, 137–158.

Sherif, M. (1958). Superordinate goals in the reduction of intergroup conflict. *American Journal of Sociology, 43*, 349–356.

Slavin, R. E. (1995). Enhancing intergroup relations in schools: Cooperative learning and other strategies. In W. D. Hawley & A. W. Jackson (Eds.), *Toward a common destiny: Improving race and ethnic relations in America* (pp. 291–314). San Francisco: Jossey-Bass.

Spencer, M. B., Swanson, D. P., & Cunningham, M. (1991). Ethnicity, ethnic identity, and competence formation: Adolescent transition and cultural transformation. *Journal of Negro Education, 60*, 366–387.

Steele, C. (1988). The psychology of self-affirmation: Sustaining the integrity of the self. *Advances in Experimental Social Psychology, 21*, 261–302.

Stevenson, H. C., Jr. (1995). Relationship of adolescent perceptions of racial socialization to racial identity. *Journal of Black Psychology, 21*, 49–70.

Tajfel, H., & Turner, J. (1979). An integrative theory of intergroup conflict. In W. G. Austin & S. Worchel (Eds.), *The social psychology of intergroup relations* (pp. 33–47). Monterey, CA: Brooks/Cole.

Thorne, B. (1993). *Gender play: Girls and boys in school.* New Brunswick, NJ: Rutgers University Press.

Vanderslice, V. J. (1995). Cooperation within a competitive context: Lessons from worker cooperatives. In B. B. Bunker, J. Z. Rubin, & Associates (Eds.), *Conflict, cooperation, and justice: Essays inspired by the work of Morton Deutsch* (pp. 175–204). San Francisco: Jossey-Bass.

Weis, L. (1990). *Working class without work: High school students in a deindustrializing economy.* New York: Routledge.

Weis, L. (1991). Disempowering White working class females: The role of the high school. In C. Sleeter (Ed.), *Empowerment through multicultural education* (pp. 95–120). Albany: State University of New York Press.

Weis, L., & Fine, M. (Eds.). (1993). *Beyond silenced voices: Class, race, and gender in United States schools.* Albany: State University of New York Press.

Weis, L., & Fine, M. (1996). Narrating the 1980s and 1990s: Voices of the poor and working-class White and African American men. *Anthropology and Education Quarterly, 27*, 493–516.

Wells, A. S., & Serna, I. (1996). The politics of culture: Understanding local political resistance to detracking in racially mixed schools. *Harvard Educational Review, 66*, 93–118.

Winant, H. (1997). Behind blue eyes: Whiteness and contemporary U.S. radical politics. In M. Fine, L. Weis, L. Powell, and L. M. Wong (Eds.), *Off-white: Readings on race, power, and society* (pp. 40–53). New York: Routledge.

Wolf, D. P., & Spicer, W. (1994). *Evaluation of world literatures course.* Unpublished manuscript.

PART 4

GRADE SPECIFIC/SUBJECT SPECIFIC APPLICATIONS OF MCE

CHAPTER 16

MULTICULTURAL EDUCATION IN EARLY CHILDHOOD (1982)

Patricia G. Ramsey

"How can we teach children about other cultures when they don't even know what their own ethnic heritages are?" "I have real problems finding materials that don't stereotype cultural or ethnic groups." Questions and comments such as these are frequently voiced by early childhood teachers in response to advocates of multicultural education. Theoreticians and practitioners can point to ample evidence that young children cannot grasp the concept of different countries nor the relationships and correspondences among different cultural groups within a country. In his study of children's views of their homeland, Piaget (1951) found that children before the age of six could not relate the concept of town, state, and country. Many teachers have reported that their children enjoyed the variety of activities involved in United Nations Week programs but were unable to understand the categories of different countries and cultures. Finding information about ethnic groups in this country that is simple enough for children to understand and yet not superficial and stereotypical is another challenge to teachers who integrate multicultural education into the curriculum for young children.

At the same time, there is evidence that children's attitudes toward their own race and toward other racial groups start to form in the preschool years (Goodman 1964; Porter 1971). Infants recognize differences in social objects (Thurman and Lewis 1979) and negative stereotypes appear to be readily absorbed by young children. We once had an Algonquin woman visit our school. Several three-year-olds began to cry and shriek with fright as soon as the visitor mentioned that she was an Indian. Similar accounts of children's stereotyped misconceptions are frequently described by teachers (Califf 1977; Ramsey 1979). During the early years, children are forming their initial social patterns and preferences and their basic approaches to learning about the physical and social worlds. Thus, the difficulties of designing effective multicultural education for young children appear to be considerable; however, there is compelling evidence that in order to influence children's basic racial and cultural attitudes, we must start with the very young.

Challenging some misconceptions

How can we resolve this apparent contradiction? First, there are several prevalent misconceptions about the nature of multicultural education and the rationale for it that need to be challenged. One prevailing idea is that multicultural education should focus on information about other countries and cultures. Plans for implementing multicultural education are often reminiscent of the geography or history lessons that we learned as children. There is an emphasis on names of countries, their capitals, flags, exports, typical artifacts, and famous people. Efforts to have International Week or to cover a country a week often fall into the trap of teaching children facts for which they have no context. We frequently stress information that is meaningful to adults but not necessarily to children. Moreover, the emphasis on exotic differences often accentuates the "we" and "they" polarity. Thus, in many respects, this type of curriculum may actually work against the goal of understanding the shared experiences of all people.

A second misconception is the notion that multicultural education is only relevant in classrooms with students who are members of the cultural and racial groups to be studied. When I suggested the topic of multicultural education for a workshop I was to give, the teachers quickly said that because they did not have any Blacks or members of other minority groups in their classrooms, such a workshop would be irrelevant. These responses reflected a limited view of the effects and responsibilities of intergroup relationships. The fact that teachers and children in this country feel disassociated from issues related to race and culture underscores the importance of multicultural education for children of all cultural groups.

From an early age children who grow up in culturally mixed settings or as members of minority groups are exposed to the idea that our society is comprised of many groups. Through television, books, and school they have been exposed to the life styles and expectations of the Anglo-American middle class. From their own experiences they may also be aware of the existence and effects of discrimination. Many American children however, can grow to adulthood unaware of and insensitive to the experiences of other cultural groups. The extent of this isolation is illustrated by the following incident. Recently, in Boston, a Black, high school football player was shot during a game in a White community. In a subsequent discussion in a class of student teachers, the people working in the inner city talked about the questions and reactions expressed by their young students. In contrast, the students teaching in the suburbs a few miles away reported that neither the teachers nor the children mentioned the incident.

In order to increase the potential for positive relationships among groups of people, all children need to expand their realm of awareness and concern beyond their immediate experience. Since education in this country traditionally has been dominated by the Anglo-American point of view, one important task of multicultural education is to try to balance this lopsided learning by helping children look into and beyond their relatively insulated environments.

A third misconception, that there should be a unified set of goals and curriculum for multicultural education, contradicts the underlying purpose of multicultural education to provide relevant and meaningful education to children from all cultural backgrounds. Many books and activity kits designed for multicultural education describe curriculum with no mention of the cultural backgrounds and attitudes of the children in the class. In order to design effective multicultural education, teachers need to learn about the racial, cultural, and socio-economic background of children in their care, what experiences they have had with people from other groups, and their attitudes toward their own and other groups. In order to respond to these variations, the goals and the curriculum will differ considerably from classroom to classroom.

For instance, in a classroom of children from diverse backgrounds, the primary goal might be to help the children understand the extent of their similarities and the nature of some of their differences. Learning how to communicate if there is not a shared language might also be a major focus of the classroom. However, for a group of White middle-class children who have grown up in a relatively monocultural environment, the emphasis would be in seeing the diversity that exists among the group members and grasping the idea that there are many other cultures and ways of life. For children from low-status groups, one initial goal would be to foster their respect and appreciation for their own culture. Children of high-status groups often need to become more realistic about the relative value of their own culture. The social and political climate of the school and community should also be taken into account. The state of intergroup relationships and the prevalence of negative or positive perceptions of the groups influence the children's attitudes. While published multicultural materials can be used as resources for information and, in some cases, activities, each education program should be designed to fit the backgrounds, awareness levels, and attitudes of the particular group of children in each class.

Finally, the misconception that multicultural education is a set of activities added on to the existing curriculum needs to be reexamined. Multicultural education embodies a perspective rather than a curriculum. Just as teachers constantly assess and address children's social skills, emotional states, and cognitive abilities, so should teachers consider children's cultural identities and attitudes. This type of learning can occur every minute of the day. Effective teachers are ingenious at incorporating language skills, problem-solving abilities, and social experience into all activities. Likewise, teachers can seize opportunities to foster the children's awareness of their immediate and broader social world. A child's comment about a picture of an unfamiliarly clothed person, the arrival of a child who does not speak English, a conflict between two children, the advent of a holiday season, and a visiting grandparent are a few of the many moments that can become opportunities to introduce and reinforce the idea that people share many of the same feelings and needs yet express them in many different ways. In addition to incidental teaching moments, all aspects of the planned curriculum can incorporate a multicultural perspective. Decisions about materials, program structure, the role of parents, and the selection of curriculum topics all reflect attitudes toward cultures.

The role of the teacher

The design and implementation of multicultural education rests, in large part, with the attitudes, skills, and knowledge of the teacher. One initial step is for teachers to become aware of their own cultural backgrounds, their relationships with the larger society, and their attitudes toward other people. This process requires a great deal of honesty and is often painful. However, it is important that we all recognize our biases and ignorance. It is tempting to deny our prejudices and to claim that we find all children equally appealing. Many teachers, in their efforts to minimize differences, maintain that children are all alike. While such comments emerge from genuine intentions to be fair and impartial in their perceptions and their relationships with children, they also reflect a naiveté about the power and effects of social attitudes and conditions. As teachers we need to accept the fact that we, like our young charges, have inevitably been influenced by the stereotypes and the one-sided view of society that prevail in the schools and the media.

I spent several weeks observing in an elementary school noted for its humanistic, child-centered approach to learning. The teachers had met the challenges of mainstreaming special needs children with commitment, sensitivity, and imagination. However, in our conversations, there were frequent disparaging allusions to the "foreign student element." Clearly frustrated by the extra work that these recent immigrants required, the teachers tended to dwell on the things that the children "didn't even know." Differences in life style and language were interpreted as ignorance. Neither the school nor the individual teachers attempted to learn about the diverse cultures of the children or to incorporate that richness into the classrooms. These kinds of attitudes obscure our own biases and restrict our realm of knowledge. Thus, it is important that we dispel the illusion that we are totally without prejudice and recognize that there are many valid ways of life beyond our immediate experience. Humility and a genuine desire to know more about other people are absolute prerequisites for designing and implementing multicultural education. From this perspective, we can genuinely learn about the children's cultural backgrounds and attitudes and start to form effective and reciprocal collaborations with parents and people in the community. This knowledge can then provide the base to design ways of promoting cultural identity and positive attitudes toward various cultural and ethnic groups. Once a multicultural perspective has been incorporated into our view of children and educational goals, many ways of implementing it in our classrooms become obvious.

Guidelines for integrating a multicultural perspective

The possibilities for a multicultural program suggested here are by no means exhaustive. However, it is hoped that these concrete ideas will enable teachers to see more clearly how appropriate forms of multicultural education can be woven into their programs.

Enhance self-concept and cultural identity

The development of a positive self-concept is a major goal of early childhood programs. Usually the curriculum related to this goal consists of activities to enhance awareness and appreciation of each child's feelings and competencies. Stories, art projects, and discussions about families, homes, likes and dislikes, and other related topics are frequent. Each child's cultural, ethnic, and racial identity can easily be incorporated into these activities. Activities can focus on how all the children's lives are similar and yet different. This enhances identification with one's own culture as well as awareness of other cultures. For minority children, this theme is ideal for stressing the value of their culture and for neutralizing the impact of negative stereotypes.

In classrooms that are monocultural, the differences among the children may be limited to family size, personal experiences, and physical appearance, but still the idea that people are both similar and different can be explored. For children who have had little or no experience with people from other cultural backgrounds, the notion that people who look different from them have similar needs can be woven into discussions about families and feelings. Photographs in *The Family of Man* (Steichen 1955) and *This Is My Father and Me* (Raynor 1973) help convey the concept that all people have common needs, feelings, and relationships even though they may look, dress, and speak in many different ways. The goal here is not to teach about particular cultures or countries but to incorporate into the children's own framework images and experiences that support the development of cultural identity and the awareness of diversity.

For children, kindergarten age and younger, these activities should be very concrete. Having the children bring in photographs of their families and themselves as babies will provide very immediate ways to talk about the children, their growth, their similarities, and differences. Visiting parents and siblings can also make the children aware that everyone has a family; yet each one is unique. Activities in the role-play area can further stimulate discussion of variations among the children's families.

For primary-age children, these concepts can be incorporated into early language arts activities. Children can write and share stories about their own backgrounds and family. Books that appropriately reflect the different backgrounds of the children in the class should be available. Bringing in family trees and stories can make the idea of background more real. Trips to neighborhoods, museums, and community organizations may also enhance children's awareness of the cultural groups in their class and community. For second and third graders, maps, globes, and simple histories might also be introduced within the context of knowing more about themselves and their classmates.

Develop social skills and responsibility

The ability to recognize that another person has a point of view, state of mind, and feelings that are distinct from one's own is an important area of development. Through maturation and social experience children learn how to identify, predict, and respond to others' points of view. Clearly, the ability to see and appreciate others' perspectives are important skills for understanding and relating to different cultural groups. While these skills are emerging in very young children, they develop quickly as children progress to kindergarten and the primary grades. Flavell et al. (1968) found that children often do not choose to use their abilities to see what others are experiencing. He suggested that there are some ways that we can motivate children to practice and expand these skills. The first one is making provisions for frequent social interaction. Second, we can consistently call the children's attention to the existence of other points of view. Third, children should be encouraged to communicate so that others can understand them. Finally, the presence of younger children may make the reality of others' needs and points of view more concrete. Consideration of these factors would influence both the physical and social structure of the classroom.

Young children spend a great deal of time exploring social relationships. Initially, they watch each other, then play beside, and gradually make attempts to play together with varying degrees of success. Rivalries, inseparable pairs, exclusive "gangs," bullies, and transient friendships all emerge, change, and end in rapidly shifting events. Classroom equipment and activities can be set up to provide many opportunities for cooperative activities, where children have to coordinate their actions to achieve a common goal. Equipment such as seesaws, pulleys, and hoists that require two people, large blocks, double slides, and horizontal tire swings, all facilitate social play. A stimulating and attractive role-play corner invites many group interactions. Almost all activities in the art, construction, and science areas can be adapted to incorporate a cooperative dimension. In creative movement, children can be asked to synchronize their motions in many ways that increase awareness of each other.

Classroom chores such as cleaning up, moving furniture, transporting materials, preparing snack, collecting litter, and emptying the wading pool can all provide increased opportunity for social interaction, communication, and the experience of other (often conflicting) points of view. Conflicts over materials are excellent opportunities to help children express their own feelings and listen to those of their opponents. In helping to resolve these disputes, teachers can guide the children toward cooperation. All too often, we settle conflicts by simply giving the children another object so they can each have one or by telling them to play separately. By emphasizing cooperation rather than individual achievements in our plans and guidance, we can foster the development of social awareness and communication skills.

When children enter the primary grades, teachers tend to focus on children's academic skills. During lunch, recess, and after school children work out their social hierarchies, rivalries, friendships, and cooperative ventures. In many respects, children at this age have gained enough control, awareness of others, and communication skills to manage without a lot of adult supervision. However, there are many classrooms where scapegoating, excluding, bullying, and rivalry go unchecked. Moreover, little time and attention are paid to helping children further develop their skills in cooperating and communicating. Classroom projects such as plays, murals, sculptures, newspapers, and construction projects can provide opportunities to expand social contacts and skills as well as to practically apply academic skills. At recess and gym, cooperative games can be introduced to balance the societal emphasis on competition (Orlick 1978). Certainly in classrooms where there are tensions among racial and cultural groups, it is crucial that teachers take an active role in establishing a positive social climate and helping children explore and resolve their differences.

The inclusion of younger and/or special needs children in classrooms may provide opportunities for children to be aware of others' needs and to learn when it is appropriate to offer help. In age-stratified groups, children usually receive attention, help, care, and teaching from adults and rarely are in situations where they can contribute to the knowledge or welfare of others. Not only is this awareness and concern for others basic to the goals of multicultural education, it is also relevant to recently emerging concerns about the self-centeredness of the me generation. While the presence of special needs and younger children may make the idea of social awareness and responsibility more concrete, these expectations can be incorporated into any classroom. Young children can be encouraged to help each other get dressed to go outside, pick up spilled crayons, carry the trikes onto the porch, etc. For primary age children, this involvement might be extended to raising money or contributing work for community people who need help. These activities are vehicles for fostering cooperation, social responsibility, and awareness of other people. It is important, however, that the children do not view the recipients of their efforts as "less good" or the "needy poor," but rather as people who, like themselves, sometimes need assistance.

Children's orientation to the social world, which begins with their earliest friendships, must be considered as part of any efforts to integrate multicultural education into the curriculum. Efforts to expand children's awareness of others, their capacity to communicate, their willingness and ability to cooperate, and their sense of social responsibility should be emphasized throughout their lives.

Broaden the cultural base of the curriculum

In addition to considering the children's self-concept, cultural identity, and their basic social orientation, teachers also need to broaden the cultural awareness of their students. Here the goal is not to teach children *about* other groups or countries but rather to help children become accustomed to the idea that there are many life-styles, languages, and points of view. Two factors appear to influence children's concepts of other groups (Lambert and Klineberg 1967). One is their perception of their own group. If their view is unrealistically superlative, then it creates an attitude of superiority toward others. Second, if children learn about other groups only in terms of contrasts, then they see them as being more different than groups about which they know nothing. Thus, it is important that teachers present a realistic view of the children's own group and stress the similarities among all people. Furthermore, children are more likely to integrate new information when they see it in relation to their previous knowledge (Forman and Kuschner 1977).

In a culturally diverse classroom, children can experience this relationship in a concrete way. "When Jorge talks to his mother, I can't understand him; when he talks to me, I can. When we play with cars, he calls them 'carros' so I call them 'carros' too." In these situations, teachers can incorporate a wide cultural content in the curriculum by including experiences and materials that reflect the children's cultural groups. While the teachers need to establish the basic framework for such a curriculum, the children, parents, and community can provide many resources.

In a monocultural group, these concepts are more difficult to convey. The fact that there are many different ways that people look, eat, work, cook, speak, etc., has to be more consciously introduced into the classroom. By concretely experiencing many different ways of doing things it is hoped that children will become more acclimated and receptive to variations among people. Children may develop more flexible expectations of human behavior, which, in turn, will enable them to approach contacts with less familiar people with a more respectful and open-minded attitude.

In early childhood classrooms, there are many opportunities to introduce variations in clothing, cooking, work, music, etc., into the classroom in very concrete ways. For instance, young children can be encouraged to try many ways of carrying objects using their backs, hips, heads, and in a variety of containers. These activities can be encouraged by having pictures that show people carrying objects in many different ways. The message would not be "The people in India carry containers of water on their heads," nor would it be "We do it *this* way, they do it *that* way." Instead, the idea that "All people carry things in many different ways and you can try some of them" would be emphasized. This same principle and format can be applied to include a variety of clothing, tools, and utensils in the role-playing corner. Singing and dancing from many different cultures are lively ways of conveying this concept. Other languages and nonverbal forms of communication can be introduced in the language arts program with songs, dramatics, books, and pictures. Foods, cooking, and eating are popular vehicles for incorporating unfamiliar experiences in a comprehensible context. Holidays provide high-interest occasions for incorporating cultural experiences into the classroom. There are many similar celebrations across cultures. Seasonal festivals (planting, harvesting, the celebrations of light at the winter solstice, the arrival of the new year) and commemorations of independence and other historical events occur in virtually every culture. Observances of familiar holidays can be greatly enriched by incorporating many cultural expressions of similar themes (Flemming, Hamilton, and Hicks 1977; Ramsey 1979).

In primary classrooms, many similar activities can be introduced in greater depth. Cooking activities, celebrations of holidays, and learning new languages can stimulate a great deal of interest and involvement in all areas of the curriculum.

For these older children, teachers may want to make more information available about various groups, but it is important not to get involved in trying to convey information that is not meaningful to the children. When the children seem ready, teachers can start helping them to see the correspondences between their own lives and activities and those of others. When attempting to draw comparisons, it is important to avoid the we/they dichotomy or any suggestion that the unfamiliar forms are inferior. One important factor in reducing ethnocentrism is to see our own behaviors and responses as simply one way of doing things, not the only nor the best way.

Young children can experience in many concrete and meaningful ways the rich variety of human experience. Far from contradicting the goals and practice of early childhood education, this inclusion will enrich and expand them.

Study a particular group

Studying the cultures represented in any group of children is an important contribution to their cultural identity and understanding of their classmates. If there are children in the group who have recently immigrated to this country, then studying their homeland may be a way of easing the newcomers' entry into the classroom. This approach makes the adjustment and learning process a mutual and reciprocal one instead of being the sole responsibility of the recent arrival. Teachers might also want to focus on a particular culture or country if the children express a great deal of interest and/or many misconceptions about that group of people. In this country, this phenomena often occurs about Native American peoples. Teachers have tried and reported some success in their efforts to reduce negative stereotypes and to promote authentic understanding and appreciation of Native Americans (Council on Interracial Books for Children 1977).

When developing a focus on a particular group of people, it is important that the *people*, not the stereotypes or exotic differences, are studied. The fact that they are individuals who share many of the feelings and needs that children have experienced can be conveyed with photographs, stories, and if possible, actual contact with people from that group. Whenever children learn about a life style that differs from their own, they need to be given a context in which to understand why that particular system was developed. They need to understand all human behavior as reasonable responses to the environment, not simply as isolated actions. Also, the distinctions between the contemporary life styles and historical ones need to be drawn clearly, so that children do not confuse different cultures with different historical periods. For example, they need to understand not just that "The Sioux people lived in tepees," but that "The Sioux people *used* to live in tepees because they needed to have homes that they could move easily as they followed the herds of buffalo. *Now* some of the people live in houses on reservations and others live in cities and suburbs." It is important that we do not convey a romanticized post card image of other people. Some sense of the political and social realities should be incorporated into the curriculum. For instance, it would be a misrepresentation to study Cambodia without some discussion of the present plight of the people there. As mentioned previously, the depth and complexity of the information will obviously depend largely on the age and experience of the children involved. However, efforts to simplify information should not impair its authenticity.

The activities that are developed as part of this curriculum should be concrete and comprehensible to the children. As described earlier, much of this information can be incorporated into materials and experiences that are already familiar. For preschoolers, this immediacy is particularly important. For primary age children, information should be offered only as long as they appear to understand it. Because of the complexity of many of the concepts involved, teachers should carefully monitor the children's responses to insure that they are forming authentic and differentiated perceptions of the people being studied.

Conclusion

Multicultural education can be incorporated effectively into every aspect of early childhood programs. While multicultural education may seem to be most immediately relevant to classes with minority children, it is even more important that all children in this country understand the culturally pluralistic nature of our society. Teachers need to be conscious of their own views and the limits of their knowledge in order to learn about the backgrounds and attitudes of the children in their classes. Using this information, they can design appropriate goals and curricula.

The concept of shared human experience and cultural diversity can be woven into all aspects of the curriculum. The emphasis on social and emotional development can be expanded to incorporate the enhancement of children's cultural identity and their awareness, concern, and respect for other people. Through a variety of materials and activities, young children can become accustomed to the idea that there are many ways of doing things. For primary school children, there should be a continued emphasis on the development of self-concepts, cultural identities, and social skills. As these children start to express curiosity about the world and gain skills to seek information, they should have access to materials that will foster their awareness of the diversity of human experience as well as its common themes.

Despite the complexity of its issues and content, multicultural education is far from incompatible with early childhood education. In fact, by incorporating one with the other, we can enrich and expand the lives of the children with whom we work.

References

Califf, J. "What One Teacher Has Done." In *Unlearning "Indian" Stereotypes*. New York: Council on Interracial Books for Children, 1977.

Council on Interracial Books for Children. *Unlearning "Indian" Stereotypes*. New York: Council on Interracial Books for Children, 1977.

Flavell, J. H.; Botkin, P. T.; Fry, C. L.; Wright, J. W.; and Jarvis, P. E. *The Development of Role Taking and Communication Skills in Children*. New York: Wiley, 1968.

Flemming, B. M.; Hamilton, D. S.; and Hicks, J. D. *Resources for Creative Teaching in Early Childhood Education*. New York: Harcourt, Brace & Jovanovich, 1977.

Forman, G., and Kuschner, D. *The Child's Construction of Knowledge*. Monterey, Calif.: Brooks/Cole, 1977.

Goodman, M. E. *Race Awareness in Young Children*. New York: Collier, 1964.

Lambert, W. E., and Klineberg, O. *Children's Views of Foreign Peoples*. New York: Appleton-Century Crofts, 1967.

Orlick, T. *The Cooperative Sports and Games Book*. New York: Pantheon, 1978.

Piaget, J. "The Development in Children of the Idea of the Homeland and of Relations with Other Countries." *International Social Science Journal* (Autumn 1951): 561–578.

Porter, J. D. R. *Black Child, White Child: The Development of Racial Attitudes*. Cambridge, Mass.: Harvard University Press, 1971.

Ramsey, P. G. "Beyond Turkeys and 'Ten Little Indians': Alternative Approaches to Thanksgiving." *Young Children* 34, no. 6 (September 1979): 28–32, 49–52.
Raynor, D. *This Is My Father and Me*. Chicago: Whitman, 1973.
Steichen, E. *The Family of Man*. New York: Simon & Schuster, 1955.
Thurman, S. K., and Lewis, M. "Children's Responses to Differences: Some Possible Implications for Mainstreaming." *Exceptional Children* 45, no. 6 (March 1979): 468–470.

Suggested resource books

Cole, A.; Haas, C.; Hellen, E.; and Weinberger, B. *Children Are Children Are Children*. Boston: Little, Brown, 1978.
Gold, M. J.; Grant, C. A.; and Rivlin, H. N. *In Praise of Diversity: A Resource Book for Multicultural Education*. Washington, D.C.: Association of Teacher Educators, 1977.
Schmidt, V., and McNeill, E. *Cultural Awareness: A Resource Bibliography*. Washington, D.C.: National Association for the Education of Young Children, 1978.
Shepard, M., and Shepard, R. *Vegetable Soup Activities*. New York: Citation, 1975.

CHAPTER 17

ON BEHALF OF CHILDREN (1979)

A curriculum design for multicultural education in the elementary school

Geneva Gay

Today's children are born into a world in which ethnic, cultural, and social pluralism is vigorously alive and active. They are children of the universe, thanks to electronic media and transportation technology. The world is virtually at their fingertips. With the flick of a switch or the turn of a knob, the child can travel to the far corners of the world without ever leaving his or her living room. Within the space of minutes, he or she can "visit" a Navajo reservation in Arizona, a Chicano barrio in San Antonio, Chinatown in New York City, Russian urbanites in Moscow, a disco in Tokyo, an Australian aborigine village, or the black belt of the Mississippi Delta. They can "see" apartheid in South Africa and abject poverty in Haiti. Young children "experience" the world daily in all of its diversity, but "know and understand" preciously little about what they are "experiencing." Children have a right to expect school instructional programs to help them develop skills for understanding this universe of pluralistic peoples and experiences, and to help them maximize their potential for achieving socially constructive and personally fulfilling lives in this highly diversified world.

Children of elementary school age are impressionable and malleable. They are still formulating attitudes, values, and impressions about the different peoples and experiences they encounter. "Oh, it is such a lovely thing to see a child blossoming," said Marjorie Kahl Lawrence.[1] The impressions and orientations about ethnic diversity and cultural differences they form during the first few years of their formal education can have lasting effects upon their social perspectives and interpersonal capabilities.

Children are the most valuable human investment for the future, and it is a worthy deed for teachers to build children's early educational experiences on a strong foundation of ethnic diversity and cultural pluralism. Jordan and Bush tell us that,

> [Children are] the people of new life. They are the only ones always willing to make a start; they have no choice. Children are the ways the world begins again and again. . . . What's more, if we hear them, they will teach us what they need; they will bluntly formulate the tenderness of their deserving.[2]

The elementary grades constitute the most crucial period in children's formal education. It is a time when children are initiated into school norms and protocols, and formative skill development essential to education and schooling.

Subsequent school experiences are merely refining processes. Since the elementary years are both formative and directive in shaping students' learning attitudes and skills, special care should be taken to insure that all things considered important to the comprehensive educational development of children are included in the curricula. Given their commitments to facilitating individual development, social cohesion, human dignity, and world citizenship, schools have a moral and ethical obligation to include ethnic diversity and cultural pluralism among their *primary* curricular offerings. While important at all levels of schooling, this mandate is crucial to elementary education.

The inclusion of multicultural education (that is, the study of the cultures, heritages, experiences, life styles, and histories of different ethnic groups) in elementary school instructional programs provides a means for children to acquire accurate knowledge, develop positive attitudes, and learn respect and appreciation for ethnic diversity. If acknowledgement, examination, and promotion of ethnic diversity and cultural pluralism are part of the total educational experiences of children from the time they enter school onward, they will learn to accept diversity as a normal part of learning and living. If ethnic diversity is an integral component of young children's learning experiences during the formative years of schooling, they will come to accept it as fundamental to American life, world culture, and the human condition.

The value of diversity

Of what benefit is multicultural education to the elementary school child? Is it possible that introducing the study of ethnic, cultural, and social differences among groups and individuals will be more detrimental than beneficial to the elementary student? Is there any benefit to be gained from multicultural education beyond its own merits for the betterment of the general education of the child?

Like most other Americans, children live in ethnic enclaves. While they often play together, and are encouraged to do so by teachers and other adults, neither their teachers nor their parents capitalize upon the natural opportunities provided by play activities to explore and examine ethnic and cultural differences with children. Therefore, even though many children of elementary school age are experientially aware of some ethnic differences, they lack the conceptual and cognitive frameworks necessary to fully understand these differences. Multicultural education has the potential for filling these cognitive voids.

One of the first benefits to be derived from multicultural education on behalf of elementary school children is an increased sensitivity to and appreciation of humanity and humanness. This sensitivity comes through acquisition of some knowledge and understanding about one's own ethnic and cultural heritages as well as about the cultures and life styles of other ethnic groups. As a knowledge base about ethnic diversity is established, children can begin to penetrate the walls of ethnic isolation and ignorance which surround them, and begin to learn how their ethnic neighbors in the nation and the world live, love, think, behave, and believe. The study of ethnic diversity provides a foundation for children to better understand their individuality, their Americanness, and their humanness. Multicultural education can create a "bridge" between ethnic enclaves for students to "cross over" as they emerge from their own ethnocentricism and ethnic illiteracy into a more constructive ideational and experiential world of cultural exchange and understanding among different ethnic groups.

Second, multicultural education benefits children by helping them develop a more reality-based understanding of the presence and influence of ethnic diversity in the development of the history, life, and culture of American society, the world, and humankind. Children should begin early in their educational careers to learn not to be fearful of or intimidated by different ethnic groups' life styles and experiences, to understand the social-cultural factors that account for human differences, to accept human diversity as a fact of life, and to understand how and why diversity is a catalyst for improving the quality of societies and the lives of individuals. Through multicultural education programs, children can also learn how their personal lives, and their own ethnic group's actions and experiences are inextricably linked to the lives and experiences of other ethnic groups and individuals. Such insights lead to understanding the concept of social and cultural interdependence among ethnic individuals and groups.

Furthermore, multicultural education helps children develop skills, attitudes, and values necessary to understand and appreciate the beauty of human diversity. For example, the child learns that diversity exists—that it is *real*, that human differences have positive social and creative potential, that ethnicity is an influential component of one's humanness, that no ethnic group or life style is inherently better or worse than another. Children discover that instead of being apologetic for their ethnic identities and trying to repress them, they should applaud who they are. Children learn how they are like all other individuals, yet very different, and that this "diversity within unity" constitutes the beauty of humankind. Thus, multicultural education helps the child develop a more accurate understanding of and authentic appreciation for the humanity of everyone.

Third, multicultural education can function as an instructional vehicle for improving the quality of general education for elementary school children. Many children whose cultural values and identities are strongly rooted in their traditional ethnic heritage experience alienation and isolation in American schools. This disaffection is often manifested in situations of classroom management, conflicting expectations about school behaviors, lack of interest in instructional activities, and low level academic performance.

Feelings of disaffection and alienation among ethnic students can be minimized, and the potential for increasing their academic achievement improved, by incorporating multicultural education in the instructional programs provided for students. How can this be done? First, by using content and materials written by and about a variety of different ethnic groups to teach basic literacy skills and common core subjects. This technique allows ethnically different students to identify more closely with school learning activities and, thereby, increases their senses of ownership in the educational process. The child's self-image, pride in ethnic heritage, and interest in classroom activities improve. Children who are secure in their identity, feel good about themselves, and are excited about what is happening in the classroom, are more likely to engage eagerly in learning activities and achieve higher levels of academic performance than those who find the classroom hostile, unfriendly, insensitive, and perpetually unfamiliar.

Multicultural education is as much knowing the cultural experiences, values, beliefs, and expectations of ethnically different groups, and using this knowledge in making decisions about the education of children, as it is teaching accurate information about ethnic groups and cultural differences. Therefore, multicultural education contributes to improving the quality of children's general education by familiarizing teachers with the cultural conditioning, value systems, learning styles, and prior experiences which influence ethnic children's intellectual potential and classroom behaviors. Teachers so informed can make more viable decisions about the educational needs of ethnically different children, make more realistic assessments of students' intellectual potential and academic performance, and create learning activities and alternatives to complement different ethnic learning styles and experiential frames of reference. These modifications will help children to channel more of their mental energy toward intellectual pursuits instead of expending that energy in a continuing struggle to make cultural transitions, avoid cultural collisions, and/or battle intrapsychic traumas caused by inconsistencies between the cultural inclinations, values, norms, and behaviors of schools and home life styles.

The ecological environment in which teaching and learning occurs influences the quantity and quality of learning achieved by students. A classroom atmosphere that is receptive to ethnic and cultural diversity, that encourages ethnically different individuals to be themselves and celebrate their ethnicity, and whose symbolic decorations praise and promote diversity creates a living laboratory in which children can experiment with pluralistic living. The indirect, informal teachings provided by pluralistic classroom atmospheres reinforce the teachings of the formal curriculum. Thus, a variety of options is created for children to "buy" into learning about ethnic differences at their own personal levels of attitudinal, ethnic identification, and intellectual developmental readiness. For those children who have a strong sense of ethnic identity, the class becomes an arena for them to share their ethnicity with others, to learn about others' ethnicity, and to begin to move toward becoming functional bi- or multi-culturalists. For those students who have not had previous close encounters with ethnic and cultural diversity the pluralistic classroom atmosphere is an adventure in ethnic exploration and discovery. They learn about diversity as they go about their daily routines of living in the classroom. Ethnic diversity is unavoidable for it permeates the entire ecological contexts in which all living and learning occur. For those children who need tangible evidence of the acceptability and worth of their ethnicity, it is on public display in the classroom. If children are accustomed to living with ethnic diversity in the classroom and within the instructional process, they will learn that cultural and ethnic differences need not be restrictive or a cause of hostilities, but can enrich their lives both as students and as individuals. As the poem, "A Child," says:

> If a child lives with encouragement he learns to be confident.
> If a child lives with praise he learns to be appreciative.
> If a child lives with approval he learns to like himself.[3]

Multicultural education also assists teachers to be better counselors to students. Knowledge of ethnic group life styles, values, customs, cultures, and traditions is invaluable to teachers who wish to better understand the personal problems of their ethnic students, and maximize their effectiveness in providing counseling and guidance to them. Without this knowledge, it is questionable whether classroom teachers and school counselors can fully appreciate the concerns, perceptions, and problems ethnically different students encounter in adjusting to schools. Nor is it possible to establish a trusting relationship between students and teachers. Conversely, teachers who understand different ethnic life styles and cultures are able to communicate and empathize better with ethnic students; can recognize cultural expressions in ethnic students' classroom behaviors; can minimize cross-cultural conflicts among students and teachers; and can develop constructive, facilitative strategies to assist students in their personal and intellectual growth and development. Informed and sensitive teachers are invaluable forces for creating warm, receptive, non-threatening classroom environments that are conducive to learning. They can also incorporate into their counseling routines techniques and materials which will facilitate the growth of ethnic awareness and cultural consciousness about self and others for the students they serve. Multicultural education thus serves the child, through his teachers in their counseling capacity, to better understand how one's personal problems, needs, interests, and potentials are conditioned, in part, by his or her ethnic group membership, existential situations, experiential backgrounds, and cultural heritages.

Multicultural education has much to offer elementary school students. The kinds of experiences they have and what they learn about ethnic diversity at this juncture in time will be indelibly imprinted in their minds and hearts for the rest of their lives. The importance of multicultural education in elementary schools is captured cogently in the symbolism of Milton's proverb, "The childhood shows the man, as morning shows the day."[4]

Multicultural curriculum design for elementary education

The greater proportion of instructional time and emphases in most elementary schools are devoted to introductory and formative intellectual skill development. The curricula concentrate on the development of certain attitudes and skills which are the bases for the attainment of literacy and the foundations of intellectual maturity. These skills may be classified as social, learning or intellectual, basic literacy, and functional survival skills. Social skills include the development of such abilities as human relations, work and study habits, adaptive behaviors, empathy, cooperation, social and civic citizenship, and individual autonomy and responsibility. Intellectual skills, sometimes referred to as process skills, include problem solving, data collection, decision making, critical thinking, and conflict resolution. Communication, reading, and computation are typically identified as basic literacy skills. Functional survival skills are usually associated with vocational competency, coping with the challenges of daily living, personal control and good judgment, physical fitness, avoidance of unnecessary dangers, and constructive use of leisure time.

The same categorical skills (i.e., social, intellectual, literacy, functional survival) that constitute the core of general education are equally applicable to multicultural education. In order to understand ethnic diversity and cultural pluralism in American society and the world, students must apply the basic skills of general education when studying different ethnic groups' life styles, histories, cultures, and experiences. The complexity of the cognitive information and learning activities about ethnic groups that are designed for elementary school children must be consistent with their social, emotional, intellectual, and experiential levels of development. Therefore, a large percentage of multicultural elementary education should operate on the instructional levels of introduction, awareness, and conscious raising. This is particularly true of the primary grades. As children enter the intermediate grades, the multicultural content and general skill development should likewise mature and broaden to include such emphases as cognitive depth, analysis, and evaluation. These developmental patterns of elementary children and the interactive potential between general education and multicultural education provide the theoretical framework for recommending an *Integrative Multicultural Basic Skills* (hereafter, IMBS) curriculum design for achieving multicultural education in the elementary school.

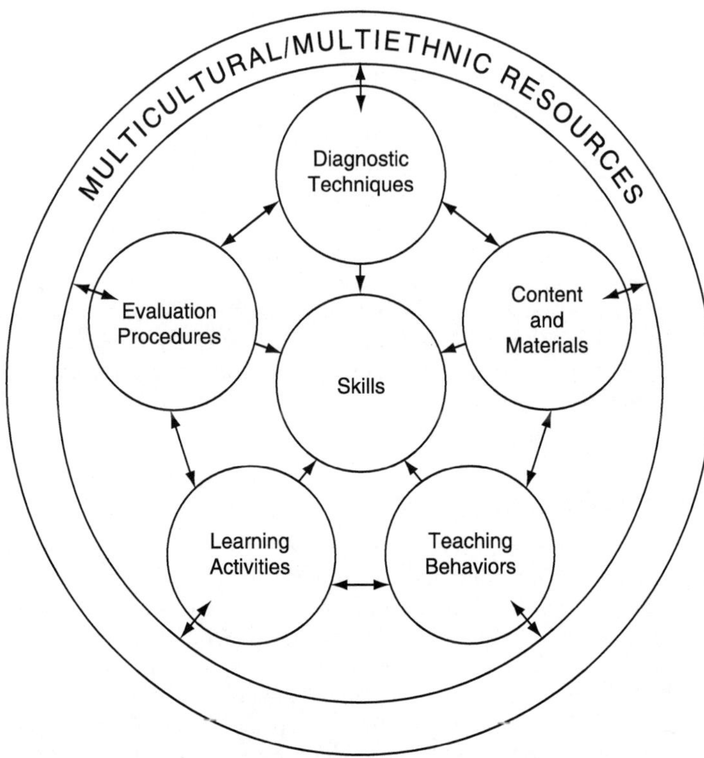

Figure 17.1 Integrative Multicultural Basic Skills Curriculum Design

A visual representation of the IMBS is presented in Figure 17.1. The key to the implementation of this curriculum model is the use of cultural perspectives, content, materials, and experiences from a wide variety of different ethnic groups in teaching basic educational skills. The basic skills (i.e., social, intellectual, literacy, functional survival) represented by the center circle of the diagram, form the core, or hub, of the IMBS curriculum design. Several different pedagogic actions are applied in teaching any skill. The five circles surrounding the "skills" circle identify these actions. In other words, the teaching of any educational skills area (for example, the basic literacy skills of reading, communication, and computation) requires the employment of some kinds of diagnosis of needs, content and materials, teaching behaviors, learning activities, and evaluation processes. No instructional unit or learning skill can be taught effectively without the interactive application of these pedagogic actions, for what occurs in any one of them affects what happens in all others. These relationships are represented in the diagram of Figure 17.1 by the double headed arrows linking the pedagogic actions, and the single headed arrows leading from the pedagogic actions to the skills area. The outermost ring of the diagram, labeled multicultural/multiethnic resources, is linked to the pedagogic actions by double-headed arrows. These arrows signify that the relationship existing between multicultural/multiethnic resources (e.g., experiences, histories, cultures, contributions, values, life styles, perspectives, etc., of different ethnic groups) and the pedagogic actions (i.e., diagnosis, content and materials, teaching behaviors, learning activities, evaluation procedures) is one of reciprocity, with each affecting and influencing the other. Multicultural/

multiethnic resources are linked to the skills areas by way of the pedagogic actions, suggesting that the skills themselves are not unique to multicultural education; nor are they inseparable from multicultural education, since both the skills and the pedagogic actions are encased by the multicultural/multiethnic resources.

According to the IMBS curriculum design, no teacher in the elementary school can claim to have taught adequately and effectively any general education skill if he or she has not incorporated multicultural education into the teaching of that skill. Stated in another way, when this curriculum model is used to design and implement instructional programs for children, no student can succeed in learning any fundamental skill of general education without, in the process of so doing, learning about ethnic and cultural diversity. Therefore, the child is served comprehensively by multicultural education while learning basic skills, for the IMBS curriculum design requires not only the use of multiethnic content and materials in teaching general education skills, but that ethnically diverse knowledge, perspectives, and experiences penetrate diagnostic techniques, teaching behaviors, learning activities, and evaluation processes as well.

Application of the IMBS curriculum model

Some examples from each of the four basic skills areas of general education are provided below to demonstrate how the IMBS curriculum design operates. These examples are merely illustrative, for the number of conceivable examples is limitless. The primary onus for operationalizing the curriculum model rests with the instructional leaders, much more so than with more conventional curriculum designs. Teachers must become so familiar with different ethnic groups' life styles, cultures, values, and experiences that the inclusion of these in *all* their instructional behaviors is automatic. They can then go beyond the ideas and examples included in the written curriculum document (such as those explained below) and create their own interfaces between basic skill development and multicultural education. This action can personalize the curriculum to particularized classroom "ethnic complexions," thereby heightening its potentiality to serve the educational needs and interests of the children in culturally pluralistic ways. The readers are cautioned not to allow themselves to become too distracted by the specifics of the examples provided and lose sight of the fact that they are intended not so much as exemplars, but as illustrations of the underlying principle of the IMBS curriculum model. That principle is the *interactive instructional interface* between multicultural education and basic skill development of general education.

Part of reading instruction at any grade level includes vocabulary building and comprehension. The teaching of these skills is readily conducive to the incorporation of multicultural education. A variety of ethnic literature, such as poetry, short stories, folklore, fiction, drama, song lyrics, and biographies and autobiographies should be used to develop vocabulary building skills. As the students read these selections they should make lists of ethnic terminology unfamiliar to them. These words and phrases can then be defined and used in sentences. This activity can be extended to include identification of synonyms for the unfamiliar terms, and use of the terms in spelling exercises. These reading skill building activities take on a multicultural character when the reading selections chosen are written by ethnic authors about ethnic experiences. They are "interactive and integrative" in that they facilitate the development of a skill essential to reading while simultaneously exposing students to ethnic literature, contributions of ethnic groups to the literary world, and to those aspects of ethnic groups' experiences, cultural traditions, values, and beliefs embedded in the selected readings. Other reading skills, such as interpretation, comprehension, and translation, can be taught as well.

In developing comprehension skills within a multicultural context, teachers might consider using these three approaches. First, ask students to read selections from traditional Black folklore written in Black dialect. Then have the students translate what they have read into Standard English written compositions or oral expressions. The teacher might also have students read and listen to disc-recordings of traditional folklore from a variety of different ethnic groups. Then have the students identify what animals appear most frequently in which ethnic folktales, explain the symbolism of the animals' roles, and compare the animal symbolism across several ethnic groups. A third multicultural technique for teaching comprehension involves allowing students who are bilingual and/or bi-dialectical to use their first linguistic styles to express their understanding of reading assignments. The reading materials can be selected from standard textbooks in different content areas and/or particular ethnic materials and experiences. The emphasis, however, is on the medium used for demonstrating comprehension, not the materials per se. For example, Black students who are speakers of Black dialect and Mexican American or Puerto Rican students fluent in "Spanglish" are encouraged to use Black dialect and Spanglish respectively in expressing their understanding of what they have read. Or, those students who are more culturally oriented toward individualistic effort and written expression are allowed to demonstrate their comprehension in individualized written projects, while those who are more cooperatively and verbally oriented have the option to "perform" their comprehension through role-playing, story-telling, sociodrama, and/or audio recordings.

In using these kinds of techniques to teach comprehension, teachers are more concerned with finding out what students understand from what they have read than on measuring their competency in producing Standard English (that emphasis is reserved for another time!). They teach multicultural education by allowing students who have different linguistic styles as their "first languages" and different cultural learning patterns to use these without reproach in the formal context of teaching and learning. Ethnically different children benefit twice-over. They are allowed some opportunities to "act naturally according to cultural inclinations" without apology, embarrassment, or punishment, and there is no need for them to divide their mental energies between producing Standard English and mastering the task of comprehension. Therefore, on task performance is likely to be higher, and the child's general sense of well-being much more positive.

A teaching exercise in reading readiness which illustrates the use of the IMBS curriculum design is ethnic word/item association. Identify a list of items, such as foods, musical instruments, words, etc., common in American culture that originated from different ethnic groups. On one sheet of paper draw pictures of each of the items. On a different sheet, list the names of the items. On a third sheet, list the names of the ethnic groups and countries of origins of the items. Provide opportunities for the students to, first, associate the names of the items with the pictures, and subsequently, to associate the ethnic groups and countries of origin with the items. The teacher might even help students learn to locate these countries on a world globe. After the children have mastered each individual aspect of the activity (i.e., can easily associate maize with American Indians, rodeo with Mexican Americans, etc.), the learning activity can be modified to allow for increasing cognitive complexity. List each picture, name, ethnic group, and country of origin of each item on a different card, keeping the cards separated by category. Jumble the names, country of origin, and ethnic group cards so that they do not appear in a sequence consistent with the picture cards. Divide the class into groups of three or four, making sure each group is ethnically mixed, if at all possible. Each group receives four sets of cards, with instructions to match the appropriate names, country of origin, and ethnic group with the corresponding pictures of the items.

These activities have multiple skill development potential. Not only are the students learning about ethnic groups and some of their contributions to American life while developing word/item association skills, they are also gaining experience in manual dexterity, studying ethnic world geography, and learning how to work cooperatively with ethnic others for the attainment of a common goal.

All upper elementary school students are expected to develop such computational skills as percentages and ratios. The teaching of these skills can be made multicultural by using data about ethnic diversity as curriculum content which students use in learning how to compute ratios and percentages. The actual composition of the classroom can provide the data base for the skill development. For example, a math activity in figuring ratios and percentages might proceed in this way: "There are thirty students in class. Of that number six are Black American, three are Vietnamese, two are Chinese American, three are Jewish American, and the remainder are Anglo-American. What percentage of the total class membership is Black, Vietnamese, Chinese American, Jewish, and Anglo?" Or, "if 10% of the total class population of thirty is Jewish and 20% is Black Americans, what is the total number of Jews and Blacks in class?"

This activity can be modified to match the intellectual maturity of the students involved. For younger children it can be restricted to the skills of addition and subtraction, and the concepts of "less than" and "more than." For instance, multiethnic math learning activities might include such problems as the following: "If there are 9 Blacks, 4 Mexican Americans, 3 Italian Americans, and 7 Anglos in our class, what is the total number of students in class?" Or, "there are 25 students in class. Six of these are Polish American, 8 are German American, and all the others are Anglo. How many Anglos are there? Is the number of Polish Americans and German Americans combined less than or greater than the total number of Anglos?"

To accommodate more cognitively sophisticated students, the boundaries of the problem focus on ethnic compositions can be extended to the level of the city, state, region, or country. The principles operating and the skill development techniques (i.e., integrating meaningful and pragmatic ethnic content into the teaching of basic math skills) are the same in both the simplified and the sophisticated versions of the learning activity. The main differences are found in the quantity of data students must manipulate and the complexity of the skills they are expected to master.

The same content (ethnic populations of cities, states, regions, schools, classes, nations) can provide the context for developing such intellectual or process skills as data collection, analysis, and processing; problem solving, and critical thinking. Learning to plot information on and interpret charts and graphs are common skills of most social studies instruction to assist in the development of problem solving abilities and critical thinking. Once students have collected their raw data on the distribution of ethnic populations, they can then be instructed to plot their findings on a bar, line, or pie graph; and, by reading these graphs, answer such questions as: How does the ethnic distribution of Mississippi, Wisconsin, and Arizona, or of Chicago, San Francisco, and Atlanta compare with each other?

The expansion of graphing ethnic population distributions to include a comparative dimension broadens the base of that particular skill development, while introducing opportunities for developing another intellectual skill—problem solving. Comparing ethnic populations of cities, states, and regions of the country may lead the perceptive teacher and student to ask: Why are there lots of Japanese Americans in San Francisco but very few in Atlanta? Why is there a sizeable number of German Americans and Polish Americans in Wisconsin, but virtually none in Mississippi? Why are there so many Blacks in Detroit, but very few in Honolulu? These questions lead naturally to hypothesizing about ethnic group settlement patterns. They cannot be examined adequately or thoroughly without eventually taking a look at original ethnic immigration patterns to the United States. They can also lead to questions and explorations about how or if the numerical size of an ethnic group in a given location affects its political potential and socioeconomic status, and other peoples' attitudes, beliefs, opinions, and behaviors toward that ethnic group.

The examination of these kinds of issues is illustrative of the interface which occurs when content about ethnic diversity provides the *substantive context* for the development of basic educational skills. Because the students are acquiring knowledge about multiethnicity in the process of developing data collection and analysis, problem solving, and critical thinking skills, both the student's learning about ethnicity and mastery of basic education skills are better than if the two were taught separately.

The socialization functions of elementary schools frequently get translated into a host of social skills, such as value analysis, developing respect for others, and accepting their right to be. These skills are particularly conducive to the application of the IMBS curriculum design. Helping students to get to know ethnic others without prejudices and stereotypes, through understanding their cultures, life styles, experiences, contributions, and traditions, is a major function of multicultural education. In order to truly respect people who are ethnically and culturally different, students should understand those socializing systems which shape and regulate the beliefs and behaviors of different ethnic groups. To help students understand these socializing systems, as a foundation for developing respect for others, the elementary school curriculum should include the study of different ethnic child-rearing practices, value systems, communication styles, interrelational patterns, and sex-role socialization. Students must also analyze and clarify their attitudes and values about ethnic diversity. Studying various ethnic rites of passage, using values clarification exercises and moral dilemmas focusing on ethnic issues and experiences, and exploring ethnic customs, traditions, and beliefs are essential to developing respect for others. Students might also examine such issues as the reasons people stereotype others, the prejudices and stereotypes different ethnic groups hold about each other, how mass media contributes to the institutionalization of stereotypes of ethnic groups, the identification of behaviors and beliefs which facilitate or inhibit cross-cultural and inter-ethnic group relations, and how these can be improved.

Another way teachers can help students to learn respect for ethnic others is by *deliberately* having racially, ethnically, and culturally mixed groups of students working together on common learning tasks, and using such instructional techniques as sociodrama, moral dilemma exercises, and role reversals in role playing activities. Or, the class could establish a pen pal relationship with another class in another part of the city, state, or country, preferably one with a dissimilar ethnic composition. For example, class A in School Y, which is urban and predominantly Puerto Rican might become a pen pal to class B in School Z across town (or in another city or state), which is rural and totally Anglo. The children, as a collective, would share with each other information about issues that are relevant to them at their developmental levels, and pertinent to "getting to know and respect ethnic others." They might want to know what negative beliefs Anglos have about Puerto Ricans, and Puerto Ricans about Anglos; what they like, dislike, and respect about each other's ethnic group; who their respective heroes and heroines are, and why them; how they spend their leisure time; what their favorite musical groups, records, games, and books are; what behaviors cause them to be punished by their parents, and what kinds of punishment are they likely to receive for what misdeeds; what they like or dislike about school; etc. It is important for the students themselves to direct their own pen pal relations, by making their own decisions about what questions to ask, what information to exchange, and how the exchanges will occur.

Experiences of the "pen pal" sort are invaluable for elementary school students, especially those who have had minimal contact and interaction with ethnic groups other than their own. They have the advantage of putting an abstract idea like "respecting others" on a level that elementary school children can personalize and internalize. And, they have numerous subsidiary learning skills embedded in them. They are fun. They involve data gathering and decision making. They deal with distribution of resources, recognizing differential individual abilities, assuming responsibility, and negotiating rights and obligations to achieve common goals. They require the application of basic literacy and intellectual skills. They demand collective effort and working together and provide a means for students to get to know others of their own age group but from different ethnic, cultural, and social backgrounds. Students can discover levels of similarities and differences among themselves through personal sharing. By using a group context to address a learning task, pen pal experiences offer security, support, and even anonymity for those students who are timid and somewhat unsure about exploring ethnic diversity with members of those ethnic groups of interest to them.

The constructive use of leisure time is increasingly becoming an important functional survival skill for citizens of a chaotic, constantly changing, and technological society and world. Implicit in this growing significance is the idea that living in a highly depersonalized, technological society can cause psychosocial disequilibrium, and the wise use of leisure time can function as an equalizing or balancing force. How leisure time is spent can be a means of maintaining psychological well-being for individuals, improving the overall quality of one's life, and, thus, enriching his or her humanness.

The Integrative Multicultural Basic Skills curriculum design can facilitate the development of skills in constructive use of leisure time by using experiential learning as the means for students to explore ethnic leisure activities. Several possible learning activities are available to the inventive, imaginative teacher. Among these are playing a variety of different types of ethnic music during "quiet time" in the school day, and having children learn, by doing, different ethnic games. By participating in ethnic games, students will better understand different kinds of ethnic recreation, how and why some form of recreation is important to all people, and that attitudes toward and choices of recreation are frequently influenced by ethnic group membership, cultural heritages, and social status.

The curriculum can also specify a time in each week's schedule for "undirected reading from the ethnic book corner." This reading center should be equipped with a wide variety of materials in terms of form (written, audio, and visual), genre (prose, poetry, folklore, drama, fiction, autobiographies and biographies, etc.), and ethnic groups represented (both minority and majority).

Ethnic folk dancing (including contemporary social dance as a form of folk dancing) can be very beneficial to upper elementary school students. Dance is a legitimate form of leisure and recreation, and it can teach some additional social skills of major importance to upper elementary school students. Folk dancing allows students to enjoy themselves while learning and examining dance in historical, cultural, ethnic, and regional perspectives. This is possible since the students should explore all kinds of folk dances, from the minuet, waltz, polka, samba, and square dance to the stroll, hustle, disco, and the rock steady. Instruction in folk dance can be incorporated into the physical education program. Not only does ethnic dance provide an exciting booster for the physical education curriculum and contributes to developing an enjoyable leisuretime activity, it also helps students learn some basic skills about interpersonal relations, cooperative efforts, motor coordination, body movement, physical fitness, and multicultural education. Furthermore, in the process of learning ethnic dances, students may gain some insights and skills that are applicable to any form of social dancing. This can be of invaluable assistance to fifth and sixth graders who are approaching puberty and are beginning to think about the possibility of dating, since social dancing plays a significant role in these rites of passage.

Conclusion

The above examples of how multicultural content and ethnic experiences can be incorporated into learning activities are merely illustrative of the underlying principle of the Integrative Multicultural Basic Skills curriculum design for elementary schools. That principle is the creation of an *interactive interface* or "marriage" between cultural content and experiences about ethnic diversity and the basic skills development of general education typical of elementary school programs. Such a "marriage" has many advantages for the student, the teacher, and the education process in general. It allows for teaching multicultural education without necessarily adding more content to an already overburdened curriculum. It dispels the misconception that multicultural education and basic skills are competitors—that is, teaching one jeopardizes the teaching of the other. It is pedagogically and politically sound, for it incorporates the study of ethnicity and cultural pluralism into patterns of instructional organization that are consistent with proven school practices, principles of curriculum development, learning theories, and human development. It improves the authenticity, realism, and motivational potential of learning experiences for students from various ethnic and experiential backgrounds. It legitimizes and institutionalizes multicultural education by making it and general education inseparable entities. Most important, the IMBS curriculum design honors that part of the "Bill of Rights for Children" which grants to *all* children, "the right to a school program which offers sound academic training, plus maximum opportunity for individual development and preparation for living."[5] And, it begins to respond to the plea made by Georgia Douglas Johnson in her poem, "Interracial":

Let's build here and there
  Or sometimes, just a spiral stair
That we may come somewhat abreast
  And sense what cannot be exprest,
And by these measures can be found
  A meeting place—a common ground
Nearer the reaches of the heart
  Where truth revealed, stands clear, apart;
. . . Oh let's build bridges everywhere
  And span the gulf of challenge there.[6]

Notes

1 Majorie Kahl Lawrence, "Childhood," in *Shining Wings* (New York: Exposition Press, 1959), p. 50.
2 June Jordan and Terri Bush, *The Voice of the Children* (New York: Holt, Rinehart and Winston, 1970), pp. 92–93.
3 "A Child," in Maryjane Hooper Tonn (ed.), *Children's Issue Ideals* (Milwaukee, WI: Ideals Publishing Company, July 1970), n.p.
4 Quoted in Tonn (ed.), *Children's Issue Ideals*, n.p.
5 "Bill of Rights for Children," in Tonn (ed.), *Children's Issue Ideals*, n.p.
6 Georgia Douglas Johnson, "Interracial," in Langston Hughes and Arna Bontemps (eds.), *The Poetry of the Negro, 1746–1970* (Garden City, NY: Doubleday and Company, 1970), p. 78.

CHAPTER 18

ISSUES-CENTERED APPROACHES TO MULTICULTURAL EDUCATION IN THE MIDDLE GRADES (1992)

Valerie Ooka Pang and Cynthia Park

> As a result of omitting, or downplaying, the importance of social movements of the people in our history—the actions of abolitionists, labor leaders, radicals, feminists, and pacifists—a fundamental principle of democracy is undermined: the principle that it is the citizenry, rather than the government, that is the ultimate source of power and the locomotive that pulls the train of government in the direction of equality and justice. Such histories create a passive and subordinate citizenship.
>
> Howard Zinn, *Declarations of Independence*, pp. 61–62

Human progress is dependent not only upon an informed citizenry but also upon a committed citizenry willing to struggle to protect the rights of all people to life, liberty, equality, and the pursuit of happiness (Zinn 1990). We hope that children will become adults who are passionate about their role as citizens and will become actively involved in creating new solutions to public issues. We know that the health of democracy is dependent upon the ability of all citizens irrespective of their cultural or ethnic background, to work together with civility toward justice. Many schools often state that their goal is to nurture students who will mature into empowered, responsible citizens, but what do they mean by empowerment? What should these citizens be empowered to do in a democracy? What is a democratic society? In this article, we look at aspects of these crucial questions and show how issues-centered education can help prepare middle school students for citizenship in a multicultural society.

How does issues-centered education strengthen a multicultural education program?

Issues-centered education is consistent with our national ideals as part of the exercise of democratic values. It fosters examination, discussion, and resolution of public issues in the context of a multicultural society. The issues-centered approach activates a search through the public swamp of conflicting values and competing choices. The bottom is never clear, and it is sometimes difficult to describe one's personal and community ethics, morality, and values because they have not been tested or applied to real life situations. Teachers often throw out such terms as equality, freedom, and justice in classroom discussions, but it is through the struggle with and resolution of social issues that these values are genuinely defined.

Underlying assumptions of issues-centered education are compatible with multicultural education. The following five assumptions support and recognize the complexities of a culturally diverse democracy. First, issues-centered education prizes multiple perspectives. This is especially important in a culturally diverse society where the views of women, ethnic groups, and gays and lesbians have historically been denied legitimacy. Bateson writes that diverse viewpoints have been rejected because "sexual, racial, and cultural chauvinism all rest on the same traditional assumptions of dominance based on difference" (1990, p. 72). The reflective process of issues-centered education validates new perspectives and encourages divergent thinking because the status of all groups is equalized. In this way, students from disenfranchised groups cultivate their own "voice" without the filter of another group. The issues-centered approach advocates students listening to each other and respects the knowledge that each student brings to school. Differences between students are seen as a contributing strength to a community rather than as a divisive element. For students, this may mean respecting and listening to the views of groups as diverse as African-American women and white supremacist males.

Multiple perspectives can give more depth to an issue. Should the ethnic caricature of a group be used as a mascot for a sports team? Some schools, after intense dialogue, have chosen to move from using an American Indian representation to other symbols. At Stanford University (Wassaja 1980), native American students declared,

> A human race is not entertainment. There is little chance that those who regard the term "Indian" as a team name will ever realize the importance of socio-economic problems, the traditional life-styles, and the religious practices which are central to an understanding of today's Indian people.
>
> People will fail to understand the human side to being Indian as long as they can't choose instead to see only the entertaining aspects of Indian life. (p. 45)

Middle school students can examine the discussions held at other schools regarding ethnic mascots and discover the dissimilar ways in which this conflict has been resolved.

The second assumption is that issues-centered education encourages an open-ended attitude toward social problems that facilitates higher-order thinking and development of problem-solving skills. An issues-centered curriculum does not have preset solutions. The context of open-ended inquiry encourages children to engage in the higher levels of cognition. Bloom (1956) discussed the importance of children developing skills at the application, analysis, synthesis, and evaluation levels of knowledge. These levels are important in the process of problem solving. In an open-ended process, students control their own learning and can tackle real life issues. Students must bring together their skills from a variety of content areas and combine both knowledge and value judgments in creation of a resolution (Wolfinger 1984). In this way, the teacher stimulates a quest for reflection.

The third assumption of issues-centered education in a multicultural society reinforces the perennial nature of change in society and the need for continuous reinterpretation, reevaluation, and reform of societal values. Society and its citizens are continually in flux. This does not mean that decisions may change at the drop of a hat or that people are jello-like in their thinking. New world views on issues may surface that give rise to reevaluation of previous solutions. In a democratic nation, values should be continually tested in order to make them applicable to current tensions. For example, affirmative action was initially instituted during the 1960s as part of the civil rights legislation that represented a broad collective move toward social equality. Today, some affirmative action programs have met increased opposition because more people believe the protection of individual freedom should take precedence over group wants (Alexander 1991). Presently, many people believe that state and federal intervention should be limited when addressing racial and cultural gaps in employment, housing, income, and education.

The fourth assumption is that issues-centered education uses culturally familiar analogies and content that will help children make the bridge between their lives and broader social issues. For example, teachers can ask students to describe the circumstances under which scapegoating occurs in everyday life and in history. In everyday life, students may become frustrated when something goes wrong and blame another student who has already been seen as being different. This difference could be due to skin color or language diversity. On a larger scale, the United States presently wrestles with large numbers of immigrants from other countries who come seeking jobs and a better lifestyle. The question could be, should citizens fear the increasing numbers of immigrants? Scapegoating often occurs when diverse groups are competing for the same jobs.

The fifth assumption is that issues-centered education can assist in building a strong sense of community among individuals and cultural groups. Individual effort to improve society within the context of community is reinforced in an issues-centered approach. Middle school children are challenged to define their personal values within the context of their community. One of the major challenges for middle school students is to create compassionate connections with others. As Bateson (1990) has written,

> I grew up in a New York neighborhood where I learned to step around drunks on the sidewalk, to think of them as failures or dropouts whose predicaments were unconnected to me, rather than generated by the same social system that supported me. (p. 150)

We live in an interdependent society: When individuals come together committed to making a better society through dialogue and collaborative action, bonds between people are nurtured and strengthened. Middle school students are more likely to find new ways of addressing public issues when they are interacting and negotiating with each other. An issues-centered approach to social education fosters a shared vision of the protection of human rights for all citizens. When more than twenty-five percent of children under six in the United States live in households that are at the poverty level or lower (Reed and Sautter 1990), the future of these children and the United States as a whole is jeopardized. Middle school students can build community projects where their efforts make a difference. One project might involve planting, tending, and harvesting a garden in science classes and donating vegetables to homeless shelters. Middle school students have also been the catalyst for clothing drives in their local communities. When adolescents see that they can contribute to the community, they develop a continuity between their ideals and their social actions that is an important stage in their maturation (Erikson 1963).

An example of a multicultural issue: should warpowers or the rights of citizens take precedence during wartime?

Although most textbooks have several sentences that describe the incarceration of members of Japanese-American communities from the West Coast and some individuals from the Hawaiian Islands, it is not presented as an issue or question. Textbooks seldom raise the central issue whether warpowers should take priority over due process during time of war?

Background information

After Japan bombed Pearl Harbor in 1941, the United States entered World War II. Two months later, Japanese-American communities all along the West Coast were ordered by Franklin D. Roosevelt in Executive Order 9066 to leave their friends, homes, businesses, and their property. They were forcibly moved under armed guards to relocation camps and later internment camps. Japanese-Americans were prisoners of their own government, the United States.

In order for middle school students to get some sense of what happened to the Japanese-American community, students can read the following case.

> Marie Horiuchi had just turned twelve years old. She lived in Seattle, Washington, and went to Washington Middle School. One day when she came home from school, her mother had all their books on the living room floor and was ripping out pages and throwing entire books in the fireplace. Tears ran down her face.
>
> "What are you doing?" Marie asked.
>
> "The government thinks that we are traitors because we are Japanese. We must get rid of anything with Japanese writing in it," said her mother in a quiet voice. "All of us must leave Seattle soon. I don't know when, but soon. They are sending us away."
>
> Marie couldn't understand what was happening. "But we haven't done anything? How can they do this to us? What are they going to do to us? Mom, I'm a citizen. I was born here in Seattle. What about the Constitution?"

The teacher could then begin asking students what they know about the internment of Japanese-Americans. After the children volunteered their information, the teacher can say, "I would like to pose two questions for you to think about. Should wartime powers take priority over the constitutional rights of citizens? Can you find evidence that supports or refutes the wartime need for taking away the civil rights of Japanese-Americans?

The teacher can then direct the students to read about the internment from the following materials: "Rite of Passage: The Commission Hearings 1981," *Amerasia Journal; Personal Justice Denied—Report of the Commission on Wartime Relocation and Internment of Civilians; The Bamboo People: The Law and Japanese-Americans;* "Gordon Hirabayashi v. United States." in *The Courage of Their Convictions; Desert Exile; Justice at War*, and *Japanese-American Journey*.

After several days, when students have had the opportunity to read and conduct research, a discussion similar to the following might occur:

> *Teacher:* Our charge is to decide whether a) warpowers should have taken priority over the rights of Japanese-Americans during World War II

or b) whether the civil rights of Japanese-Americans should have been protected.

Joey: I don't think that the warpowers should take over during wartime, but maybe by putting the Japanese in camps, the government protected them from the prejudice that lots of people felt for them.

Joy: That's true. The Chinese wore "I am Chinese" buttons so that others would know they weren't Japanese-Americans. People were hysterical after the bombing of Pearl Harbor, and many Americans were afraid that the Japanese would bomb the West Coast.

Eric: I found racial prejudice against Japanese-Americans was terrible then. In fact, General DeWitt who was in charge [of] moving the people, said before Congress, "A Jap's a Jap."

Teacher: Why did most Americans favor the relocation?

George: The Japanese bombed Pearl Harbor and we were at war. How did they know who would be loyal? Many Japanese-Americans didn't speak English and they sent their children to Japanese language class on Saturday. We had to be sure that they didn't do anything to help the enemy. People were really scared. If the Japanese hadn't been put in camps, we might have lost the war.

Jenni: Not all Americans wanted the Japanese put in camps. In fact, Henry Stimson, secretary of war, did not believe that the United States should evacuate the Japanese because they hadn't done anything wrong.

Jose: Clark argued that if all Japanese-Americans were moved because of their ethnicity, this would conflict with the due process clause of the Fifth Amendment, which calls for trial before anyone can be put in prison. We must always uphold our laws. We can't let war tell us no one has rights. That isn't fair.

Latoya: Judge Black in Washington state did not believe that the individual rights of a few people should be more important than the rights of a whole nation. He was sure that Japanese parachutists would drop into Seattle and sneak into the airplane factories and cause problems. So he ruled that Gordon Hirabayashi did not have the right to protest the evening curfew or the relocation of the community.

Mark: And the Supreme Court even upheld the need for the internment in the Fred Korematsu case, saying the internment was justified because there was evidence of disloyalty.

Rosa: Weren't there other alternatives?

Sam: I guess the United States could have let the Japanese stay in their homes and not let them write letters to anyone in Japan.

Matt: Why should we have done that? There was never even one case where a Japanese-American was found to be a spy. What evidence did the Supreme Court justices use? I read that Kenneth Ringle, a Navy officer who spoke Japanese, didn't find any reason to worry about the Japanese, and he told this to the Navy in his report.

Akbar: That is why on August 10, 1988, President Reagan signed the Civil Liberties Act of 1988. The law required the United States to pay each Japanese-American who was interned and was still living, $20,000 for the mistake the government made. In addition, an official apology from the United States would be written and a cultural center would be created to remind us not to ever allow this to happen again.

Jenni: I don't think any of us can imagine how horrible it had been for Japanese-Americans. I read a lot of testimony of Japanese-Americans. I can't believe the United States put them in jail because of their ethnicity. They lost everything because of racism. One man named Thomas Kinaga was taken to Lone Heart Mountain concentration camp, and he volunteered to serve in the all Japanese-American 442nd Infantry Regiment. He thought it was wrong that all the Japanese-Americans were put in camps, and he suffered terrible mental anguish. Here he was in the army, serving his country, while his family was living behind barbed wire. When he went to visit his family during a furlough, he found himself locked up in the concentration camp in his army uniform.

Susan: But what other choice did the president have? Imagine Russia attacking the U.S. Wouldn't we fear Russian spies?

Nancy: I don't think it was right to take away their rights as citizens because of their ethnic background. That doesn't sound fair to me. That's like telling me I can't go to the store because I'm a sixth grader. I have freedoms and rights, that's what it means to live in a democracy.

Rosa: I was surprised to find Japanese-Americans had so many rights taken away; like the right to a lawyer, the right to vote, the right to assemble, freedom of speech, and freedom of the press.

The teacher should then ask students to put themselves in the context of the times and continue the discussion with more specific questions. The teacher's questions might include:

What prejudices existed against Japanese-Americans?
Were these fears based on facts?
Why were Japanese-Americans interned?
What crimes did they commit?
What constitutional rights were violated?
What are the consequences of denying citizens their rights?
What could have been done? Were there alternatives?
How do these violations affect all Americans, not just Japanese-Americans?

Teachers can conclude the set of lessons by asking students what should have been done. Student responses will vary from saying that what was done was justified to saying nothing should have been done. The balance between warpowers and constitutional rights is an issue that continues to arise. Similar fears arose during the Iranian conflict and Iraqi war.

Conclusion

Middle school children have many challenges ahead of them. As the conflicts between cultural groups continue and social inequities widen, these young citizens must be better equipped than past generations to solve devastating social problems. Issues-centered education is one avenue through which public dilemmas can be addressed in schools. The constant quest toward ideals suggests a continuous struggle in which students need tools to help them sort out conflicting choices among competing values. Issues-centered education engenders a nonviolent approach toward conflicts because people with divergent and, often times, opposing views find common ground in a collective effort towards resolution. All participants gain strength and creative power from ethnic and cultural diversity. As Martin Luther King, Jr., stated,

> Injustice anywhere is a threat to justice everywhere. We are caught in an inescapable network of morality, tied in a single garment of destiny. What affects one directly, affects all indirectly. (National Council for the Social Studies 1990, p. 15)

References

Alexander, J. 1991. American dream at a turning point. *Los Angeles Times*, September 15, San Diego edition, pp. M1, M6.

Bateson, M. C. 1990. *Composing a life*. New York: Penguin Books.

Bloom, B. (ed.), 1956. *Taxonomy of educational objectives: The classification of educational goals. Handbook I: The cognitive domain*. New York: MacCay.

Erikson, E. 1963. *Childhood and society*. New York: Norton.

National Council for the Social Studies. 1990. *The Social Studies Professional* 99, Jan./Feb.: 15.

Reed, S., and C. Sautter. 1990. Children of poverty. *Phi Delta Kappan* 71: K1–K12.

Wassaja. 1980. The football dispute. *The Indian Historian* 13(3): 45.

Wolfinger, D. 1984. *Teaching science in the elementary school*. New York: HarperCollins.

Zinn, H. 1990. *Declarations of independence*. New York: HarperCollins.

CHAPTER 19

BIG PICTURE TALKERS/WORDS WALKING WITHOUT MASTERS (1991)

The instructional implications of ethnic voices for an expanded literacy

Carol D. Lee

Jody Starks, a major character in Zora Neale Hurston's *Their Eyes Were Watching God* (1937/1990), is accused by his wife Janie, the story's protagonist, of being "too busy listening tuh yo' own big voice" (p. 82). Janie believed that God made humans each with a special spark and that God intended each spark to shine. Because Jody Starks was too full of his own big voice, he was unable to see Janie's shine. An analogy can be drawn between the fictive Jody Starks and the academy of both researchers and classroom teachers. The academy is so full of its own big voice that it diminishes and (more often than not) tarnishes the shine of those children who are not White and middle-class. The voices of America's diverse ethnic populations each have a linguistic power that too often only the creative writer—the novelist, the poet, the dramatist, and creative essayist—hears and appreciates.

The present article offers an example of the voice of one such community: the African American community. It attempts to describe the craft with which that community's talk is sculpted and re-created at another level by creative writers who consciously acknowledge the voices of those whom Hurston calls "big picture talkers"—adults and youths from the porch stoops and street corners of African America—as a source of inspiration. Lest anyone fear that I am simply joining the ranks of those who rancor for the inclusion of African American literature in schools because of the positive self-esteem that Black youth can gain from reading such literature, let me caution that this article attempts to stake out new territory. I offer herein that the union of novice readers and ethnic literature provides a great deal more than ethnic pride. Rather, it can support a pedagogical scaffolding between reader and literary text capable of building the skills of literary analysis that most youth in American schools simply miss (Lee, 1991b). The most recent National Assessment of Educational Progress (NAEP) scores indicate that the best of America's students have difficulty reading below the surface meaning of texts, and most cannot support their inferences about what they have read with evidence (Mullis et al., 1990). Marshall's (1989, 1990) field studies present a picture in which teachers dominate classroom talk about literature, while students in inner-city literature classes barely talk at all. The potential promise of ethnic literatures in concert with ethnic community voices expands the hope of what schools can do for all youth when it comes to teaching literature.

My argument rests on some basic assumptions. First, literacy is not a single, amorphous set of skills that are evenly applicable across any circumstances requiring reading or across any text. Rather, as Scribner (1984) and Resnick (1990) both claim, literacy is a set of social practices situated in specific sociocultural contexts. As sets of social practices, specific literacies are evident in the ways people talk, read, write about, and otherwise use a variety of printed texts. Literate behavior involves attitudes toward language and uses of print that readers in particular communities bring to the material they read. These "interpretive communities" (Fish, 1980) may be ethnic communities, religious communities, work communities, or other configurations; and a person may be a member of a variety of such communities and practice a variety of literacy skills. Second, any text requires a minimal breadth of prior knowledge of facts as well as conceptual knowledge of processes and networks of associations. For example, although I consider myself quite literate in the generic sense, I cannot fathom stock market results in the Sunday newspaper and quite literally shudder at the thought of reading the manual for any new computer program I obtain.

The present article focuses on a particular set of literacy practices for which appropriate knowledge of human social relationships is necessary, namely, the reading of literary texts. The bare bones of my argument is that there are routine practices within the cultural life of communities that schools can draw upon to assist students in constructing concepts in a given domain the schools seek to teach. The challenge is to find that powerful match between the contours of the knowledge that is socially constructed in the community as well as the family context and those constructs introduced in the context of the classroom.

Social practices and schooling: prior research

Many very careful ethnographies of the processes through which young people acquire socially constructed knowledge have been completed over the past 20 years by researchers in cultural psychology. These researchers have been influenced by work in both anthropology and cognitive psychology, and their cross-cultural investigations have provided in-depth pictures of social practices outside of traditional Western schooling. They have identified and measured the cognitive consequences of these practices, i.e., Vai (a Liberian kinship group) literacies in three scripts (Scribner & Cole, 1981, 1988); Brazilian children's candy selling (Saxe, 1988; 1991); the uses of literacy and the interplay of oral and written mediums in a southern African American and White working-class community (Heath, 1983, 1988); and the construction of mathematical strategies in the work environment of a dairy factory (Scribner, 1984a), to name a few. From the standpoint of anthropology and psychology these studies provide meaningful insights into the texture and nuances of the interplay of culture and cognition. As Saxe (1991) puts it, culture and cognition "co-construct" one another.

What is missing, however, in terms of enriching the links between everyday practice and schooling, are specific descriptions of the knowledge structures taught in school as they relate to the knowledge structures constructed within nonschool social settings. The interplay of existing structures of knowledge generated by social activity outside classrooms and structures of knowledge embedded in school learning is potentially powerful because the resulting network of associations is richer in both its specificity and its generalizability. This interaction can be viewed in Vygotskian terms as the cross-fertilization of scientific and spontaneous concepts (Vygotsky, 1986).

Links between literature and talk in the African American community

In the instance of the discourse practices within the African American community and the genre strategies of at least one significant and powerful body of African American literature there exists a bridge of not only socially meaningful motifs but an intimate overlay of rhetoric that links oral talk and literary language. Gates (1988) employs the term "speakerly text"[1] to refer to such works, in which Black English—with its relish for playing on the meanings of words and its flair for figuration, innuendo, verve, and style—is transformed in literature. Gates further explicates the links between the talk of ordinary people and the speakerly text. This link between ordinary talk and literature, although explicated through the example of African American discourse, may have unexplored reverberations for other communities of talk.

In my work with African American novice readers and such speakerly texts (Lee, 1991a), it has been precisely the rhetoric of the text which has engaged these readers and which they have used as points of analysis to construct and critique the significant themes and symbols within the works. Traditionally, African American literature critically reflects the historic and personalized experiences of African Americans. African American writers carry on the role of the traditional African griot, or communal story teller, who is seen by the community as imbued with the gift of insight and provocative introspection. Many African American writers from DuBois (1903) to Walker (1983) have publicly avowed their role as tellers of the stories of their people, interpreters of the sociopolitical realities their people experience, and maintainers and shapers of their language.

Knowledge required to interpret literature

Literature is a powerful source of school study for those who have distanced themselves from or have been distanced by the academy. Reading literature requires at least two categories of knowledge. The first is social knowledge regarding human relationships, the motivation of people in particular circumstances, and the relationship between human goals and human action. Moreover, as the diversity of human cultures attests, what may appear reasonable human behavior in one cultural context or particular historical moment may be ridiculous or unthinkable in another. Scholes (1985) calls such social and cultural knowledge the cultural codes of a literary text. Writers do not compose in a vacuum but within (or perhaps against) a tradition that is inherently cultural in nature. Thus, one cannot adequately read the literature of a people without knowing something of the culture and historical circumstances of that people.

The second category is knowledge of the literary conventions operating in the text. The literary conventions within the narrative, for example, may include manipulation by the author of the point of view of narrators and characters; of imagery and detail to create mood and setting; of rhetorical strategies to create ironic effects; or the juxtaposition of characters, relationships, and events to suggest commentary or interpretation beyond surface meaning. Literary texts represent the vividness of social experience through dialogue, imagery, and stylistic strategies aimed at engaging the emotional involvement of the reader. These same strategies are employed in everyday conversation (a point illustrated in detail by Tannen [1989]). Writers of literary texts, especially narrative texts, elevate and hone these strategies of everyday talk to representational or symbolic levels that derive their meaning from the context of the text. They sculpt dialogue, imagery, and concrete detail to construct a scaffold for broader meaning and significance. As a result literature generates symbols that stand both within and beyond the text.

Thus, if we are to shape effective readers of literary texts, we must make certain our students understand the cultural codes of the literary text (i.e., the social knowledge and cultural values upon which it rests). We must also teach the use of specific interpretive strategies that represent the "technology" of interpreting literature. Scholes (1985) argues that the technical aspects of interpreting literature fall into three broad categories: (1) basic reading comprehension, (2) interpretation, and (3) criticism. According to Scholes:

> The supposed skill of reading is actually based upon a knowledge of the codes that were operative in the composition of any given text and the historical situation in which it was composed. . . . The ideal reader shares the author's codes and is able to process the text without confusion or delay. Such a reader constructs a whole world from a few indications, fills in gaps, makes temporal correlations, performs those essential activities that Umberto Eco has called writing "ghost chapters" and taking "inferential walks"—all without hesitation or difficulty. (p. 22)

Progression from basic comprehension of a work of fiction to interpreting it involves the movement "from a summary of events to a discussion of the meaning or theme" (p. 22). Criticism, "involves a critique of the themes developed in a given fictional text, or a critique of the codes themselves, out of which a given text has been constructed" (p. 23). Scholes concludes that a major function of teachers of literature should thus be to help students "identify their own collectivities, their group or class interests, by means of the representation of typical figures and situations in fictional texts" (p. 23).

Signifying in the streets and school

Although Potts (1989), an African American ethnographer who situated himself as an intimate participant observer in a housing project community in Chicago, made a very different set of observations, Heath (1989) bemoans what she observes as a decline in the amount and complexity of verbal interaction between young African American mothers in an urban housing project and their young children. However, despite the dearth of language stimulation in the earlier years, Heath notes that these Black adolescents are experts at "signifying," a practice that has been formally defined by many scholars, writers, and activists (Mitchell-Kernan, 1973; Gates, 1984, 1988; Abrahams, 1970; Andrews & Owens, 1973; Kochman, 1972; Brown, 1969; Major, 1970; Hurston, 1935; Cooke, 1984). Smitherman (1977) summarizes the formal properties of signifying as follows:

> . . . indirection, circumlocution; metaphorical-imagistic (but images rooted in the everyday, real world); humorous, ironic; rhythmic fluency and sound; teachy but not preachy; directed at persons or persons usually present in the situational context (siggers [signifiers] do not talk behind yo back); punning, play on words, introduction of the semantically or logically unexpected. (p. 121)

Signifying has been defined by some in structural terms as a speech act with delineated functions (Abrahams, 1970; Kochman, 1972). Others define it as a rhetorical stance, an attitude toward language, and a means of cultural self-definition (Mitchell-Kernan, 1973; Gates, 1984, 1988; Smitherman, 1977; Cooke, 1984). I do not see these categories of definitions as being mutually exclusive; all are vital to the argument of this article. As a valued traditional form of African American discourse, signifying has been maintained across generations and across both rural and urban environments. It has been traced back to the period of the African American Holocaust known to many as slavery (Gates, 1988). It is precisely because signifying is so highly valued and so widely practiced within the African American community that it has the potential to serve as a bridge to certain literacy skills within the school environment.

Gates (1984, 1988) and Mitchell-Kernan (1973) both point to the specialized meanings attributed by African Americans to the word "signify." Both contrast the Eurocentric, dictionary-based definition with the Afrocentric definition. In the latter, to signify means to speak with innuendo and double meanings, to play rhetorically upon the meaning and sounds of words, and to be quick and often witty in one's response. There is no parallel usage of the term within other ethnic English-speaking communities. Moreover, according to Gates (1984), signifying may be called or classified by many names: "marking, loud-talking, specifying, testifying, calling out (of one's name), sounding, rapping, and playing the dozens" (p. 286). Other terms include "shucking," as in "shucking and jiving," and "talking shit."[2] Mitchell-Kernan describes signifying as a "way of encoding messages or meanings which involves, in most cases, an element of indirection" (p. 311). She emphasizes that dictionary meanings of words in an act of signifying are not sufficient for constructing meaning; rather, one must recognize "implicit content or function, which is potentially obscured by the surface content or function" (p. 314).

Popular forms of signifying include playing the dozens (i.e., "talkin' about yo' mama," as in: "Yo' mamma so skinny, she do the hula hoop in a Applejack!") and "capping" or "sounding" (a verbal duel of friendly insults, as in the following exchange: "I went to your house and wanted to sit down. A roach jumped up and said, 'Sorry, this seat is taken.' " Response: "So, I went in yo' house and stepped on a match and yo mama said, 'Who turned off the heat?' "). Signifying can also be metaphoric and serve functions other than insults. The following example is taken from Mitchell-Kernan (1981):

> (Grace has four kids. She had sworn she was not going to have any more babies. When she discovered she was pregnant again, she wouldn't tell anybody. Grace's sister came over and they had the following conversation.)
>
> Rochelle: Girl, you sure do need to join the Metrecal-for-lunch bunch.
>
> Grace: (noncommittally) Yea, I guess I am putting on a little weight.
>
> Rochelle: Now look here girl, we both standing here soaking wet and you still trying to tell me it ain't raining. (p. 323).

Extended signifying dialogue may be either metaphoric or ironic. Smith (1987) and Booth (1974) identify strategies by which an expert reader may both identify a passage in a literary text as ironic and reconstruct the passage's intended meaning. I have demonstrated elsewhere (Lee, 1990) that these same strategies may be used to identify a selection of extended signifying dialogue as ironic and to reconstruct its intended meaning. According to Booth, to perceive the irony intended by an author, the reader and the author must share linguistic knowledge of the rules of verbal interventions as well as common cultural and reading experiences. Similar knowledge is required for participants to understand the irony of extended signifying dialogue, except that the shared reading experiences are replaced with knowledge of the speakers and the rituals of signifying. For novice African American readers, speakerly texts of African American literature can bridge that gap between processing irony in literature and irony in social discourse. This is important because understanding irony in literature is a difficult and often unmastered skill (Booth, 1974; Hillocks & Smith 1988; Smith, 1989).

The properties of signifying may be broadly classified under the scope of metaphoric or figurative language and ironic talk. African American adolescents regularly produce and interpret such talk. Indeed, in many social settings within the African American community, the person, particularly the adolescent, who cannot signify is viewed as having neither status nor style and is judged as a kind of outsider incapable of participating in social conversation. African American creative writers in the speakerly text tradition frequently appropriate and refigure this attitude toward language and discourse form.

Research by Delain et al. (1985), Taylor (1982), and Ortony et al. (1985) examines the relationship between the predominance of this figurative talk (specifically "sounding") among adolescents in the African American community and comprehension of figurative language in school texts. Their studies indicate that, for White students, comprehension of figurative language in a text is directly related to general verbal ability. For Black students, however, "black language ability affects sounding skill, which in turn [directly] affects figurative language comprehension" (Delain et al., p. 170). As Delain et al. further conclude: "skills acquired 'in the streets,' so to speak, do transfer to school settings" (p. 171).

My research (Lee, 1991a) extends the findings of Delain et al. to the comprehension of speakerly texts of African American fiction. I have demonstrated that African American students' skill in interpreting figurative language and ironic verbal constructions can serve as a scaffold to learning the more complex skill of interpreting complex implied relationships in literary texts (Hillocks & Ludlow, 1984). The problem with the implications for school achievement of my research is the evidence that teachers generally do not respect or support any demonstrations of Black English in classrooms (Delpit, 1990; Rist, 1970; Smitherman, 1977; Taylor, 1982). Michaels's (1981, 1986) work on storytelling in primary-level classrooms shows how Black English discourse practices are devalued. Michaels delineates two story-telling strategies: a topic-centered style used by middle-class White children, and a topic-associative style used by poor and working-class African American children. Michaels concludes that teachers identify the topic-associative style as deficient and incoherent, and consequently do not assist students who employ this style to develop the strategies of being explicit and linear, that is, the strategies emphasized by the school. Cazden (1988) makes similar observations in her comparison of White and Black teacher ratings of student stories. While both Black and White teachers identified the topic-associative stories told by the Black youngsters as deficient, the Black teachers recognized the strength of the use of detail in the stories.

Gee's (1989) analysis aligns perfectly with my overarching argument that there is strength in the social and linguistic knowledge as well as the story schema that many African American children, especially the poor, bring to schools. In critiquing a topic-associative story composed by a 7-year-old Black girl (who had been sent to the school psychologist for consistently composing such stories), Gee automatically presumes its coherence. He asserts that all humans tell the stories of their personal experiences with some presumed logic which they may or may not make explicit, depending on the cultural tradition of storytelling from which they come. Moreover, as one who has studied the dimensions of the cultural discourse of the African American community, Gee recognizes the literary qualities of the story: its use of imagery, concrete detail, and parallelism in its syntactic structure as well as shifts in points of view and the representation of an emotional state by showing actions which demonstrate it. Thus, Gee looks on as a kind of expert who has explicit knowledge of the storytelling form of which the child, as a novice, has only intuitive, fledgling, and incomplete knowledge. That is to say, the child in question certainly would not say about her story what Gee says. Gee, were he the teacher, would have the responsibility of slowly scaffolding this novice storyteller into an explicit knowledge of the strategies she uses unknowingly and incompletely. He would help her to make explicit, for the school context, the links that tie together the episodes she reports. The child may not even be cognizant of these links until she has had an opportunity to complete the story, but such scaffolding would result in a story structure that is more literary, more detailed, and more complex than the linear structure that teachers traditionally emphasize in schools. Tannen's (1989) explication of the rhetoric empowering the text of Jesse Jackson's oratory at the 1988 Democratic convention looks at the expert end of the spectrum of African American storytelling tradition, whereas Gee's analysis of the seven-year-old girl's stories reveals the formative buds of that tradition.

As I continue to construct this Vygotskian framework, it is equally important to investigate how African American oral strategies such as signifying are represented in the expert domain of literature. In Hurston's *Their Eyes Were Watching God* I have identified and classified almost two hundred statements as either metaphoric, proverbial, or oxymoronic. These statements convey the implicit themes, symbols, and ironies within the text. Each of these statements fall within the purview of the indigenous oral tradition of African American discourse typified by signifying. Indeed, Hurston's and many other texts within the speakerly tradition are replete with signifying (see Smitherman, 1977; and Gates, 1988, for specific examples). In *Their Eyes Were Watching God*, however, the speech act of signifying becomes a metaphor for the empowerment of the female protagonist and a mirror for viewing the ironic pettiness as well as largesse of ordinary folk. Hurston refers to the signifiers as "big picture talkers . . . using a side of the world for a canvas." She describes the ordinary folk who signify on the porch as:

> [t]hese sitters [who] had been tongueless, earless, eyeless conveniences all day long. Mules and other brutes had occupied their skins. But now, the sun and the bossman were gone, so the skins felt powerful and human. They became lords of sounds and lesser things. They passed nations through their mouths. . . . They made burning statements with questions, and killing tools out of laughs. . . . A mood came alive. Words walking without masters; walking altogether like harmony in a song. (pp. 1–2).

In earlier studies (Lee, 1991a, 1991b) I reported on a process that expanded students' signifying skill such that they were able to scour the rhetoric of Hurston's 1937 novel and the more contemporary speakerly text, *The Color Purple* by Walker (1982), which also makes artistic use of signifying. I could not have been more impressed with the insights and skills these students brought to these texts. These African American high school seniors, whose reading scores ranged from 60% to a dismal 2% of the national percentiles, unravelled questions regarding their understanding of the texts that Scholes would surely have classified above the level of basic comprehension and at the levels of interpretation and criticism. The questions were ones for which there were no simple right or wrong answers. They were questions that required them to infer meaning from clues across the text and that focused on the figurative language of the texts. The students achieved statistically significant gains from pretest to posttest over control classes that were taught texts from the more traditional literature curriculum.

Two brief examples taken from the transcripts of the final class discussion are offered to illustrate the level of insight these students achieved. Again, it is important to remember that not one of these students had a reading score above the 50th percentile. Discussion about why Walker's book was called *The Color Purple* elicited the following comments:

> [Student 1] God does not want people to go through life looking at the material things and the unnecessary things that make life impossible. He wants people to look at life as a gift and they should cherish that gift. The color purple is a pass way for people to look and realize that life is not a toy but a gift to the earth. Alice Walker to me is the messenger through this book to tell that life is a gift or treasure . . . The (unintelligible) is an example of life and how life (unintelligible) through a young girl's life like saying one purple flower is an individual and are individuals like yourself. That's all I wrote.

> [Student 2] I said that *The Color Purple* as [the protagonist] Celie's life and how she behaved all through the whole book. I came to this conclusion from what Shug had said about it pisses God off when you walk through the color purple in a field and don't notice it. On the next page Celie says that her eyes were opened. And Sofia went through the color purple, too. I think that the color purple was just like a depression or trying period and she went through when she was in jail and she was working for Miss Millie and she transformed into someone else. When Celie came out of her shell when she signified on "Mr." And I think that the red, they always put red and purple together, I think that would represent a transformation from being in a depression and coming into something new.

The skills these students addressed went beyond their personal reactions to the speakerly text and beyond any ethnic pride they may have felt as a result of reading it. Rather, the appropriateness of the prior social and linguistic knowledge these students brought to these texts, combined with pedagogical strategies aimed at teaching the independent use of specific strategies of literary interpretation, allowed for powerful academic scaffolding. This scaffolding can be viewed as an apprenticeship comparable in many respects to the Vygotskian framework of semiotic mediation in a zone of proximal development (Vygotsky, 1986). By analyzing the transcripts of class sessions I traced both the shifts in students' conceptions of the task of literary analysis and the instructional efforts to draw upon their existing prior knowledge (i.e., cultural and linguistic knowledge) to bring them closer to the formal strategies that lead to constructing interpretations of themes and symbols in fictional texts (see Table 19.1).

What also occurred in this instructional unit was a form-function shift such

Table 19.1 Shifts in conceptions of the task: Signifying as a scaffold to literary interpretation

PHASE ONE	
Novice:	Right or wrong answers; unconscious, superficial, and literal processing of concepts; views signifying as being applicable only to the streets
Teacher:	Conception of literary task is just the opposite of the student's, yet teacher must understand and appreciate what the student knows and believes and determine how to map new associations onto the student's existing conceptions
PHASE TWO	
Novice:	Begins to adjust concepts and views of the task
Teacher:	Begins to draw on the student's knowledge and to raise to a conscious level the strategies the student uses to process signifying dialogue
PHASE THREE	
Novice:	Begins to apply his or her existing knowledge about signifying to the new domains of literary interpretation
Teacher:	Provides student with speakerly texts of fiction that elevate signifying to the level of a literary tool with metaphoric functions
PHASE FOUR	
Novice:	Through application to new domains, begins to adjust his or her conceptual framework of signifying to accommodate new variables
Teacher:	Raises critical questions that force student to consolidate new concepts, look at unexplored connections and relationships, and consider disconfirming data; observes student carefully to learn how his or her concepts are changing and to inform the teacher's own scope of knowledge about the concept or task
PHASE FIVE	
Novice:	Begins more independent applications of concepts
Teacher:	Begins to remove levels of support and observe student's independent applications

as that described by Saxe (1991). Over the course of the instructional scaffolding the form and the function of signifying slowly changed for these students (see Table 19.2). The association of new characteristics with signifying in the context of literature evolved to include literary uses of figurative language. This form-function shift was directed by the explicit scaffolding of the teacher and the affective cooperation of the student.

A key question, then, is: why does the student cooperate? Does the cultural context of the text and the discourse form influence the level of affective cooperation? I would argue that it does.

I have argued two core premises: (1) literature instruction should teach students the technology of literary interpretation and criticism; and (2) the potentially privileged relationship between novice African American readers and speakerly

Table 19.2 Form-function shift in student's concept of signifying

FORM	FUNCTION
Level One	
Views signifying as mostly "sounding" (i.e., "Yo' mama so skinny she can walk through the cracks in the door")	Sees signifying as tool to embarrass or tease in verbal competition; for street use (not at school, home, or church)
Level Two	
Understands signifying as having a variety of forms and can assign metalabels to each form	Understands cross-generational historical functions of signifying, its political overtones, and its utility in expressing double meanings, innuendo, exaggeration, and comparison
Level Three	
Recognizes signifying embedded in literature (fiction)	Sees signifying as serving psychological function for characters, as having symbolic function within the text, and as a structural tool of identity and class affiliation

texts of African American fiction shows great promise for teaching this technology. The significance of this approach is highlighted by Purves's (1984) observation:

> In secondary schools in the United States, . . . students in literature learn that it is most appropriate to talk about the content of the text rather than its form, to talk about the text's meaning and moral rather than its aesthetic effect. This situation extends to other subjects, where the rhetoric of a text is virtually ignored except in the occasional lesson on propaganda. (p. 99)

Because the academy is too busy listening to its own big voice, it does not hear the voices of ethnicity which the poor in particular bring to the classroom. Students from poor and/or ethnically diverse communities need desperately to assume a voice—not a monolithic point of view—with which they can critically analyze the assumptions (i.e., about values and appropriate or inappropriate roles) that underlie a story. Certainly, a critical reader is what a democracy demands and is what Woodson (1933), Freire (1970), Giroux and McLaren (1989), and others call for in their conceptions of critical pedagogy.

As the character Celie in Walker's *The Color Purple* puts it: "Look like to me only a fool would want you to talk in a way that feel peculiar to your mind" (p. 223). If we are liberal we say it is important to acknowledge the language of the child, yet we do not talk about how. As researchers we have not assisted teachers in finding ways to bridge the knowledge brought by these children when they enter the classroom door. As Heath (1989) states:

> The school has seemed unable to recognize and take up the potentially positive interactive and adaptive verbal and interpretive habits learned by Black

> American children (as well as other nonmainstream groups), rural and urban, within their families and on the streets. These uses of language—spoken and written—are wide ranging, and many represent skills that would benefit all youngsters: keen listening and observational skills, quick recognition and nuanced roles, rapid-fire dialogue, hard-driving argumentation, succinct recapitulating of an event, striking metaphors, and comparative analyses based on unexpected analogies. (p. 370)

There are cognitive consequences to this social and linguistic knowledge which can both assist, inform, and broaden the scope of knowledge validated by schools. The act of teaching students to exercise criticism over literary texts by framing perspectives that are beyond the merely personal (and likely to be both cultural and political) is an empowering act for schools to fulfill. Baldwin, in his speakerly text, *Go Tell It On the Mountain* (1952), captures the possibility and promise of culturally sensitive texts in classrooms:

> She did not know why he so adored things that were so long dead [to the classroom]; what sustenance they gave them, what secrets he hoped to wrest from them. But she understood, at least, that they did give him a kind of bitter nourishment, and that the secrets they held for him were a matter of his life and death. (p. 166)

Notes

1 The term was originally coined by Hurston, who perhaps remains the master of this voice to this day.

2 As my students reminded me recently, however, these terms are old-fashioned. Nonetheless, while the current labels are not yet under my grasp, the fundamental taxonomy of forms remains stable.

References

Abrahams, R. D. (1970). *Deep down in the jungle: Negro narrative folklore from the streets of Philadelphia*. Chicago: Aldine.

Andrews, M., & Owens, P. T. (1973). *Black language*. Los Angeles, CA: Seymour-Smith.

Booth, W. (1974). *A rhetoric of irony*. Chicago: University of Chicago Press.

Brown, R. (1969). *Die nigger die!* New York: Dial Press.

Cazden, C. (1988). *Classroom discourse*. Portsmouth, NH: Heinemann.

Cooke, M. (1984). *Afro-American literature in the twentieth century: The achievement of intimacy*. New Haven, CT: Yale University Press.

Delain, M. T., Pearson, P. D., & Anderson, R. C. (1985). Reading comprehension and creativity in Black language use: You stand to gain by playing the sounding game. *American Educational Research Association Journal*, *22*(2), 155–173.

Delpit, L. (1990). Language diversity and learning. In S. Hynds & D. L. Rubin (Eds.), *Perspectives on talk and learning* (pp. 247–266). Urbana, IL: National Council of Teachers of English.

DuBois, W. E. B. (1903). *The souls of Black folk*. Chicago: A. C. McClurg.

Fish, S. (1980). *Is there a text in this class? The authority of interpretive communities*. Cambridge, MA.: Harvard University Press.

Freire, P. (1970). *Pedagogy of the oppressed*. New York: Seabury.

Gates, H. L., III. (1984). The Blackness of Blackness: A critique of the sign and the signifying monkey. In H. L. Gates, III (Ed.), *Black literature and literary theory* (pp. 285–321). New York: Methuen.

Gates, H. L., III. (1988). *The signifying monkey: A theory of Afro-American literary criticism*. New York: Oxford University Press.

Gee, J. (1989). The narrativization of experience in the oral style. *Journal of Education, 171(1)*, 75–96.
Giroux, H., & McLaren, P. (Eds.). (1989). *Critical pedagogy, the state and cultural struggle*. Albany, NY: State University of New York Press.
Heath, S. B. (1983). *Ways with words: Language, life and work in communities and classrooms*. Cambridge: Cambridge University Press.
Heath, S. B. (1988). Language socialization. In D. Slaughter (Ed.), *Black children and poverty: A developmental perspective* (pp. 29–42). San Francisco: Jossey-Bass.
Heath, S. B. (1989). Oral and literate traditions among Black Americans living in poverty. *American Psychologist*, 44(2), 367–373.
Hillocks, G. (1986). *Research on written composition*. Urbana, IL: National Conference on Research in English.
Hillocks, G., & Ludlow, L. (1984). A taxonomy of skills in reading and interpreting fiction. *American Educational Research Journal*, 21, 7–24.
Hurston, Z. N. (1935). *Mules and men*. New York: Harper & Row.
Hurston, Z. N. (1990). *Their eyes were watching God*. New York: Harper & Row. (Original work published 1937)
Hynds, S. (1990). *Questions of difficulty in literary reading* (Report Series Number 4.6). Albany, NY: Center for the Learning and Teaching of Literature.
Kochman, T. (Ed.). (1972). *Rappin' and stylin' out: Communication in urban Black America*. Urbana, IL: University of Illinois Press.
Lee, C. (1990). *Signifying in the zone of proximal development*. Unpublished manuscript, Department of Education, University of Chicago.
Lee, C. (1991a). *Signifying as a scaffold to literary interpretation: The pedagogical implications of a form of African-American discourse*. Unpublished doctoral dissertation, Department of Education, University of Chicago.
Lee, C. (1991b, April). *Signifying as a scaffold to literary interpretation: The pedagogical implications of a form of African-American discourse*. Paper presented at the annual meeting of the American Educational Research Association, Chicago, IL.
Major, C. (1970). *Dictionary of Afro-American slang*. New York: International Publishers.
Marshall, J. D. (1989). *Patterns of discourse in classroom discussions of literature* (Report Series Number 2.9). Albany, NY: Center for the Learning and Teaching of Literature.
Marshall, J. D. (1990). *Discussions of literature in lower-track classrooms* (Report Series Number 2.10). Albany, NY: Center for the Learning and Teaching of Literature.
Michaels, S. (1981). Sharing time: Children's narrative styles and differential access to literacy. *Language in Society, 10*, 423–442.
Mitchell-Kernan, C. (1971, February). *Language behavior in a Black urban community* (Monograph Number 2). Berkeley, CA: Language Behavior Laboratory, University of California, Berkeley.
Mitchell-Kernan, C. (1981). Signifying, loud-talking and marking. In A. Dundes (Ed.), *Mother wit from the laughing barrel*. Englewood Cliffs, NJ: Prentice-Hall.
Mullis, I. V. S., Owens, E. H., & Phillips, G. W. (1990). *Accelerating academic achievement: A summary of findings from 20 years of NAEPs*. Princeton, NJ: Educational Testing Service.
Ortony, A., Turner, T., & Larson-Shapiro, N. (1985). Cultural and instructional influences on figurative language comprehension by inner-city children. *Research in the Teaching of English, 19*(1), 25–35.
Potts, R. (1989, April). *West side stories: Children's conversational narratives in a Black community*. Paper presented at the biennial meeting of the Society for Research in Child Development.
Purves, A. C. (1984). The potential and real achievement of U.S. students in school reading. In N. Stein (Ed.), *Literacy in American schools: Learning to read and write* (pp. 85–110). Chicago: University of Chicago Press.
Resnick, L. B. (1990). Literacy in school and out. *Daedalus, 199*(2), 169–186.
Rist, R. (1970). Student social class and teacher expectations: The self-fulfilling prophecy of ghetto education. *Harvard Educational Review, 40*, 411–451.
Rosenblatt, L. (1978). *The reader, the text, the poem*. Cambridge, MA: Harvard University Press.

Saxe, G. B. (1988). The mathematics of child street vendors. *Child Development, 59*, 1415–1425.

Scholes, R. (1985). *Textual power, literary theory and the teaching of English*. New Haven, CT: Yale University Press.

Scribner, S. (1984a). Literacy in three metaphors. In N. Stein (Ed.), *Literacy in American schools: Learning to read and write* (pp. 7–22). Chicago: University of Chicago Press.

Scribner, S. (1984b). Studying working intelligence. In B. Rogoff & J. Lave (Eds.), *Everyday cognition* (pp. 9–40). Cambridge, MA: Harvard University Press.

Scribner, S., & Cole, M. (1981). *The psychology of literacy*. Cambridge, MA: Harvard University Press.

Scribner, S., & Cole, M. (1988). Unpackaging literacy. In E. R. Kintgen, B. M. Kroll, & M. Rose (Eds.), *Perspectives on literacy* (pp. 57–70). Carbondale, IL: Southern Illinois University Press.

Smith, M. (1989). Teaching the interpretation of irony in poetry. *Research in the Teaching of English, 23*(3), 254–272.

Smith, M., & Hillocks, G. (1988, October). Sensible sequencing: Developing knowledge about literature text by text. *English Journal, 96*, 44–49.

Smitherman, G. (1977). *Talkin' and testifyin': The language of Black America*. Boston, MA: Houghton Mifflin.

Tannen, D. (1989). *Talking voices: Repetition, dialogue, and imagery in conversational discourse*. Cambridge: Cambridge University Press.

Taylor, M. (1982). *The use of figurative devices in aiding comprehension for speakers of Black English*. Unpublished doctoral dissertation, University of Illinois, Urbana, IL.

Vygotsky, L. (1986). *Thought and language*. Cambridge, MA: MIT Press.

Walker, A. (1982). *The color purple*. New York: Pocket Books.

Walker, A. (1983). *In search of our mothers' gardens: Womanist prose by Alice Walker*. New York: Harcourt Brace Jovanovich.

Winner, E. (1988). *The point of words: Children's understanding of metaphor and irony*. Cambridge, MA: Harvard University Press.

Woodson, C. G. (1933). *Miseducation of the Negro*. Washington, DC: Associated Publishers.

Wright R. (1972). Blueprint for Negro writing. In A. Gayle (Ed.), *The Black aesthetic* (pp. 315–326). Garden City, NY: Doubleday.

CHAPTER 20

FROM REMEDIAL TO GIFTED (1995)

Effects of culturally centered pedagogy

Rosa Hernández Sheets

Fabiola and Lupe,[1] fluent native-born Spanish speakers, rarely came to class. They could not read or write in Spanish, believed their Spanish was substandard (or "Mexican," as they referred to it), and ended up failing second-year Spanish. Their student records indicated a pattern of non-attendance and academic failure. I knew part of the problem was poor attendance, but it just did not make sense to me that Spanish-speaking students failed beginning Spanish.

The following September, I recruited Fabiola, Lupe, and three other Spanish-speaking students for a newly-developed, advanced Spanish class. Naturally, they did not want to enroll. "How can we pass an advanced class if we can't even pass Spanish 2?" they argued. "You will. It was my fault you failed last semester. I promise you'll pass. All you have to do is try and come every day." Finally they agreed. This time I was determined that textbook driven, grammatical concepts would not decide success.

A semester later, these five students passed the College Board Advanced Placement (AP) Spanish Language exam, earning college credit while sophomores and juniors in high school. A year later these students passed the prestigious AP Spanish Literature exam, which is comparable to a third-year college course. Over a 3-year period, as a result of intervention. Latina and Latino students, previously labeled "at risk," performed at a level usually expected of honor or gifted students.

This article documents the program's history and examines the results of an accelerated academic model interconnected with culturally relevant learning and teaching. Compensatory or basic skill models are frequently the type of intervention used for students labeled LEP (limited English proficient). This is also a category in which students from groups of color are overrepresented (Slavin, Karweit, & Madden, 1989). This article posits that these students may have demonstrated behaviors that fall within the construct of "giftedness" when procedural constraints[2] are removed.

A culturally relevant Spanish program

Year one: 1989–1990

In 1989, I decided that my classes would have to change if native speakers were to succeed. The solution was to enroll them in my advanced Spanish class, which traditionally was a small class. The focus of this new class would be conversation through literature and culture instead of emphasis on reading and writing through grammar. I rationalized that the language fluency of my regular students would increase by having native speakers in the class and the ability to speak Spanish could technically count as 3 years of Spanish courses.

For a whole semester no one knew this class existed. In a large urban public school system, asking permission to start a new program sometimes means the stifling of ideas. I knew I would be told that we had compensatory and transitional bilingual programs in place to meet the needs of at-risk, linguistically-different students. Yet Latino students, 6 percent of the student body, accounted for 13 percent of the disciplinary action, and 50 percent of them were below grade level.

Five native Spanish-speakers were simply enrolled in an advanced Spanish class with regular students. All five students qualified for the Federal Reduced or Free Lunch Program, three were from single parent homes, and two were on welfare. All were a year or more behind, based on credits earned, and had established non-attendance patterns. Aside from attendance issues, they did not experience disciplinary problems. None of the students participated in extra-curricular activities at school, and three held part-time jobs. All came from homes where parents spoke little or no English. Although Spanish was their first language, they could not read or write in Spanish.

The first thing they learned was that Spanish was an asset. In the small groups with regular students, they used their cultural knowledge to describe, translate, and explain concepts in Spanish. This verbal dexterity placed them in high demand during group work. They sensed that along with their peers, I too believed they were capable. Within a short time, they began to believe in themselves. The change was incredible to witness. By March, as a result of their success and enthusiasm in the classroom and a notice about registration for the advanced placement tests, I was inspired to challenge them further. I asked them if they wanted to register for the AP exam in May.

I explained that the test was difficult. We watched the movie, *Stand and Deliver* (Warner Brothers, 1988), which documents the success of East Los Angeles Latino students in AP calculus. I made it clear that it was impossible to prepare adequately in 3 months with one class hour per day. They knew we would have to spend many hours after school and on Saturdays. ("Sí.") I would call their families and in some cases make home visits. ("Sí.") We could work around their work schedules.

They learned the placement of accents and wrote essays in Spanish. They practiced 2-minute orals, listened to 10-minute lectures, and answered multiple choice questions. We were determined. Surprised that it was fun to study, they often laughed and commented, "Can you imagine! Me, studying? *¡Es incréible!*"

Then, one Saturday in April, we came early to take the 5 1/2-hour 1985 version of the Spanish language test. The results indicated passing scores. It was exciting to watch them run and scream up and down the empty halls, throwing their mock test scores high in the air. The school counselor used the Saul Haas Fund[3] to pay the required test fees, and that May, five students took the exam. Notices in July from the Advanced Placement College Board indicated the students had passed.

The College Board scores students on a scale of 1–5, with scores of 3–5 guaranteeing college credit. Miguel and Fabiola received "4s," earning 10 college credits. Lupe, Carmen, and Luis each received perfect "5s," worth 15 college credits. Lupe, Miguel, and Fabiola were only sophomores in high school. Carmen was a senior who had no chance of graduating due to excessive absenteeism in the past, and Luis was a junior.

In June, I was awarded a PIPE Education Grant,[4] valued at approximately $3,000. I ordered and scrounged for material for the advanced placement Spanish literature class and spent the summer reading the five required authors: Gabriel García Márquez, Jorge Luis Borges, Ana María Matute, Federico García Lorca, and Miguel de Unamuno. I took the sample literature exam, barely passing with a low "3."

Year two: 1990–1991

The PIPE Grant provided funds for test fees, field trips, and curricular materials. I actively recruited as many native speakers as possible. I knew the academic program could take some students 1–3 years to accomplish, but gains in self-concept and empowerment were immediate. The students gave each other positive peer support, the class provided a natural "mentoring" environment, and we unwittingly became a family.

During the second year of the program, students who had passed the AP Spanish language exam were joined by new native speakers. In addition there were four non-native speakers in their third year of Spanish and 32 first-year Spanish students, totaling 45 students in one class period during the first semester. Having 32 first-year students made learning and teaching difficult that fall. The second semester, the 13 advanced Spanish students were assigned to a separate class.

This group, although similar to the original group ethnically, economically, and culturally, was different. They attended classes, won school academic achievement awards, and joined extracurricular school activities. We formed a touring Ballet Folklórico. The students choreographed traditional Mexican folk dances, designed authentic costumes, and performed for their peers and students in the greater Seattle area.

The *West Seattle Herald*, a Seattle neighborhood weekly, and *La Voz*, a Washington State monthly Spanish newspaper, ran articles and pictures of their success. As members of the yearbook staff, the honor society, the soccer team, and the volleyball team, they were no longer marginal. They did not hug the walls as they moved from class to class. I remember Lupe's loud voice and happy laughter in the halls and recall the strange pain I felt when she casually stated, "You know, I used to be afraid to walk down the middle of the hall. I didn't belong. I used to touch the wall with my finger or walk around the building on the outside, even in the rain. But now everybody knows me. They say, 'Hi.' "

As May approached, students prepared for either the AP Spanish language or the AP Spanish literature exam. A teacher strike in April not only took away valuable school time but made it impossible to find suitable places to study. Without access to the school and computers, important information carefully recorded on disks was useless. Most of the time, the 3–4 hours scheduled for studying were lost to the constant interruptions encountered at the places where we met. I constantly worried that perhaps I was not preparing them adequately.

Only Lupe and Marisol were ready for the difficult literature test. We spent the previous night studying until 11 p.m. at Marisol's home. We reviewed all five authors, five novels, three plays, 30 or so short stories, and 30–40 poems. They knew characters, themes, literary terminology, and the structural analysis and writing style of each author. They also had a basic understanding of the era in which each author wrote and the major cultural and historical influences in their lives.

The literature exam was scheduled in the early afternoon. They had spent the morning sitting on the floor outside my room cramming and waiting for my substitute to arrive. We had no time for lunch. The exam was to be given at the downtown district offices. Five long hours later, the exam ended. They walked out softly. Carefully and casually on the ride to a restaurant to celebrate, I inquired, "How was it? I'm really proud of you guys!" I made sure my tone indicated that at this point the result did not matter.

"Rosa, it feels like a heavy cloud has been lifted from my soul. I can't express how glad I am to have it over with." Marisol crossed her arms over her chest and held her shoulders emotionally as she spoke in Spanish, lightly and poetically. She had taken the AP Spanish language exam the week before and had prepared for both simultaneously.

Lupe emerged from her stupor. She was more expressive and realistic. She worked 30–40 hours a week at a fast-food restaurant, bought her clothes and food, and even paid part of the rent. "I'm glad that stupid test is over, Rosa. Now you can't mess with me! If I had known it was going to be this hard, I would have never done it. It was pure hell!" She laughed.

"Do you think you passed?" I asked timidly. "I don't know. Parts of it. . . ." Marisol tried to recall the test. "Who cares! Let's go celebrate!"

In July, the report from the College Board indicated that all five students passed the Spanish language test. One received a "4" and the other four had perfect "5s." Lupe and Marisol passed the Spanish literature exam with a score of "4" for Lupe and a "3" for Marisol.

That summer I was awarded a Mellon Grant designed to provide training for teachers in inner city schools to establish AP classes for students from under-represented groups. I attended the University of Northern Colorado where I learned that the literature exam was one of the most prestigious AP exams, with a high failure rate for mainstream students (18%) and an even higher failure rate for "Chicano/Mexican American" students (22%). In May 1991, 3,146 students took the AP Spanish literature exam compared with 23,643 students taking the AP Spanish language exam (AP Program, 1992). Had I known in September what I found out in June, I might not have even attempted the literature exam. We were the only students in the state of Washington taking this exam.

Year three: 1991–1992

The 5-hour "mock test" in March indicated that 15 students were ready to take the advanced placement exams in May. Feelings of pride were mixed with fear and knowledge that many long hours would be spent studying. No one chose to back out. Lessons were held every day after school during March and April. Sometimes I provided snacks and pop. On the days that we stayed really late, parents brought "pot luck." A traditional highlight was an all-day Saturday study session at my house complete with jalapeño pizza.

In the third year of the program, four students passed the Spanish literature exam and four students passed the Spanish language exam. Two students scheduled to take the language exam were unable to do so because of personal issues beyond their control, and three students moved prior to exam day. Over a 3-year period, 20 out of 29 of the Latina(o) students who participated in the program received college credit by passing AP exams.

Opportunity to learn

The program described above allowed Latina(o) students access to AP Spanish language and Spanish literature courses usually designed for and offered to "gifted" or "honors" English-speaking students. At no time were the students who participated in the program tested for or identified as gifted. The class was offered in the world language department and, therefore, was not part of the ESL (English as a second language) or transitional bilingual program. All classroom interactions were conducted in Spanish. In this program a culturally centered pedagogy included: the use of the Spanish language as the medium of instruction, affirmation and validation of ethnic identity, development of self-esteem, curricular content emphasis on the students' cultural heritage, history, and literature, and implementation of learning strategies that matched preferred learning styles (e.g., oral language, cooperative learning, peer support, and family involvement).

¿Qué pasa? "What happens" when classroom events become important to students? Along with student performance on the AP tests, five factors in the classroom climate and curricular process emerged as indicators of student success: learning-teaching strategies, development of ethnic identity and self-esteem, student-teacher relationships, student-student relationships, and bridging of home to school. In addition, student focus discussion groups, open-ended questionnaires, and interviews provided information about student perception of their ability to succeed in a national AP exam, their academic skills, and the personal, social, and academic value of the program.

Learning-teaching strategies

Students worked in small groups, and the level of proficiency in reading and writing determined each student's contribution to the group activity. All written work (exams, literary critiques, and reflective essays) led to a single document produced by a collaborative group. Emphasis was placed on the development of intellectual competence by actively involving the student in critical reflection, analysis, and interpretation of literature using appropriate terminology.

For example, they understood, identified, and discussed primary and secondary themes, and used and applied literary terms such as paradox, hyperbole, onomatopoeia, juxtaposition, ellipse, and alliteration. By reasoning, weighing evidence, and thinking originally, they discussed the structural elements of the author's work, including writing styles, literary periods, and the influences of the historical, cultural, and political era in which the author wrote and lived.

At first, students listened or followed the text as I read. Little by little they learned to read and write words, phrases, and sentences in Spanish. They helped each other translate, summarize, and write analytical papers in Spanish, full of spelling and grammatical errors but intellectually sophisticated, drawing conclusions from the literature in a creative, complex, and in-depth analysis from their own intuitive frame of reference. They did not appear to feel inadequate or unaware of what they could do intellectually.

The goals and substance of each lesson were embedded in higher level thinking skills, using a variety of learning strategies and styles and incorporating literary concepts to actively engage the students both intellectually and emotionally. Students were invited to clarify their thoughts, assumptions, and feelings by, for example:

- Discussing the traditional role of the mother, the concept of family honor, and the influences of Catholicism.
- Identifying, comparing, analyzing, and inferring similar themes in Federico García Lorca's trilogy: *Yerma, Bodas de Sangre*, and *La Casa de Bernalda Alba* (see Lorca, 1967).
- Analyzing the influences of the Harlem Renaissance literary period and the American economic depression on Lorca's poetry.
- Identifying themes in Gabriel García Márquez's work that reflected the political and economic unrest in South America, U.S. imperialism, the African American Caribbean influence, and his socialistic political orientations.
- Examining concepts such as existentialism, metaphysics, immortality, fatalism, solitude, circular and linear time, fanaticism, the supernatural, sexual frustration, power, magical realism, violence, and spiritual beauty in relationship to literary themes, protagonists, and individual tone and style of an author.

"Basic skills," such as spelling, vocabulary, grammar, punctuation, and paragraph writing were never taught in isolation, as separate disciplines, nor were they determined by what I thought the students needed. I modeled reading and decoding by writing student inquiries on the overhead projector or on scraps of paper. The connection from verbal to written form was made whenever possible. In a speech at a nearby school district, I explained how literacy was addressed: "I honored the fragile game we played. They pretended they knew how to read. I pretended I didn't know they couldn't read."

As students demanded to know how difficult words were pronounced, why accents appeared, the structure of a paragraph, or why various phonetic spelling occurred, explanations were given. Difficult words were broken down into syllables, and phonics was slipped in as students struggled to read as much as possible. They continued teaching and learning from each other. When they asked to be taught to read, they learned to read in two sessions. The following scenario is representative of the general style and mood of the learning climate that prevailed.

Student: Rosa, why am I being marked down on "organization of ideas"? What do you mean? It's almost four pages long!
Teacher: You're not using paragraphs to show a change of ideas. The paragraphs you use don't have a main idea or supporting sentences. Read my comments! You guys better get it together. I'm running out of ink!
Student: I indented. See I indented here, and then I indented here. See.
Teacher: But, *mi amor*, that's not a paragraph.
Student: What's a paragraph?
Teacher: Do you want to know? [He nods.] Now?
Student: *¡Sí!*
Teacher: Anyone who wants to know paragraphs, please come up.

It was evident they thought a paragraph meant: indent, write a little, indent, write a little. These high school students, schooled in remedial ESL classes with English language acquisition as the major dimension, did not know the basic elements of a paragraph, a concept usually taught at the elementary level. Nor did they know what a main idea was, or what supporting sentences were. They thought a paragraph was physical or spatial. It took less than 15 minutes for students to learn the elements in paragraph writing when they identified a need and determined the time and place for teaching and learning. It was incredible to watch their enthusiasm, their insatiable desire to learn, and the excitement created when new skills were attained, especially knowing they had a choice whether or not to attend these informal sessions. It was an established pattern crucial to the learning climate. Students appeared hungry for writing mechanics and reading skills. One student exclaimed, "I can't believe it! This is fun. It feels like when I first learned how to drive. I remember I could hardly wait."

Development of ethnic identity and self-esteem

Emphasis was placed on developing a positive ethnic identity. Ethnic identity in this case is defined as a sense of self determined by racial and cultural variables and embedded in a social and historical context. A positive ethnic identity was enhanced with an awareness of their cultural background, but equally important were addressing social and political issues such as the causes and effects of racism.

Although student ethnic and linguistic differences were affirmed in this program, the students still perceived these differences as negative. An incident that occurred is illustrative. A student stated she was ashamed of her accent when she spoke English and that she did not even speak "real Spanish." A world map was shown to demonstrate all the places in the world where Spanish was the dominant language. The elements of a living, spoken language with variations by geographical location were discussed. Students were encouraged to be proud they were bilingual. It was noted that all students in the class spoke at least two languages. Common English and either Spanish, Tagalo, African American English, or Chinese. I emphasized: "An accent only proves that you can speak at least two languages. Do you know that the United States is the only country in the world where a person who speaks only one language is considered educated?"

The development of self-esteem was an important element of the program. Self-esteem is defined as a personal judgment of one's worthiness, capability, success, or significance and the accompanying feelings of approval and disapproval (Pascarella & Terenzini, 1991). Thus, it was directly related to identity development and critical in this program.

While students were intellectually challenged, they were not subjected to situations where failure was possible. Tasks were designed to be verbal, and students were assessed orally until they learned reading and writing. When field trips were taken, students representing all ethnic groups were invited to participate. This was a way to model acceptance of cultural and ethnic diversity that would perhaps transfer to acceptance of self. Students met and were publicly praised by the famous Puerto Rican lawyer and talkshow host, Geraldo Rivera, when he was in town. They attended motivational lectures by Jaime Escalante and Henry Cisneros and saw Cesar Chavez at El Centro de la Raza.[5] They attended dance and music performances at the University of Washington and visited selected university classes to help them realize that a college education was possible. Spanish literature professors allowed them to participate in third-year college literature classes and told them their own college students might not be able to pass the AP literature test.

The local papers ran articles and pictures of their success. *Focus*, the monthly newsletter for the Seattle Public Schools, referred to them as "stand and deliver Seattle-style" ("Stand and deliver," 1992) stressing that their differences were assets. Marc Ramirez, a *Seattle Times/Seattle Post-Intelligencer* newspaper reporter, followed them throughout the year and reported their ultimatc success. They were featured on the cover and dominated the September 1992 back-to-school issue of *Pacific Magazine*, the *Seattle Times/Seattle Post-Intelligencer* Sunday magazine. Ramirez described how hard they studied, the strengths of using their first language and culture as resources rather than hindrances, their vulnerability, and their fear and nervousness on test day. He captured their feelings of family, buoyancy, expectation, and joy while they ripped apart the envelopes containing their AP passing scores.

Student-teacher relationships

The traditional roles of the student and teacher were altered. Working as a family team, both students and teacher were equally involved in the content, process, and context of the lessons as well as in the establishment of assessment criteria. Students determined the focus of a given lesson. I provided opportunities to learn through materials, resources, and experiences. As active participants in the learning process, they decided whether or not to take the AP tests. They taught each other and determined the level of excellence required. Student literary analyses were bound into booklet form to be used for "cramming" weeks before the exam. Students graded the essays and determined acceptance for booklet inclusion. They helped develop the class syllabus by selecting the content and sequence of instruction.

After-school study groups were scheduled by students. In the typical 3-hour study sessions, students debated and confronted each other, supporting their arguments with citations. They laughed, took copious notes, and expressed their fear of failure. One student remarked at the end of one of these study sessions: "I used to worry about whether or not I would ever finish high school. Now I worry if I can get enough money to go to the university. I want to go to Berkeley. Maybe be a lawyer."

When the discussion of assessment took place, we quickly realized that grades were not the issue, learning was. We decided that all students would receive an "A" on their high school transcript. However, the more important measure of success would be the AP test score. I evaluated the critical essays written by students on a nine-point scale using the College Board AP assessment rubric as agreed. Students received two grades on all assignments, one for assignment completion, the other reflecting AP standards. The goal was to narrow the gap between the two scores.

Cooperation was actualized and internalized. For example, students were more concerned with helping and encouraging each other in order to decrease the point spread in their grades than competing for the highest grade. They collaborated to identify weak areas in their essays and helped each other make needed revisions. Competition, if any, was self-directed. Ultimately, we accepted that students would be evaluated as "proficient" if they passed the AP exam; likewise, I would be deemed "competent" if my students passed.

Student-student relationships

For most students this was the first time they were together in a class where they could speak Spanish freely. They helped each other learn to read and write, and seemed at ease seeking peer assistance. In the second year of the program, the addition of the 32 first-year students in the advanced Spanish class created a natural situation for the development of strong student-student relationships. The first-year students demanded, dominated, and required teacher contact time. The Latina(o) students, lacked the skills necessary to read independently and attend to task assignments without assistance from me.

To accommodate the first-year students, 3 days a week the Latina(o) students worked as tutors with the beginning Spanish students. In return the beginning Spanish students did seatwork or worked on orals while 2 days a week were devoted to the advanced students. This worked only as a schedule on the blackboard. In reality, a semester was lost for the advanced students. However, the lack of continual student-teacher interaction resulted in a natural peer mentoring process. The student-selected motto "*Sí queremos, podemos*," roughly translated to mean, "If we want something, we can achieve it," reflected their feelings of togetherness, unity, community, and family. This class was never an individual effort!

Bridging of home to school

Home visits were made. Parents and extended families attended functions such as Ballet Folklórico performances, academic achievement assemblics, and University of Washington MeCHA[6] award presentations. Parents often provided unsolicited snacks for the late after-school sessions. I was invited in for coffee when driving the students home in the evening.

Repeatedly, students were amazed by the pride their parents expressed because they were studying literature in their own language. The students' fear of failure was validated since parents bragged to everyone about the test. One student commented:

> My Mom and Dad always want to know what happens next in the story. I even caught my Dad trying to read *El General en Su Laberinto*. I liked it when my whole family even my aunt came to see us dance the jarabe. My dad bought me a red carnation. My mom tells everyone that I can read and write in Spanish.

Student perception

Student interviews generated perceptions about ethnic identity, self-esteem, personal academic expectations, and home-cultural expectations. Students felt this class allowed them to be themselves, a place where no one laughed at their English competency, and where everyone supported each other. They felt this class promoted a healthy ethnic identity, allowing them to take pride in their cultural heritage and linguistic abilities. Students related:

> I think my pride for being Latino was the most important thing that happened to me. That made me study as hard as I could to be the leader in that program.
>
> I feel part of my culture in this class. I was proud when I learned to read and write all those hard words in Spanish. I didn't even know there were so many hard words in Spanish.

Being in this class improved their self-esteem, allowing them to participate fully in the school's regular and extracurricular activities. They felt they were treated as individuals with unlimited abilities and resources, expected to perform at an optimal level while at the same time feeling secure. This climate of acceptance gave them the confidence to excel. For example:

> I liked it when Rosa said I was brilliant. It made me want to work harder. I wanted to be the best in the class. This was hard because everyone wanted to be the best. So we just worked together and studied harder.
>
> Being in this class was a tough challenge, but I knew that I could make it. We were very supportive of each other and willing to help, and when we were ready to take the test, I knew I was going to pass the exam.

Of additional interest were the students' responses to the questions, "What does gifted mean to you?" and "Do you think you are gifted?" This was the first time the word gifted was used explicitly. Their responses included the following:

> A person who knows a lot, thinks a lot, and knows almost everything. . . . Who knows? I might just be so. I am intelligent. I only need to develop my capacity.
>
> A child that has superior qualities, more than others of his age and sometimes more than adults. . . . I think so, not in an intellectual aspect but in my self-value and in the power of my self-determination. In terms of my intellect I function at an adequate level.
>
> A gifted student for me is a student who always reaches his potential. This person knows how to learn. . . . Yes, I think so. Well maybe not but I do know I can pass the test because I studied hard and I tried to do the best I can.

Conclusion

The Spanish program used student resources as strengths by providing Latina(o) students with a class that maintained their native language and increased language fluency by developing thinking, oral, and written skills in Spanish. Before involvement in this program, the opportunity to learn appeared to be compromised by the inaccessibility of culturally relevant instruction in Spanish and by students' lack of opportunity to enroll in advanced placement classes, even when these classes were offered in their school.

This program illustrated a multicultural claim that programs planned and executed to meet the cultural needs of students succeed. However it requires changing traditional roles of teachers and students, building bridges between home and school, and moving from a compensatory to a challenging, academically demanding model with high expectations. In addition, learning and teaching of skills based on student perceived need as learning gaps emerge not only can decrease the amount of time needed to attain skills but also illustrates that a fragmented, decontextualized approach to teaching basic skills may not be pedagogically sound.

The change that occurred in these students resulted in equity of educational opportunities and in equitable academic outcomes. Most importantly, it attended to the affirmation and validation of ethnic identity and intended growth in self-empowerment.

¡Si queremos podemos!

Notes

1 All names in this article are pseudonyms. The data for this article is derived from my teaching experience from 1989 to 1992. The research I conducted for this program was presented at the 1994 National Association for Bilingual Education in Los Angeles, CA, and at the 1994 American Educational Research Association annual meeting in New Orleans, LA. The author is appreciative of Seafirst Bank, Seattle, WA, for a pre-doctoral fellowship, which provided support toward her studies.
2 Students who participate in "gifted programs" undergo identification and labeling through assessment procedures, such as IQ tests, achievement tests, academic achievement history, and/or teacher recommendations (McKenzie, 1986). Students who are considered gifted are characterized by IQ scores in the upper 3–5 percent of the population. In gifted programs the differentiated curriculum includes achievement at an accelerated academic level and the use of higher level thinking skills in the learning process.
3 The Saul Haas Fund is special moneys used in the Seattle Public School District to pay educational expenses for students who would be denied participation because they are unable to afford such expenditures.
4 PIPE stands for Partners in Public Education, an organization affiliated with the Greater Seattle Chamber of Commerce, which awards financial assistance to worthwhile innovative educational projects in Seattle Public Schools on a competitive basis.
5 El Centro de la Raza is a community center serving the Latina and Latino population in Seattle, WA.
6 MeCHA is a Mexican Chicano student organization at the University of Washington.

References

Advanced placement program, The college board: National and Washington state summary reports. (1992). New York: College Entrance Examination Board.
Lorca, F.G. (1967). *Obras completas.* Madrid: Aguilar.
McKenzie, J.A. (1986). The influence of identification practices, race and SES on the identification of gifted students. *Gifted Child Quarterly, 30*(2), 93–95.
Pascarella, E.T., & Terenzini, P.T. (1991). *How college affects students: Findings and insights from twenty years of research.* San Francisco: Jossey-Bass.
Ramirez, M. (1992, September 6). Rhyme & reason: In this class, Spanish is an asset, not a hurdle. *Seattle Times/Seattle Post-Intelligencer Pacific Magazine*, pp. 12–20.
Slavin, R.E., Karweit, N.L., & Madden, N.A. (1989). *Effective programs for students at risk.* Boston: Allyn & Bacon.
Stand and deliver: Seattle schools-style. (1992, October). *Focus*, p. 2.
Warner Brothers. (1988). *Stand and deliver.* [Film]. Burbank, CA: Author.

CHAPTER 21

MULTICULTURAL SCIENCE EDUCATION (1993)

Perspectives, definitions, and research agenda

Mary M. Atwater and Joseph P. Riley

Introduction

Setting: Panay, an island in the Visayas, one of a group of islands that comprise the middle of the Philippine archipelago

A sun-bleached, crushed-shell walkway cuts through the tropical vegetation and leads to the open door of a woven grass and bamboo structure. Inside are grey, hand-hewed, double-seater desks, weathered but sturdy. About 40 children sit quietly at the desks, bare feet on the dirt floor, their plastic sandals arranged in orderly rows outside the door. The translucent shell shutters are pushed back as far as they will go. The room is dark and cool. Batteries, bulbs, and wires lie on the desks untouched by the hands covering each face.

The teacher, a foreigner, is an American white. He had read about and seen this disturbing student behavior before. It is termed "nahuya," and while it has no direct translation in English it captures what we might describe as a mixture of shyness and respect. Nahuya is expected and rewarded in this culture. With an accent guaranteed to bring out smiles behind the hands, he starts the lesson. "Maayong aga sa tanan tanan." With encouragement, the hands slowly creep down and hesitantly reach for the batteries and bulbs.

Setting: an inner-city school bordering Washington, DC

A concrete wall and chain-link fence surround the large brick turn-of-the-century building, separating it from the urban sprawl of three-decker houses, iron-barred shop windows, and abandoned stores. Inside about 35 children, all African-American, noisily talk at their desks. The desks are wooden surfaces with cast iron sides, placed in rows and bolted to the floor. The students have just returned from recess. The teacher is preparing to teach the same lesson on batteries and bulbs. The class behavior is nervous and anxious. Something is in the air. It seems everyone—but the teacher—can feel the tension. The students are avoiding Princeton, moving away from him. All eyes are on Beatrice, who reigns from the back of the class and whose domain extends throughout the school and beyond the fence. Chaos explodes as the first battery crashes against the wall. Students scramble for cover as Beatrice and Princeton circle the classroom hurling batteries at each other, reloading at each desk. In time, order is restored. The science lesson resumes. The batteries, bulbs, and wires, confiscated and hidden away, are replaced with safe ditto sheets.

Discussion

In episode one, the teacher had the advantage of cultural preparation as part of his preservice science teaching program. He had training so he could understand and speak the language. He understood the culture, geography, and economy of the region and ways this local structure fit into national and international contexts. He knew the history of this culture. He knew their heroes and heroines—the warrior Lapu Lapu, the statesman Dr. Jose Rizal, and General Bonifacio. He believed that from these 40 barefoot children could come doctors, teachers, farmers, and nurses. All things were possible for these children.

In contrast, the teacher in the second episode did not speak the language. He knew nothing of the culture, the community in which he taught, nor the children's heroes and heroines. He had concern for their education, but little faith that successful professional careers would develop for this group. How could there be optimism when sixth-grade students were three to four years behind grade level and used a form of English unintelligible to the teacher?

Both examples featured the same teacher working in two different paradigms. The first episode was cross-cultural. The teacher knew he was teaching in a different culture. He was given preservice training that encouraged him to accept, respect, and understand the cultural, religious, linguistic, and socioeconomic differences he would encounter in the setting.

In the second setting, the teacher did not recognize that he was teaching in another culture. Instead of working within a cross-cultural framework, he was operating in a deficit paradigm (Valentine, 1971). This supports the position that African-American behavior be judged not as it is but as it deviates from accepted standards. Teachers are inundated with literature and preservice experiences that subtly reinforce the deficit theory. As a result of this exposure, teachers enter the classroom with stereotypic characterizations about students of color.

With these predominant beliefs, teachers, children, and schools fail. In the second episode, a culturally aware teacher, who knew the dialect and the body language, would have been able to pick up the cues and anticipate and defuse the situation. He or she could have conducted the lesson as planned. If teacher educators were charged with preparing science teachers for overseas teaching assignments, preparation in the culture in which they are to teach would be balanced against the content and methodology in program development. Yet, teacher education programs in this country send students out to teach with little or no preparation for the real-world classrooms that are more culturally divergent each year.

As science educators approach the 21st century, it is imperative that they understand that precollege settings will be different from those of 20th because of the changing composition of the student population in the United States. The schools' student population in the United States is increasingly diverse (Snyder, 1987). In 1972, overall "minority" enrollment in public school was 21.7% of the total school population; by 1981, that figure had increased to 26.7%. It has been predicted that by the year 2000 African-American, Asian American, Hispanics, and Native American students are expected to make up over 33% of school enrollment.

In the 32 largest school districts in the country, 75% of the 5,000,000 students are representatives of these groups. Florida, for example, has had an increase in its Hispanic and Asian/Pacific Islands student enrollments; southeastern states, such as Georgia, Louisiana, and Alabama, continue to experience increases in their

African-American student populations. In the southwest, in such states as California and New Mexico, Hispanic enrollment in schools is rapidly increasing. In many cities in these states, ethnic groups now constitute a majority of the student enrollments (Matcznski & Joseph, 1989).

However, unfortunately few of these ethnic students enroll in advanced science courses and aspire to careers in the sciences. Few African-Americans, Native Americans, and Hispanics receive doctorates in the sciences or become science teachers. While the composition of the school population is changing in this country, many ethnic groups are still not fully experiencing the "American dream" (Atwater, 1986).

Definitions

The term *multicultural education* was introduced in the 1960s and has been defined by a variety of researchers in fields other than science education. Over the course of 30 years, the definition of multicultural education has been refined. In addition, other terms have become a part of this research area such as *multiethnic* and *cross-cultural education*.

Banks and Banks (1989) defined multicultural education as an idea, and educational reform movement, and a process whose major goal is to change the structure of educational institutions so that male and female students, exceptional students, and students who are members of diverse ethnic and cultural groups will have an equal chance to achieve academically in school. He maintained that the power relationships, curriculum materials, and attitudes and beliefs of school staff must be altered in ways that will allow the school to promote educational equity for students from diverse groups. Hence, the total educational environment must change for a wide range of cultural groups to experience equitable educational opportunities and educational success. The implication is that changes in instructional methodology and program development in all subjects must occur.

Baptiste and Baptiste (1979) agreed that multicultural education must be regarded as a philosophy and a process that guides the total enterprise called education. At its most sophisticated level, multicultural education exists as a product, a process, and a philosophical orientation guiding all persons involved in the educational process. The National Council for Accreditation of Teacher Education (NCATE) has strong standards for both preservice and graduate teacher programs related to multicultural education. According to NCATE, multicultural education is defined as follows:

> . . . the preparation for the social, political, and economic realities that individuals experience in culturally diverse and complex human encounters. This preparation provides a process by which an individual develops competencies for perceiving, believing, evaluating, and behaving in different cultural settings. Thus, multicultural education is viewed as an intervention and an ongoing assessment process to help institutions and individuals to become more responsive to the human condition, individual cultural integrity, and cultural pluralism in society. (Baptiste et al., 1980, pp. 2–3)

Thus, multicultural education emphasizes the development of communication skills for cross-cultural and interethnic group interaction. It endorses the development of perceptual, analytic, and application skills of teachers, which can be applied in both formal and informal, personal, and institutional settings. In the past, the concern for multicultural education was fundamentally a concern for maximizing individual ability to use communicative and interactional skills to improve the quality of life in a culturally pluralistic, multiracial, and highly technological society. In 1979, NCATE required its member institutions to include multicultural components in their teacher education programs. However, the lack of agreement over what constitutes multicultural education resulted in teacher education programs that have been generally misinterpreted, weakly conceptualized, and poorly designed (Rodriguez, 1984). The missing element in multicultural education is that it is thought of as subject matter and not as a curriculum-wide consciousness. Multicultural education should be included in every facet of teacher education: "Every teacher educator, even those in sciences . . ., needs to develop a clear multicultural perspective" (Rodriguez, 1984, p. 48).

Tiedt and Tiedt (1986) contended that multicultural education deals with morality, attitudes, and values. These are the underlying philosophies of teaching that guide the behaviors of teachers. Multicultural education is to be delineated in goals and objectives that deal with factual information, controversy inherent in stereotypes and prejudices, and the basic need for enhancing. Therefore, multicultural education is viewed as interdisciplinary and cannot be taught in isolation from other instruction.

To develop a multicultural perspective, one must first recognize the need that exists for this perspective even in science education. Yet, *multicultural science education* as a concept has been defined even though it is a new term. Thus, multicultural science education is a construct, a process, and an educational reform movement with the goal of providing equitable opportunities for culturally diverse student populations to learn quality science in schools, colleges, and universities (Atwater, 1991). The National Science Teachers Association (NSTA) has created a standing committee called the Committee on Multicultural Science Education and an elected position, Director of Multicultural Science Education. The charge of this committee is as follows:

> Assume responsibility for reviewing, coordinating, initiating as appropriate or making recommendations for NSTA activities dealing with multicultural science education. Provide general recommendations to the President and the Board of Directors regarding NSTA policy in the area of multicultural science education. (NSTA, 1992, p. 23)

NSTA has developed a position statement on multicultural science education. It has defined as one of its goals to ensure that "culturally diverse children . . . have . . . access to quality science education experiences that enhance success and provide the knowledge and opportunities required for them to become successful participants in our democratic society" (NSTA, 1992, p. 159).

These professionals also claim that it is a *process* that must be modeled by teachers and students as we move toward short- and long-term goals. Multicultural education affects all people as they strive to gain understanding of themselves, develop feelings of self-esteem, and understand and appreciate the other people who make up the population of their classroom, state, country, and world.

Multicultural science education should be considered a vital part of the field of science education. A body of knowledge about multicultural science education does exist, even though it may be scanty. This body of knowledge includes our understandings of group identification, culture, and science. It relates to science learning and achievement, science instruction, and the involvement of different cultural groups in the sciences. Both qualitative and quantitative methods are appropriate in generating new knowledge in this field. Researchers with a variety of skills and backgrounds are needed to enhance the knowledge in this area.

Professionals involved in science education may have different perspectives of this new concept. The science teacher educator, the science education researcher, the scientist, and the science teacher may view this area differently. Science teacher educators may align themselves with the NCATE definition. They are committed to the preparation of multicultural science teachers, persons in science education who can teach science to diverse groups of students (Atwater, 1989). Thus, science educators are committed to the model programs for the development of multicultural teachers of science and equity issues as they relate to science instruction.

Smith (1989) has called for a new direction in multicultural education for teacher educators. That new direction is "research based," believing that

> . . . the central core of multicultural education should become the knowledge base for effective minority education; that is, . . . there exists a "research-based" body of knowledge on minority achievement and learning, the parameters of which have never been defined and the content of which has never been placed in a broad theoretical framework that can be taught effectively in teacher education programs. (p. 3)

He proposed that the knowledge base for multicultural education includes: (1) effective school research findings; (2) effective teaching research; (3) learning styles research; (4) teaching style research; (5) research on language acquisition; (6) research on the cultural dimensions of minority learning and motivation; (7) research on minorities and subject-specific learning; (8) research on social and cultural values as inhibiting and enhancing learning factors; (9) research on restructuring schools for minority learning; (10) research on cross-racial interpersonal relationships and their effects on minority group children; (11) policy research studies related to minority achievement; (12) research on the effects of role models and mentors on minority students; (13) research on exceptional and gifted minority students; and (14) research on curriculum and minority students.

On the other hand, the science teacher would be much more interested in science curriculum materials for diverse groups of students, appropriate teaching strategies for the different groups of students, motivating students from different groups, and the science learning for all students. The science teacher would ideally apply the research findings in multicultural science education to improve science instruction in classrooms.

Chemists, physicists, biologists, and geologists would also be consumers of multicultural science education research findings. These natural scientists may be interested in the factors influencing the achievement of different groups in the sciences at the college level and also factors related to the involvement of different groups in science. It is expected that they would use the research findings to improve their instruction and aid students in becoming involved in science. However, few of these natural scientists would be involved in generating research in this area.

Grant and Millar (1992) have delineated several reasons to account for the lack of research on multicultural education and educational research that focuses on multiculturalism. These reasons include the following:

1. There is little diversity in higher-education faculty; therefore, few faculty members are knowledgeable about multicultural education.
2. Science multicultural education has been poorly defined; this allows research critics to ignore research efforts in multicultural education.
3. Financial support for multicultural education research is limited.
4. Because the research work of multicultural education scholars is judged as unscholarly and/or is not relevant to the majority of education scholars, few risk their academic careers in this areas.
5. Few researchers attend conference presentations on multicultural education. Therefore, this "ghettorization" inhibits research in this area (p. 10).
6. Few seminars and forums of analysis and debate about multicultural education exist at the graduate level. Because little conceptualization in multicultural education research occurs, few young scholars emerge in this field.
7. A lack of leadership by scholars of color has caused a paucity of multicultural education research (pp. 8–10).

In the field of science education, all of these barriers exist; however, multicultural science education is a legitimate field for research study. Thus, research studies should be conducted in the areas of schooling, learning, teaching, and the effects of science educational policy and practices as it relates to multicultural science education.

Relevant research themes in science education might include the following:

1. views of science held in European and non-European cultures;
2. beliefs and attitudes toward science and science teaching of different groups of students;
3. beliefs and attitudes toward science and science teaching of teachers;
4. learning styles, cognitive styles, ways of knowing, teaching styles, and science learning for different groups;
5. student–teacher interactions in diverse groups of students;
6. communication styles in the teacher–student verbal and nonverbal interactions and science learning;
7. science teacher education models at the preservice and in-service levels for producing bicultural and multicultural science teachers;
8. evaluation for different groups of science students and science teachers.

Multicultural education has a long history in the United States and British Commonwealth countries (Lynch, 1983). Multicultural science education is an emerging area within science education; therefore, its development will require time. However, it is imperative that organizations, such as the National Association for Research in Science Education, stimulate research in this area. The world has always been composed of different cultural groups; it is imperative that science education researchers acknowledge and respond appropriately to this fact.

References

Atwater, M. M. (1991, April). *Reform in science education: Multicultural education.* Paper presented at the annual meeting of the National Association for Research in Science Teaching, Fontanna, WI.

Atwater, M. M. (1986). We are leaving our minority students behind. *The Science Teacher, 53*, 54–58.

Atwater, M. M. (1989). Including multicultural education in science education: Definitions, competencies, and activities. *Journal of Science Teacher Education, 1*, 17–20.

Banks, J. A., & Banks, C. A. McG. (1989). *Multicultural education—issues and perspectives*. Boston, MA: Allyn and Bacon.

Baptiste, Jr., H. P., & Baptiste, M. L. (1979). *Developing the multicultural process in classroom instruction. Competencies for teachers*. Lanthem, MD: University Press of America.

Baptiste, Jr., H. P., Baptiste, M. L., & Gollnick, D. M. (1980). *Multicultural teacher education: Preparing educators to provide educational equity*. Vol. I. Washington, DC: American Association of Colleges for Teacher Education.

Grant, C. A., & Millar, S. (1992). Research and multicultural education: Barriers, needs, and boundaries. In C. A. Grant (Ed.), *Research and multicultural education: From the margins to the mainstream*. Washington, DC: The Palmer Press.

Lynch, J. (1983). *The multicultural curriculum*. London, UK: Batsford Academic and Education.

Matcznski, J. J., & Joseph, E. A. (1989). Minority shortage: A proposal to correct the lack of activity. *Action in Teacher Education, 10*, 42–46.

National Science Teachers Association (1992). *NSTA Handbook 1991–1992*. Washington, DC: Author.

Rodriguez, F. (1987). Multicultural teacher education: Interpretation, pitfalls, and commitments. *Journal of Teacher Education, 35*, 47–50.

Smith, G. P. (1989, February). *Remarks on the directions for multicultural education for the 1990's*. Paper presented at the ATE Special Interest Group ATE Annual Conference, St. Louis, MO.

Snyder, T. D. (1987). *Digest of education statistics*. Washington, DC: U.S. Government Printing Office.

Tiedt, P. L., & Tiedt, I. M. (1986). *Multicultural teaching: A handbook of activities, information, and resources*. Boston, MA: Allyn and Bacon.

Valentine, C. A. (1971). Deficit, difference and bicultural models of Afro-American behavior. *Harvard Educational Review, 41*, 137–157.

CHAPTER 22

MUSIC AS A MULTICULTURAL EDUCATION (1983)

Jack P. B. Dodds

If we believe that music is essentially concerned with living and life, music cannot be separated from education. Its elements are present in an embryo state in all children. And from them music elicits responses on various levels, whatever the children's cultural backgrounds and irrespective of whether they are intellectually gifted or suffering from a mental or physical handicap.

Music is not an international language, but it is a universal medium of expression for the deepest feelings and aspirations that belong to all humanity. It provides this medium through various means—traditional and folk music, jazz, the works of individual composers, and the popular music that speaks so powerfully for and to the young.

Many young people are being educated musically without our help. The music to which they listen, emanating from radios, record players, televisions, and concert stages, is not of one uniform type, and much of it shows influences from many cultures. They take it all in stride. Some of it they like; some they reject. What to an older generation were "exotic" sounds imported from foreign parts do not seem strange or bizarre to the young. The sounds are a natural part of their auditory experience. This is not entirely a new phenomenon. A friend who grew into adolescence when George Harrison was introducing the sitar into his song "Within You, Without You," told me recently that she had not thought of that sound as "exotic." It was just one of the many fascinating sounds to be enjoyed.

A lot of music making and listening, then, is going on out of school. How far is this accepted and extended in the activities of the classroom? Can we fit yet another area of music into an already crowded music scheme? Or does our music education require a type of conceptual approach that is not based on thinking about the addition of extras, but on the recognition that there are many manifestations of music, all of which can be drawn on freely to illuminate basic elements of any scheme of music education. If the latter is true, where do we begin?

Start with sound

All musics' impact is made directly by the experience of sound, whatever the system through which that sound is conveyed. And so it is sound per se that must be the starting point for music education. The differences between the various systems can be understood and cherished later, as can the context in which they were conceived and reasons for their creation. So let us start with sound and silence, rather than system, letting our children investigate sounds and themselves as sound producers. Sound is our common property, and the savoring of a single sound is the beginning of musical wisdom. As we experiment with sounds—of children's own environment, of human voices, of instruments (homemade, purchased, electronic, or acoustic), of whatever sort we wish to include in our soundscape—we begin also to explore pitch, rhythm, timbre, texture, and structure.

As children's imagination catches fire they become creators, making from the raw material satisfying patterns and structures, working together, whatever their cultural backgrounds. The more we place emphasis on creation rather than imitation, re-creation, or transmission, the quicker any prejudices we may have about the validity of certain music systems will disappear.

It is at this stage that the wealth of the world's music—folk, high art, popular—can be of such value in helping to extend pupils' musical experience. In a multicultural society such as ours there are many resources already at hand. They are all to be welcomed. The sounds and sound producers of the minority groups, together with the natural sounds of their homelands, still retained in the memories of the older members of their families, can be shared in the classroom. This always depends on the teacher's sensitivity to the origins and associations of those sounds within the cultures from which they come.

We can learn from each other, not allowing ourselves to be blown off our indigenous feet, but being refreshed by new sources of inspiration—and that means new sources of life. This can only happen if we ensure that all those minority groups are encouraged to make their own music, to share it with others, and to know its value, both for itself and for its contribution to the total pattern of music making.

Understand styles

Having absorbed the sounds that make up the music, children can be helped in trying to understand styles of the music itself. This may force us as teachers to question some of our own preconceptions. It there, for example, as we sometimes suggest, a correct style of singing voice that all children should aim to produce in the classroom? If so, what is it? As we listen to voices of a cathedral choir, Cathy Berberrian, members of the Peking Opera, and Mick Jagger, is the answer quite as straightforward as we had thought—or are we beginning to discover something about style and appropriateness?

What can students gain?

What then, are we hoping that our children will gain as they move away from their home base and meet the music of other cultures?

1. Students will gain new musical experiences and an extension of their means of expression through the enlargement of their vocabulary, as they use scales, rhythmic groupings, tone colors, textures, and structures that before were unfamiliar to them.
2. They will achieve an appreciation of diversities and, at a deeper level, of similarities.
3. They will participate in different ways of making music together. In the West we shall particularly benefit from group music making that depends

on interaction between the members of the group—listening to and relating to each other or to an instrumental leader within the group, instead of following the visual directions of a conductor or printed notation. In so doing there will be a development of their aural perception through an approach more akin to that used in folk, jazz, rock, and other popular forms of music. Spontaneity and improvisation will play more important roles, and composer and performer will often be the same person.

4. They will come to understand the influences of nonindigenous music on twentieth-century composers, popular music, jazz, and rock. Students who wish to study these musics in depth need to know about their sources and the social situations that gave them birth.
5. Students will see the relatedness of the arts. That divisions between music, dance, and other arts are less strong, or are nonexistent, in many cultures provides a lesson to those of us who perpetuate these divisions by our specialist approaches.
6. Social involvement and audience participation with direct emotional expression will restore to music its function of bringing together people from varying backgrounds in celebrations, seasonal festivities, and other domestic rituals.
7. Pupils will gain the intellectual stimulus that working within new systems gives and may later wish to embark upon the serious study of a nonindigenous culture in order to become scholars in their own chosen area.
8. Students will develop tolerance and respect, leading to an attitude that, it is hoped, will find expression in their relationship with people of other races, cultures, and geographic areas.

This, then, is music education for all schools—not just those in areas with a concentration of pupils from nonindigenous cultures. Perhaps it is even more important in isolated rural areas from which young people will of necessity go to industrial areas in search of work. If they have had no contact with people from different cultures and are hardly aware of their existence, they will take with them a limited view of life. Attitudes bred in isolation can easily succumb to persuasive racist propaganda.

If music education is to meet more adequately the needs of our own age and environment, we must decide what there is in our tradition to which we must hold fast and determine what human and material resources are required to effect necessary change.

We certainly need many more musicians and teachers from nonindigenous cultures to play key roles in music education. We also need indigenous teachers prepared for new thinking and processes of working. But changed attitudes, good will, tolerance, and understanding are not enough. In order for their attitudes to be translated into practical reality, teachers need material resources and a knowledge of other musics that is the result of experience, practice, and involvement.

I am not referring to the training of musicologists. I am asking, rather, for a broadening and deepening of the education of all musicians. Nor is this a concern for initial training only. In-service courses must be established to develop a new orientation for all teachers. More is required than lectures on multicultural music. These may be informative, but they do not always lead to practical action. There must be opportunities for all musicians and especially music teachers to be immersed in the music of nonindigenous cultures as part of their everyday training. For this purpose we need centers where music of specific cultures is performed within as appropriate a setting as possible. There must be close links between the centers to avoid duplication, and a regular flow of performing musicians from the centers to other colleges and institutions where teaching about the music is given.

Wherever possible, the music must be live, When this is not possible, we shall have to rely on tapes, records, videos, and films made by the carriers of the traditions represented. This is where close cooperation with ethnomusicologists is important, so that the resources are authentic and are not diluted. The songs that are sung, the instruments that are used, and the music that is played on them all need the careful scrutiny of the ethnomusicologist, especially where there is no practicing member of the tradition at hand. It is equally important for the ethnomusicologist to understand the aims and intentions of the music teachers and limitations within which they have to work. One of the most valuable contributions ethnomusicologists can make is to help bring about an understanding of the culture from which a music comes, its significance to those who make it, and its function in their society. At later stages we also need more opportunities for exchange visits, so that young people can experience the music in its home setting. One of the disquieting features of the present is that just when unrestricted travel and the exchange of students could be of such importance in helping young people to get to know each other, governments seem keen on erecting barriers. As musicians we must do all within our power to resist the erection of such barriers between peoples and groups. Music is not just an art to be practiced within the education of a multicultural society. It is, in itself, a truly multicultural education.

APPENDIX 1: OTHER SUGGESTED READINGS

Asante, M. K. (1991). The Afrocentric idea in education. *Journal of Negro Education, 60*(2), 170–181.

Bailey, D. B., & Harbin, G. L. (1980). Nondiscriminatory evaluation. *Exceptional Children, 46*(8), 590–596.

Banks, J. A. (1995). Multicultural education: Historical development, dimensions, and practice. In J. A. Banks (Ed.), *Handbook of Research on Multicultural Education* (pp. 3–24). New York: Macmillan.

Christensen, L. (1989). Writing the word and the world. *English Journal, 78*(2), 14–18.

Cortes, C. (1980). The role of media in multicultural education. *Viewpoints in Teaching and Learning, 56*(1), 38–49.

Cortes, C. E. (1976). Need for a geo-cultural perspective in the bicentennial. *Educational Leadership, 33*(4), 290–292.

Deyhle, D. (1985). Testing among Navajo and Anglo students: Another consideration of cultural bias. *Journal of Educational Equity and Leadership, 5*(2), 119–131.

Dilworth, M. (1986). Teacher testing: Adjustments for schools, colleges, and departments of education. *Journal of Negro Education, 55*(3), 368–378.

Ellsworth, E. (1987). Educational films against critical pedagogy. *Journal of Education, 169*(3), 32–47.

Garcia, P. A. (1986). The impact of national testing on ethnic minorities: With proposed solutions. *Journal of Negro Education, 55*(3), 347–357.

Gilmore, P. (1983). Spelling "Mississippi": Recontextualizing a literacy-related speech event. *Anthropology and Education Quarterly, 14*(Winter), 235–255.

Gordon, E. W., & Rubain, T. J. (1980). Bias and alternatives in psychological testing. *Journal of Negro Education, XLIX*(3), 350–360.

Greene, M. (1986). In search of a critical pedagogy. *Harvard Educational Review, 56*(4), 427–441.

Johnson, N. B. (1977). On the relationship of anthropology to multicultural teaching and learning. *Journal of Teacher Education, 28*(3), 10–15.

Koza, J. E. (1992). Picture this. *Music Educators Journal, 78*(7), 28–32.

Laosa, L. M. (1977). How psychology can contribute. *Journal of Teacher Education, 28*(3), 26–30.

McCormick, T. E., & McCoy, S. B. (1990). Computer-assisted instruction and multicultural nonsexist education: A caveat for those who select and design software. *Computers in Schools, 7*(4), 105–124.

Pang, V. O. (1991). The relationship of test anxiety and math achievement to parental values in Asian-American and European-American middle school students. *Journal of Research and Development in Education, 24*(4), 1–10.

Ravitch, D. (1993). Launching a revolution in standards and assessments. *Phi Delta Kappan, 74*(10), 767–772.

Rist, R. C. (1970). Student social class and teacher expectations: The self-fulfilling prophecy in ghetto education. *Harvard Educational Review, 40*(3), 411–451.

Tate, W. F. (1994). Race, retrenchment, and the reform of school mathematics. *Phi Delta Kappan, 75*(6), 477–484.

Wills, J. S. (2001). Missing in interaction: Diversity, narrative, and critical multicultural social studies. *Theory and Research in Social Education, 29*(1), 43–64.

APPENDIX 2: JOURNAL PUBLISHERS AND CONTACT INFORMATION

Action in Teacher Education
Association of Teacher Educators
1900 Association Drive, Suite ATE
Reston, VA 20191–1502
(703)620–2110; (703)620–9530
http://www.ate1.org

American Association of Colleges for Teacher Education
1307 New York Avenue, NW Suite 300
Washington, DC 20005–4701
(202)293–2450; (202)457–8096 (Fax)
www.aacte.org

American Educational Research Association
1230—17th Street NW
Washington, DC 20036
(202)223–9485, × 100; (202)775–1824
http://aera.net

American Journal of Education
University of Chicago Press
Permissions Department
1427 East 60th Street
Chicago, IL
(773)702–6096; (773)702–9756

American Sociological Association
1307 New York Avenue, NW Suite 700
Washington, DC 20005–4701
Jill Campbell
Publications Manager
(202)383–9005, × 303; (202)638–0882
www.asanet.org

Anthropology and Education
Anthropology and Education Quarterly
University of California Press
Journals and Digital Publishing Division
2000 Center Street, Suite 303
Berkeley, CA 94704

Association for Supervision and Curriculum Development
1703 N. Beauregard Street
Alexandria, VA 22311–1714
(703)578–9600; (703)575–5400 (Fax)
www.ascd.org

Banks, Cherry A. McGee
Professor, Education
University of Washington, Bothell
18115 Campus Way NE Room UW1 244
Bothell, WA 98011–8246

Banks, James A.
University of Washington
Box 353600, 110 Miller Hall
Seattle, WA 98195–3600
(206)543–3386; (206)542–4218 Fax
http://faculty.washington.edu/jbanks

Comparitive Education Review
University of Chicago Press
Permissions Department
1427 East 60th Street
Chicago, IL
(773)702–6096; (773)702–9756

Curriculum and Teaching
James Nicholas Publishers
PO Box 244
Albert Park, Australia, 3206

Education
Dr. George E. Uhlig
PO Box 8826
Spring Hill Station
Mobile, AL 36689

Education and Urban Society
Corwin Press, Inc.
2455 Teller Road
Thousand Oaks, CA 91320–2218
(805)499–9734; (805)499–0871 (Fax)
http://www.sagepub.com

Educational Horizons
National Association for Ethnic Studies, Inc. &
American Cultural Studies Department
Western Washington University
516 High Street—MS 9113
Bellingham, WA 98225–9113
(360)650–2349; (360)650–2690 (Fax)

Educational Leadership
Association for Supervision and Curriculum Development
PO Box 79760
Baltimore, MD 21279–0760
(703)578–9600; 1–800–933–2723; (703)575–5400 Fax
www.ascd.org

Educational Research Quarterly
113 Greenbriar Drive
West Monroe, LA 71291
(318)274–2355
hashway@alphagram.edu

Educators for Urban Minorities
Long Island University Press (No longer in operation)
Eugene E. Garcia, Ph.D.
Vice President Education Partnerships
Professor of Education
Arizona State University
Eugene.Garcia@asum.edu

English Journal
1111 W. Kenyon Road
Urbana, IL 61801–1096
(217)328–3870; (217)328–9645 (Fax)
http://www.ncte.org

Exceptional Children
Council for Exceptional Children
Permissions Department
1110 North Glebe Road Suite 300
Arlington, VA 22201–5704
(703)264–1637

FOCUS
Joint Center for Political Studies
1301 Pennsylvania Avenue, NW
Washington, DC 20004
(202)626–3500

Ford Foundation
320 East 43rd Street
New York, NY 10017

Gibson, Margaret A.
Professor of Education and Anthropology
Department of Education
University of California, Santa Cruz
1156 High Street
Santa Cruz, CA 95064
(831)459–4740; (831)459–4618 (Fax)

Harvard Educational Review
Harvard Graduate School of Education
8 Story Street, 1st Floor
Cambridge, MA 02138
(617)495–3432; (617)496–3584 (fax)
www.hepg.org

HarperCollins Publishers
10 East 53rd Street
New York, NY 10022
(212)207–7000

Interchange
Nel van der Werf
Assistant Rights and Permissions/Springer
Van Godewijckstraat 30
PO Box 17
3300 AA Dordrecht
The Netherlands
31 (0) 78 6576 298; 31 (0) 78 6576 323 (Fax)
Nel.vanderwerf@springer.com
www.springeronline.com

Journal of Curriculum Studies
Routledge (Taylor & Francis, Inc.)
4 Park Square, Milton Park
Abingdon, Oxon OX14 4RN United Kingdom
44–1235–828600; 44–1235–829000 (Fax)
http://www.routledge.co.uk

Journal of Curriculum and Supervision
Association for Supervision and Curriculum Development
1703 North Beauregard Street
Alexandria, VA 22311–1714
(703)578–9600/(800)933–2723; (703)575–3926 (Fax)
http://www.ascd.org

Journal of Teacher Education
American Association of Colleges for Teacher Education
1307 New York Avenue NW Suite 300
Washington, DC 20017–4701
(202)293–2450; (202)457–8095 (Fax)
www.aacte.org

Journal of Research and Development in Education
Julie P. Sartor, Editor
Office of the Associate Dean for Research,
Technology, & External Affairs
UGA College of Education
(706)542–4693; (706)542–8125 (Fax)
jsartor@uga.edu

Journal of Negro Education
Howard University Press
Marketing Department
2600 Sixth Street, NW
Washington, DC 20059
(202)806–8120; (202)806–8434 (Fax)

Journal of Literacy Research (formerly *Journal of Reading Behavior*)
Lawrence Erlbaum Associates, Inc.
10 Industrial Avenue
Mahwah, NJ 07430–2262
(201)258–2200; (201)236–0072 (Fax)

Journal of Educational Thought
University of Calgary
Faculty of Education – Publications Office
2500 University Drive N.W.
Education Tower, Room 1310
Calgary, Alberta, Canada T2N 1N4
(403)220–7499/5629; (403)284–4162 (Fax)
www.ucalgary.ca

Journal of Teacher Education
American Association of Colleges for Teacher Education
1307 New York Avenue NW 300
Washington, DC 20005–4701
(202)293–2450; (202)457–8095 (Fax)
www.aacte.org

Language Arts
The National Council of Teachers of English
1111 W. Kenyon Road
Urbana, IL 61801–1096
(217)278–3621
permissions@ncte.org

Momentum
National Catholic Educational Association
1077—30 Street, NW Suite 100
Washington, DC 2007
(202)337–6232; (202)333–6706 (Fax)
nceaadmin@ncea.org

Multicultural Education
Gaddo Gap Press
3145 Geary Boulevard PMB 275
San Francisco, CA 94118
(414)666–3012; (414)666–3552
http://www.caddogap.com

National Catholic Educational Association
1077—30 Street, NW Suite 100
Washington, DC 20007
(202)337–6232; (202)333–6706 (Fax)
nceaadmin@ncea.org

National Council for the Social Studies
8555 Sixteenth Street, Suite 500
Center for Multicultural Education
Silver Spring, MD 20910
(301)588–1800 × 122;
(301)588–2049 Fax

National Educational Service
1252 Loesch Road
PO Box 8 Department V2
Bloomington, IN 47402

Negro Educational Review
NER Editorial Offices
School of Education
1601 East Market Street
Greensboro, NC 27411
Alice M. Scales (scales@pitt.edu)
Shirley A. Biggs (biggs@pitt.edu)

Peabody Journal of Education
Lawrence Erlbaum Associates
10 Industrial Avenue
Mahwah, NJ 07430–2262

Phi Delta Kappan
Phi Delta Kappa International
408 N. Union Street
PO Box 789
(812)339–1156; 800–766–1156; (812)339–0018 fax

Race, Class, and Gender
Southern University at New Orleans (No Response)
Carl contact Jean Belkhir (jbelkhir@uno.edu)

Radical Teacher
Center for Critical Education
PO Box 382616
Cambridge, MA 02238
Saul Slapikoff, Permissions Editor
slap2@comcast.net

Researching Today's Youth: The Community Circle of Caring Journal
Dr. Carlos E. Cortes
Professor Emeritus
Department of History
University of California,
Riverside, CA 92521–0204
(951)827–1487
(951)827–5299 fax
carlos.cortes@ucr.edu

Review of Educational Research
American Educational Research Association
1230—17th Street NW
Washington, DC 20036–3078

Sage Publications, Inc.
Corwin Press, Inc
2455 Teller Road
Thousand Oaks, CA 91320
(805)410–7713; (805)376–9562 (Fax)
permissions@sagepub.com

Southeastern Association of Educational Opportunity Program Personnel (SAEOPP)
75 Piedmont Avenue NE
Suite 408
Atlanta, GA 30303–2518
(404)522–4642

Teachers College Record
Blackwell Publishing
PO Box 805
9600 Garsington Road
Oxford OX4 2ZG United Kingdom
44 (0) 1865 776868; 44 (0) 1865 714591 Fax
www.blackwellpublishing.com

Teacher Education and Special Education
Dr. Fred Spooner, Editor
Teacher Education and Special Education
SPCD/College of Education
University of North Carolina at Charlotte
Charlotte, NC 28223

(704)687–8851; (704)687–2916 Fax
fhspoone@email.uncc.edu

The American Scholar
1606 New Hampshire Avenue NW
Washington, DC 20009
(202)265–3808; (202)265–0083

The Educational Forum
Kappa Delta Pi
3707 Woodview Trace
Indianapolis, IN 46268–1158

The High School Journal
The University of North Carolina Press
PO Box 2288
Chapel Hill, NC 27515–2288
(919)966–3561; (919)966–3829
www.uncpress.unc.edu

The Journal of Educational Research
Heldref Publications
1319 Eighteenth Street, NW
Washington, DC 20036–1802
(202)296–6267; (202)296–5146 (Fax)
www.heldref.org

The New Advocate
Christopher-Gordon Publishers, Inc.
1502 Providence Hwy, Suite 12
Norwood, MA 02062–4643
(781)762–5577; (781)762–7261
http://www.christopher-gordon.com

The Social Studies
Heldref Publications
1319 Eighteenth Street, NW
Washington, DC 20038–1802
(202)296–6267; (202)296–5149 (Fax)
permissions@heldref.org

The Teacher Educator
Ball State University
Teachers College
TC 1008
Muncie, IN 47306
(765)285–5453; (765)285–5455

The Urban Review
Nel van der Werf
Assistant Rights and Permissions/Springer
Van Godewijckstraat 30
PO Box 17
3300 AA Dordrecht
The Netherlands
31 (0) 78 6576 298; 31 (0) 78 6576 323 (Fax)
Nel.vanderwerf@springer.com
www.springeronline.com

Theory into Practice
Lawrence Erlbaum Associates, Inc.
10 Industrial Avenue
Mahwah, NJ 07430–2262

Viewpoints in Teaching and Learning
Indiana University
School of Education
Education Building 109
Bloomington, IN 47405

Young Children
National Association for the Education of Young Children
1313 L Street, NW, Suite 500
Washington, DC 20036–1426
(202)232–8777; (202)328–1846 (Fax)
http://www.naeyc.org

PERMISSION CREDITS

Part 1: State, Local, and Classroom Assessment

Bill Bigelow, "Why Standardized Tests Threaten Multiculturalism." *Educational Leadership,* 56:7 (April 1999), 37–40. Copyright © 1999 by the Association for Supervision and Curriculum Development. Reprinted with permission. The Association for Supervision and Curriculum Development is a worldwide community for educators advocating sound policies and sharing best practices to achieve the success of each learner.

Richard A. Figueroa and Eugene Garcia, "Issues in Testing Students from Culturally and Linguistically Diverse Backgrounds." *Multicultural Education,* 2:1 (Fall 1994). Copyright © 1994 by the Caddo Gap Press. Reprinted with permission.

Renée Smith-Maddox, "Defining Culture as a Dimension of Academic Achievement: Implications for Culturally Responsive Curriculum, Instruction, and Assessment." *Journal of Negro Education,* 67:3 (1998), 302–317. Copyright © 1998 by the Howard University Press. Reprinted with permission.

Eugene E. Garcia, Myriam Casimir, Xiaoquin (Alice) Sun Irminger, Ann Marie Wiese, and Erminda H. Garcia, "Authentic Literacy Assessment (ALA) Development: An Instruction Based Assessment That Is Responsive to Linguistic and Cultural Diversity." *Educators for Urban Minorities,* 1, 1999. Copyright © 1999 by Long Island University Press. Reprinted with permission by Eugene E. Garcia.

Linda Darling-Hammond, "Performance-Based Assessment and Educational Equity." *Harvard Educational Review,* 64:1 (Spring 1994), 5–30. Copyright © 1993 by the Ford Foundation. Reprinted with permission. This article was originally presented at the Ford Symposium "Equity and Educational Testing and Assessment." Washington, DC, March 11–12, 1993.

Part 2: Instruction

G. Orville Johnson, "Organizing Instruction and Curriculum Planning for the Socially Disadvantaged." *Journal of Negro Education,* 33:3 (1964), 254–263. Copyright © 1964 by the Howard University Press. Reprinted with permission.

Phil Chinn, "Curriculum Development for Culturally Different Exceptional

Children." *Teacher Education and Special Education,* 2:4 (1964), 49–58. Copyright © 1964 by *Teacher Education and Special Education.* Reprinted with permission.

Charles R. Payne, "Multicultural Education: A Natural Way to Teach." *Contemporary Education,* 54:2 (Winter 1983), 98–104. Copyright © 1983 by the Indiana State University. Reprinted with permission.

Lisa D. Delpit, "The Silenced Dialogue: Power and Pedagogy in Educating Other People's Children." *Harvard Educational Review,* 58:3 (1988), 280–297. Copyright © 1988 by the President and Fellows of Harvard College. Reprinted with permission.

Kathryn H. Au, "Social Constructivism and the School Literacy Learning of Students of Diverse Backgrounds." *Journal of Literacy Research,* 30:2 (1998), 297–319. Copyright © 1998 by Lawrence Erlbaum. Reprinted with permission.

Tonya Huber, "Of Pigs and Wolves at the OK Coral." *Multicultural Education,* 3:4 (Summer 1996), 4–7. Copyright © 1996 by Caddo Gap Press. Reprinted with permission.

Cherry A. McGee Banks and James A. Banks, "Equity Pedagogy: An Essential Component of Multicultural Education." *Theory into Practice,* 34:3 (1995), 152–158. Copyright © 1995 by Lawrence Erlbaum. Reprinted with permission.

Part 3: Examples of Practice

Luis C. Moll, "Some Key Issues in Teaching Latino Students." *Language Arts,* 65:5 (September 1988), 465–471. Copyright © 1988 by the National Council of Teachers of English. Reprinted with permission.

Gloria Ladson-Billings, "Toward a Theory of Culturally Relevant Pedagogy." *American Educational Research Journal,* 32:3 (1995), 465–492. Copyright © 1995 by the American Educational Research Association. Reprinted with permission.

Michelle Fine, Lois Weis, and Linda C. Powell, "Communities of Difference: A Critical Look at Desegregated Spaces for and by Youth." *Harvard Educational Review,* 67:2 (1995). Copyright © 1995 by the President and Fellows of Harvard College. Reprinted with permission.

Part 4: Grade Specific/Subject Specific Applications of MCE

Patricia G. Ramsey, "Multicultural Education in Early Childhood." *Young Children,* 37:2 (1982), 13–24. Copyright © 1982 by the National Association for the Education of Young Children. Reprinted with permission.

Geneva Gay, "On Behalf of Children: A Curriculum Design for Multicultural Education in the Elementary School." *Journal of Negro Education,* 47:3 (1979), 324–340. Copyright © 1979 by Howard University Press. Reprinted with permission.

Valerie Ooka Pang and Cynthia Park, "Issues-Centered Approaches to Multicultural Education in the Middle Grades." *The Social Studies* (1992), 108–119. Copyright © 1992 by Heldref Publishing. Reprinted with permission.

AUTHOR INDEX

SUBJECT INDEX